THE KILLING TRAP

The Killing Trap offers a comparative analysis of the genocides, politicides, and ethnic cleansings of the twentieth century, which are estimated to have cost upwards of forty million lives. The book seeks to understand both the occurrence and magnitude of genocide, based on the conviction that such comparative analysis may contribute to prevention of genocide in the future. Manus Midlarsky compares socioeconomic circumstances and international contexts, and includes in his analysis the Jews of Europe, Armenians in the Ottoman Empire, Tutsi in Rwanda, black Africans in Darfur, Cambodians, Bosnians, and the victims of conflict in Ireland. The occurrence of genocide is explained by means of a framework that gives equal emphasis to the non-occurrence of genocide, a critical element not found in other comparisons, and victims are given a prominence equal to that of perpetrators in understanding the magnitude of genocide.

MANUS I. MIDLARSKY is the Moses and Annuta Back Professor of International Peace and Conflict Resolution at Rutgers University, New Brunswick, NJ. He has authored or edited eleven books and sixty-five articles and book chapters. Most recently he has published *The Evolution of Inequality: War, State Survival, and Democracy in Comparative Perspective* and the edited volumes *Inequality, Democracy, and Economic Development* (Cambridge), and the *Handbook of War Studies II.*

THE KILLING TRAP

Genocide in the Twentieth Century

MANUS I. MIDLARSKY

CAMBRIDGE
UNIVERSITY PRESS

CAMBRIDGE UNIVERSITY PRESS

Cambridge, New York, Melbourne, Madrid, Cape Town, Singapore, São Paulo

CAMBRIDGE UNIVERSITY PRESS

The Edinburgh Building, Cambridge CB2 2RU, UK

Published in the United States of America by Cambridge University Press, New York

www.cambridge.org
Information on this title: www.cambridge.org/9780521815451

First published 2005

Printed in the United Kingdom at the University Press, Cambridge

A catalogue record for this book is available from the British Library

ISBN-13 978-0-521-81545-1 hardback
ISBN-10 0-521-81545-2 hardback
ISBN-13 978-0-521-89469-2 paperback
ISBN-10 0-521-89469-7 paperback

For Liz, with extreme gratitude, and for Tali: May she and her generation never bear witness to genocide.

Right or wrong, we must win. It is the only way ... And once we have won, who is going to question our methods?

Adolf Hitler

Evil, violent, iniquitous, and inhuman means, even supposing that they had an appearance of immediate utility at the moment of crisis, leave behind ... long and disastrous traces.

Charles Augustin Sainte-Beuve

CONTENTS

PREFACE

I write this book after a 46-year gestation period. This does not mean that my thinking about the book spanned nearly five decades. Instead, my experiences as a seventeen-year-old were formative and ultimately decisive in the decision to do the research and writing.

For many years, I avoided the issue of the Holocaust, despite an intense training in Orthodox Judaism and a household deeply affected by the news of the Holocaust. Although both sides of my family were originally from Eastern Europe, site of the most extensive massacres, we were fortunate in that none of our immediate relatives was murdered by the Nazis. To my knowledge, not even a first or second cousin of mine succumbed to this bestiality. Yet, as in most American-Jewish households of that period, feelings ran deep, especially as the full extent of the horrors had been so recently revealed. At the age of seventeen, I was afforded the opportunity to experience them vicariously.

On Yom Kippur in Israel, in 1954, I visited an uncle (through marriage), who escaped from eastern Poland with his immediate family to live with relatives in Voronezh, in the depths of Russia. Virtually all of his relatives who remained in Poland perished in the Holocaust. Now in Israel after leaving the displaced persons camp in Germany, he was living in one of the last of the Israeli transit camps (Maabarot). Most of the younger couples with children had already been placed in new housing, leaving only the older people who remembered only too well the extent of their losses. When it came time for the Memorial Service for the Dead (Yizkor), the extent of their agony became abundantly clear. I have never before, or since, heard such anguished weeping. It was as if the many dead in the full extent of their suffering had entered the consciousness of the living, and we were now hearing their cries of horror at experiencing their wholly unjustified fate.

Such intensity of feeling was simply too much for a seventeen-year-old relatively sheltered American. For the next thirty years, I blocked out this memory. It was revived only after my wife, Professor Elizabeth Midlarsky of

Teachers College, Columbia University, who was then in the midst of a research project on helping during the Holocaust (supported by the National Institutes of Health) and editing a special issue of the *Humboldt Journal of Social Relations* on that topic, asked that I contribute an article. I was exceedingly reluctant for reasons already given; the subject also was then outside my field of expertise. Yet perhaps it was the memory of that Yizkor service long ago, now revived, that was decisive in my ultimate agreement to write the article. As it happens, the article received a favorable citation in a review article on altruism in the 1990 *Annual Review of Sociology*, thereby allaying fears over my handling of this important and sensitive topic. Subsequent research on ethnic conflict brought me closer professionally to the topic of genocide, the subject of this book.

These heightened sensitivities to the Holocaust then led to an increased awareness of other genocides, including, of course, the Armenian and Tutsi, as well as the Cambodian politicide. All are explored in this volume.

My first and heartfelt thanks go to my wife, Liz, for dragging me kicking and screaming to face the reality of my recent heritage. She also was immensely helpful in suggesting better ways to frame the arguments, and to make them more coherent and accessible. My children, Susan, Miriam, and Michael, all contributed through their questions and concern within this long gestation period, Miriam perhaps most of all. In her rabbinical studies at the Jewish Theological Seminary, Miriam (now Rabbi Miriam Midlarsky Lichtenfeld) has continually raised important issues about the future of Judaism and the Jewish people in light of the Holocaust. These conversations fueled much of the thinking that fed into the writing of this book.

Acknowledgments and thanks are extended to Laura Ahrens, Yaïr Auron, Joseph Bendersky, Claudio Cioffi-Revilla, Helen Fein, Brian Ferguson, Joseph Grieco, Max Herman, Jan Kubik, Jack Levy, Roy Licklider, Robert Melson, Alexander Motyl, Jack Porter, Scott Straus, Anna Stubblefield, and Benjamin Valentino for their comments on portions of the book. For their efforts, the book is stronger. All errors, of course, are my own.

Research support of the Back family to the Moses and Annuta Back Chair of International Peace and Conflict Resolution at Rutgers University, New Brunswick, NJ, made this effort possible. For that too, I am extremely grateful.

Last, but certainly not least, are the secretarial and administrative efforts that were needed to complete the manuscript. Isabel La Venuta and Sonya Riley rendered extremely competent service that frequently went beyond the call of typical office work. Sonya especially displayed a loyalty to the project and reliability of effort that led to completion of the manuscript in a timely fashion. She deserves the highest praise for her work.

One point needs to be made with great clarity. Although the primary purpose of this book is social science explanation, I hope that this analytic emphasis does not prove to be offensive to the survivors of genocide. The attempt to explain mass murder, which often involves understanding the perspective of perpetrators of great evil, can sometimes appear to be callous by those who experienced the full impact of that evil. Theory, with its necessary mode of abstraction, itself can be viewed as offensive by people who lost whole families and even entire societies. The question of abstraction pales before that of existence. Even the children and grandchildren of survivors can harbor justifiable sensitivities on this issue. Yet to explain is not to condone. Explanation has the virtue of perhaps establishing the foundation for the future prevention of mass murder. Without such explanation, certainly the probability of the future repetition of genocide is increased. It is my hope that social science analysts and genocide survivors, ultimately, are not members of disjoint sets on this issue. Hopefully, they can agree on the utility of the analytic mode, even when it appears to be abstracted from the immense brutalities of everyday existence in concentration camps or other killing traps.

PART I

Introduction

1

Preliminary considerations

On the morning of April 11, 1922, Hans Morgenthau presented a speech in honor of the duke of Coburg, leader of an autonomous duchy within Weimar Germany. This was an honor traditionally conferred on the top-ranked eligible student at the local *gymnasium*. No Jew had ever been selected for this honor; indeed, Morgenthau was the only Jew enrolled at this elite institution. Yet, there was no getting around the fact that Morgenthau merited this distinction and so the duchy allowed him to present the speech. That morning, citizens of Coburg distributed anti-Semitic leaflets including demeaning distortions of his Jewish-sounding name and urging a boycott of the speech. Later, Morgenthau wrote: "Nobody would speak to me ... And people would spit at me and shout at me. People would shake their fists at me and shout imprecations or anti-Semitic insults, and so forth. It was absolutely terrible, absolutely terrible ... probably the worst day of my life."[1] During the speech, the duke and other notables held their noses in a show of disgust. After his emigration, Morgenthau's classic *Politics Among Nations* would establish the study of international relations as a distinct field of inquiry in the United States.

Is this an illustration of virulent anti-Semitism that Daniel Goldhagen would argue quickly morphed into "eliminationist"[2] anti-Semitism prior to and during the Holocaust? Or are there other answers that provide a more compelling explanation? Despite a long history of German anti-Semitism,[3] the overtly anti-Semitic political parties experienced a steep decline prior to World War I. By 1912, together they captured less than 1 percent of the vote.[4] We also know that, for most supporters of Nazism during the early 1930s, the principal attraction of the NSDAP (Nationalsozialistische Deutsche Arbeiterpartei, or Nazi Party) was not anti-Semitism, but the perceived need for radical solutions to the country's economic and political chaos. Perceived

---

[1] Frei 2001, 22.   [2] Goldhagen 1996.   [3] Hilberg 1985.   [4] Melson 1992, 119.

injustices of the Treaty of Versailles also fed into support for policies of the NSDAP.[5] The April 1, 1933, economic boycott of Jewish-owned businesses sponsored by Hitler's government was particularly unsuccessful.[6] Why, then, the atrocious treatment of Morgenthau, among other Jews, at this time? Answers are to be found in the wider setting of European society at the end of World War I, as will be emphasized in this book.

Purposes of the book

In the broadest sense, this book is about *threat* (the fear of potential loss)[7] and *vulnerability*, two necessary conditions for the occurrence of genocide. The targeted population needs to be perceived as threatening, or at least have a tenuous connection to external threatening agents, whatever the reality of that perception, and the targeted population must be vulnerable to mass murder. At the same time, the potential perpetrators of genocide also must experience some vulnerability to generate their real or fantasized images of threatening civilian populations. Any process that simultaneously increases both threat to the state and its vulnerability, as well as vulnerability of a targeted civilian population, also increases the probability of genocide. It is for this reason, among others, that all of the cases examined here, even those that are ultimately excluded from lengthy consideration, occur during time of war, interstate or civil. Threat management by the state can be understood as a critical function of realpolitik (defined as policies designed to preserve and strengthen the state),[8] while vulnerability of states or potential civilian targets is most frequently signaled by loss. Realpolitik and loss are the twin theoretical foci of this book.

Understanding the dynamics of genocide at the moment of decision is at best incomplete, for models of genocide etiology have been put forward infrequently.[9] Thus far, two basic approaches have been taken to understanding the annihilation of European Jewry, the exemplar of

---

[5] Abel [1938] 1986; Merkl 1975.   [6] Friedländer 1997.

[7] For the impact of external threat on domestic societies, see M. Midlarsky 2000b, 2002, and 2003; see also chapter 5.

[8] Waltz 1979, 117.

[9] Raul Hilberg 1985 (originally published in 1961) put forward perhaps the earliest model of the Holocaust in the form of the sequence: definition–expropriation–concentration–extermination. More recent and comprehensive models of genocide are found in Fein 1979, 1984, 2000; Kuper 1981; and Harff 2003.

twentieth-century genocides because of its magnitude and the absence of identifiable Jewish provocation. The first is the "intentionalist"[10] that posits an ultimate intention on the part of Hitler and his henchmen to destroy all of Europe's Jews. The second is the "functionalist" argument[11] that points to the coercive build-up (by the Germans) of Jewish populations in unsanitary ghettos, which were not only disease-prone but also required the material support of the occupying German forces, as the root cause. With so many "unwanted" Jews excluded from the economy and the bickering between bureaucratic agencies of the Third Reich as to the ultimate responsibility for their welfare, the decision to liquidate them was made.

Neither of these two explanations, nor others such as Saul Friedländer's most recent emphasis on "redemptive anti-Semitism,"[12] explains the essentially dynamic circumstance of the increasing propensity to murder Jews as World War II progressed. In other words, this book seeks to explore the transition from genocidal behavior – the tendency to massacre *some* people having a particular ethnoreligious identity – to genocide itself wherein the mass murder is systematically extended to include *all* people with that identity.

This distinction is not merely a matter of definitional semantics, for the lives of millions of people were forfeited in the transition from the more limited behavior to the far more extensive one. Massacres[13] can be used to terrorize and cow a hated civilian population, as occurred in the large-scale murder of both Polish and Jewish leaders (Communists, high church and army officials, rabbis, professors) after the invasion of 1939. Indeed, the murder of the Polish leaders occurred prior to that of the Jews because of the greater threat of Polish anti-German agitation given their much larger numbers, yet this murderous behavior is distinct from the later Holocaust both in kind and scale. Or consider the massacre of approximately 200,000 Armenians by the Ottoman authorities in 1894–96. This large-scale massacre is qualitatively distinct from that of the genocide of 1915–16 when as many as 1 million or more Armenians were systematically murdered. One can make similar distinctions between the episodic massacre of Tutsi by Hutu in Rwanda and the genocide of 1994 in which a likely maximum of 800,000 Tutsi were killed.

---

[10] Dawidowicz 1986; Jäckel 1981; Fleming 1984.
[11] Fraenkel 1941; Neumann 1942; Broszat 1981.   [12] Friedländer 1997.
[13] For comprehensive treatments of massacres, see Levene and Roberts 1999.

The emphasis on change over time, particularly during a war, might appear to be self-evident, yet major public and scholarly figures have largely ignored it. In addition to the distinction between "intentionalists" and "functionalists," journalists such as Sebastian Haffner, himself a non-Jewish anti-Nazi refugee from Hitler who has been called "the conscience of post-war Germany," argued that over and above everything else, including victory, the principal goal of Nazi Germany was destruction of the Jews.[14] More recently, Omer Bartov, who has emerged in recent years as one of the leading Holocaust historians, also affirmed that, "when all other plans fell through, even when the fronts were collapsing and Germany was about to be invaded, the Jews remained what they had been from the very beginning: Germany's first and *primary* target."[15] As we shall see, the analyses here will belie this presumed constancy of motivation.

Contingency also is one of the major emphases of this book. Genocide, I argue, is a contingent event, one made more probable by the earlier experience of loss and its consequences. In contrast to John Lewis Gaddis, who argues for the absence of patterns in contingent events ("By contingencies, I mean phenomena that do not form patterns. These may include the actions individuals take for reasons known only to themselves: a Hitler on a grandiose scale, for example"),[16] this book demonstrates that patterns of contingency in genocide do occur.

This book, then, attempts to solve two puzzles in the study of genocide. First, how does the pattern of massacre, sometimes random, oft-times organized for specific purposes, become transformed into genocidal policy organized at the state level? Terror is often used to achieve specific purposes. Potentially hostile civilian populations need to be cowed into submission; even on the battlefield, technical changes are sometimes introduced solely in order to induce terror and a consequent demoralization of opposing forces. The fitting of shrieking sirens to the wings of German Stuka dive bombers in World War II is a case in point. And terror is often sufficient to achieve neutralization, even complete submissiveness. Active Czech opposition to the German occupation effectively ceased after the massacre of the male population and internment in concentration camps of the women and children, as well as physical destruction of the town of Lidice near the assassination site of Reinhard Heydrich, protector of Bohemia-Moravia and an architect of the "Final Solution." More generally, as Edward Luttwak notes,

[14] Haffner 1979.   [15] Emphasis added; Bartov 2003, 93.   [16] Gaddis 2002, 30–31.

"The reprisal policy of the German forces during World War II was very effective in minimizing the results that guerrillas could achieve, in most places, most of the time."[17] Genocide of the Czech population was unnecessary and did not occur.

European Jewish populations had for centuries trained themselves to be utterly submissive to Christian secular authorities in the expectation, frequently realized, that even severe oppression ultimately would pass, and the Jewish community would survive. Orthodox, especially Hasidic Jewish communities in eastern Poland, Belorussia, and Ukraine were singularly indifferent to the secular authority of the moment. Their lives were intensely spiritual and predominantly concerned with doctrinal Jewish matters. In the face of such manifest indifference or surrender, why institute genocide?

Second, why does genocide persist? One of the oldest recorded genocides, the Melian of the Peloponnesian War, occurred almost 25 millennia ago, while the most recent, the Tutsi, took place within the past decade. And these genocides appear not to have conferred any tactical or strategic advantage on the perpetrator. All of the major instances of the past century, as well as the prototypical Melian case, were committed by the losing side in a major war. Indeed, instead of incremental gain, genocide appears to have incurred substantial losses, as in the Holocaust when German transport and personnel had to be diverted from the principal task of waging war against an increasingly formidable array of opponents. A rational choice decision calculus emphasizing instrumentality appears not to have been decisive in choosing the genocidal option, an argument that will be developed more fully in chapter 4.

The past is unalterable. This painful axiom of invariance sets the stage for attempts to confront and then roll back the dictates of history. Based on some understanding of the past, frequently flawed as in the canard of Jewish responsibility for Germany's defeat in World War I, genocide emerges as a radical solution to the perception of an unacceptable, indeed intolerable, historical circumstance. Genocide is not an inevitable consequence nor is it a frequent one. But when certain sociopolitical conditions coincide, genocide has ensued. The task of this book is to delineate these conditions in three almost universally acknowledged genocides: the Holocaust of 1941–45, the Armenians of 1915–16, and the Tutsi of 1994. By confining the analysis to cases of maximum

---

[17] Luttwak 1987, 133.

victimization (in the 66–70 percent range),[18] I also allow for the possibility of ferreting out variables that have the strongest impact on extensive mass killing. The role of the state, realpolitik, and loss will turn out
to be crucial. These variables also allow for the possibility of specific
policy recommendations – included in the concluding chapter – an
outcome frequently denied to the more macro variables typically
found in large-N analyses.[19] Later, a politicide – the mass murder of
designated enemies of the state based on socioeconomic or political
criteria – the Cambodian politicide of 1975–79, will be shown to have
a different etiology, stemming from an equally flawed understanding of
historical causation.

I choose these instances not only because there is little debate about
their status as genocides in contrast to many other potential candidates,
but also because much information is available for the analyst to draw
upon. This is especially true of the Holocaust. Its sheer magnitude of
6,000,000 dead, and the absence of any identifiable Jewish provocation
render it unique and almost endlessly attractive to historians, social
scientists, and philosophers who seek to explain the apparently inexplic-
able. The literature on the Holocaust, therefore, is far more extensive
than that found in other cases. Yet explain it we must, because it is too
important an event to leave to the mystifiers who contend that it simply
cannot be explained in the temporal realm. The Holocaust also has a
much wider geographical range of occurrence than do any other genocides including the Armenian and Rwandan. It took place in twenty
European countries (including Britain, in the collaboration of local
government with the Nazis on the Channel Islands)[20] with varying
degrees of collaboration or defiance among their leaders and populations, and over a longer time period. This plethora of data allows for the
examination of a wide variation of behaviors among countries and even
among the Jewish ghettos in Poland between 1940 and 1944. This
behavioral variation, too, is absent in other cases. For these reasons,
the Holocaust receives greater emphasis. By studying it in its entirety, we

[18] Fein 2004 lists the Holocaust, the Armenian, and the Tutsi genocides in that category.
Only the Herero are also to be found in the category of maximum victimization but, as
we shall see in chapter 2, the ambiguous extent of state involvement and combatant
status lead to its exclusion.

[19] See, for example, the important association between political upheaval and genocide
found in Harff 2003. Political upheaval, of course, allows for a large number of
manifestations that lacks the specificity required for policy recommendations.

[20] For an artistic rendering of this collaboration, see Pascal 2000.

simply learn more from the varieties of behavior found across most of the European continent.

In order to maximize explanation, we must listen to the voices of perpetrators and rescuers alike. Voices of the victims have mostly been stilled by mass murder and the ravages of time, but their rage, sorrow, powerlessness, and, for the survivors, a lifetime of pain, assuaged only intermittently by new families and personal achievements, have been recorded in memoirs and oral histories. Where appropriate, their evidence can help us as well.

This book is about loss in two important senses. First, in the enormous losses of human life, possibility, and culture visited on the world by genocide. The three genocides examined here resulted in the direct deaths of approximately 8,000,000 people; the aftershocks and contagion processes led probably to a minimum of another 4–5 million dead. This number is greater than the number of combat deaths in World War I, with the obvious difference that nearly all of the World War I combat dead were male. Genocides in the twentieth century made no provision for the rescue of women and children.

Entire cultures were lost. The vibrant Yiddish-based culture of East European towns and cities is no more. There are no longer any Armenian communities in eastern Anatolia; their church bells no longer ring for Sunday services. In Rwanda today, only with some effort can one find a Tutsi who was living in Rwanda in 1994. Most Tutsi in Rwanda now are returnees or migrants who arrived after the genocide. The enormity of the losses can perhaps best be appreciated by those who directly experienced them or their relatives or ethnic kin. Yet all of us can at least cognitively understand the monstrous dimensions of these losses.

The second meaning of loss is more analytic, for it provides a basis for understanding the behavior of many of the perpetrators. Indeed, loss is the single common thread that undulates throughout the several theoretical foci that are used here to understand the onset of genocide. Loss is understood as either (1) the transfer of territory, population, authority, or some combination of any of the three to another political entity, or (2) significant casualties in political violence (e.g., war) that either are about to be or have already been incurred.

Why should a political scientist like myself, in addition to personal reasons, seek to study the origins of genocide? After all, genocide is a profoundly human condition involving the deaths, in the aggregate, of millions of people, often by extraordinarily barbaric means. In that, it is first and foremost a human tragedy and justifiably it has been treated as such. Yet to understand the etiology of genocide, and that is my principal concern in this book, we must look to the foundations of policy making, namely politics. And these political processes often involve threats to the security of fairly newly established states, specifically the possibility of loss. Germany embarked on its genocidal path in 1941 after only seventy years of independent united existence, a period during which it experienced three incarnations – imperial Germany, the Weimar Republic and the Nazi state – the last, of course, the newest and in certain respects the least established in August 1941 when genocide began in earnest. The state, then, and policies designed to ensure its continuity – a fundamental component of realpolitik defined as success in preserving and strengthening the state[21] – loom large in the following analyses.

Genocide is understood to be the state-sponsored systematic mass murder of innocent and helpless men, women, and children denoted by a particular ethnoreligious identity, having the purpose of eradicating this group from a particular territory. More detailed reasons for this choice will be presented in chapter 2. *Genocidal behavior* is understood to be mass murder short of eradicating the entire group, but including a significant subset of that group in the killing.

In understanding the behavior of perpetrators, explanation will not be restricted to the political realm. Theories will be drawn from social psychology, economics, cognitive science, and other sciences committed to understanding the human condition. And the perpetrators, however well deserved their odious reputations, were primarily human beings. It does no good to label them as monsters and simply forget about them after their consignment to the trash heap of history. Certainly the perpetrators committed monstrous deeds. Yet, we do far better to explain their descent into atrocity as human beings than as some mutated creatures whose behaviors defy understanding. In the latter instance, we will claim no purchase on explanation and possible prevention, whereas in the former we may find some hope for the future. To humanize is to understand, but certainly not to absolve or condone.

As the Israeli poet and Holocaust survivor Dan Pagis wrote in his poem "Testimony":

---

[21] Waltz 1979, 117.

No no: they definitely were
human beings: uniforms, boots.
How to explain? They were created
in the image.
I was a shade.
A different creator made me.

And he in his mercy left nothing of me that would die.
And I fled to him, floated up weightless, blue,
forgiving – I would say: apologizing –
smoke to omnipotent smoke
that has no face or image.[22]

The moral stigma will remain whatever our level of understanding, for the barbarities and immensities of human loss lay beyond any absolution, however limited. Notwithstanding their intent, unless perpetrators are genuinely deranged, are psychologically disconnected from their surroundings, or are coerced with deadly force, judgments are based on actions, not motivations.[23] In the final analysis, I pose the question: can we afford to treat the perpetrators as human beings instead of monsters? The answer is simply that we can't afford *not* to. Too much is at stake in the explanation of genocide and perhaps prevention of future mass killings.

The role of theory

If we view genocide as a human perversion, certainly in the moral realm, it is useful to seek answers in the perverse. One hint of the source of such perversion is found in the Message to the Assembly that Dr. Ismar Schorsch, chancellor of the Jewish Theological Seminary in New York, delivered at the 2001 graduation ceremony of the Cantorial and Rabbinical School. Chancellor Schorsch suggested that one of his favorite Hebrew words was "tzimtzum," meaning contraction. To be an effective leader, a rabbi must frequently contract her sphere of influence in order to stimulate creativity in others. Her contraction provides the intellectual/spiritual space for congregants or colleagues to explore their own capabilities, thereby enhancing the creative process.

The identification of contraction with creativity in Schorsch's interpretation contrasts sharply with the effective identification of contraction with destruction in the minds of genocidal leaders. For example, in

---

[22] Quoted in Bartov 2003, 113.   [23] Neiman 2002.

his speech of June 25, 1931, Hitler stated that: "The parties of the middle say: everything is collapsing; we declare: what you see as collapse is the beginning of a new era. There is but one question about this new era: will it come from the German people ... or will this era sink toward another people? Will the Jew really become master of the world, will he organize its life, will he in the future dominate the nations? This is the great question that will be decided, one way or the other."[24] The "space" created by the collapse of the center parties is to be occupied not by a political creation of the Nazi Party, but by the destruction, or at least neutralization, of the Jewish "menace."

In all of the genocides considered here, the perpetrators had already experienced losses in the form of substantial spatial contractions, or were reasonably certain that such contractions were impending. Instead of a creative response, they entered upon a manifold intensification of the destructive process indiscriminately applied to innocent men, women, and children. Creativity of the intellectual and spiritual domains empha-sized by Schorsch provides a stark contrast with the wholesale violence associated with genocide.

Explanation of the onset and magnitude of genocide is the main purpose of this book. And such an analysis at the outset cannot be firmly in the nomothetic camp because of the relative absence of theorizing in the field of genocide. This unfortunate situation is due to at least two reasons, not entirely independent of each other.

First, the preponderance of research in the field of genocide studies has been by professional historians, almost always on a single case of genocide, most frequently the Holocaust. And, until now, this is as it should have been. Even the Holocaust, as by far the most extensive genocide of the twentieth century, even in all of recorded history, had received very little attention from historians until the Eichmann trial in Israel and the virtually simultaneous publication of Raul Hilberg's magisterial study of the Holocaust in the early 1960s.[25] Only then, and with the gradual disappearance of the generation of German perpetra-tors, as well as the even more recent end of the Cold War, did historians, especially German ones, take a serious interest in the Holocaust. The passing of the survivors also has quickened the pace of Holocaust research, before their oral testimony and the writing of their memoirs will no longer be added to the store of evidence. Even a basic issue such as the timing of Hitler's decision to murder *all* of Europe's Jews, not just

[24] Quoted in Friedländer 1997, 103.   [25] Hilberg 1985, a new edition of his 1961 work.

those in the Soviet Union presumably infected with the Bolshevik bacillus, has only received a modicum of consensus among historians in the past several years. Interestingly, this issue will arise later in connection with the uses of theory.

The need for comparison in theory development

As a result of this emphasis on single cases, important as they are, generalizability has suffered greatly. This limitation on generalizability – a hallmark of empirical validity – has impeded the development of theory. The fact that the third most extensive genocide of the twentieth century, that of the Tutsi in Rwanda, occurred only during the past decade has also retarded theory development because its recency prevented its inclusion in comparative analyses. This brings me to my second concern, the relative absence of comparative analyses (statistical or small-N) without which theory building either cannot proceed or is sterile.

Because of its extent and manner of occurrence, the Holocaust has been claimed to be unique. And it *is* unique in the unthinkable number of dead and the innocence of any malevolent intent toward Germany among the vast majority of those killed. Indeed, because of the derivation of Yiddish from Middle High German (when taught in the absence of Judaic studies, it is almost always included among the Germanic languages), it was far and away the most popular choice among Jews as a "foreign" language of study in the early part of the last century. At the personal level, my mother and her American-born siblings all studied German in high school, my aunt having won the German medal, a matter of some family pride.

German was the official language of the first Zionist Congresses prior to World War I, and it is clear that no more patriotic group could be found in Germany than its Jews. Nearly 100,000 Jews had served in the German army during World War I: 80,000 experienced combat, 35,000 were decorated for bravery, and 12,000 were killed, numbers out of all proportion to the estimated 500,000 Jewish citizens living in Germany at that time.[26] A horribly ironic sidelight on the Holocaust is the relative warmth that many older Warsaw Jews felt for the Wehrmacht soldiers immediately upon German arrival in 1939.[27] These Jews recalled the substantially better treatment meted out to them by the German

---

[26] Fischer 1998, 120.   [27] Abramowicz 1999.

occupying troops of World War I, in comparison with the overtly anti-Semitic tsarist authorities they replaced.

This positive sentiment certainly did not exist among the other cases of genocide considered here. The Armenians had created at least two anti-Ottoman revolutionary groups – the Dashnaks and Hunchakists – by the turn of the century, and many Tutsi (but certainly not all) were sworn enemies of the Hutu-dominated Rwandan government.

This is not to say that there exists a justification for genocide. Any single death as the result of murder, mass or single, is one death too many. The vast majority of Armenians and Tutsi murdered in their respective genocides were wholly apolitical, as were the Jews in the Holocaust. These people wanted nothing more than to live in peace with their neighbors. Yet one cannot ignore the existence of opposition to the *anciens régimes* in the Ottoman Empire and Rwanda that genuinely provoked these governments.

I chose a comparative analysis because, despite the Holocaust's uniqueness, this mode of inquiry is more likely than any other to yield insights into the origins of not only genocide generally, but even the Holocaust in particular. One case in point is the role of a particular theoretical orientation in helping to pinpoint the moment of decision to murder all of Europe's Jews found within the boundaries of German governance or occupation. This theory, to be developed more fully in chapter 5, concerns the impact of increasing losses on state insecurity, and the consequent increase in the probability and intensity of political violence directed against civilian populations.

A related issue is that of the use of social science theory in an effort to generalize across cases. Realpolitik, prospect theory, and other perspectives on loss will be introduced as means of understanding the onset of genocide within the context of earlier state losses and high risk. This emphasis reverses the understandable tendency to view genocide as principally a domestic enterprise.[28] After all, did not the ideological bases of the Holocaust and other instances of mass murder arise within the borders of states such as Germany? The answer to this question obviously is yes, but with an important qualification. Although the rise of such murderous sanctioning ideologies was necessary to the commission of routinized mass murder, it was not sufficient. We shall see how the experience of loss by perpetrators bridges the chasm between ethno-religious hostility that traditionally was expressed in the form of legal

---

[28] Melson 1992.

exclusions, personal beatings, even occasional murder, on the one hand, and genocide, on the other. Clearly, other conditions had to be present. This book will focus on the largely neglected international context.

Does this effort at abstraction detract from what is essentially a humanistic enterprise? Abstract theory is very far removed from the individual Jews and their entire communities burnt alive inside their wooden synagogues. Or Armenian families hacked to death inside their churches. Or Tutsi children slaughtered with machetes in front of their parents before they themselves were killed. Or later, as we shall see, Cambodians murdered simply because they wore glasses. The analytic enterprise does not concern itself with these micro-level aspects of mass murder, yet in a larger sense the analysis *is* humanistic if it helps us understand why human beings engage in such notoriously savage behavior. To understand is not to condone or to forgive. We understand as the result of social scientific explanation. Part of that explanation includes the conditions under which people are willing to jettison their moral universe and clearly transgress the bounds of ethical conduct. Yet, at the same time, we can and must insist on the firm maintenance of those boundaries, even under the trying conditions to be detailed in the following chapters. Not to do so is to sacrifice the essential part of what makes us human.

Theory as explanation can also help us get around the "mystification" obstacle to understanding. Even as accomplished a historian as Jan Gross (author of *Neighbors*) can state that "the Nazi-conceived project of the eradication of world Jewry will remain, at its core, a mystery."[29] Although sensitive to Elie Wiesel's deep concerns on this issue and of course his horrific experiences in Auschwitz, nevertheless Yehuda Bauer takes issue with Wiesel's well-known mystification of the Holocaust.[30] If we seek to know what is in the heart of every single member of the *Einsatzgruppen* operating in eastern Poland and the Soviet Union (or the Ittihadists or members of the Interahamwe), or even the Polish peasant guarding against Jewish escape from the mass murder at Jedwabne, the subject of Gross's book, then the mystery probably will remain unsolved. Motivations can range from outright sadism, to the desire for loot, to the obedience to authority, to the settling of old business scores, to the utter absence of empathy, or to ideological fanaticism, to name but a few. The biographical case study approach to the study of perpetrators' motivations thus far has yielded little explanatory traction. Even after

[29] Gross 2001, 132.   [30] Bauer 2001, 15.

some 100 biographies, we still are not absolutely certain why, at bottom, Hitler chose this singularly destructive path. But if we stick with the observable behaviors of state decision-makers and perpetrators, particularly those at the highest levels and extending down through the mid-range (e.g., army captains), noting the patterns amenable to explanation, then at least progress can be made.

There may exist enduring principles underlying the human condition that govern this murderous choice – otherwise, why is genocide repeated? Answers are to be found in the principles and practices of realpolitik, especially the imprudent variety, and the empirical findings associated with prospect theory, one that emphasizes loss aversion and risk acceptance as essential components of decision making under risk and uncertainty. Additional consequences of loss lie in the realm of emotional reactions to loss including anger, brutality, desire for revenge, and class envy. Altruistic punishment will help explain large-scale coop-eration with the genocidal enterprise, even if only among the *génoci-daires* themselves, and abetted by many bystanders sympathetic to the mass murder.

A contribution of this book is the finding that a statement of *desire* or *intent* to commit genocide is not the key variable leading to its onset. Whatever the virulence of the ideological underpinnings, the actual events occurring just prior to the genocide and the relevant geopolitical setting are crucial. In some cases, they can contribute to the making of the final decision to commit genocide as in Germany in December 1941, or to its prevention, or at least minimization of the genocidal urge, as in Anatolia in 1915–22 and the survival of almost the entire Anatolian Greek community. This is not to deny the relevance of ideology. It is important and necessary to the genocidal enterprise. It simply is not sufficient.

Genocide, the wholesale elimination of a perceived enemy, is an idea that has been around since biblical times and the writings of Thucydides. Yet only on rare occasions do we find its actual occurrence. That relative rarity is to be explained by the confluence of events suggested by the theoretical approaches to be introduced shortly.

Research strategy

A "top-down" strategy is chosen here, namely to identify the most general precursors of genocide and then to narrow the choices to specific influences. The funnel of causality is widest at the top and very narrow at the bottom. The most general influences at the top are those that can have many possible outcomes, including genocide, while at the bottom are variables that are more specific in their genocidal effects.

Theoretical conditions can yield different outcomes depending on the specific application. Realpolitik as policy prescription, emergent from realism for example, was at one time ubiquitous. Emphasis on state needs characteristic of realpolitik was a policy foundation for most European as well as independent Asian powers prior to World War II. Thereafter, many newly independent countries also adopted this policy prescription. Yet, under certain constraining conditions, realpolitik can have horrific outcomes. It is the imprudent–brute force form of realpolitik as distinguished from the prudent type[31] as well as from a third type, the cynical variant, that can increase the probability of genocide. Victim vulnerability is greatly increased by cynical realpolitik. One of the constraints imposed by the theoretical approach adopted here – loss – is a critical component of prospect theory. Specifically, it is the magnification of perpetrator loss suggested by prospect theory, anger at the presumptive "other," or other consequence of loss leading to the use of an imprudent realpolitik, and impact of the cynical variant, that can yield the genocidal outcome.

Still further down the funnel is the concept of altruistic punishment as the basis for cooperation between genocidal leaders and followers. In the face of overwhelming odds and/or likely defeat in war, why were genocidal perpetrators not deterred from continuing, in fact accelerating the mass murder? This theoretical perspective can shed light on what at first appears to be highly anomalous behavior.

This book, then, employs theoretical perspectives to explain the typically complex behavior associated with genocide. The conjunction of several processes is required in order for the genocide to take place. In this, the book is in the tradition first adumbrated by Theda Skocpol in her *States and Social Revolutions*,[32] and employed by me in *The Onset of World War* and "Preventing Systemic War."[33] This approach has been further developed theoretically by Charles Ragin.[34]

Why erect this formidable theoretical scaffolding upon which to construct the explanation of genocide? After all, was not the virulence of Nazi anti-Semitism, Ottoman "Turkism," and Hutu extremist "anti-Hamitism" sufficient to explain the genocides? They hated, so they killed, runs the argument. But this argument belies the considerable

---

[31] Garver 1987.   [32] Skocpol 1979.   [33] M. Midlarsky 1984, 1988a.   [34] Ragin 1987.

variation in the killing over time and over space in all of the genocides. Whatever their murderous fantasies, they could be enacted by the perpetrators only under a certain confluence of sociopolitical conditions. It is the task of this book to detail the nature of these conditions, insofar as possible.

In two senses, the book is isomorphic to the phenomenon it seeks to explain. First, the outcome of genocide seldom is the result of a single decision. It tends to be a cumulative process in which earlier violence directed against civilians can make later mass murder more likely to occur. Second, genocide is not a neat one-size-fits-all happening. Genocides differ in their extent, rapidity of occurrence, and asymmetries in patterns of killing both within and between genocides. In its attention to these differences, this book seeks to be an accurate reflection of genocide. Only in the commonalities of human failing across all three of the genocides is there symmetry, perhaps pleasing to the analyst, but nevertheless suggesting deep pessimism about the unfettered human condition. Only with the appropriate political institutions can human beings master the homicidal impulses unleashed in genocide.

Finally, all of these processes and events occur within an international context that can be critical in either promoting or abetting genocide, or preventing it altogether. Indeed, aside from the absence of loss or its compensation by nonviolent means, the only variable consistently identified as a genocide preventive – the existence of powerful affine ethnoreligious groups or governments – arises from the international setting. Thus, the contextuality of genocide is emphasized here. Events occurring within a single country certainly are not sufficient for genocide to occur. Even an emphasis on a single dyad of countries would not be sufficient. It is the regional and international context that is crucial for an outcome of this magnitude, or its prevention.

Plan of the book

A definition of genocide,[35] its justification, and more detailed case selection (including reasons for excluding certain candidates) are found

---

[35] The term genocide was coined by Raphael Lemkin 1944, 79. This definition provided the basis for the somewhat later one devised by the United Nations. Rudolph Rummel 1998, 1–13, has coined the term *democide* to refer to the killing of large numbers of people by the state. See also Rummel 1997. Issues of comparative genocide are treated in many of these sources, but see especially Rosenbaum 1998. For additional perspectives, see Krain 1997 and Valentino 2000.

in chapter 2. Part II presents theoretical foundations for understanding perpetrator behavior. First, the experience of killing and its validation, including the important role of identification with earlier victimizers prior to the genocides, are detailed in chapter 3. The experience of massacre itself, especially without significant negative consequence for the perpetrator, makes the later genocide more likely to occur.

Chapters 4 and 5 present alternative theoretical perspectives such as classical rational choice theory and utopianism, reasons for their rejection, and justification for the choice of realpolitik and loss as central components of the theory. Empirical findings in the field of Bayesian decision making are helpful in this regard. Chapter 4 also includes two prototypical cases that aid us in theory development.

Most critical to the transition from massacre to genocide are realpolitik and loss. Because realpolitik (especially involving threats to state security) is such an important variable, three types of realpolitik are identified in chapter 5; five consequences of loss are suggested, all leading to the onset of genocide.

Part III consists of empirical applications of the theory. First, in chapter 6, realpolitik in the form of threat to the state is associated with ethnic cleansing in Ireland, Poland, and Bosnia, but not genocide (excepting Srebrenica). With the addition of loss, the expanded theory is examined in the contexts of the onset of the Holocaust, and the Armenian and Tutsi genocides (chapter 7). The etiology of genocide is distinguished from that of ethnic cleansing principally in the presence of recent loss in the former instance.

In chapter 8, altruistic punishment is put forward as a means of effecting unity in a fractious population, as a way of answering a question initially posed by Michael Marrus,[36] namely why so many followed the genocidal leader down his nihilistic path. Expanding empirically, perpetrating states, that is states participating in the Holocaust – Italy, Vichy France, and Romania – are all found to have experienced severe territorial losses and refugee migration, as did Germany and Austria prior to World War II (chapter 9).

Unique to this book is the systematic effort in part IV to identify conditions that increase victim vulnerability. Although Christopher Browning has recently presented detailed and invaluable histories of mass murder during the Holocaust[37]– a significant departure from

---

[36] Marrus 1987.   [37] Browning 2004.

earlier concentration by Holocaust historians on the perpetrators – this evidence in itself does not readily translate into identifying the antecedents of vulnerability. New variables, or more specifically variations on those used earlier in the book, are required to explain victim vulnerability, especially increases in the magnitude of the killing and manner of dying.

Chapter 10 details the cynical realpolitik of international agents that increases the vulnerability of potential victims, thereby undoubtedly increasing the magnitude of the killing. Cynical realpolitik is further examined in the context of the refusal to admit refugees from almost certain death, an important factor influencing the magnitude of the killing (chapter 11).

The subsequent chapters (12–14) focus on high victimization rates, inequality, identification, and potential for revolt within ghettos, with detailed considerations of perpetrators and victims. Here again, the extent or magnitude of the killing is at issue. The full sweep of the Holocaust with its twenty-country involvement is given its due. Although the Holocaust was orchestrated from Berlin, nevertheless the considerable variation in local implementation deserves separate treatment. Again, altruistic punishment will be critical in understanding the onset of widespread rebellion in one Jewish ghetto, but not in others also located within the old pale of East European Jewish settlement.

Part V analyzes exceptions to the patterns of genocide identified earlier. A single case of politicide, Cambodia, also having a relatively small genocidal component – the ethnic Vietnamese – is explored in chapter 15. Victimization of the ethnic Khmer was vastly increased by Khmer Rouge ideological affinities with Maoism and Stalinism, and a consequent Cambodian ability to seal itself off from international scrutiny and influence that could have diminished the extent of the killing. Cases of the "dogs that didn't bark," instances where genocide might have been expected to occur, but did not, are explored in chapters 16 and 17. The roles of realpolitik and the absence of loss are examined in the cases of Bulgaria and Finland, exceptions to the pattern of collaborating European states. A form of prudent realpolitik, affinity, is developed to explain the absence of genocide in certain instances – Greeks in the Ottoman Empire, Jews in Eastern Europe before December 1941, Poland at the time of the Partitions, Roman Catholic Irish in Ireland after World War I, and Israel during Intifada II – where genocide seemed possible, even likely. Vulnerabilities of target populations are substantially reduced in the presence of powerful affine ethnicities in other countries, or powerful sympathetic governments.

Potential losses in human life from genocide are simply too vast to ignore the necessity to generalize and extrapolate from the findings here. In one sense, this book seeks to be an antidote to death and nothingness. Genocide is intended to achieve precisely that outcome for the victimized group. Yet, by understanding the genocidal process, the hoped-for prevention of future genocides suggests that the murdered did not die completely in vain. Which are the sociopolitical conditions most likely to influence both the onset and magnitude of genocide and how may we best avoid them? The concluding chapter (18) suggests generalizations and extensions of the analysis. Connections with cognate scholarly work and policy making are developed. Most important, the frequently incalculable consequences of genocide are examined in some detail, followed by implications of the analysis for the prevention of genocide.

2

Case selection

As stated in the introduction, genocide is understood to be the state-sponsored systematic mass murder of innocent and helpless men, women, and children denoted by a particular ethnoreligious identity, with the purpose of eradicating that group from a given territory.[1] Vulnerability of the targeted group and a real or purported connection with threats to state security (e.g., ethnic kin in an enemy state) are necessary conditions for the genocide to occur.

Two elements are critical in defining genocide. First is the matter of state policy. Was it the policy of the perpetrating state to commit mass murder with exterminatory intent? If so, then the number of people murdered would be vastly greater than if such a policy were absent. Second, were non-combatants of a particular ethnoreligious identity subject to the mass murder? If large numbers of men were killed on the battlefields of Flanders or elsewhere during World War I, it is a substantially different matter than if they, as civilians, were killed along with their families in the Nazi gas chambers of World War II. In the former instance, they are typically (but not always) men fighting on behalf of their country. In the latter, they are victims of an exterminatory state policy. Thus, the two elements critical for selecting cases for analysis are the existence of a state policy demanding the systematic mass murder of an ethnoreligious group and the implementation of that policy.

---

[1] I distinguish between genocide as the systematic mass murder of people based on ethnoreligious identity, and politicide as the large-scale killing of designated enemies of the state based on socioeconomic or political criteria. Although genocide can be understood to be a species of politicide (but not the converse), in practice, genocidal (i.e., ethnoreligious) killings tap into much deeper historical roots of the human condition. In this distinction, I follow Harff and Gurr 1988, 360. For other conceptualizations and definitions of genocide, see Bauer 2001, 8–10; I. Horowitz 2002, chapter 2; Fein 1990, 2–31, and 1979, 3–4; Kuper 1981, chapters 2–3; Charny 1994; Chalk and Jonassohn 1990, 3–32; Melson 1992, 22–30; R. Smith 1987; Katz 1994, 125–39; Chorbajian 1999, xv–xxii; Huttenbach 2002; Straus 2001; and Staub 1989, 3–8.

Although other definitions certainly exist,[2] this one has the advantage of including only those cases that are almost universally acknowledged to be genocides – the Holocaust, for example – in contrast to partial efforts at mass murder that have other intentions. Massacres intended to induce flight and ethnic cleansing frequently are denied the status of genocides.[3] However, *genocidal behavior* in intensity of the killing stands somewhere between massacre and genocide. It is understood to be mass murder short of the aim of eradicating the entire group, but including a significant subset of that group in the killing. The mass murder of Muslim males in Srebrenica in 1995 is a prototypical example. So too is the transition from the massacre of Jews in Ukraine during the Russian Civil War to genocidal behavior by the *Einsatzgruppen* early in the summer of 1941 (only Jewish males subject to mass murder), followed by genocide throughout Europe after December 1941. This issue will be examined at length in the following chapter.

Accordingly, it is possible to categorize cases of genocide on the two dimensions: exterminatory state policy and the selection of non-combatants (including prisoners of war of a certain ethnicity) for annihilation. However, one case is much less easily categorized than the other two. It is the one anomaly that not only suggests some ambiguities in the understanding of exactly what constitutes state policy and even what constitutes a combatant, but also points in certain analytic directions for understanding the etiology of genocide.

Table 2.1 presents such a categorization based on the two dimensions. Where state policy of systematic ethnoreligious mass murder is clearly present and is implemented in the killing of non-combatants, we have three incontrovertible cases of twentieth-century genocide, the Armenians in 1915–16, the Holocaust of 1941–45, and the Tutsi of Rwanda in 1994. It is clear that in all three instances state policy was exterminatory and was implemented with deadly effect. Cambodia will be examined later as a case of exterminatory state policy and its implementation in the killing of non-combatants, but without a substantial ethnoreligious dimension, which demonstrates a different etiology from the other cases. It will be treated as a politicide.

Occasionally, politicides aim at a particular ethnoreligious group, but with overtly political goals. The massacre of approximately 100,000–200,000 Hutu in Burundi in 1972 had the goal of preventing their political ascendance based on their majority status. Thus, Tutsi

---

[2] Straus 2001.   [3] Levene and Roberts 1999; Schabas 2000, 197–201.

Table 2.1 *Dimensions of genocide and politicide*

		Victim status	
		Combatant	*Non-combatant*
Exterminatory state policy	*Present*	Herero?	Armenians Holocaust Tutsi [Cambodia]*
	Absent	World War I	Bosnia Nanjing

Note: *Cambodia is an example of politicide.

leaders "saw the annihilation of all educated Hutu elements as the most sensible course to make Burundi safe for the Tutsi minority. By striking at all Hutu elites, students, and schoolchildren indiscriminately, even at the least suspicion of subversive intentions, they aimed . . . to decapitate a potential counterelite."[4]

Not only is the differing etiology important, but genocides and politicides frequently yield different outcomes. Genocide is not only exterminatory, but aims at *annihilation*. I prefer this term to extermination, although to signify intent I will use *exterminatory* to describe state policy; extermination implies that the noxious insect could somehow return in which case the "exterminator" would have to be brought in again. Annihilation implies a total erasure of any human or physical remnants (e.g., synagogues, Armenian churches) that could remind the perpetrator of the victim. The eradication is complete.

In contrast to genocides, politicides – the mass murder of designated socioeconomic or political enemies of the state – not only typically leave the majority of the population intact after purging the economic or political "offenders," but do not necessarily destroy the cultural infrastructure of the victim. Even if attacked and partially destroyed, enough of the infrastructure survives to build anew as in the former communist countries that experienced this form of state-sponsored mass murder. The same cannot be said of the minuscule Jewish communities of Eastern Europe, the Armenians of Anatolia, or the surviving Tutsi in Rwanda (in contrast to returning Tutsi refugees). As one would expect,

[4] Lemarchand 1996, 101–02.

proportions of the victimized populations differ greatly. Whereas the percentages of murdered Armenians, Jews, and Tutsi within the targeted country areas centered around 66–70 percent, that of Cambodians was approximately 20 percent.[5]

Another clear-cut case of the absence of genocide is World War I where the vast majority of deaths, especially on the Western front, were incurred on the battlefield. Although the deaths in Bosnia and Nanjing were mainly those of non-combatants and extermination was not state policy, both cases require discussion because of their occasional treatment as genocides.

Excluded cases

The definition of genocide and the use of the two dimensions to select cases may be clarified by considering the three cases that are excluded – Bosnia, Nanjing, and the Herero. Each provides a cogent example of mass murder. However, none meets all of the criteria. Later, in the concluding chapter, the recent ethnic cleansing of black Africans with possible genocidal behavior in Darfur in western Sudan will demonstrate some resemblance to the Bosnian case.

Bosnia

Although sometimes categorized as a genocide, the Serbian actions against the Bosnian Muslims would not fit the definition adopted here. According to the 1948 United Nations Convention on the Prevention and Punishment of the Crime of Genocide, any "acts committed with intent to destroy, in whole *or in part*, a national, ethnical, racial or religious group"[6] would be sufficient to label as genocide an instance of mass violence but, in the absence of state policy mandating wholesale extermination, would not be included here. My view of the United Nations Convention is that it is too broadly inclusive, for it does not distinguish between killing with the purpose to terrorize and perhaps effect an ethnic cleansing through mass flight of the victims on the one hand, and deliberate wholesale extermination on the other. Genocide is a form of ethnic cleansing, but ethnic cleansing does not have to entail the presence of genocide. Emigration and other forms of

[5] Fein 1979, 2004; Melson 1992; Kiernan 1996.
[6] Emphasis added; Chalk and Jonassohn 1990, 44.

population removal, even if coerced and/or effected by terror, do not
constitute annihilation.

The number of dead in Bosnia-Herzegovina has been estimated by the
Bosnian Institute for Public Health to be 146,340, a number that is in
approximate agreement with that given by Mustafa Imamović: 144,248,
mainly Muslims.[7] These estimates have been challenged by George
Kenney, who argues for a number between 25,000 and 50,000 total
deaths. And the highly respected Stockholm International Peace
Research Institute (SIPRI) essentially agrees with Kenney's view in
putting forward a figure of 25,000 to 55,000 total deaths, excluding
those incurred by fighting between the Bosnian Serb and Bosnian
Croat armies.[8] More recently, officials of the Demographic Unit,
Office of the Prosecutor, International Criminal Tribunal of the former
Yugoslavia, estimated the total number of dead at 102,622, broken down
into 55,261 civilian and 47,360 military.[9] Even assuming that all of the
civilian deaths were Muslim, a somewhat unsafe assumption, the total
number of deaths due to ethnic cleansing or to genocidal activity is
maximally in the 50,000 range, in agreement with SIPRI.

Clearly even the highest estimates here do not match the number of
Armenians killed in the massacres of 1894–96 (approximately 200,000)
that, despite their horror, were really only a precursor to the genocide of
1915–16. I am reluctant to appear to be playing a "numbers game" here.
Yet one must distinguish between exterminatory state policies that have
the capacity to murder many hundreds of thousands, if not millions, as
in the case of the Holocaust, and the absence of such policies. In the
latter instance, the death tolls are invariably much smaller. Additionally,
and most importantly, the etiologies of massacres and genocides likely
differ, if only because state sponsorship of the former, more limited type
of violence frequently is absent.[10]

The absence of exterminatory intent on the part of the Serbs (or
Croats) does not mitigate the tragedy of the displacement of between
one-third to two-thirds of the Bosnian population, most of whom are
Muslim. The Bosnian Institute of Public Health found that nearly one of
every two persons living in the federation was displaced, and many of

---

[7] Burg and Shoup 1999, 169.   [8] Ibid., 170.   [9] Tabeau and Bijak 2003.
[10] See, for example, D. Horowitz 2001. More directly relevant to our concerns here is the
finding by Klier and Lambroza 1992 that many of the late nineteenth- and early
twentieth-century pogroms that had been thought to be sponsored by the tsarist
state, in fact, were of spontaneous origin.

them are now living abroad. A crime against humanity had been committed, but "The practice of expelling Muslims from Serb-controlled territories and the tendency to single out men and boys for execution – while in themselves despicable – seem contrary to an intent to destroy the Muslim people *as such*."[11]

Absence of exterminatory intent is further indicated by the fact that, in 1990 and 1991, Serbs actually spent much time and effort in attempting to woo the Bosnian Muslims.[12] The Serb leaders thought that, despite the threatened secession of Croatia and Slovenia, Muslims might choose to remain within the federation, thus creating a viable, if smaller, political entity. Should the Muslims decide to stay, even the departure of the dissident republics ultimately might be avoided. Only later, after the hounds of war had been let loose, did the killing begin, with the main purpose of inducing the flight of as many Muslims as possible.

According to William Schabas in his comprehensive treatment of genocide in international law,[13] the drafters of the UN Genocide Convention resisted efforts to include ethnic cleansing under the rubric of punishable acts. Further, after a detailed analysis of the Bosnian case, Schabas concludes, "it is incorrect to assert that ethnic cleansing is a form of genocide, or even that in some cases, ethnic cleansing amounts to genocide."[14]

Thus far, as of early 2004, the United Nations war crimes tribunal for Yugoslavia agrees. Three defendants accused of genocide have been acquitted of the charge; the third is Milomir Stakic, a Bosnian Serb and former mayor of Prijedor in northeast Bosnia. Although responsible for the deaths of 1,500 persons and the forcible removal of 20,000 non-Serb civilians from the town, the tribunal refused to convict him of genocide. Instead, he was convicted of five counts of crimes against humanity and war crimes, receiving the maximum possible sentence of life imprisonment.[15] At the same time, the Bosnian Serb general Radislav Krstic was found guilty of genocide for his involvement in the Srebrenica massacre, and the sentencing appeal was recently denied. As we shall see in chapter 6, even within cases of predominantly ethnic cleansing, genocidal behavior can be identified, especially where earlier losses are experienced by the perpetrator.

---

[11] Emphasis in original; Burg and Shoup 1999, 183.   [12] Judah 2000, 196.
[13] Schabas 2000, 196.   [14] Ibid., 200.   [15] *New York Times*, August 1, 2003, A8.

Distinguishing between behaviors that are principally ethnic cleansing from those that yield full-fledged genocides can help us predict and
perhaps even prevent their occurrence in the future. As we shall see, an
accentuated sense of recent or impending loss beyond any found in the
instances of ethnic cleansing or episodic massacre characterizes all three
cases of genocide.

Nanjing

The second excluded case is the massacre that occurred in Nanjing in
December 1937. The claimed murder of several hundred thousand
(between 200,000 and 250,000) has led some analysts to view it as a
genocide,[16] a perception that is understandable especially in light of the
many atrocities committed by the Japanese troops. Nevertheless, the
Rape of Nanjing, although aptly named, does not meet the criteria
adopted here.

In the matter of scale, the Rape of Nanjing is maximally in the
category of several hundred thousand dead. Masahiro Yamamoto, on
the other hand, gives a much lower range of 15,000 to 30,000 fatalities.[17]
Even if we accept Iris Chang's maximum estimate, this still would put
Nanjing in the same category as the maximum estimated number killed
in the Bosnian ethnic cleansing and the Armenian massacres of 1894–96.
But this is not decisive. What is decisive, as table 2.1 implies, is the
absence of Japanese state policy mandating such action. Apparently the
horrific events occurred at the instigation of local commanders who
violated the orders even of the military general responsible for the
overall entry of Japanese troops into the city. Accordingly, General
Matsui Iwane, himself a devout Buddhist, ordered only a few well-
disciplined battalions into the city with instructions to complete the
occupation so that the army would "sparkle before the eyes of the
Chinese and make them place confidence in Japan."[18] While ill, he called
a meeting of his staff officers to his sickbed and stated:

> The entry of the Imperial Army into a foreign capital is a great event in
> our history ... attracting the attention of the world. Therefore let no unit
> enter the city in a disorderly fashion ... Let them know beforehand the
> matters to be remembered and the position of foreign rights and interests
> in the walled city. Let them be absolutely free from plunder. Dispose

[16] Chang 1997, 4.   [17] Yamamoto 2000, 282.   [18] Chang 1997, 39.

sentries as needed. Plundering and causing fires, even carelessly, shall be punished severely. Together with the troops let many military police and auxiliary military police enter the walled city and thereby prevent unlawful conduct.[19]

Matsui had just been promoted to general supervisor of the entire central China theater, and his replacement in command of one of the three major columns about to enter Nanjing was a relative of the Emperor Hirohito, Prince Asaka Yasuhiko. Being a member of the royal house would give him extraordinary freedom of action. His acquaintance with the other two commanders from their joint stay in Paris as military intelligence officers would further facilitate a common policy.

With nearly 300,000 Chinese troops about to surrender in Nanjing and without the food to feed them, or even sufficient Japanese force to contain them and prevent reprisals, an order was sent from Asaka's command to "kill all captives."[20] The murder of these Chinese troops was the basis of the atrocity that then quickly spread to the wholesale rape and in many cases subsequent murder of women and even of female children.

The killing and rape subsided only when Matsui Iwane, although still not fully recovered, entered the city for a ceremonial parade. When he discovered what had happened, he sharply rebuked his officers including the royal Asaka Yasuhiko. Shocking those present, Matsui even went so far as to tell an American foreign correspondent (the United States was not yet in the war) that "the Japanese army is probably the most undisciplined army in the world today."[21]

Clearly, those mass murders were not mandated by the Japanese state. Yet, in one sense, they began to point in the direction of understanding how genocide as state policy can begin in wartime. What the Rape of Nanjing, Bosnia, and the mass murder of the Herero (to be discussed shortly) and our three principal cases hold in common is the emergence of unexpected threat experienced by ultimately victorious troops in local engagements.

Earlier in the 1930s, the Japanese boasted that they could conquer mainland China in as little as three months. The Chinese army was nowhere near as modern or as well equipped as the Japanese. Nor were its leaders as experienced or well schooled in the practice of warfare. Yet in the summer of 1937, after the outbreak of war, instead of falling

[19] Ibid., 39–40.   [20] Ibid., 40.   [21] Ibid., 51.

almost immediately to the Japanese, the city of Shanghai held out for months. Setbacks to the Japanese included the deaths of several hundred men as the result of a Chinese artillery ambush of the soldiers as they were being landed on the Shanghai docks. A cousin of the Empress Nagako died in that clash.[22] The Japanese approach to the capture of Nanjing, the Chinese capital, would now be far more brutal than anyone anticipated.

The Herero

The third case to be excluded is the Herero. Although genocidal behavior did occur in 1904, it differs in important ways from the cases that are included. At the same time, this case is even more convincing in the impact of emerging threat, and is more complex, especially in the understanding of what constitutes state policy and even combatant status. Moreover, in contrast to the cases considered in this book, the killing took place in an explicit colonial context, German-governed South-West Africa (today Namibia), involving racially distinct perpetrators and victims. Although important in providing a justification for the brutalization and ultimate genocidal behavior, racism itself was not decisive. Other, more immediate and more compelling factors were to build on this racist edifice and yield the mass destruction.

In response to the continued expropriation of land and cattle by German settlers, and despite some last-minute attempts at reform by the administration of the governor, Major Theodore von Leutwein, the Herero, realizing that expropriation would continue, "rose as one man under the leadership of their Supreme Chief Samuel Maharero."[23] The blatant racism of the Germans in virtually eliminating Herero civil and human rights was an important factor stimulating the uprising. Although von Leutwein sought to limit the German military response to the initial Herero success, he gave way to the tactical choice of General Lother von Trotha, newly arrived in South-West Africa. In a letter to von Leutwein, he wrote: "I did not receive any instructions or directives on being appointed Commander-in-Chief in South-West Africa. His Majesty the Emperor only said that he expected me to crush the rebellion by fair means or foul and to inform him later of the causes that had

---

[22] Ibid., 33.   [23] Drechsler 1980, 132.

provoked the uprising."[24] Earlier the kaiser had forbidden the opening of negotiations with the Herero, demanding instead unconditional surrender, which von Trotha was determined to achieve.[25]

Accordingly, in order to unconditionally quell the rebellion, until then quite successful, von Trotha adopted a new strategy. He ordered the Herero in the Waterberg (including women and children) surrounded on three sides, with the fourth side only weakly garrisoned, facing the desert. This was the only direction open for escape from the Germans. Facing German forces including thirty pieces of artillery and twelve machine guns on three sides, the Herero had no choice but to retreat to the Omahake desert, where many died of thirst and starvation. A study by the German General Staff later concluded that this battle inflicted a far worse fate on the Herero than "German arms ever could have done, however bloody and costly the battle."[26] As a result of this and other actions against the Herero and later the Nama, another rebelling tribe, by 1911, fully 80 percent of the Herero and 50 percent of the Nama had died.[27]

Three factors are important to consider. First, the initial Herero successes were startling to the Germans, as was the Chinese success (albeit limited) in Shanghai to the Japanese invaders. The Herero had learned to fight the Germans in repeated ambushes leading to successive German losses. Von Leutwein, to all appearances, had failed to come up with a military strategy to counter these successes. That a "primitive" tribe of Africans, undoubtedly viewed as racial inferiors by the Germans, should be so successful militarily was anathema to the Germans. As a consequence, the far harsher genocidal policy of von Trotha was substituted for von Leutwein's reliance on pure military tactics.

The deaths of women and children in the Omahake desert raise the second of our issues, the nature of a combatant. Given the customs of Herero society, it would have been virtually impossible to separate the men from the women and children, for the families tended the cattle together. When von Trotha surrounded the Herero in the Battle of Waterberg, the women and children were present together with the men and the cattle they were tending. Thus the avoidance of frontal clashes and movement of the Herero closer to the desert inevitably entailed the transfer of women and children as well.

Yet, after the battle when so many Herero had died and the power of this people appeared to be broken, von Trotha still followed an

---

[24] Chalk and Jonassohn 1990, 241.   [25] Ibid., 239.   [26] Ibid., 243.   [27] Ibid., 246.

exterminatory policy. In a report to the chief of the Army General Staff, General Alfred von Schlieffen, von Trotha laid out his strategy:

> Since I neither can nor will come to terms with these people without express orders from His Majesty the Emperor and King, it is essential that all sections of the nation be subjected to rather stern treatment. I have begun to administer such treatment on my own initiative and, barring orders to the contrary, will continue to do so as long as I am in command here ... Before my departure yesterday I ordered the warriors captured recently to be court-martialled and hanged and all women and children who sought shelter here to be driven back into the sandveld ... To accept women and children who are for the most part sick, poses a grave risk to the force, and to feed them is out of the question. For this reason, I deem it wiser for the entire nation to perish than to infect our soldiers into the bargain and to make inroads into our water and food supplies.[28]

Von Schlieffen himself approved of von Trotha's intentions in terms of a "racial struggle" that required an effort either to "wipe out the entire nation or to drive them out of the country," but he had doubts about the effectiveness of von Trotha's strategy. Von Schlieffen desired a surrender of the Herero that von Trotha's intention of shooting "each and every Herero" male would complicate enormously.[29]

The imperial chancellor desired further limitations on von Trotha that stemmed from the inconsistency of a genocidal policy with "Christianity and Humanity," the impracticality of von Trotha's strategy, the indispensability of the "natives for the colony's potential development and the [fact that this] policy was demeaning to your [German] standing among the civilized nations of the world."[30] Kaiser Wilhelm II initially had ruled out negotiations, demanding unconditional surrender instead,[31] and apparently approved of the harshest measures to be taken against the Herero. However, after five days of hesitation, he agreed to a version of Chancellor von Bülow's suggested policy that surrendering Herero be shown mercy. Eight days later, he assented to von Bülow's specific request that the lives of surrendering Herero be spared.[32]

Here we see a split between the civilian and military components of the German government, with the kaiser initially leaning toward the military side, but ultimately malleable on the issue. This disjunction between the German military and civilian sectors will reappear in

---

[28] Drechsler 1980, 161.   [29] Ibid., 163.   [30] Ibid., 164.   [31] Ibid.   [32] Ibid.

the later cynical realpolitik of Germany in the Armenian genocide of 1915–16 (see chapter 10). Essentially, the state in the form of the kaiser and von Bülow had stepped back from the precipice of authorizing genocide. This was, of course, little comfort to the Herero now confined to reservations and subject to indiscriminate brutality and outright murder, albeit unauthorized, by German soldiers. Without their traditional hierarchy and cattle-based way of life, the Herero experienced a catastrophic demoralization. One year after the Battle of Waterberg, only 25 percent of the Herero existing in 1904 were still alive;[33] seven years later, that number declined to 20 percent. Although many were later murdered, further demographic attrition was based principally on declining fertility and poor living conditions in the enforced dwellings.

Because of the absence of state policy authorizing genocide, and the status of virtually all Herero including women and older children at least as combat associates especially during the Battle of Waterberg, this case of genocidal behavior will not be included in the following analyses. Yet the violation of expectations – and the possibility that the Germans could have actually experienced defeat at the hands of the Herero – is an important clue to the conditions under which genocide may be initiated. The invocation of the domain of losses and realpolitik as important sources of genocidal behavior[34] are also represented here. Additionally, von Trotha's treatment of the Herero in the Battle of Waterberg could have served as a model for German military advice to the Ottomans during the Armenian genocide (see chapter 10).

Why concentrate on genocide as state policy? Why not focus instead on the fortuitous opportunistic mass murders, or genocidal behavior, found in Bosnia, Nanjing, and German South-West Africa? An initial answer is to be found in my concern for understanding the behavior of the perpetrators, in addition to factors that increase the rate of victimization. By emphasizing the saved, films like *Schindler's List*, *The Pianist*, or *The Killing Fields* become luminous works of art that help keep the issue of genocide as well as the perversity and depredation of the perpetrators alive in the public consciousness. Sadly, however, they tell us little about the overwhelming majority of victims who went to their deaths. By understanding the perpetrators, we can address the causes of the mass killings that took so many lives and, thus armed, perhaps

---

[33] Bridgman 1981, 131.
[34] See the governor of South-West Africa's advocacy of the use of realpolitik in dealing with rebellious "natives"; Drechsler 1980, 241.

prevent similar occurrences in the future. And the vast majority of those murders took place *after* a policy decision had been made to commit genocide. If in Serb-occupied Bosnia, Japanese-occupied China, and German South-West Africa, the governing authorities had decided to kill *all* indigenous peoples, then certainly many times more people would have died than in the absence of such a policy. State-generated genocidal policies put at the disposal of the perpetrators the tools of modern mass killing – machine guns, gas chambers, ovens, or "only" a highly developed communications infrastructure that could be used to coordinate the mass murders, as in Rwanda.

Three cases of genocide

The three cases of genocide included in this analysis are the Holocaust, the Armenians, and the Tutsi. All were selected because they meet the criteria of state-sponsored systematic mass murder of a targeted ethnoreligious group and of non-combatant status of the victims. More will be said later about these cases, especially in the course of presenting the empirical analyses. For now, certain bare outlines can be given.

The Holocaust

Despite the onset of the war in September 1939, Jews were not murdered en masse until the German invasion of the Soviet Union in June 1941. However, immediately after the invasion, specially trained murder squads called *Einsatzgruppen* began murdering Jews throughout the conquered areas of the Soviet Union. At first only males were killed. In mid-August, women and children were included in the systematic killing. In some instances, local populations enthusiastically took part in the massacres of men, women, and children. For example, in a December 1, 1941, report by Karl Jäger, commander of *Einsatzgruppe* 3, he described in summary fashion the eradication of the majority of Lithuania Jewry:

> I can confirm today that *Einsatz Kommando* 3 has achieved the goal of solving the Jewish problem in Lithuania. There are no more Jews in Lithuania, apart from working Jews and their families. These number: in Shavli about 4,500, in Kovno about 15,000, in Vilna about 15,000.
>
> I wanted to eliminate the working Jews and their families as well, but the Civil Administration [Reichskommissar] and the Wehrmacht attacked me

most sharply and issued a prohibition against having these Jews and their families shot. The goal of clearing Lithuania of Jews could be achieved only through the establishment of a specially selected Mobile Commando under the command of SS Obersturmführer Hamann, who adopted my aims fully and who was able to ensure the co-operation of the Lithuanian Partisans and the Civil Authorities concerned. The carrying out of such *Aktionen* is first of all an organisational problem. The decision to clear each sub-district systematically of Jews called for a thorough preparation for each *Aktion* and the study of local conditions. The Jews had to be concentrated in one or more localities and, in accordance with their numbers, a site had to be selected and pits dug ... The Jews are brought to the place of execution in groups of 500, with at least 2 kms distance between groups ... All the officers and men of my command in Kovno took active part in the *Grossaktionen* in Kovno. Only one official of the intelligence corps was released from participation on account of illness.

I consider the *Aktionen* against the Jews to be virtually completed. The remaining working Jews and Jewesses are urgently needed, and I can imagine that this manpower will continue to be needed urgently after the winter has ended. I am of the opinion that the male working Jews should be sterilised immediately to prevent reproduction. Should any Jewess nevertheless become pregnant, she is to be liquidated.[35]

By March 1942 the first facilities with permanent gas chambers were built in Belzec in eastern Poland. Shortly thereafter, Auschwitz (Oświęcim)–Birkenau in Silesia also was operational and gassing Jews transported to its extermination camp (Birkenau). Approximately 1.2 million Jews died there. Other extermination camps, also in Poland, were Sobibór established in May 1942, Treblinka (July 1942), and Majdanek (autumn 1942). The latter two were responsible respectively for the mass murder of the large Jewish concentrations in the Warsaw and Lublin areas.[36]

Throughout Europe, Jews were transported either directly to these camps or to the Polish ghettos that were already in existence, from there to be taken to the death camps at a later time. This entire process was prefigured by the infamous speech of December 16, 1941, by Hans Frank, the governor-general of the Polish Generalgouvernement (the German administration in Poland), in which he stated, "One way or another – I will tell you that quite openly – we must finish off the Jews. The Führer put it into words once: should united Jewry again succeed in

[35] Wistrich 2001, 93–94.   [36] Ibid., 100.

setting off a world war, then a blood sacrifice shall not be made only by
the peoples driven into war, but then the Jew of Europe will have met his
end." Frank then concluded his speech:

> We must destroy the Jews wherever we meet them and whenever the
> opportunity offers so that we can maintain the whole structure of the
> Reich here ... The Jews batten on to us to an exceptionally damaging
> extent. At a rough estimate we have in the Generalgouvernement about
> 2.5 million people [Jews] – now perhaps 3.5 million who have Jewish
> connections and so on. We cannot shoot these 3.5 million Jews, we
> cannot poison them, but we can take measures that will, one way or
> another [*so oder so*], lead to extermination, in conjunction with the large-
> scale measures under discussion in the Reich.[37]

The timing of this speech will prove to be important in understanding
the etiology of the Holocaust in its gruesome entirety.

The Wannsee conference of January 20, 1942, was convened shortly
thereafter to implement the extermination process under the aegis of
Reinhard Heydrich, chief of the security police and the SD (intelligence
arm of the SS), and "Plenipotentiary for the Preparation of the Final
Solution of the Jewish Question."[38] Altogether, the process of shootings,
gassings, starvation, and epidemic diseases among the malnourished
residents of the Jewish ghettos led to the deaths of approximately
6,000,000 Jews between 1941 and 1945, the principal genocidal component of the Holocaust, which also included among its victims Roma,
homosexuals, and Soviet prisoners of war.

The Armenians

Here again, state authorization of the systematic mass murder of ethnoreligiously targeted non-combatants is found. On April 24, 1915, the
leaders of the Armenian community in Constantinople and elsewhere
were rounded up and deported. This event signaled the beginnings of
the Armenian genocide that would lead to the deportation and deaths of
approximately 1,000,000 Armenians. The German pastor Johannes
Lepsius in 1919 recorded that the earliest deportations began in
March, but in May were begun in earnest. The following is a partial
list of the deportations beginning in eastern Anatolia closest to the

---

[37] Ibid., 101.   [38] Ibid., 102.

Russian border, continuing into central Anatolia and northern
Mesopotamia, and ending in western Anatolia.[39]

May 15, 1915	The rural parts of Erzeroum [Erzerum]
June 15–July 15 and	
July 26, 1915	The city of Erzeroum
June 26, 1915	Harpout [Kharput] and Trebizond
June 27, 1915	Samson
July 10, 1915	Malatia
Deportations from Cilicia	
July 27, 1915	The seashore areas in Cilicia Antioch
July 28, 1915	Aintah
Deportations from western	
Asia Minor	
August 10–19, 1915	Brusa
August 16, 1915	Konia

Able-bodied Armenian men were drafted into the Ottoman army
where they were eventually disarmed and given menial tasks to perform.
Deprived of younger male protection, remaining inhabitants of villages
were exposed to massacre and deportation. Only the city of Van in the
heartland of Armenian Anatolia successfully defended itself initially
against the deportations, although it succumbed later. Armenians who
survived the village massacres were deported to the Mesopotamian
desert and then left to die a horrible death of starvation and disease.
En route, the few possessions they had were stolen by successive mar-
auding tribesmen until virtually nothing was left. The younger and more
attractive women were either abducted and subjected to forced conversion to Islam or repeatedly raped and left to die.

One of the witnesses, Edith Woods, a nurse in Kharput and Malatia
described the consequences of the deportations:

> It was like an endless chain ... The children would often be dead before
> I had taken their names. Forty to fifty of the older women died each day.
> You see starvation, exposure, exhaustion ... Their mouths were masses
> of sores, and their teeth were dropping out. And their feet, those poor,
> bleeding feet. The Turks were doing nothing at all for them. In Malatia
> the dead lay around in the streets and fields. No attempt was made to bury
> them ... Deportation is sure death – and a far more horrible death than

---

[39] Boyajian 1972, 104–05. The full list was initially recorded in 1915 by Johannes Lepsius,
a German pastor working in Anatolia.

massacre. Unless one sees these things it is difficult to believe that such monstrous cruelty and barbarity exist in the world. Making women and children suffer that way until they die seems incredible. But that is Malatia.[40]

The majority of the deportations ended in 1916, but even as late as 1920, atrocities took place in portions of Russian Armenia occupied by the Turks, leading to a minimum of another 100,000 dead.[41] Only the intervention of a Soviet army stationed nearby prevented continued slaughter of the Armenians. Today there are few, if any, Armenians remaining in their former heartland of eastern Anatolia.

The Tutsi

Eradication of an ethnoreligious group also became state policy in the Hutu extremist-led Rwandan state. Of the three genocides considered here, the most rapidly executed was that which occurred in Rwanda between April and July 1994. Estimates range between 500,000[42] and 800,000[43] dead, mostly Tutsi, but including thousands of Hutu moderates who wanted no part of the genocide. Most of the killing was done between April and May, a killing rate that exceeded that of the Nazi death camps during World War II. Rapidity of the killing distinguished the Rwandan genocide, although extent could still be claimed by the Nazis.

The genocide began soon after the April 6 assassination of the Rwandan president Juvénal Habyarimana. The military, National Police (*gendarmes*), and communal police actively led the genocidal attacks, with civilians, especially those in the Interahamwe (militia), then becoming active participants.[44]

At first, only targeted individuals, either Tutsi leaders or prominent Hutu moderates, were murdered. Soon they began the distinctive process of driving Tutsi from their homes to government offices, churches, schools, or other public sites, which appeared to confer safety, but actually became sites of wholesale massacre.[45] The mass killings at the church in Kaduha is typical of many. At first, Hutu neighbors and friends were allowed to bring food and livestock to the assembled Tutsi at the church. But after April 17, and the instigation of a more aggressive national policy, food could no

---

[40] Quoted in Marashlian 1999, 131.   [41] Dadrian 1999, 159.   [42] Des Forges 1999, 1.
[43] Gourevitch 1998, 3.
[44] Des Forges 1999, 8. For a recent description of the genocide including the training of the Interahamwe and the French role in that process, see Melvern 2004.
[45] Ibid., 9–10.

longer be brought in, and people were no longer allowed to leave the church. On April 20, a Hutu crowd tried to steal the livestock but were prevented from doing so by the Tutsi defenders. On April 21, assailants threw grenades at a house containing Tutsi refugees, which apparently signaled the start of the massacre. A witness reported:

> I could hear gunfire and the explosion of grenades and the cries of people being killed. The attackers fired their guns and threw grenades into the crowd and then groups of killers with traditional weapons came in and killed those who were still alive. This began early in the morning on the 21st and it continued all day Thursday and all day Friday. On Friday, they mostly searched for people who were hiding.[46]

Another witness commented on the role of the National Police:

> The National Police who were supposed to protect us were lodged in the agricultural school. When we awoke and found we were surrounded, we tried to defend ourselves. We were more than they and so we were able to force them back by throwing rocks. But the National Police came to reinforce them ... They began to organize the crowd. They fired their guns and threw grenades.[47]

Scenes of this type were repeated many times over in Rwanda until the Tutsi population was decimated. Rape, torture, and physical mutilation often preceded the killing, which not infrequently included beheading by machete.[48] Only those who were able to flee successfully, find effective hiding places, or were fortunate enough to be befriended by a Hutu sympathizer survived. Today the vast majority of Tutsi living in Rwanda are not survivors of the 1994 genocide, for they are few in number, but returnees from the Tutsi refugee communities in surrounding countries.

Because of its status as primarily a politicide, although including a genocidal element, the Cambodian case will be described in its entirety in chapter 15. All of the cases of genocide and politicide share the properties of state sponsorship of the systematic mass murder of a selected population. At the same time, individual persons were required to perform the mass murders. The following chapters explore the etiology of the killing from the perspectives of decision makers, actual killers, and the victims themselves. But, before these issues are addressed, we need to establish the theoretical foundations of this inquiry.

---

[46] Quoted ibid., 341.   [47] Quoted ibid.   [48] Gourevitch 1998, 131.

PART II

Explaining perpetrators: theoretical
foundations

3

Continuity and validation

In order to understand the onset of genocide, we must look at moments during which the vulnerability of victims was clearly established, and at the conditions that established vulnerability in the minds of the perpetrators. In this chapter, I first discuss continuity as one such condition. Later, validation – the absence of serious consequences for perpetrators – is presented as a second condition. In succeeding chapters, explanations will be offered for the transition from massacre to genocide.

Continuity, whether through experience or identification with the mindset associated with mass murder, is supplemented by validation. Validation occurs when a morally reprehensible act, even a heinous act, goes unpunished. If the perpetrators of previous murders were not punished, then to all intents and purposes, in a purely pragmatic sense, the killings were justified by their tacit acceptance.

Continuity of the killing in the three cases

By continuity, I mean prior experience with massacre or identification with the aims and mindset of those associated with mass murder. Genocide as a thoroughgoing eradication requires preparation. And it is not only pre-paration in the material sense of building gas chambers or buying large numbers of guns and machetes. It is the *experience* of massacre that is crucial. To be sure, this is not a historical awareness as in Hitler's reference to the genocide of the Armenians in his speech to army commanders prior to the invasion of Poland. Nor does this experience require the perpetrators of genocide themselves to have murdered in the past. What is required is that perpetrators be aware that there have occurred massacres of elements of the victim population in the recent past, and that they identify with the political goals and mindset of the earlier perpetrators. Identification can provide a bridge between the recent past and present, and makes subse-quent mass murder more likely to occur. Vulnerability of the victims, a necessary condition for genocide, has been clearly established.

The East was a major preoccupation of Nazis such as Hitler and Himmler. Therefore, these leaders would have been aware of the Russian generals' plan to deport substantial numbers of Jews from Poland to the Don basin during World War I because of their status as "security risks."[1] The Nazi leadership would also have known that, after World War I, the stridently anti-Semitic Polish National Democratic Party sought to limit citizenship in the new Poland to those who could prove that there had been no Jews in their families for at least three generations. In this respect, anti-Semitic Poles anticipated the Nazis by about fifteen years. The National Democrats also sought to forcibly eliminate or reduce the Polish-Jewish population.[2] And the economic boycott of Polish Jews that had begun under the Russian administration in 1912 was continued after Polish independence,[3] again anticipating the Nazi boycott of 1933 by more than a decade.

And if Russian or Ukrainian nationalists as opponents of Bolshevism saw fit to murder Jews en masse, then certainly the current (i.e., Nazi) cognoscenti of racial superiority and extreme anti-Bolshevism could, under the appropriate political conditions, at least follow the earlier example, or even better it. Because this linkage between massacre by the Ukrainian or Russian anti-Bolshevists and the later activities of the *Einsatzgruppen* (German killing squads) in the East typically is not emphasized in earlier studies of the Holocaust, it receives a substantial share of attention here. Similarly, in the Ottoman Empire and Rwanda, many of the same people who had earlier participated in the massacres, or the descendants of those people, participated in the genocide at the local level.

Identification with past murderers and/or their political goals works to disinhibit the genocidal perpetrators from the moral restraints that typically prevent mass killing. Of course, ideologies justifying mass murder can serve a similar function, but the view that the victims in the recent past somehow deserved to die, and the murderers were justified in the mass killing, can further remove inhibitions against systematic murder. Intimations of genocidal possibility are presented.

The Holocaust

In his otherwise finely wrought treatment of the *Einsatzgruppe* massacres of East European Jewry, Richard Rhodes gets one thing wrong. He

---

[1] Black 1993, 268.   [2] Ibid., 274.   [3] Ibid., 275.

explicitly connects the activities of the *Einsatzgruppen* with the origins of the Holocaust as in the title of his book – *Masters of Death: The SS-Einsatzgruppen and the Invention of the Holocaust*.[4] In fact, one cannot begin to understand the onset of the Holocaust without examining the Russian Civil War period. In those years, approximately 10 percent of Ukrainian Jewry died[5] under circumstances not terribly different in kind, although massively different in scale, from those existing in the summer and fall of 1941. The earlier massacres of 1919–20 heralded those of the early 1940s. Events within Ukraine in the early 1930s further exacerbated matters immeasurably. It is to that processual continuity that we now turn.

It has been estimated that between 1918 and 1920 as many as 150,000 Jews were murdered by Bolshevik armies (2.3 percent), Petlura's Ukrainian nationalists (53.7 percent), and Denikin's Volunteer Army (17 percent). The remainder was killed by local bands of renegade soldiers and other anti-Semites.[6] These estimates include deaths due to massacre-induced disease or starvation. More recent estimates based on newly available Russian records judge the percentage killed by the Volunteer Army to be much higher, perhaps as high as 50 percent.[7]

At the end of World War I, the withdrawal of German troops left a vacuum that no existing force could adequately fill. The Bolshevik Red Army under Leon Trotsky had not yet been fully formed, and the interventions of the tsarist White Russians under leaders such as Anton Denikin and Aleksandr Kolchak were just beginning. Just as the Poles and Finns were mobilizing for independence from the tsarist empire, so too were the Ukrainians under nationalist leaders like Simon Petlura. His forces were to commit atrocities against the Jews that were comparable in kind to those later committed by the Nazi *Einsatzgruppen* in alliance with Ukrainian nationalists.

Many were the number of reported atrocities. Only several are needed to communicate their level of barbarity. At Chernobyl, famous for its failed nuclear reactor, Jews were forced into streams; those who attempted to avoid drowning were shot. Typical of several appeals from towns such as Kostichev, Volochek, or Khemlnik (sic) was a message from the Jews of Trokinitz to the rabbi of Kaminski:

---

[4] Rhodes 2002.   [5] Baron 1976, 184–85.   [6] Gergel 1951, cited in Vital 1999, 722.
[7] Kenez 1992, 302.

> The misfortunes which fall upon the Jews of our town of Trokinitz are indescribable. Savage bandits have murdered, massacred and torn to pieces four-fifths of the Jewish population. It is a real wonder that some of them have been able to escape the massacre. The money, the beds, the clothes, the furniture, the wares, everything has been robbed and plundered. Houses have been demolished. Windows and stores broken and hacked to pieces. Here are now several hundred Jewish widows and thousands of Jewish orphans.[8]

As in the later Holocaust, many towns had virtually their entire Jewish populations murdered en masse. In the town of Tetiev on March 25, 1919, as was their custom in times of trouble, 2,000 Jews sought sanctuary in their large wooden synagogue. This time, the building could not protect them, for it was set afire by Cossack troops under the command of Colonels Kurovsky, Cherkovsky, and Shliatoshenko. Indeed, this was the prototype for the later mass murder by fire of Polish Jews in their wooden synagogues during the Holocaust. According to one eyewitness, "Of the synagogue nothing remained except walls blackened by fire and a few charred bodies which it was no longer possible to identify. All around the place, hands, feet and other human remnants were seen."[9] Elsewhere in the town, "Infants were tossed up into the air and their bodies dashing against the pavement squirted blood on the murderers."[10] A group of peasants tried to intercede on behalf of one Jew, at which point Kurovsky stated "He may be the best of them, but since he is a Jew he must be killed."[11]

Approximately 4,000 of Tetiev's 6,000 Jews were murdered in this pogrom. Towns with smaller Jewish populations had even a larger proportion of their Jews killed. In Dubovo on June 17, 1919, 800 of the town's 900 Jews were murdered in assembly-line fashion. Under the supervision of invading Cossack troops, two executioners stood at the head of the stairs leading to the basement of one D. Feldman. With their sabres, they proceeded to decapitate the Jews who were forced to approach the staircase. Shortly, the basement filled with the fragments of corpses.[12]

When the malevolence approached Kiev, with its sizable Jewish population, even an avowed anti-Semite, U. V. Shulgin, was appalled:

---

[8] Quoted in S. Friedman 1976, 22.   [9] Quoted ibid., 11–12.   [10] Ibid., 12.
[11] Quoted ibid.   [12] Ibid., 11.

> A dreadful medieval spirit moves in the streets of Kiev at night. In the general stillness and emptiness of the streets, a heartrending cry suddenly breaks out. It is the cry of the Jews, a cry of fear. In the darkness of the street appears a group of "men with bayonets." At this sight, large five and six story houses begin to shriek from top to bottom. Whole streets, seized with mortal anguish, scream with inhuman voices.[13]

According to various reports, the murderers systemically cordoned off streets and then moved from building to building as they bayoneted, bludgeoned, or shot the Jews to death. Jewish intellectuals appear to have been the early targets, as in the later Holocaust.

Before the end of the reign of terror, the Ukrainian nationalist forces led by Petlura were responsible for 493 separate massacres.[14] Nationalists assumed that the Jews were Bolshevik supporters, committed to the Sovietization of the entire former tsarist empire including, of course, Ukraine. The anti-Semitic nationalist spokesman Shulgin declared that "if you have some Jews who are very rich, who are very great financiers, the majority are very poor. They live in the small towns and villages and they live miserably. They became communists."[15]

True, many prominent Bolsheviks such as Leon Trotsky, leader of the Red Army, were Jews. Other prominent Jewish Bolsheviks included Jacob Sverdlov, president of the Central Committee of the Soviet Communist Party, and Grigori Zinoviev, president of the Third International. Yet the equation of Jews and communism, later to be even more emphatically propagandized by Hitler, was a canard. In 1922, only 5.2 percent of Soviet Communists cited themselves as Jews and, of these, many, such as Trotsky (né Bronshtein), had taken Slavic names, and no longer identified themselves in any fundamental way as Jewish.[16] Also in 1922, of a total Ukrainian-Jewish population of 1,773,000 only 8,250, less than half of one percent, identified themselves as Communists.[17] Indeed, the vast majority of Ukrainian Jews were poor artisans, traders, and shopkeepers. As such, they deeply opposed the collectivization policies of the Bolsheviks to the extent that initially many even welcomed the arrival of Denikin's White forces,[18] as some Jews welcomed German forces in 1941 because of their loss of businesses under Bolshevik rule. Thus, for example, in Vinnitsin in 1941, an elderly Jew who had his inn confiscated under Soviet governance requested that it be restored by the Germans because of his recollection of their

---

[13] Quoted ibid., 13–14.   [14] Ibid., 365.   [15] Quoted ibid., 193.   [16] Ibid., 196.
[17] Committee of the Jewish Delegations 1927, 43.   [18] Kenez 1992.

relatively benign rule during World War I. The Germans tied him to a horse and dragged him through the city to his death.[19]

In addition to common anti-Bolshevik sentiments, two factors were to strengthen the Ukrainian nationalist–Nazi connection. First, Stalin's forced collectivization of agriculture was to have disastrous consequences in Ukraine. At least several million, perhaps as many as 5,000,000, Ukrainians died as the result of famine directly induced by the collectivization process.[20] Whether Stalin actually intended this draconian outcome in order to counter Ukrainian nationalist activity, or the famine came about as the result of Soviet incompetence, the widespread devastation exacerbated Ukrainian anti-Semitism. In addition to the perception of Jews as Bolshevik supporters, the famine differentially impacted Ukrainian non-Jews. By the mid-1930s, the majority of Ukrainian Jews were urbanized, or at least lived in towns and villages. In contrast, the majority of Christians were rural peasant farmers – the precise target of the agricultural collectivization. Thus, they died in far higher numbers and proportions of their populations than did the Jews. And if the target was Ukrainian nationalism with its correlative separatist tendency, as writers such as Robert Conquest argue, then, historically, the Jewish population would have been far less susceptible to this particular ideological appeal with its strong overtones of Orthodox Christianity.[21] Thus, from this perspective, too, Jews would have been targeted less than Christians.

It was during this period of 1930–33 that in a Ukrainian newspaper *Meta* on April 17, 1932, the following exhortation was found: "Ukrainian Nationalism must be prepared to employ every means in the struggle ... not excluding mass physical extermination, even if millions of human beings, physical entities, are its victims."[22]

Also in the early 1930s, overt cooperation developed between the Nazis and the Organization of Ukrainian Nationalists (OUN), the civilian successor to the Ukrainian Military Organization that emerged after World War I and was now headquartered in Berlin. This was the second factor leading to the World War II alliance of Nazis and Ukrainian nationalists, at least in relation to the mass murder of Jews. Many members of the OUN were Nazi agents acting on behalf of Nazi Germany from locations in eastern Poland (western Ukraine) with its predominantly Ukrainian population, and even within the Soviet

---

[19] Rhodes 2002, 149–50.   [20] Conquest 1986, 303.   [21] Conquest 1986.
[22] Gartner 1991, 231.

Union. "Espionage information provided by the OUN network in the Western Ukraine before World War II was utilized by the Third Reich to its best advantage when it invaded the Soviet Union."[23] Thus, even before the war, Nazis and Ukrainian nationalists were in close covert cooperation, which facilitated their later overt cooperation during the Holocaust. The following incident is an exemplar of their early cooperation:

> During the first three days of July 1941, the "Nightingale Battalion," composed almost entirely of Ukrainians under the direction of the Gestapo, slaughtered seven thousand Jews in the vicinity of Lwow (Lemberg). Before their executions, Jewish professors, lawyers, and doctors were made to lick all the steps of four-story buildings and to carry garbage in their mouths from house to house. Then, forced to run a gauntlet of men who wore blue and gold armbands (coincidentally the colors of the Petlurist Republic), they were bayonetted to death in what was officially termed *Aktion Petlura*.[24]

Early massacres of this sort suggest that the Nazi–OUN collaboration yielded information concerning the intense anti-Semitism they found throughout Ukraine prior to any action against the Jews or any other European nationality. The Nazis were very careful to gather as much information as possible as the counterpart to Goebbels's dissemination of propaganda to the targeted country. Both intense awareness of the enemies' circumstances as well as propagandistic influence were hallmarks of the Nazi regime. Thus, the task of annihilating Soviet Jewry was greatly facilitated by the Ukrainian nationalist collaboration.

In addition to the Ukrainian nationalist pogroms of 1918–19, there were those emanating from a very different quarter but with the same outcome for the Jews. In the summer of 1919, taking advantage of strategic errors by the Red Army, Denikin's Volunteer Army occupied virtually the whole of Ukraine. As a tsarist army, its goals of defeating the Bolsheviks while maintaining the empire intact obviously conflicted with the separatist purposes of the Ukrainian nationalists. But the Cossacks of both armies held in common their hatred of Jews and propensities toward looting and rape. The tsarist officers in command of Denikin's army allowed the Cossack troops considerable leeway in their initiation of pogroms throughout areas of Ukraine under their command.

[23] Sabrin 1991, 4.   [24] S. Friedman 1976, 374.

A typical pogrom began with the officers and men divided into groups of five or ten each. They would beat and rob Jews on the street followed by entry into their houses and the extortion of money and valuables. Rape and murder would follow:

> Methods of murder varied greatly. Generally the Cossacks shot or bayo-neted their victims, but hanging, burning, drowning in wells, and live burials also occurred. There were recorded instances of people buried up to the necks in the sand and then killed by horses driven over them. Many victims were not killed outright but wounded and left to die. Thousands died of hunger, disease, and exposure after their houses were burned down and they had no one to turn to for help.[25]

An important distinction needs to be addressed: that between the locally raised Ukrainian forces, which sometimes acted like little more than a rabble, and the Volunteer Army, which was thoroughly professional, consisting mainly of officers from the old Russian army in command of Cossack forces. Describing this army, David Vital writes:

> All ranks within it were politically united in their dedication to the re-establishment of the Autocracy and genuinely imbued with the connected, driving conviction that at the root of Russia's tragedy and their own political discomfiture as a military class lay the Jews. If their Russia was ever to rise again from the ashes in which it now languished, the Jews, so ran their common and exceedingly tenacious belief, needed to be punished, indeed destroyed. Given the spirit moving them and the armed power at their command, it was inevitable that the consequences should go well beyond the Cossacks being allowed a few days' amusement – as Denikin's subordinates were apt to put it – in the Jewish quarters of the towns and villages through which they swept when advancing towards the centre of the country and again, in darker mood, early in 1920, as they retreated. In the view of the thinking members of the Volunteer Army, there lay upon them a positive duty to rid Russia, and by extension Christian Europe generally, of "the Jew" – "the Jew" in general, that is to say, conceived generically and without regard to his or her actual sex, or age, or station in life, or political affiliation (if any at all). No explicit obligation to kill was laid upon Denikin's officers in the field. So far as is known, no central, binding order to do away with the Jewish population was ever issued. But the climate of opinion in which they were engulfed encouraged it.[26]

[25] Kenez 1992, 299–300.   [26] Vital 1999, 724–25.

Although organized Jewish self-defense was sometimes successful against the Ukrainian nationalists, it was hopeless against the Volunteer Army. Here for the first time in modern memory, apparently without orders to do so, disciplined uniformed military forces were engaged in the massive destruction of a civilian population on the continent of Europe. Clearly this is a prototype for the later uniformed cadres of the SS and Wehrmacht, who in even more disciplined fashion managed to kill many times the number of Jews murdered by Denikin's forces.

Were the Nazis of the post-World War I period aware of these murderous anti-Semitic activities in the East and, if so, how salient were they? That they were aware cannot be disputed if only because of the large-scale immigration of Polish and Galician Jews into Germany during this period. Germany appeared to be a safe haven after the extreme depredations of Petlura and Denikin. Coming at the time of the Great Disorder, over 70,000 recent Jewish immigrants from the East were found in Berlin alone, most of them illegally. Many of these Jews, without proper means of support, along with large segments of German society, were engaged in black marketeering, which further alienated many Germans already inclined to anti-Semitic thinking. "By 1920, the term *Volksschädling* had become a widely accepted code word for the Jew, a term used to identify those who injured the people but which also suggested a noxious insect whose elimination could only serve the public good."[27]

From another perspective, we also can appreciate the salience of the East in the Nazi mind. The first districts in Germany to go over to the Nazis in free elections were those in East Prussia and Silesia.[28] East Prussian origin was highly overrepresented among early members of the Nazi Party.[29] East Prussia and Silesia were closest geographically to the East and indeed would be absorbed into a newly reconstituted Poland at the end of World War II.

Another indication of the importance of the East comes from a major study of early members of the Nazi Party.[30] Of the 581 Nazi respondents to a survey by Theodore Abel, those from East Prussia and other Eastern regions are overrepresented.[31] Military-civil servants comprising 23 percent of the sample[32] along with business and professional people[33] saw the Weimar Republic as Jewish-run. Disproportionate numbers of those who

---

[27] Feldman 1993, 203.   [28] Merkl 1975, 110, 189.   [29] Ibid., 17.
[30] Abel [1938] 1986; Merkl 1975.   [31] Merkl 1975, 17.   [32] Ibid., 51.   [33] Ibid., 690.

viewed Weimar as the *Judenrepublik* participated in or sympathized with the beer hall putsch or belonged to *völkisch* social groups or parties.[34] More than 61 percent of the early Nazis either had some direct experience with the war or were enthusiastic "victory-watchers."[35] Most of the dynamic marcher-proselytizers among them were of the war generation.[36] Fully two-thirds of the concentration camp commandants had served in the army before joining the Nazi Party.[37]

Military experience of this type could serve as a conduit of attitudes and behavior experienced in the East. Peter Kenez tells us that:

> The beginning of antisemitic agitation cannot be dated, for the Ukraine had not been without it for centuries. During 1918, however, when the country was occupied by the Germans and the Austrians, agitation accelerated. The occupying authorities contributed to antisemitism by their proclamations, which singled out the Jews. These proclamations attacked the Jews for black marketeering and for the spread of anti-German rumors. An Austrian commander, for example, forbade Jews under pain of death to have any contact with his soldiers; he was afraid that the Jews would somehow corrupt them.[38]

Local attitudes and behaviors, whether or not stimulated by the German occupying authorities, must have left a deep impression on the German (and Austrian) soldiers returning from the front. The many quasi-legal militias that sprang up in Germany after World War I (e.g., the *Freikorps*) must have been fertile arenas for the exchange of experiences at the front. Attitudes in Ukraine leading to the loss by murder or pogrom-induced disease of approximately 10 percent of the Jewish population, the rape of Jewish women, and the destruction by fire of 28 percent of all Ukrainian Jewish houses[39] must have communicated themselves forcefully to the German occupying soldiers. Anti-Semitic ideas developed first in Western Europe, especially Germany, found fertile ground among many of the Russian intelligentsia in the nineteenth century,[40] and then, having been acted upon in Ukraine in 1918–20, returned to Germany as a model for genocide. A White secret service agent reported from Ukraine:

> No administrative step would help; it is necessary to neutralize the microbe – the Jews ... As long as the Jews are allowed to do their harmful work, the front will always be in danger ... The Jew is not satisfied with

---

[34] Ibid., 483.   [35] Ibid., 157.   [36] Ibid., 371.   [37] Segev 1987, 60.
[38] Kenez 1992, 294–95.   [39] Baron 1976, 184–85.   [40] Klier 1995, 407–16.

corrupting the soldier. Lately he has been paying even greater attention to officers. But he is most interested in young people. Clever [Jewish] agents, under the cover of patriotism and monarchism, mix with young soldiers, and with the help of cards, women and wine they lure the debauched youth into their nets.[41]

The "microbe" analogy is compatible with the worst of Nazi propaganda a decade or two later. As Peter Kenez comments:

> This new and passionate antisemitism was born out of a need to explain, not so much to others, as to themselves, why the revolution had occurred. In the view of the reactionary officers it was the alien Jews who were primarily responsible. They were the microbes that destroyed the healthy body politic of old Russia. Antisemitism was not simply an element in their *Weltanschauung*; it was the focal point. It alone enabled them to make sense of a world that to them seemed senseless. In this respect, at least, the White officers were precursors of the Nazis.[42]

Analogy to the distress of German soldiers puzzling over the defeat of 1918 and its aftermath is striking. How could a powerful European empire descend to the level of chaos and near-dissolution with left-wing leaders governing in place of the hereditary monarchy? The same question was asked in both the German and Russian instances; the answer was identical. It is no wonder that the great Soviet-Jewish writer, Isaac Babel, upon observing the devastation of Jewish villages in western Ukraine remarked, "Is it not bound to be our century in which [the Jews] will perish?"[43] This foreboding also is reflected in one of the Red Cavalry stories, *Zamość*, dated September 1920 in which a *muzhik* (peasant) shares his views with the author:

> "The Jew is guilty before all men," he said, "both ours and
> yours. There will be very few of them left when the war is
> over. How many Jews are there in the world?"
> "Ten million," I replied and began to bridle my horse.
> "There'll be two hundred thousand of them left,"
> the muzhik exclaimed.[44]

The Holocaust in fact began in the East as a continuation of the shootings and other individualized methods of murder used at the end of World War I. In the opening stages, most of the killing was done by local

---

[41] Quoted in Kenez 1992, 304. [42] Ibid., 310–11. [43] Babel 2002, 408.
[44] Babel 1998, 206.

populations, as in Lithuania where only eight to ten German soldiers were required to kill approximately 130,000 Jews between July and December 1941; virtually all of the killing was done by Lithuanians in mobile machine gun units.[45] Later, the killing police battalions[46] and the use of gas in industrialized mass killing would add a Western (German) organizational touch, gas first having been used in the earlier eugenic killings. Thus, the uniquely German methods and those more "native" to the East would be combined in the mass slaughter of innocent men, women, and children. Interestingly, only after the first use of the more primitive methods principally by the local population, almost as a test case, do we find application of the industrialized chemical-based methods.

In Munich, the hotbed of Nazism, were found former participants in the 1905–06 pogroms, members of the reactionary Black Hundreds, and the later more deadly 1918–20 pogroms, all now refugees from the 1917 revolution. They brought with them the *Protocols of the Learned Elders of Zion*, the infamous tsarist forgery used as an important basis of Nazi propaganda. Also brought to Munich were many Baltic Germans from the former Russian Empire, among them Alfred Rosenberg who would soon become the chief ideologist of Nazism, a close collaborator of Hitler, and an "expert" on the East, Russia, and the Jews.[47]

Heinrich Himmler, the chief implementer of the Holocaust, was known to have been obsessed with the East. In 1921, he attended a lecture by Count Colmar von der Goltz, a general who had continued to fight in the East after the end of World War I. Himmler confided in his diary that "Now I know more definitely: if there is a campaign in the East again, I will go along. The East is the most important thing for us. The West dies out easily. We must fight and settle in the East."[48] In his biography of Himmler, Richard Breitman comments that "Anti-Semitism and German conquest of land in the East were to remain two of his great lifelong causes."[49] Thus, in Himmler's mind as well as Hitler's, the joining of these two obsessions was paramount in their genocidal policies. As Oscar Hamman commented in the immediate post-World War I period, "Our resurrection will to a great extent depend upon the shape things will assume in the East."[50]

---

[45] Neshamit 1977, 293.   [46] Browning 1992.   [47] Malia 1999, 351.
[48] Quoted in Breitman 1991, 16.   [49] Ibid.   [50] Quoted in Weinreich 1999, 11.

The Armenians

In the case of the Armenian genocide, elements of continuity also are prominent. Approximately 200,000 Armenians were massacred in the Ottoman Empire during the period 1894–96. One authoritative estimate puts the total as high as 250,000.[51] The first of these massacres occurred in the mountainous region in the vicinity of Sassoun; its cause was similar to earlier local revolts in the Balkans surrounding the issue of taxation.

Many Christian minorities throughout the Ottoman region were subject to double taxation, especially in rural areas in eastern Anatolia. Local Kurdish tribal chiefs exacted tribute from the Armenian peasantry, as did the Ottoman authorities. The combination of the two often was sufficient to deprive the peasants of even a subsistence livelihood. Additionally, one of the Armenian revolutionary groups that emerged during this period, the Hunchakists, agitated for an armed uprising. Although a widespread uprising did not take place, there was isolated resistance to the Kurds and Ottoman support troops, in addition to the refusal of approximately seventy or eighty houses of a village to pay taxes. Ottoman authorities attempted to implicate the Kurds as entirely responsible for the massacre, but evidence exists for the presence of the Fourth Army Corps acting under orders of Sultan Abdulhamit II. The commander of the Fourth Army Corps later was decorated by the sultan for his "laudable services and excellent and able efforts."[52] There even exists the suspicion that the Kurds were encouraged to raise their taxes so that, when the Armenians objected, the Ottoman authorities would have a pretext to stage the massacre.[53] According to Vahakn Dadrian, "The Sassoun massacre was the first instance of organized mass murder of Armenians in modern Ottoman history that was carried out in peacetime and had no connection with any foreign war. It lasted 24 days (August 18–September 10, 1894)."[54] It was to be but the opening stage of a series of massacres.

The following year, in October 1895, a demonstration in Constantinople, the Ottoman capital, was to have additional consequences. Organized by the Hunchakists, a peaceful demonstration took place against the Sassoun massacre, the precarious situation of the rural Armenian peasantry, and the inaction of the Ottomans. The 4,000 demonstrators were set upon by the Turks, and many of them were

[51] Dadrian 1997, 155.   [52] Ibid., 115.   [53] Marriott 1947, 399.   [54] Dadrian 1997, 117.

killed. Shortly thereafter, in late October, an uprising occurred at Zeitoun in the Armenian highlands. It was apparently occasioned by a warning from some friendly Turks that a massacre was about to take place. Military units had actually begun to destroy Armenian villages when the defenders of Zeitoun mounted their insurrection. A furious battled ensued, leading to a negotiated settlement. But elsewhere in the fall of 1895 most Armenian communities were attacked and devastated resulting in the final conflagration at Van, the center of Armenian life in eastern Anatolia. A nine-day battle followed that saved the vast majority of the Armenians in the city from Ottoman massacre, but further from the city the losses increased exponentially. Approximately 20,000 Armenians were killed in these depredations.[55]

The last of the major events of this period was the capture of the Ottoman State Bank in August 1896. This time, the Dashnaks, another Armenian revolutionary group, organized the action. Although audacious in its planning and execution, the consequences were bloody in the extreme for thousands of Armenians in the capital. The insurgents were allowed to leave the country after returning the bank to its directors, but many innocent Armenians were not so fortunate. Not only Armenians in Constantinople were murdered but even those in distant cities such as Egan in the interior of Turkey did not escape massacre.[56] Typical of these massacres is one related by an Armenian pastor, Abraham Hartunian:

> On Sunday morning, November 3, 1895, the church bells were silent. The churches and schools, desecrated and plundered, lay in ruins. Pastors, priests, choristers, teachers, leaders, all were no more. The Armenian houses, robbed and empty, were as caves. Fifteen hundred men had been slaughtered, and those left alive were wounded and paralyzed. Girls were in the shame of their rape ... On Thursday, November 7, the fifth day of our imprisonment, we were taken out and driven to the courtyard of a large inn. As we moved along in a file under guards, a crowd of Turkish women on the edge of the road, mocking and cursing us like frenzied maenads, screeched the unique convulsive shrill of the zelgid, the ancient battle cry of the women of Islam – the exultant lu-lu-lulu filled with the concentrated hate of the centuries.[57]

Although different from the massacres of Jews in Ukraine in precise etiology, there exists a strong underlying similarity. While the threat of

---

[55] Ibid., 137.   [56] Ibid., 148.   [57] Quoted in Staub 1989, 177.

Jewish equality motivated the pogroms of 1918–20 – Jews had joined socialist and communist political groups in sizable numbers and had organized self-defense forces partially effective against the Ukrainian nationalists – the threat of Armenian equality was at least as important in 1894–96. A response to the British and French insistence on Christian, especially Armenian, equality at the end of the Crimean War (1856) was the prediction of "a great slaughter" by then Grand Vizier Reşid.[58] In the Turkish view, by appealing to the European powers for juridical equality, Armenians had overstepped their bounds as *dhimmis*, subject people whose lives and property could be protected only under Muslim hegemony.

In Adana, in 1909, another massacre took place in which approximately 30,000 Armenians died.[59] The occurrence of this massacre after the Young Turk Revolution of 1908 suggests that the extreme anti-Armenian policies of the Ottoman state would continue. Once they had challenged that hegemony, their lives and property could be forfeit.[60] Many of the massacres occurred on a Friday when Muslims were gathered in their mosques for prayer:

> [The massacre's] objective, based on the convenient consideration that Armenians were now tentatively starting to question their inferior status, was the ruthless reduction, with a view to elimination of the Armenian Christians, and the expropriation of their lands for the Moslem Turks. Each operation, between the bugle calls, followed a similar pattern. First the Turkish troops came into a town for the purpose of massacre; then came the Kurdish irregulars and tribesmen for the purpose of plunder. Finally came the holocaust, by fire and destruction, which spread, with the pursuit of the fugitives and mopping-up operations, throughout the lands and villages of the surrounding province. This murderous winter of 1895 thus saw the decimation of much of the Armenian population and the devastation of their property in some twenty districts of eastern Turkey ... Cruellest and most ruinous of all were the massacres of Urfa, where the Armenian Christians numbered a third of the total population ... When the bugle blast ended the day's operations, some three thousand refugees poured into the cathedral, hoping for sanctuary. But the next morning – a Sunday – a fanatic mob swarmed into the church in an orgy of a slaughter, rifling its shrines with cries of "Call upon Christ to prove Himself a greater prophet than Mohammed." Then they amassed a large pile of straw matting, which they spread over the litter

---

[58] Dadrian 1997, 147.   [59] Miller and Miller 1993.   [60] Ye'or 1985, 101.

of corpses and set alight with thirty cans of petroleum. The woodwork of the gallery where a crowd of women and children crouched, wailing with terror, caught fire, and all perished in the flames. Punctiliously at three-thirty in the afternoon the bugle blew once more, and the Moslem officials proceeded around the Armenian quarter to proclaim that the massacres were over ... the total casualties in the town, including those slaughtered in the cathedral, amounted to eight thousand dead.[61]

Much of this hatred for Christians, as we shall see in chapters 5 and 7, must have stemmed in part from the refugee status of many Ottoman Muslims who had fled from newly independent Christian lands. But the mobilization and direction of this hatred by the Ottoman authorities had a geopolitical base. If the Armenians remained subservient as was traditionally the case, then matters could continue as before. But with the rise of Armenian revolutionary groups and agitation for equality, autonomy, or even political independence, the Anatolian base of the Ottoman Empire appeared to be threatened. Spread out among all six Anatolian provinces and with a large presence in the east at the Russian border, "another Bulgaria," split from the empire, appeared to be in the offing. The vast majority of Armenians had no such expectations. They simply wanted to continue to live in peace in their ancestral villages, as did the Ukrainian Jews.

By the end of the nineteenth century, the traditional empire with one ethnoreligious group in perpetual ascendancy simply became untenable. The Soviet Union, as a reincarnation of the tsarist empire in centralized and industrialized garb, prolonged the agony of dissolution for another seventy years. It did so in part by promising and then partially fulfilling the promise of equality, but outside the rubric of ethnoreligious nationalism so common in that era and indeed our own. But some people, namely Russian Communist leaders, were more equal than others; the promise of equality was not sustained beyond the 1920s, and only through the vehicle of national self-determination could individual Soviet republics feel they could fulfill that promise.

The Ottoman Empire had no new incarnation. It was reduced to the dimensions of modern Turkey by World War I. Genocide of the Armenians and expulsion of the Greeks yielded a homogeneous Muslim Turkish state, but one that adopted a secular government. Ethnoreligious equality as a major issue – Greek and Armenian

---

[61] Kinross 1977, 559–60.

dominance of the nonagricultural economy – no longer existed beyond the early 1920s, with one exception. Only the Kurds, confessionally the same, but ethnically different, persisted as a threat to the integrity of the Turkish state in eastern Anatolia. Paradoxically, the Kurds were highly useful to the Ottomans in establishing a united Islamic front versus the Armenians, especially in critically important eastern Anatolia. Now that religious homogeneity was no longer an issue, the Kurds constituted a separatist threat.

Ironically, only the Jews, despite episodic persecutions in virtually all of Europe and especially in tsarist Russia, escaped harm. Their small number and absence of any affinities of religion, ethnicity, or politics with competing great powers rendered them harmless. Their proportion of valuable economic holdings in the Ottoman Empire also was substantially less than that of Greek or Armenian Christians.[62] This too, rendered them less visible and therefore less liable to persecution. Interestingly, the Zionist Jews in Palestine with their potential for separatist activity and Russian origins were viewed with far greater suspicion by the Ottoman authorities. Zionist support for the Allies in World War I in part stemmed from these sentiments.

Rwanda

Equality also is a component of continuity preceding the Rwandan genocide. One cannot understand the genocide of 1994 without first examining the sources and consequences of the "revolution" of 1959, and the first massacres of Tutsi in 1963–64.

Gradually, over time, the Tutsi, who were pastoral herders, began to assert political dominance over the Hutu, who were settled agriculturalists. By the eighteenth century, the polarization between rulers and ruled was complete. Power was increasingly defined as solely a Tutsi prerogative.[63] But it was under colonial rule that the distinctions between the two groups were hardened into virtually hermetic racial categories. First under the Germans and even more emphatically after World War I under the Belgians, the Tutsi became the handmaidens of colonial rule. The Belgians especially found it useful to appoint Tutsi to be heads of various prefectures and other positions of leadership. The Roman Catholic Church, by now the dominant religion, also was disproportionately staffed by Tutsi in leadership positions. With

[62] Issawi 1980.   [63] Mamdani 2001, 63.

independence nearing in 1959, and the Tutsi only a 15 percent minority in Rwanda, violent opposition against the Tutsi chiefs developed. Several were killed and others forced to resign. To forestall even more violence by the Hutu, and major Tutsi reprisals, the Belgians moved to install a Hutu-led government. Many Tutsi went into political exile, only to return in the early 1960s as the *inyenzi* or "cockroaches," Tutsi armed guerrillas who targeted Hutu leaders. An early Hutu reprisal had the following consequence: "Between 1000 and 2000 Tutsi men, women and children were massacred and buried on the spot, their huts burned and pillaged and their property divided among the Hutu population."[64]

The year 1963 witnessed further *inyenzi* attacks, and the level of violence escalated dramatically. Early estimates of the number of dead were low but have now been substantially revised. Careful scholarly estimates put the number killed at between 10,000 and 14,000, while Human Rights Watch estimates that close to 20,000 Tutsi were murdered.[65] The revolution, followed by attempts at restoration and bloody reprisals, set the stage for the genocide of 1994. Even much of the killing pattern was the same as in the disposal of Tutsi bodies in the Nyabarongo river.[66] Not only was this a fairly efficient method of disposing of the large number of Tutsi killed, it had symbolic value as well. The river was seen to flow in the direction of the Horn of Africa where the Tutsi were presumed to have their origins. Now these "foreigners" were being sent back to the region from whence they came. By 1966, the *inyenzi*, sickened by the number of their ethnic brethren butchered by the Hutu, ceased their incursions.[67]

Although Rwanda would not again experience massacres of this intensity until the early 1990s, nevertheless responses to external events took the form of massacre. In 1972, in response to an attempted Hutu student-led uprising in Burundi, the Tutsi-led army murdered approximately 200,000 Hutu.[68] In Rwanda, Hutu students at the National University in Butare began agitating against their Tutsi colleagues. Tutsi students began to leave, along with Tutsi employees of targeted firms. Several hundred Tutsi were murdered. Now the hostility of the Hutu population, most of whom were poor, began to be directly leveled not only at the Tutsi, but at all of those who were presumed to be rich (mostly the Tutsi).[69] Ethnopolitical violence now merged with class warfare. Although the number of murdered was small relative to the

---

[64] Ibid., 129.   [65] Ibid., 30.   [66] Des Forges 1999, 85.   [67] Gourevitch 1998, 66.
[68] Mamdani 2001, 137.   [69] Ibid.

previous decade, continuity of massacre was preserved until the Rwandese Patriotic Front (RPF) invasion of 1990.

The political system facilitated the occurrence of massacre, and later of genocide. In July 1973, following a period of attacks by Hutu against Tutsi, partly to minimize growing differences between northern and southern Hutu, General Juvénal Habyarimana seized power in a blood-less coup. Two years later, he officially made Rwanda a single-party state under the Mouvement Révolutionnaire National pour le Développement (MRND). Increasingly, he and his cohort included the leadership of the army, corporate heads, and the hierarchy of the Rwandan Roman Catholic Church. Of the nine bishops in place at the time of the genocide, seven were Hutu. The Anglican hierarchy and the Baptist Church also supported him.

Within this larger circle of the elite was a smaller one called the *akazu* or "little house" consisting of corporate heads and military officers. Among them was Colonel Théoneste Bagosora, a principal organizer of the 1994 genocide. Habyarimana's rule was increasingly harsh, especially against political opponents. Although evidence of increasing corruption and favoritism along with economic decline forced the establishment of a nominal multiparty system in 1990, Habyarimana still held the levers of power until the genocide four years later.

Validation

Continuity presupposes proximity in time of similar acts, committed by like-minded perpetrators, acting in roughly comparable circumstances. Thus, the *Einsatzgruppen* are exemplars of the German continuation of earlier reactionary Russian barbarism in Ukraine and Belorussia in 1918–20, but of course on a much larger scale. The near-elimination of the Herero and Nama tribes by German colonial authorities in South-West Africa around the turn of the century also provides an earlier element of continuity in German policy toward "alien" people whom the Germans perceived to be "troublesome."[70] Continuity establishes a temporal causal nexus via the identification of genocidal leaders with the policies of earlier prototypes of the same nationality or at least similar ideological disposition. Thus Nazi leaders could identify with the elimi-nationist policies of earlier German colonial authorities, as they could with the virulent and murderous anti-Semitism of anti-Bolshevik

---

[70] Arendt 1951.

Ukrainians and White Russians. The Ottoman Turks at the start of the Armenian genocide could identify with the behaviors of the minions of Abdulhamit II in the massacres of Armenians in 1894–96, and the Hutu extremists in 1994 were able to identify with the earlier murderous behaviors of their political forebears in 1959–64 and in 1972. Essentially, in each case, the goals were the same – the mass murder of ethnically different people who did not share the worldview of the prevailing political authority.

Validation, on the other hand, refers to the consequence of an act for the actor. Validation occurs when morally repugnant and heinous behaviors result in few if any negative consequences for the perpetrators. The mass killing of Armenians by Turks during World War I and of kulaks by Stalin during the early 1930s yielded no appreciable negative consequences for either the Ottoman or Soviet leaders. However disgusted Western leaders were with the Ottoman and Stalinist policies (and some actually praised the latter), none in the West was willing or able to act against them. Indeed, from the standpoint of an amoral autocratic observer, massacres simply resulted in a reinforcement of the power of the political leadership. As Hitler stated in his speech to German generals on the eve of the invasion of Poland in September 1939 justifying the killing of Polish civilians, "Only thus shall we gain the living space [*Lebensraum*] which we need. Who after all, speaks today of the annihilation of the Armenians?"[71] Hitler need not have identified with the policies of the Ottoman leadership. Certainly he saw no continuity between the policies of his leadership and those of the Turks in 1915. Yet their actions, whatever the degree of verbal condemnation they incurred, had no adverse external consequences for them. In other words, the end genuinely justified the means, a more extreme but nevertheless commonly understood precept of realpolitik.

Similar but not identical arguments apply to the Armenians and the Tutsi. The massacres of 1894–96 in the Ottoman Empire led to very few, if any, consequences for the Ottoman leaders. If anything, they tended to cement the relationship between the German and Ottoman leaders (see chapter 10). The mass killings in Rwanda after 1959 also had no appreciable consequences for the extremist Hutu leadership that could deter future actions of this kind. Thus, in all three cases, the precedent of impunity was established, which validated killings on a massive scale

---

[71] Quoted in Fein 1979, 21.

and could then be applied to mass murder on the even larger scale of genocide.

Risks associated with the earlier mass murders of Jews, Armenians, and Tutsi were minimal or nonexistent; these massacres later were amplified into genocide. Conversely, if risks were greater, as demonstrated, say, by consequences for earlier massacres, then the likelihood of genocide would be diminished significantly. This theme will be developed later in the discussion of protective affine populations or sympathetic governments (see chapter 17) that significantly elevate the risk of committing genocide for potential victimizers.

Now, having established certain pre-genocidal conditions that facilitate the later onset of genocide, we can turn to the development of theory. In this, I first consider existing theories, rejecting some, and then turning to other avenues of understanding the onset and the magnitude of genocide.

4

Prologue to theory

Two existing theories, one based on goal attainment and the other based on ideology, are first examined as plausible approaches to the explanation of genocide. Respectively, they are rational choice theory and utopianism.

Rational choice theory is virtually ubiquitous in many fields of social science, especially in economics and political science, and therefore is a prime candidate for consideration. Utopianism has emerged in one major work as an exemplar of ideologically driven behavior leading to genocide. Since genocide has been claimed to be ideologically motivated at bottom, utopianism appears to be an appropriate point of theoretical departure. Later, two cases of genocidal behavior will be examined as bases for theory development.

Rational choice

Why not use rational choice theory as the primary basis on which to build theory about the onset and implementation of genocide? After presenting basic elements of the theory, I will state the blatant, somewhat coarse version of the argument against its usage, followed by a nuanced version that I believe to be more accurate. In the end, I conclude that rational choice theory has broad applicability in the everyday discourse of normal politics, but outside the domain of losses where genocides typically occur.

Two fundamental bases of rational choice theory are the existence of preferences and utility maximization. These requirements are intimately connected. Rational choice theory demands that utility be maximized or, in other words, that a clear preference exists that is to be achieved in the most efficacious manner.[1]

---

[1] See Elster 1986 and O'Neill 1999, 259–60.

As Jon Elster reminds us, if we are to agree that an act is based on rational choice, then "The agent must not act on a desire that, in his own opinion, is less weighty than other desires which are reasons for not performing the action."[2] Furthermore, according to Barry O'Neill in his award winning *Honor, Symbols, and War*, "equating rationality with possession of a utility function would go far from the normal meaning of the word, since someone can be relatively wise but fail to follow the pattern required by the utility axioms [e.g., consistency and transitivity],[3] or alternatively someone who we would call unbalanced might follow the axioms exactly."[4] To be sure, the decisive test of a theory is not its truth content but its predictive or explanatory power.[5] And there have been many successes in the application of rational choice theories, principally conceived as game-theoretic mathematical models.[6] However, here a *cost–benefit calculus*, including most importantly an evaluation of outcomes, must be introduced to assess the rationality of decision making, *independent* of any subjective perceptions of the participants.

In addition, the outcome, as well as the process, must be subjected to what Amartya Sen calls "reasoned scrutiny" and must be prudent, as we shall see shortly. As he puts it:

> Rationality is interpreted here, broadly, as the discipline of subjecting one's choices – of actions as well as of objectives, values and priorities – to reasoned scrutiny. Rather than defining rationality in terms of some formulaic conditions that have been proposed in the literature (such as satisfying some prespecified axioms of "internal consistency of choice," or being in conformity with "intelligent pursuit of self-interest," or being some variant of maximizing behavior), rationality is seen here in much more general terms as the need to subject one's choices to the demands of reason.[7]

Despite the obvious appeal in its parsimonious, even elegant formulations and successes, rational choice theory can be said to explain the onset of genocide only in the most narrow sense. Expressing a preference for genocide leads to genocide – so goes the argument. This alternative

---

[2] Elster 1986, 12.

[3] Consistency means that there are no internal contradictions in the actor's schedule of preferences; transitivity implies that given three preferences, if preference A is preferred to B and B to C, then A must be preferred to C.

[4] O'Neill 1999, 260.   [5] M. Friedman 1953.   [6] Bueno de Mesquita et al. 2003.

[7] Sen 2002, 4.

of eliminating a hated ethnoreligious group is claimed to rank first among all desiderata, as in Hitler's choice of killing the Jews above all else, including winning the war.

In addition to the arguments concerning Hitler's changes in policy over time noted in the introduction, we need not belabor the obvious point that Hitler and Himmler were perfectly willing to use valuable transport facilities and soldiers to convey vast numbers of Jews to their deaths when such equipment and personnel were desperately needed in the ever-worsening German battlefield predicament. As will be shown later, the intensity of the genocide actually was inversely related to battlefield success. In other words, winning the war as the obvious rational choice preference was subverted by the ever-intensifying desire to complete the genocide.

One has only to contrast the relatively (for Hitler) well-reasoned and benign analyses of *Hitler's Second Book*[8] with his later behaviors. Although not published in his lifetime, this book is a useful baseline for comparing his prewar, almost prudent realpolitik with the genocide beginning full force in 1942. Much of the book, written in 1928, after *Mein Kampf*, is an argument for dampening nationalist passions concerning German speakers governed by the Italian government in South Tyrol. Hitler's purpose was to maintain good relations with Italy even at the "expense" of the South Tyrolean ethnic Germans. Hence, when a Nazi government took office, fascist Italy could be its first European ally.

For the most part, Hitler's arguments are embedded in rational discourse – a prudent realpolitik. He examines all possible great power allies and, through historical example and geopolitical argument, especially concerning vulnerability of Germany's borders,[9] he arrives at the choice of Italy. Contrast the several chapters on Italy with the relatively small amount of space (five pages) at the end of the book devoted to the "Jewish Question." And, even here, he ties this issue with that of Italy's relative freedom from "Jewish domination" that makes other candidates such as Britain less desirable as allies. Although a screed, and one based on the utterly false premise of a worldwide Jewish conspiracy, beyond that fatal flaw, the argument is reasonably well presented. In contrast, as we shall see, when the human and material costs of the Soviet invasion escalated dramatically as early as mid-August 1941, this kind of reasoned scrutiny was abandoned. Because of these changes over time, a single

---

[8] Weinberg 2003.   [9] Ibid., 137–38.

analytical approach, such as rational choice theory or any other perspective that assigns primary motivation, cannot be adopted.

Recognizing Hitler's (and other genocidal leaders') changes in outlook over time suggests the more nuanced argument concerning rational choice. Adopting a Bayesian approach to human reasoning can help explain the transition from Hitler's relatively well-reasoned arguments of 1928 to the apparent irrationality of late August 1941 and the start of the Holocaust in the East. Recent findings suggest that human decision making depends on sensory feedback – that which we observe at the moment of decision – combined with prior knowledge or memory.[10]

The greater the uncertainty at the time of observation, the greater the reliance on prior knowledge of similar phenomena. Complete uncertainty would yield complete dependence on memory, while certainty of outcome would lead to the disuse of prior knowledge. As we shall see, the uncertainty of the war's outcome, especially after the difficulties encountered by the Germans in Russia in mid-August 1941, led to Hitler's reliance on prior knowledge of loss emanating from the defeat of World War I. Indeed, the vast shrinkage of German and Austro-Hungarian governed territories in Europe after June 1918 could be repeated again in the early 1940s. In June 1918, all of Central and Eastern Europe, as well as portions of Ukraine, France, and Belgium were held by German forces, or their allies. Hence, the rational calculations of 1928, dependent on the then current and predictable geopolitical environment, could give way later during the extreme uncertainty of 1941–42 to dependence on prior knowledge of loss or, as we shall see, the domain of losses with its own horrific consequences.

Even for a leader such as Hitler, rationality can persist within relatively certain environments, but when losses are invoked as a consequence of uncertainty, the dynamics of decision making change radically. Rational choice theory, therefore, has a broad mandate outside the domain of losses but, as suggested by prospect theory (see chapter 5), it is much less applicable within the domain of losses. And, as we shall see, while prospect theory indicates asymmetry between people's reactions to gains and losses, the Bayesian findings imply that, under extreme uncertainty, current sensory inputs – the database of rational decision making – would be virtually ignored in favor of the memory of loss.

---

[10] Körding and Wolpert 2004; Leonhardt 2004.

All of the cases of genocide and politicide examined in this book were associated with wars that were lost by the genocidal states both prior to the war in which genocide occurred and within its duration. These include Germany in World Wars I and II, the Ottoman Empire in the late nineteenth and early twentieth centuries and World War I, the Hutu extremist government in Rwanda during the early 1990s, and Democratic Kampuchea (the Khmer Rouge) versus the Vietnamese, the only ethnicity actually subject to genocide in the ongoing politicide (see chapter 15). Earlier cases to be brought forward for illustrative purposes toward the end of this chapter, such as Athens in the Peloponnesian War, were also on the losing side both before (Mantinea) and after the genocide.

Interesting from the cost–benefit perspective and potentially important in understanding the etiology of genocide is the Ottoman genocidal campaign against the Armenians, in part, at least, to generate an ethnically and religiously homogeneous state in Anatolia. The large concentration of Christian Armenians in eastern Anatolia separated the Muslim Turks in western Anatolia from their coreligionists to the east. As the Ottoman Empire had been shorn of its largely Christian holdings in Europe by local (mainly Balkan) nationalisms, Arab nationalism began to make itself felt in Mesopotamia and Arabia, and European powers asserted their imperial designs in North Africa. Anatolia loomed large as the only relatively secure bastion of Turkish Muslims. Armenians, and to a somewhat lesser extent Greeks, were seen as the only obstacles to an emergent Turkish statehood.[11] The former would be, for the most part, annihilated during World War I, and the latter ethnically cleansed in the Greco-Turkish War of 1919–22. In this fashion, most of Anatolia became almost entirely Muslim and, with the exception of Kurdish communities (also Muslim), ethnically Turkish. Although the Ottomans lost World War I along with Germany and Austria-Hungary, in one sense at least they can be said to have won the peace, because they now had, in their view, the ethnic and religious basis for a viable modern state.

The force of this argument, however, rests on historical contingencies that might have developed very differently, if not for critical events, foremost among them the Bolshevik Revolution. If this revolution had not occurred, then the victorious Allies (and they would have been, given the US entry into the war) could have made common cause with

---

[11] Libaridian 1987; Melson 1992.

Russia, possibly in seeking more direct and effective retribution against Turkey for the Armenian genocide. The victorious Orthodox Church in Russia, not decimated and suppressed as under the Bolsheviks, might have taken the lead in spurring Russia and the Allies to take a far more determined stand against the Turkish leadership and possibly even the Turkish nation than they did at Sèvres in 1920.

Earlier, in February 1914, at the instigation of the Russian government, an Armenian reform agreement was signed by the Ottomans, effectively relinquishing authority over the Armenian communities in eastern Anatolia to appointed foreign observers.[12] Had the same or a similarly inclined government remained in place at the end of the war, instead of an abortive legal adjudication of Ottoman crimes against humanity, with Russian cooperation there could even have occurred a restoration of the boundaries of an autonomous Armenian region in eastern Anatolia as planned by the Allies, with implications for a decidedly weakened Turkish state. Of course, when the Ittihadists embarked on the genocide of 1915 and 1916, they could have had no way of knowing that the Bolshevik Revolution would later occur in 1917, which not only would temporarily weaken Russia considerably as the result of internecine warfare, but would blunt the potential Russian quasi-religious involvement on behalf of the Armenians.

Another consideration stems from first principles. From the outset, how did the Ottoman authorities believe that they could commit carnage of this magnitude and get away with it? Virtually complete German support for Ottoman policies, especially within the German military, provides a partial answer. Had not the Germans themselves moved the Herero to the Omahake desert in the Battle of Waterberg without major repercussions? Germany as the great power protector of the Ottomans effectively generated a permissive context for the Armenian genocide. (This argument is more fully developed in chapter 10.) But the Ittihadists did not count on the outright German defeat. Without German protection they could easily have succumbed to Allied retribution, especially from the Russians, but for the weakened state of Bolshevik Russia.

Thus, the short-term gain for Turkey was a contingent event. But even here one can question the nature of the short-term gain. Witnessing the genocide in 1915 in Kharput in central Anatolia where he was posted as US consul, Leslie Davis remarked:

---

[12] Bodger 1984, 96.

> It was literally a case of killing the goose that laid the golden egg, for there
> would be no one left to till the soil and the authorities might have foreseen
> the famine which actually did visit the land the following year ... Nearly all
> the merchants, bankers, doctors, dentists, lawyers, teachers, carpenters,
> brick-layers, tile-makers, tinsmiths, bakers, tailors, shoe-makers, and other
> artisans so essential to the life of the people were Armenians ... By one
> stroke ... the country was to be set back a century.[13]

In the long term, the loss of the Armenians (and Greeks) must certainly
be considered a major setback in light of Turkey's current ambitions to
both modernize and enter the European Union (EU). The Armenians
and Greeks (whose expulsion during the Greco-Turkish War was probably motivated, at least in part, by the successful elimination of the
Armenians during World War I) could have provided a dynamic societal
bridge between Turkey and Europe. Both Armenians and Greeks in the
Ottoman Empire were entrepreneurial and leading-edge economic
innovators in what was otherwise a traditional agrarian society.
Indeed, Reşat Kasaba argues that the Greek community, and to a lesser
extent the Armenian, was laying the foundations of an Ottoman civil
society as early as the middle of the nineteenth century.[14] Over time,
these economic communities could have had a multiplier effect on the
entire Turkish economy, making it far more eligible to join the EU.
Socially, too, the presence of significant non-Muslim groups numbering
in the millions could have muted the hostility of those in the EU who
would like to admit to membership only Christian societies. At the very
least, it would have been a partly Muslim country more palatable to
most Europeans than a homogeneous Islamic state subject perhaps to
fundamentalist tendencies. In the long run, then, modernization and
growth of the Turkish economy in concert with the EU was retarded by
the Armenian genocide and its aftereffects.

What appears "rational" may actually depend on the constellation of
power available to the protagonists. In comparison with the newly
formed, relatively weak Soviet Union and with Greece in the Greco-
Turkish War, Turkey after World War I was sufficiently powerful to
avoid any serious consequences of the Armenian genocide and expulsion of the Anatolian Greek communities. These two neighboring countries were the only ones proximal geographically and with the
ethnoreligous incentives to have responded strongly to the genocide.

---

[13] Quoted in Balakian 2003, 236.   [14] Kasaba 1999.

But the Russian Orthodox Church was now muted, and the invasion of Turkey by Greece ended disastrously for the invader. Thus a much more ethnoreligiously homogeneous Turkish society, capable of utilizing that homogeneity for state-building purposes, was not only contingent on historical events like the Bolshevik Revolution, but on the overall geopolitical power configuration that effectively allowed Turkey to "get away with it."

Germany, too, would have suffered the consequences of the Holocaust far more if not for the onset of the Cold War that gave Germans in the western zones of Allied occupation the leverage to escape much of the planned de-Nazification and potential retribution. Geographically, Germany was perceived to be essential for blocking communist expansion into Western Europe. If not for the Cold War, the consequences of the Holocaust for Germany could have been far more extreme, in addition to the earlier drain on German resources during World War II. Or, going back in time, the successful European expansions and virtual elimination of Native Americans in both North and South America depended on the gross power disparities between the invaders and indigenous populations.

Our perception of "rationality" as equivalent to "success" in the cost–benefit calculus depends very much on power relationships. The phrase "history is written by the winners" is another way of saying that the reconstruction of events by historians on the winning side follows a rational design that he or she has imposed on the events in question. Had Nazi Germany won the war, we would now be studying the success of German arms through the "rationality" prism of an absolute necessity to eliminate "racial enemies" (who could stab one in the back) prior to such a victory. Obviously such a policy was not followed in World War I, hence the German defeat. What is assumed – the Jew as racial enemy – is justified by later events, whatever the truth or falsity of the initial assumption. As we shall see in chapter 8, the altruistic punishment by Nazi leaders – self-sacrifice for the sake of destroying the "other" – can account for the much greater unity and consequent success of Nazi Germany in World War II when compared to its fractious behavior and more rapid defeat in 1918. This particular element of theory was not suggested by rational choice considerations.

Although such a redactive process challenges the rational choice approach as a way of understanding the onset of genocide, it does suggest the importance of power as a real-world mediating variable. The question becomes *not* whether the Jews had to be destroyed in order to win the war, but whether Nazi Germany had the actual power to both win the war *and* at the same time destroy the Jews. Also note the substantial power increase to Germany had Jewish scientists and mathematicians (including those with partial Jewish ancestry), such as Albert Einstein, Niels Bohr, Hans Bethe, Edward Teller, Stanislaw Ulam, or John von Neumann, remained in Europe and worked on atomic weapons for the Reich instead of for the Allies. And, here, we see that in the case of the Holocaust the decision is not explainable by a rational choice approach. Rationality would dictate instead that these scientists be put to military use in the construction of atomic or other weapons for the Axis Powers. Given the contingent nature of the Turkish escape from serious retribution after World War I because of temporary Russian (Soviet) weakness, as we have just seen, that decision, too, is not readily explainable by a rational choice methodology.

The long-term implications for Germany as a twice-defeated "cosseted" state within the EU, and ever-present reminders of its horrific past that the Germans even to this day never seem to escape, also suggest the absence of any rational choice explanations. And, in Rwanda, the replacement of the Arusha power-sharing accords by genocide of the Tutsi led to the direct downfall of the Hutu-led regime, and the loss of all political power that the Hutu extremists had fought so hard to maintain. Most became refugees living a hardscrabble and conflict-ridden existence in countries like Zaire (later renamed Democratic Republic of the Congo). And even the secondary but important consequence for the Hutu extremists of eliminating the Tutsi from Rwanda has been reversed. Within a few short years after the genocide, the approximately 10 percent share of the Rwandan population has once again been achieved by the return of pregenocide Tutsi exiles. Endemic conflict throughout Central Africa, with no end in sight, has been a longer-term consequence of the genocide.

It is conceivable, of course, that one can find historical illustrations of the "success" of genocide as a policy option without obvious costs. But in candidates such as the obliteration of Carthage in the last of the Punic Wars, the status of Carthage as a feared and once nearly victorious enemy (fighting which had cost tens if not hundreds of thousands of Roman lives)[15] blunted any sense of moral outrage that could have affected Roman politics for years to come. Although defeated elsewhere

---

[15] For obvious reasons, it is difficult to obtain exact estimates of the Roman dead in the Punic Wars. Rostovtzeff suggests that "a multitude of Roman citizens and allies lay dead

in the Mediterranean region, the Carthaginians under Hannibal were never defeated in Italy itself,[16] thus yielding a sense of loss that led M. Porcius Cato, an extremely influential veteran of the wars with Hannibal, to declare in the Roman Senate, "it is my opinion that Carthage must be destroyed."[17] Whatever the ethical standards of the day, without a seemingly prudential temporal or sacral justification, mass killing may have a negative societal impact for generations to come.

The moral dimension must be weighed in any long-term evaluation of the consequences of genocide, for simple reciprocity of kindness or hostility is a moral basis for many societies. Even game-generated scenarios such as Robert Axelrod's Tit for Tat[18] conform to this principle. Later, we shall see the importance of the moral dimension in understanding the role of altruistic punishment in establishing cooperation between genocidal leaders and followers. To blithely ignore such relationships, as in a total reliance on realpolitik, is to enter a quagmire of future uncertainty, self-doubt, and even self-hatred. Polls of West European peoples' views of themselves typically have Germans at the bottom. Ian Buruma chronicles the guilt that still pervades German society.[19]

Sen criticizes the single-minded pursuit of self-interest defined in narrow terms. Accordingly, "The need for reasoned scrutiny applies not only to accommodating moral and political concerns in personal choices and in social living, but also in incorporating the demands of prudence. Many failures to be adequately prudential arise, in fact, precisely from the absence of an adequately reasoned scrutiny."[20] Clearly, leaders such as Hitler, Talât, and Habyarimana were not prudential. In the following chapter, prudence entailing the application of reasoned scrutiny will be used to distinguish between prudent and imprudent realpolitik.

Perceptions of current well-being also are deeply influenced by past behavior. In a large-N study of non-Jewish rescuers of Jews, and of bystanders who did not help, highly significant differences were found between the two groups. Specifically, those involved in historic rescue gained a sense of deep inner contentment. Furthermore, in contrast to the bystanders, rescuers felt far more satisfied with the way they had

---

on the battle-fields of Italy" (1960, 62). Polybius, 1960, 3, 116, estimates 70,000 Roman dead at Cannae alone.
[16] Rostovtzeff 1960, 64.　[17] Chalk and Jonassohn 1990, 85.　[18] Axelrod 1984.
[19] Buruma 1995.　[20] Sen 2002, 47.

conducted their lives, and had lower rates of post-traumatic stress disorder; bystanders, on the other hand, suffered from higher rates of psychopathology, even several decades after World War II.[21]

Finally, and perhaps most importantly, rational choice perspectives tend not to be integrative. Typically, they do not suggest separate processes operating at different levels of society (required assumptions of rationality at all levels), which together may present a coherent explanatory whole. Realpolitik concerns, that is those focused on the state and indeed having a rationality component, may not be persuasive to elements of the general population, but reminders of the recent experience of loss, such as the presence of refugees and the necessity for personal sacrifice, may have such resonance. In order to explain political and social mobilization for genocide having a purpose that deviates thoroughly from accepted moral precepts, such theoretical integration is required. As will be seen in the case of Bulgaria, realpolitik has a rational component in necessary risk minimization, but within the context of the domain of losses (e.g., Nazi Germany) becomes unnecessary, is genocidal, and hence is distorted well beyond the demands of reasoned scrutiny. Outside the context of loss, realpolitik, as in other potentially rational programs, can conform to reasoned scrutiny (Bulgaria) and the absence of genocide when it might have been expected to occur. Perhaps it is this case more than any other that suggests large areas of applicability for rational choice theory in the everyday discourse of politics, but excluding the domain of losses.

Utopianism

In addition to rational choice, utopianism is a current theory that could serve as a starting point for comprehending the onset of genocide. In contrast to rational choice, which provides a social scientific basis, a focus on utopianism would provide an ideological source of genocide as a uniform substratum. This emphasis on ideology is the basis of a recently published well-written comparison of four genocides by Eric Weitz.[22] Focusing on the concept of utopia at the core of genocidal ideologies, Weitz argues for its salience as an explanation of the Soviet, Cambodian, Nazi, and Bosnian atrocities.

In considering Weitz's argument, though, it is apparent that the Marxist-Leninist cases are conflated with cases that have entirely

---

[21] E. Midlarsky and M. Midlarsky 2004; E. Midlarsky et al. forthcoming.   [22] Weitz 2003.

different etiologies. The Soviets had an elaborate ideational class-based justification for mass murder, as did the Cambodians, while the Nazi and Bosnian instances were based on ethnoreligious criteria without elaborate justification. Thus, the concept of utopia does not go very far in explaining these latter two cases. The Nazis had utopian visions of a distant past including an ostensibly racially pure Ottonian Germany, while the Communists (Soviets and Cambodians) possessed a rigorous, if deeply flawed, ideational structure that predicted a future free of class oppression and conflict.

The consequences of ethnoreligious hostilities are vastly different from those of overtly political ideation. In the former, complete eradication is most frequently the goal, while in the latter elimination of incorrigible political enemies along with reeducation of the remainder constitutes the core of the governmental program. Victimization rates, therefore, differ substantially, ranging from the approximately 67 percent of Jews murdered in Nazi-targeted areas of Europe to at most 10 percent of the Soviet and Chinese populations, and 20 percent of the Cambodian. Moreover, possibilities for reconstituting cultural and religious life were sharply circumscribed for Jews (and Armenians) after their genocides. Such limitations were much less pronounced in the Soviet and Cambodian instances; contemporary Russia, indeed, has seen a massive Orthodox revival after the earlier decimation of church officials by the Bolsheviks.

It is debatable whether the Serbs ever widely shared an ethnoreligious utopian vision of the past. And in Rwanda neither of these forms of utopianism was entertained seriously. As far back as any one could remember, even into the late eighteenth century, the Tutsi – that is, the victims – had ruled over the Hutu, not the converse. A "utopia" of Hutu governance or Tutsi absence simply did not exist. There existed no ideology to justify the genocide other than the claim of "Hamitic," hence foreign, origin of the Tutsi in some distant unrecorded past.[23] Further, issues of socioeconomic class, inequality, and regionalism have been cited as major sources of the genocide.[24] Thus, there was no "golden age" of either past or future to invoke in any coherent way as a utopian enterprise.

Even more problematic in applying utopianism is the Armenian genocide. Neither in their past nor in any realistically conceived future could the Young Turks imagine a state "purified" of other nationalities, so that an ideology justifying mass murder could not be used effectively as motivation. Certainly at the time of the Armenian genocide in 1915–16, the

[23] Mamdani 2001.   [24] Pottier 2002.

Greeks, who were somewhat more numerous than the Armenians in the Ottoman Empire and even more dominant in its economic life, were not subject to genocide. This fact will be examined at length in chapter 17.

Beyond the problem of generalizability, difficult as it is, the concept of utopianism itself certainly is not sufficient to explain genocide as a behavioral category. There have been utopian socialists of every stripe, for example, from cosmopolitans in the nineteenth-century United States and Europe, to more nationalistic ones in the kibbutzim in Israel. Hardly any had advocated, let alone participated in, genocide. In other words, utopianism can just as readily invoke benign, even reclusive visions (e.g., the Hutterites), where the last thing any of these utopians wanted to do was to kill or even bother other people.

Where utopianism does get into trouble is in its juncture with the state and especially with state power. The conjoining of the two can lead to genocidal consequences, but it is the state that is the driving force behind the utopian vision or whatever related genocidal motivation (e.g., state security) may exist at the moment of decision. Utopian belief is neither necessary nor sufficient for understanding the origins of genocide although, if strongly held, it certainly can provide the ideational basis for genocidal thinking. Yet, even when utopian ideation is an element in motivating genocide, it is not the whole story. We must insert the several variables that lie between the belief system and genocidal action in order to even approach the goal of completeness of explanation. Many of these additional variables are to be found at the level of the state and its relations with its international environment, and in relationships among state leaders and followers, as will be developed in later chapters.

Two historical cases

In the theory that will be presented more fully in the succeeding chapter, loss assumes a prominent position, along with realpolitik and altruistic punishment. Loss is fundamental, however, for it chronologically precedes the other two. At least two historical cases, Poland and ancient Athens, suggest the importance of loss in the pathway to genocide.

Poland and loss compensation

I begin with illustrations from Poland because here, prior to World War II, was the largest concentration of Jews to be found anywhere in Europe. Poland also experienced one of the highest Jewish victimization

rates, estimated at approximately 90 percent.[25] Documented spontaneous massacres occurred in Poland that can help reflect on the
underlying etiology of genocide precisely because of the removal of
such massacres from the directives of state leaders. To begin "small" is
to capture social dynamics that would otherwise escape us when we
examine the genocidal process in its entirety. At the same time, to
argue that the enormity of genocide is the net result of such "small"
incidents is not only to commit the fallacy of aggregation – the assumption that genocide is the sum total of individual discrete massacres – but
is untrue to the historical record. Leaders such as Hitler did make the
decision to commit systematic mass murder that was then handed to
subordinates for implementation. Yet before such decisions were made
and even before they rose to power, European leaders as individual
Germans, Poles, Frenchmen, and others experienced processes that
were common to many. Understanding their common mindset can
help elucidate the genocidal process, specifically in the response to loss
and its compensation.

Poland is illustrative in another way that captures the thoroughness of
mass murder committed in the East, whether by Germans or Poles. The
massacres at Jedwabne, Radziłów, Wąsosz, and other eastern Polish
towns followed the pattern of genocide adopted by the Germans during
the Holocaust (and the Hutu extremists in 1994) but differed in one
important respect from that of the Ottomans in 1915–16. Although in
practice it was frequently abandoned, theoretically there at least existed
the option of conversion to Islam for Armenians threatened with deportation and likely death. No such option existed for Jews murdered by
Germans or by Poles nor, for that matter, Tutsi killed by Hutu extremists. Indeed, when priests were approached, as at Jedwabne or at
Radziłów, they offered no help to the Jews either by openly opposing
the murders or by allowing conversion.[26]

Interestingly, only some seventeen pages removed from Jan Gross's
comment on "mystery" (see chapter 1, p. 15), we find the beginnings of
an understanding, not heretofore noted. And it comes, as many of these
things do, in the form of a puzzle, actually two related puzzles. First, why
did there occur so many pogroms in *post*-World War II Poland after the
presumably common enemy of both Jews and Poles, Nazi Germany, had
been soundly defeated? Traditional Polish anti-Semitism is the most
often-cited explanation, but the exceptional violence of the Kielce

---

[25] Fein 1979, 62.   [26] Gross 2001.

pogrom of July 4, 1946, in which forty-two Jews were brutally murdered, contrasts sharply with traditional Polish patterns of personal beatings, business discriminations, legal exclusions, and other less violently expressed forms of anti-Semitism.

The second related puzzle is quoted by Gross.[27] In response to efforts to denounce perpetrators of the pogrom leading to condemnatory statements in the press, strikes were called at factories and workshops in Łódź. Refusal to sign such statements by workers and others was widespread, even resulting in violence used against those who wanted to resume work. Strikes spread to other cities, and "In Lublin during a mass meeting of 1,500 railwaymen in this matter people were screaming, 'Down with the Jews,' 'Shame, they came to defend the Jews,' 'Bierut [the president of Poland at the time] will not dare to sentence them to death,' 'Wilno [Vilna; now Vilnius in Lithuania] and Lwów [now L'vov in Ukraine] have to be ours.'"[28]

Puzzling, if not striking here, is the juxtaposition of the typical anti-Semitic statement of "Down with the Jews" with the boundary-related "Wilno and Lwów have to be ours." Why this combination of seemingly unrelated elements? Yet they are related through the particular theoretical prisms of realpolitik and loss, for these cities with majority Polish (and Jewish) populations before the war were set to be incorporated within the new borders of the Soviet Union. Effectively, the Polish state was to be moved westward in its entirety, receiving former German lands in the west but relinquishing a much larger portion of territory in the east. A net territorial loss of 20 percent was experienced in this massive transition.[29] And, since much of the western territory had been occupied by Germans, representing historically a much more powerful political entity than Poland, the formerly German lands were only insecurely held until the very recent past. Realpolitik's emphasis on state security is significant here.

Yet, despite these territorial losses, the population density of Poland actually decreased from 1939 through 1945. This decrease resulted from the loss of nearly one-quarter of its prewar population due to death (3 million Jews, 3 million Poles) and the postwar exodus of large numbers of Germans and other minorities. With a reduced population density, why then the concern over the loss of territories in Vilna and Lwów, coupled with overt anti-Semitism? The locations of these strikes and protests suggest an answer.

Both Łódź and Lublin had very large Jewish populations before the war. Lublin, where the quoted anti-Semitic statements were made, was

---

[27] Ibid., 148.   [28] Quoted ibid., 149.   [29] Davies 1982, 489.

an especially important Jewish center prior to World War II. When, in 1928, a large Orthodox Jewish gathering was convened in Vienna to select a location for the building of a new major *yeshiva* (center of Jewish higher learning), Lublin was chosen. And when surviving Jews, having escaped to Russia, returned to Poland after the war to reclaim their stolen property or simply to assess the current situation, their destination was frequently Lublin. At one point in 1946, approximately 300,000 Jews were to be found in the Lublin vicinity. Thus, to the railwaymen of Lublin and other Poles in the region, it must have appeared as if the Jews were returning en masse; earlier efforts by individual Poles tacitly or actively supporting the Nazi genocide had seemingly come to naught. Here, the tradeoff between external territory and the immediate environment becomes apparent. The loss of Vilna and Lwów to the Soviet Union, unlikely to be recouped, was to be compensated by the sustained exclusion of Jews from Polish society. In this, the Polish railwaymen and sympathizers were successful. The vast majority of returning Jews left Poland permanently, leaving only about 25,000 concentrated in the capital city of Warsaw. Most of these remaining Jews would also leave after the governmentally inspired anti-Semitic campaigns of the late 1960s. Loss compensation, at least in one salient form, had been effected, in response to the territorially reconfigured Polish state.

Athenian loss and risk minimization

The Athenian experience during the Peloponnesian War can also serve as an introductory test case, but without the contemporary research that has distinguished our three twentieth-century cases, the Holocaust of 1941–45, the Armenian of 1915–16, and the Tutsi of 1994. If these ideas demonstrate some explanatory power here, however, then they can be applied systematically to our principal twentieth-century cases. The Melian genocide occurred in the sixteenth year of the Peloponnesian War. Most importantly, it occurred after substantial strategic losses had been experienced by Athens. Risk minimization, an important element suggested by realpolitik, is emphasized here.

In 420 BC, at the behest of Alcibiades, an Athenian general, Athens concluded an alliance with three Peloponnesian states, Argos, Mantinea, and Elis.[30] This was intended to be an important diplomatic coup against Sparta because such an alliance effectively removed the northern

---

[30] Gomme et al. 1970, 54.

section of the Peloponnesus from Spartan influence.[31] This Spartan failure led to further humiliations such as the attack on the Spartan colony, Heraclea, and personal indignities suffered at the Olympic games of that year. Warfare ensued between the Argives and Spartans, ultimately leading in 418 to the battle of Mantinea, won by Sparta and its allies, which Thucydides tells us was "certainly the greatest battle that had taken place for a very long time among Hellenic states, and it was fought by the most renowned states in Hellas."[32] Although technically at peace with Sparta because of the Peace of Nicias, Athens nevertheless sent a force consisting of 1,000 hoplites and supporting cavalry (only about one-eighth of the total) to the battle. Yet, far more important for Athens and for Alcibiades, the architect of the alliance, was the failure of this Peloponnesian policy.

Athens was now to be thrown back on its own defenses in Attica and at sea. Here, the importance of Melos comes into focus, for it was the only important island not paying tribute to Athens while attempting to remain neutral. The losses incurred on land could now be compensated by gains at sea. Athens, thrown back on its sea power, could remove all potential threats to its flanks from a recalcitrant island state. Earlier, in 426, Athens had attempted to subdue Melos by ravaging the land, but withdrew after the Melians refused to offer battle.[33] Now, in 416, after considerable Spartan success, Melos would not escape, and in fact after the genocide (and it was that) Melos would be settled by Athenians. As Russell Meiggs puts it,

> His [Alcibiades's] first grand design had been to revive the policy of Themistocles and crush Sparta with an alliance of Sparta's potential enemies in the Peloponnese. This design had collapsed on the battlefield of Mantinea. It was natural that the Athenian restlessness which Alcibiades had exploited should find an alternative outlet, by sea. The incorporation of Melos in the empire was the most attractive opportunity open to the Athenian fleet.[34]

Although they are not undisputed,[35] we have two sources, Plutarch and Andocides, who indicate that the genocidal decree either was attributable to Alcibiades or that he supported it.[36]

Certainly the Melian genocide is consistent with an earlier mass murder at Scione, another island state, but Scione had rebelled against

---

[31] Kagan 1981, 39.   [32] Thucydides 1954, 353.   [33] Meiggs 1972, 386.
[34] Ibid., 387.   [35] Gomme et al. 1970, 190–91.   [36] Kagan 1981, 153.

Athens; no such revolt ever occurred on Melos, for the Melians were never allied with Athens. "Traitors" typically receive harsher punishment than do recalcitrant neutrals. Yet Thucydides gives pride of place to the invasion and debate at Melos, signaling their importance after the defeat at Mantinea and especially just prior to the disastrous Sicilian expedition. Here, we have the second possible function of genocide, risk minimization.

We know that the Athenians had an ongoing concern with the west, especially Sicily and its city-states. Strong evidence remains of an alliance between Athens and Egesta in the west of the island dating from at the earliest 458–57, and at the latest 454–53, well before the Peloponnesian War even began.[37] During the period 427–24, several Athenian military expeditions were sent to Sicily with inconclusive consequences, partly because the Sicilian cities made peace among themselves.[38] Significantly, at around the same time, the first Athenian expedition against Melos occurred, also with inconclusive results, as the result of the Melian unwillingness to do battle and the Athenian wariness of a long siege of the city. This pairing of Melos and Sicily in the minds of Athenian decision-makers, especially Alcibiades, may have been significant in the decision to commit the later Melian genocide with the still later, important Sicilian expedition in mind. The scale of the land forces in the later expedition was to exceed the combined total of the land forces sent in 427–424.[39] It is entirely possible, as Lawrence Tritle suggests, that even as Melos was being conquered and the population destroyed (men) or enslaved (women and children), the later disastrous Sicilian expedition was being prepared.[40]

The documented role of Alcibiades in both expeditions and his opposition to the more cautious Nicias, who earlier withdrew from Melos, suggests that Melos and Sicily must have been paired in his mind. If Alcibiades wanted to succeed in the more ambitious Sicilian expedition then, given the difficulties already known to the Athenians, he would have wanted to minimize the obvious risks inherent in this undertaking. "Clearing the decks," as it were, of any opposition at Melos closer to home would have minimized the risk not only by guarding against potentially hostile Melian activity at sea, but also by example. Such a demonstration of resolve would have suggested the determination of the Athenians to succeed, at whatever moral and material cost.

[37] Meiggs 1972, 100.   [38] Ibid., 321.   [39] Gomme et al. 1970, 197.
[40] Tritle 2000, 121.

Such inflexibility of will, in the Athenian view, might have made the Sicilian Dorian cities less likely to resist the Athenian onslaught.

Prior loss at Mantinea and risk minimization for the future, critically important Sicilian expedition are paired, as are the past losses and very risky behavior of the German, Ottoman, and Hutu leaders in our cases of genocide. Thus, loss compensation derived from the Polish example and risk minimization from the Athenian are plausible constituent bases of a theory of genocide that will be developed more systematically in the following chapter. At this juncture, having examined two salient theoretical approaches – rational choice and utopianism – and two important test cases for their analytic implications, we can now turn directly to theory development.

5

A theoretical framework

Having eliminated two candidates for explanation, and seeing intimations of possibility in others as the result of our test cases, we turn
directly to theory development. Realpolitik as management of threats
to the state and losses as signals of state vulnerability now occupy our
attention. Realpolitik is understood as policies that preserve and
strengthen the state,[1] while loss is the experience of either (1) transfer
of territory, population, authority, or some combination thereof to
another political entity, or (2) military defeat or significant casualties
in political violence (e.g., war) that either are about to be or have already
been incurred. Concrete expectations of loss in the near term can yield
outcomes similar to those of loss itself. In later analyses, I will find it
useful to distinguish between threat and loss, whereby threat can be
understood as the fear of *potential loss*. This understanding will be useful
later in distinguishing between conflicts that result in ethnic cleansing,
and those that proceed further to genocide.

Brute force (imprudent) realpolitik entailing disproportionate
responses to perceived provocation, to be defined more completely
below, and prospect theory emphasizing the salience of loss are introduced as means of understanding the transformation of massacre into
genocide[2] within the context of earlier state losses and high risk.
Prospect theory will also be described in more detail. Massacre, unfortunately, is not an uncommon occurrence. While massacre may origin-
ate in many different ways,[3] its transformation into genocide is complex

---

[1] Waltz 1979, 117.
[2] Figure 5.1 is a causal diagram. In regard to massacre, it does not yield any of these
variables. Instead, massacre provides a historical context for the occurrence of genocide
in the form of continuity and validation, if the massacre has gone unpunished. Earlier
unpunished massacre increases the likelihood of later genocide, assuming the sequence
displayed in figure 5.1 is followed at the later time.
[3] Levene and Roberts 1999.

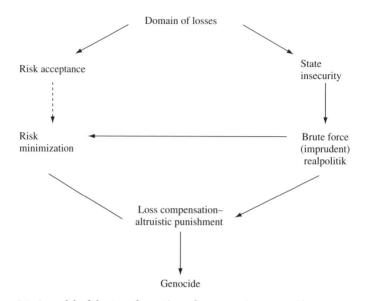

Figure 5.1. A model of the transformation of massacre into genocide

and therefore infrequent. That complexity is reflected in the following theoretical development.

Figure 5.1 presents the basic relationships suggested here. Situation within the domain of losses has two simultaneous consequences: a state insecurity that leads to brute force realpolitik, and a risk acceptance frequently resulting in risk minimization. Both of these processes together yield a loss compensation and altruistic punishment that eventuate in genocide.

On the right-hand side of the figure, situation within the domain of losses implies a state insecurity that is associated with the most extreme sorts of realpolitik. Brute force realpolitik arising from imprudence tends to be most readily invoked under conditions of state insecurity; the greater the danger to the state, the greater the likelihood of political violence and, when it occurs, the greater the intensity of violence directed against civilian populations. Threat leads to anger that will most likely target members of an ethnic group different from one's own.[4] Under conditions of extreme threat, the traditional quid pro

---

[4] Bodenhausen et al. 1994; DeSteno et al. 2004.

quo of realpolitik (as in negotiated settlements) can be transformed into a loss compensation akin to revenge that is genocidal.

On the left-hand side of the figure, prospect theory suggests reasons for the salience of loss aversion with its associated risk taking. By the tenets of prospect theory, the domain of losses – a condition of either experiencing loss or the dominance of the memory of loss[5] – gives rise to a risk acceptance that, in turn, realpolitik tells us, should be minimized to protect the increasingly insecure state. The combination of risk minimization and loss compensation (indicated by a *simple solid line, not a causal arrow*)[6] yields the genocidal outcome. Risk minimization and loss compensation can occur simultaneously, or the former can shade into the latter as the perpetrator's own battlefield and/or civilian losses mount. Altruistic punishment as self-sacrifice while punishing the perceived enemy suggests an answer to the question posed by Michael Marrus concerning reasons for the large followings enjoyed by Hitler and other genocidal leaders.

The emphasis on losses, principally to other states or societies, and realpolitik reverses the understandable tendency to view genocide as mainly a domestic enterprise.[7] After all, did not the ideological bases of the Holocaust and other instances of mass murder arise within the borders of states such as Germany? The answer to this question obviously is yes, but with an important qualification. Although the rise of such murderous sanctioning ideologies was necessary to the commission of routinized mass murder, it was not sufficient. Clearly, other conditions had to be present.

This book focuses on the largely neglected international context, which in combination with ideological justification, however primitive, forms a more complete model of genocide. The elements of the model

---

[5] A technical definition of the domain of losses will be given below, p. 104, n. 71.

[6] Although I prefer the language of probabilities, wherein a particular variable increases or decreases the probability of genocide, the testing of hypothesized relationships here can be said to constitute an as-yet-unvalidated claim for their status as necessary conditions for state-sponsored genocides, but not as sufficient ones. The later inclusion of related analyses in candidate cases where genocide did not occur may suggest the possibility of sufficiency for the entire model. For distinctions between the requirements for establishing necessity on the one hand, and sufficiency on the other, see Most and Starr 1989, esp. chap. 2, and the chapters in Goertz and Starr 2003. Cioffi-Revilla 1998 explores related issues.

[7] Although Melson 1992 emphasizes the origins of revolution within the framework of the state, he also suggests that the revolutionary state may generate international pressures leading to war that, in turn, can have genocidal consequences.

presented in figure 5.1 will be explicated beginning with the domain of losses and state insecurity. Subsequent sections of this chapter treat three types of realpolitik, followed by realpolitik, property, and loss compensation, and then the domain of losses, risk, and loss compensation. Finally, altruistic punishment will be described in some detail.

The domain of losses and state insecurity

In each of the cases of genocide, the socioeconomic space was contracted. By socioeconomic space, I mean the context within which groups live their lives spatially (meaning physical territory), economically, and in their hierarchical relations with each other. I argue that this shrinkage, especially if it occurs on all three dimensions, is the single most important long-term progenitor of genocide.

Clearly, not all states experiencing loss are expected to be genocidal. As noted in chapter 2, vulnerability of a targeted group with a real or purported connection with state security (e.g., ethnic kin in an enemy state) is a necessary condition for the genocide to occur. For example, as a result of the 1846–48 Mexican–American War, Mexico was truncated without genocide occurring. There was no vulnerable ethnic group within the boundaries of the shrunken country that could be even remotely blamed for the disaster.

The shrinkage of empire and the loss of state strength are both situated within the domain of losses and comprise international sources of state insecurity. In two of the three cases of genocide – Germany and the Ottoman Empire – the empires were contracted as the result of defeats in war. Economic catastrophe, as in the disasters of post-World War I German inflation or the extreme indebtedness of the Ottoman state, was an important factor that further magnified that insecurity. In the third, Rwanda, state insecurity was amplified by ongoing conflict that began with the virtual inception of the modern state, followed by territorial losses to the invading Rwandese Patriotic Front (RPF) after 1990, and entailed serious economic weakness as well. Further, the recent Hutu political dominance over the Tutsi was threatening to revert to the earlier, more enduring governance of Hutu by Tutsi.

In all of the following analyses of genocide, initial loss will be understood quite specifically as territorial loss. It has a concrete specification and strong consequences, not the least of which is the presence of refugees from the lost territories. World War I was to have far more intense consequences in Germany than in any other West European country, despite roughly comparable numbers of battlefield dead in the three principal contestants, Britain, France, and Germany. Territorial loss was not confined to the loss of relatively small colonial areas (relative to the British and French), principally in Africa, or to the loss of former Polish lands in the East. At the time of the armistice, Germany was still occupying large swaths of territory in Belgium and France, and especially in Russia. At the war's end, it must have seemed to most Germans that an enormous shrinking process had occurred.[8] During the later wars, genocide occurring in all three cases, loss can refer to battlefield casualties and civilian deaths.

Territorial loss also can be understood within specific national contexts that, beyond a common susceptibility to increased ethnic conflict, can yield different consequences for different countries. Contrasting Germany's sudden collapse in 1918 (see chapter 7) with France's *levée en masse* in response to French defeat by the Prussians at Sedan in 1870, Wolfgang Schivelbusch suggests that:

> The most important difference between the two was that the collapse of 1870 did not leave France in a free fall. France's safety net was its sense of national pride, which had developed over the course of two centuries of European hegemony. The vanquished Germans of 1918 lacked any comparable heritage. The memories of centuries of national inferiority, supposedly relegated to the past by the victory of 1870–71, by the founding of the empire, and by forty years of power politics, now reappeared like an unwelcome guest on Germany's doorstep.
>
> The burden of the past helps explain the response to the news of German defeat. People reacted not with manly composure, as the heroic vision would have it, but with everything from bewilderment to literal paralysis and nervous breakdown.[9]

Facing the uncertainty of the postwar era, Germany would be haunted far more by its disunified and nationally (qua nation-state) undistinguished past relative to its competitors, as the Bayesian findings – reviewed in the preceding chapter – inform us. The same holds true for the Hutu-led government in 1994, which, facing a future replete with uncertainty after territorial loss to the RPF and likely implementation of the Arusha Accords to its detriment, could only hark back to its earlier period of political servility both under the European colonial powers,

---

[8] Evans 2004, 52–53.   [9] Schivelbusch 2003, 196–97.

Belgium and Germany, and still earlier under the Tutsi since the eighteenth century. Or as Christopher Taylor concludes, colonialism "is in the hearts and minds of every ... Hutu and Twa, who imagines him or herself superior or who feels the need through the force of arms to overcome an imagined inferiority."[10]

Interestingly, when we later examine the Cambodian genocide of its ethnic Vietnamese population within the overall politicide, a similar historical context is found. Perception the Khmer Rouge that Kampuchea Krom, essentially the Mekong river region of Vietnam, had been lost to the Vietnamese was important. Earlier political subjection of the Khmer to the Vietnamese, and continued subordination even of the Communist Party of Democratic Kampuchea to its Vietnamese counterpart suggested a past that easily could be invoked in the future.

Even more decidedly, as we shall see in the empirical analysis in chapter 7, the Ottoman Empire had an unbroken series of losses, even to Balkan states that were formerly part of its empire prior to the start of World War I. There was to be no victorious referent past the eighteenth century.

At least five analytically distinct perspectives inform the consequences of loss. First, as physical space contracts, the presence of considerable numbers of refugees may lead to an emotional reaction that in turn can result in brutality or even murder. As Sandra Blakeslee put it, "People who are emotionally wrought by anger or disgust, say over ... the condition of the downtrodden, may decide that certain brutal actions are morally acceptable."[11] This conclusion is based on recent findings that decisions having moral import are far more likely to be based on emotional reactions than on reasoned deliberation.[12] Identification with the downtrodden because of ethnoreligious commonality may lead to brutal actions against those, often of a different ethnicity, who are perceived to be at fault in generating the refugee influx.

Additional evidence is found in studies indicating that anger, in contrast to sadness or a neutral emotion, increases the probability of negative reactions to people of a different ethnicity.[13] External threat can stimulate anger, which in turn is most frequently directed against members of a group different from one's own.

Second, the placing of blame for perceived or actual injury to ethnoreligious kin suggests that revenge – a kind of loss compensation – can be

---

[10] Taylor 1999, 95.   [11] Blakeslee 2001.   [12] Greene et al. 2001.
[13] Bodenhausen et al. 1994; DeSteno et al. 2004.

exacted. And recent neural findings indicate that the experience of actual or anticipated revenge activates regions of the brain associated with "feeling good."[14] Thus, revenge can be pleasurable.

Third, if those perceived to be at fault also arrive as refugees or are viewed as comfortable and wealthy, then they can be targeted for massacre or ultimately genocide. The intersection of migration, ethnoreligious identity, and social class is combustible. Refugees sharpen an existential contrast with the "other," Jews as the anti-German, Armenians as the anti-Turk, or Tutsi as the anti-Hutu, especially if the victims are, on the whole, wealthier and/or more visible than the majority. Competing for the same resources in a shrunken environment, refugees and "native" populations can come to see each other as inevitable opponents in a contracting socioeconomic space.[15]

Introducing the element of social class in the context of refugees competing with the "other," Hitler himself remarked, "our upper classes, who've never bothered about the hundreds of thousands of German emigrants or their poverty, give way to a feeling of compassion regarding the fate of the Jews whom we claim the right to expel."[16]

Fourth, as we shall see in more detail, prospect theory also tells us that losses are valued more highly than gains.[17] Experimental evidence has consistently demonstrated the asymmetry between losses and gains, even to the extent that, in contrast to gains, losses can generate extreme responses. Losses as the result of a shrinking spatial environment, therefore, may have a magnified role in the public consciousness out of all proportion to the real-world consequences of loss. Again, brutality may be justified in the mind of the observer.

Fifth, the importance of territoriality in its own right should not be minimized, especially if the presence of refugees serves as a continual reminder of the territorial loss. Territory is so fundamental to state security that massive brutalities may be justified in the name of the state. When compared with general foreign policy disputes and those involving contrasting regime types, territorial disputes have a higher probability of escalating to war than either.[18] This suggests the fundamental importance of territoriality, even in comparison with other issues that are typically thought to be critical in fomenting conflict.

---

[14] See Knutson 2004 and de Quervain et al. 2004.   [15] M. Midlarsky 1999.
[16] Hitler [1942] 2000, 397.   [17] Kahneman and Tversky 1979, 2000; Levy 2000, 203.
[18] Senese and Vasquez 2004; Vasquez 2000; Huth 1996.

A contributing element to the importance of territoriality stems from the signaling of state weakness associated with territorial loss in time of war. Territory can be used to protect the state, as in a buffer zone between the state core and its enemies. When that territory is lost, state weakness can be perceived by both defenders of the state and its external opponents. Under certain conditions, that weakness can lead to elimination of internal "enemies" in order to buttress the newly vulnerable state.[19]

There are three possible responses to the perception of a shrinking spatial environment. All three contain within them possibilities for genocide and depend in large measure on the force capability available to the potential perpetrator. First, given sufficient force capability, the perpetrator can embark on expansion to directly counter the recent contraction. The concept of *Lebensraum* that became emblematic of Hitler's drive to the East exemplifies this alternative. Instead of German-speaking refugees pouring westward into Germany after World War I, Slavic and Jewish refugees would either move eastward or, as it developed later in Nazi genocidal policy, be murdered en masse. The newly acquired space would then be safe for the perpetrator. New German settlements gradually began to occupy the eastern spaces vacated by the fleeing or murdered inhabitants.

Second, the contracting state can attempt to insure that remaining territory will remain part of the original state. Without force sufficient to expand territorial boundaries, defense of the remaining territory becomes the major focus. Any real or perceived "alien" threat to dominate that territory, as in a secession by a minority population, can generate a genocidal response. Ottoman fears of the creation of a "new Bulgaria" in eastern Anatolia by the Armenians is a case in point. Muslim refugees would no longer be forced into remaining Ottoman territory by newly independent Christian populations, but Christians (Armenians in this case) would be deported and/or murdered.

Finally, even if the national state territory can no longer be defended, at least a minority population can be prevented from governing it. In this, the case of minimal force capability, the perpetrators are losing control of national territory to enemy forces. If a kindred enemy population is destroyed, then the capability of the enemy forces to govern the conquered territory is minimal. Eventually, demographics would dictate governance. In Rwanda, after the Tutsi-dominated RPF began

---

[19] M. Midlarsky 2005.

conquering Rwandan territory at a more rapid rate, genocide of the Tutsi became the most rapidly (although not the most extensively) executed genocide of the twentieth century.

The domain of losses implies the existence of changes in state security in a negative direction. As security of the state diminishes, the probability and, when it occurs, the intensity of violence, even against hapless nonparticipant civilians, increase.

State security can be defined as the relative freedom of the state from threats to its existence emanating either from its domestic or its international environment.[20] The qualification *relative* is important because state security is often assessed by policy-makers in the context of some recent period in national history, or in some instances relative to other states. A state that has recently emerged from defeat in a major war may also experience a sense of insecurity. Of course, the ultimate condition of state insecurity is found during major war itself, when the state could be torn asunder as the result of defeat, as in fact happened to Nazi Germany at the end of World War II. And it was during wars that boded extremely ill for the state that the Ottoman Empire during World War I, Germany during World War II, and Rwanda in 1994 engaged in the most destructive form of identity conflict, genocide, respectively against the Armenians, Jews, and Tutsi.

A renewed determination and an acceleration of the killing can stem from a perceived threat to state security. Hitler apparently recognized as early as November 1941 that the war could not be won, as the Germans bogged down in their advance toward Moscow. Thus, when the Russians launched their successful counteroffensive defending Moscow on December 5, 1941, and the Pearl Harbor attack brought the United States into the war on December 7, it must have become clear to Hitler that Germany could not win the war against such an array of opponents.[21] The predicted relationship between state insecurity and political violence suggests that, shortly after these virtually simultaneous events, the Nazis would escalate the violence. And indeed, on December 12, Hitler spoke to high-level Nazi Party officials, very likely informing them of his decision to murder all European Jews.[22]

---

[20] The relationship between state insecurity and genocide is treated ibid.
[21] M. Gilbert 1989.   [22] Gerlach 2000b.

Three types of realpolitik

To begin with, one must distinguish between realism[23] as a *theory* of international politics emphasizing the national interest and state security as key explanatory variables, and realpolitik as political *practice*. The former is a positive theory that helps us understand the workings of relations among nations, while the latter is a prescription for foreign policy making, diplomacy, war, and, *in extremis*, genocide. One connection, however, is apparent. Realism in its emphasis on the national interest and state security as explanatory elements of international politics perforce single out the practice of states in maximizing their own security. Realism sensitizes us to the presence of realpolitik where it exists, but of course does not in any way mandate that it *must* exist. Theory and political practice necessarily occupy different domains of inquiry.

In the long and scabrous history of realpolitik, much has been made of its power-centered and state-centric core. Indeed, one of the most distinguished scholars of realism has based his exhaustive definition of realpolitik on the state's interest in which "success is the ultimate test of policy, and success is defined as preserving and strengthening the state."[24] Threats to state security can easily invoke the practice of realpolitik. Geopolitical considerations often lie at the core of such threats. This formulation is but one of the latest among those of a long line of like-minded theorists including Thucydides, Machiavelli, E. H. Carr, and Hans Morgenthau. Yet, surprisingly, if one examines the practice of realpolitik more closely one finds more extreme, even sinister consequences than simply the satisfaction of state interests. And we need look no further than Thucydides to find one of the more dramatic instances.

Here, in the famous Melian Dialogue, we find one of the earliest recorded instances of brute force–imprudent realpolitik, the first of our three types, which, following Amartya Sen in the preceding chapter, is defined as realpolitik *not* based on reasoned scrutiny. Conversely, the second type, prudent realpolitik, is one based on reasoned scrutiny understood as the application of reason to the empirical world. Thus,

---

[23] Among the many treatments of realism are, for example, Meinecke 1957; Waltz 1979, 2000; Jervis 1999; Snyder 1985, 1991; Posen 1984; Glaser 1996; Van Evera 1999; and Mearsheimer 2001.

[24] Waltz 1979, 117.

state policy based on a reasoned application of comparative method is very likely to be prudential. Policy that is not based on science, or indeed contradicts the findings of science, as in racially based theories, is not prudential. Consistent with this approach is that taken by Eugene Garver, who in the context of analyzing Machiavelli's thought, argued that "prudence is the ability to confront problems of the practical uses of intelligence reflexively, and in particular to make judgments about the efficacy of knowledge."[25] The reflexive element is important in connoting the ability to reflect on matters intelligently; the efficacy of knowledge here refers to policy implementations that are knowledge-based.

In his brute force–imprudent realpolitik, Hitler conflated success with protracted conflict. Accordingly, "in the life of the peoples together, the ultimate success will always be to [sic] states that fight deliberately, because conflict is the only way to increase their power."[26] Hereafter, "imprudent realpolitik" and "brute force realpolitik" will be used interchangeably.

In the Melian Dialogue, occurring after the major defeat of Athenian allies at Mantinea and just prior to the ill-fated Sicilian expedition, Athenian representatives justify their coming attack on the island of Melos, populated by Spartan colonists, but previously neutral in the Peloponnesian War. Justifying their behavior in the face of appeals to justice and fairness by the Melians, the Athenians said to them, "by conquering you we shall increase not only the size but the security of our empire. We rule the sea and you are islanders and weaker islanders too than the others; it is therefore particularly important that you should not escape."[27]

Despite Melian arguments, including the threat of Spartan retaliation, dangers of Athenian "overreaching" and the possible aggregation of outraged neutrals against Athens, the Athenians are not deterred. After siege operations, "the Melians surrendered unconditionally to the Athenians, who put to death all the men of military age whom they took, and sold the women and children as slaves. Melos itself they took over for themselves, sending out later a colony of 500 men."[28] Here we have one of the earliest illustrations of imprudent realpolitik, in the fundamental sense of maximizing state security, with a genocidal consequence. A reasoned scrutiny was not applied to this genocidal policy, for with the Melian promise of neutrality, likely to be strictly followed,

---

[25] Garver 1987, 157.   [26] Weinberg 2003, 125.
[27] Thucydides 1954, 361, Book 5, Chap. 7.   [28] Ibid., 366, Book 5, Chap. 7.

the genocide was unnecessary. Easily avoided were "alienated allies and third parties, lost hegemonia, and weakened ... power base. The Melian Dialogue and the Sicilian expedition are pathological departures from rational self-interest."[29]

Interestingly, reasoned scrutiny as part of a prudent realpolitik would also have avoided the US intervention in Vietnam. As Hans Morgenthau suggested in his public statements at the time, such an intervention could only lead to a closer alliance between China and North Vietnam, whereas a neutral stance by the United States would likely have allowed conflict between the two states – historical enemies – to develop, as indeed it did in 1979 after the war's end. In contrast to many American policy-makers at the time, Morgenthau employed a comparative historical method, contrasting the known hostile behavior of the two states during long periods without a common external enemy, on the one hand, with the likely behavior of the two in the presence of a powerful common enemy, on the other.

In the concluding chapter, more will be said about the distinction between prudent and imprudent realpolitik. For now, it is enough to suggest that when any and all methods, including the most brutal, are justified for state preservation or expansion, then an imprudent realpolitik is evident. Disproportionate responses to perceived provocation constitute imprudence. Genocide, of course, is one such illustration, as are unnecessary resorts to force when diplomacy or other peaceful methods might achieve the same or an equivalent goal.

A third version, the cynical variant of realpolitik, is also understood as "preserving and strengthening the state," but, instead of the state as a potential perpetrator of genocide, it is an onlooking bystander state that acts cynically in its own interests, disregarding the plight of potential victims.

The following instance of cynical realpolitik, although not state-based, is interesting because it is not well known, yet is richly illustrative. In 1942 and 1943, the vast majority of direct attacks against German occupying forces in France was carried out by a group called the Immigrant Workers, including many Jews, which was linked to the Communist Party's Francs-Tireurs et Partisans. Having lost families and positions and increasingly under the threat of death, they were perceived by the Communist leadership as having nothing more to lose; hence they were entrusted with the task of targeting Nazi officers,

---

[29] Lebow 2001, 551.

hotels, military convoys, and even cafes and nightclubs frequented by the German occupiers. As a result of these attacks, the Germans in Paris and elsewhere in France increasingly hid behind gated enclosures, barbed wire, and other barriers that made their lives far more difficult than they had been.

In late 1943, after Gestapo agents had followed members of the group for some time, they were arrested, and twenty-three were executed on February 21, 1944.[30] Shortly thereafter, the Nazis put up throughout Paris red posters with photographs of these resistance fighters and their names (e.g., Grzywacz, Wajsbrot, Fingerweig, Witchitz) and the question, "Des libérateurs?" (Some liberators?).[31] Of course the poster was intended to distance the French from these very foreign names and faces of Nazi opponents. Presumably, as a consequence, Parisians would identify more with the "Aryan" Germans. Yet, precisely the same logic appears to have been used by the Communists in their cynical realpolitik calculation. Although contested by some diehard Communists, the evidence points to a deliberate refusal by the Communists to rescue members of the group when they first reported being followed. Standard operating procedure in such cases was to find shelter for threatened operatives in safe houses outside Paris. Without such aid, the group was doomed. As we know, the help was not forthcoming. Why?

As the war was drawing to a close, the Communist Party leaders knew that they would be electoral opponents of Gaullists, among others, after the liberation. Given the anti-foreign sentiment of many Frenchmen, it was assumed that the emergence of such a group of foreigners after the war as Communist heroes would be detrimental to the party's electoral chances.[32] Indicative of the potential electoral climate was the following aberration: during the last year of the Third Republic, Jean Giraudoux delivered a vitriolic attack against Jewish immigrants just prior to his

[30] For a relatively complete account, see Raymond 1985, especially 13–86.
[31] Although the poster is exhibited ibid., 3, a more exact color duplication is found in Bourget and Lacretelle 1980, 162.
[32] For a thorough description of these anti-foreign sentiments, see Marrus and Paxton 1995. The betrayal of these partisans is mentioned by their leader Missak Manouchian in his last letter to his wife Mélinée ("celui qui nous a trahis ... et ceux qui nous ont vendus") and others such as Charles Tillon ("on les a abandonnés"). See Raymond 1985, 241–43. From September 1942 until the end of the war, the major clandestine Communist paper, *L'Humanité*, made not a single mention of Jewish matters. See Zuccotti 1993, 139. As late as the 1960s, the French Communist Party refused to acknowledge the non-French origin of the partisans of the *affiche rouge*. See Auron 1998, 151.

appointment as minister of information.[33] Better to have the group disappear at German hands than to suffer their electoral "liability" after the war.[34]

It is the permissive context of realpolitik that is emphasized here, following the model of cynical calculation in the satisfaction of state or, as we shall see later, church interests. This is the less obvious variant that deserves study, for it has received hardly any systematic attention. Yet the fates of entire peoples have rested on this cynical permissive variant, no less than that of brute force.

In order to understand the sources of genocide, we must look to its permissive context. Which ideational or other justification for action supersedes the traditional moral and/or religion-based inhibitions against mass murder? In the case of the brute force or imprudent realpolitik exemplified by the Melian genocide, the permission can be self-granted by the exigencies of war or the ideology of imperial expansion. An ideology of racial superiority, of course, is found in the Nazi genesis of the Holocaust.

But as in the sacrifice of the Parisian immigrant partisans by the Communist Party, larger, more powerful, and higher-status entities, acting on their own perceptions of self-interest (raison d'état or raison d'église) can facilitate the killing of ethnoreligious groups. This is seldom a matter of hatred of these groups by the higher-status entity. Indeed, in some cases there may even be strong sympathies for the victims. Yet the demands of realpolitik are such that the killing goes on.

There are two possible effects of the cynical variant of realpolitik. The first is the facilitation of the *onset* of genocide, while the second is facilitation of the *magnitude* of the killing, once begun. Influence of the cynical variant on both variables can be found in all three cases, to be treated more fully later. Although facilitation of the onset of genocide is difficult to demonstrate, nevertheless there exists evidence to that effect even in the Holocaust, the most problematic of the three in the matter of onset, for we know that the mass killing began on the Eastern front, far removed from the Vatican as the permitting agent. Yet early in the politics of Nazi accession to power, we shall see the impact of the Vatican in Hitler's own words. Nevertheless, I do not claim that the establishment of a permissive context always rises to the level of a necessary condition for the onset of genocide in all three cases, although it can. However, the magnitude of the killing *did* require the permissive

---

[33] Friedländer 1997, 213.   [34] Riding, 2001.

environment as a necessary condition, for in our three cases, the number of victims would have been reduced had the permitting agent acted differently.

Realpolitik, property, and loss compensation

Historically, realpolitik has taken on an international cast, precisely because of its emphasis on the satisfaction, even maximization, of state interests, often in conflict with competing states. Yet the word does not mean "real" in the English sense, but in German connotes "things" in opposition to principles or ideals that could govern political action. According to Machiavelli, "The desire to acquire possessions is a very natural and ordinary thing, and when those men do it who can do so successfully, they are always praised and not blamed."[35] This emphasis on possessions by Machiavelli is stated in the context of international competition for territories, principally in Italy. Accordingly, one of the major practices of realpolitik has been the use of the quid pro quo or something given in exchange for something else in negotiations. Having received a material benefit, the recipient then compensates the giver. The use of the quid pro quo in realpolitik is essentially compensatory behavior. A loss is compensated by a gain.

Realpolitik's reference to "things" has a distinguished lineage. Not only do we find it in the traditional German usage, but also Machiavelli, one of the most canny and astute interpreters of realpolitik, stated that: "When he [the Prince] is obliged to take the life of any one, let him do so when there is a proper justification and manifest reason for it; but *above all he must abstain from taking the property of others, for men forget more easily the death of their father than the loss of their patrimony.*"[36] And if any doubt exists as to Machiavelli's credentials as a theorist of realpolitik, one has only to consider Harvey Mansfield's observation that Machiavelli was "the master of politics, when politics is understood as aiming to win with no reference to a standard above politics."[37]

Property in a nationalistic age has a much wider meaning than simply personal holdings. Especially for new states such as Poland during the interwar period, all of the "patrimonial" territory is sacred and inviolable. This perspective helps explain the virtually suicidal decision of the Polish army in 1939 to defend against the impending German invasion

---

[35] Machiavelli 1950, 13 (*Prince*, 3).
[36] Emphasis added; Machiavelli 1950, 62 (*Prince*, 17).   [37] Mansfield 1996, xiii.

right at the border, despite the entreaties of expert French military advisors to withdraw somewhat to maximize tactical advantage. The loss of *any* Polish territory was intolerable to leaders of the new state. We would not expect the popular view to be any different. Indeed, the first concerted Polish reaction against Jews as a corporate body occurred in the eighteenth century after major territorial losses were experienced in the First Polish Partition of 1772.[38]

Thus, loss of the Jews internal to Poland *compensates* the Poles for their *loss* of territory to the Soviets. The earlier slaughter of the Jews of Jedwabne[39] on July 10, 1941, can be viewed as an internal compensation for the loss of sovereignty to the Germans and the doubtless reduction of the size of Poland under German tutelage. If Poland cannot have the desired territorial extent and cannot even be sovereign in its own territory, then the acquisition of an internal space must compensate for these external losses. Jews, as the most vulnerable and at the same time large enough minority, could be sacrificed.

Henryk Grynberg, a survivor of the murders at Dobre writes:

> The people of Dobre weren't monsters, and some of them sincerely sympathized with the Jews. But at bottom they were pleased. Even those who sympathized. *So many places had opened up in the town. So many goods, and such different kinds.* They couldn't help taking a quiet pleasure in this. Even the best of them, who found it hard to admit this to themselves. The Germans had known this and had certainly counted on it.[40]

It would be difficult to imagine such "quiet pleasure" by otherwise decent people, outside the context of devastating national loss and the experience of political subjugation.

To many Poles, the desirability of ethnically cleansing Jews by whatever means (see chapter 6) was enhanced considerably by the already ongoing resettlement of ethnic Germans from various locations (the old Reich, the Baltic regions, Bessarabia, Bukovina, and Volhynia) into Polish territories already ethnically cleansed of Poles.[41] After the invasion of the Soviet Union, ethnically cleansing Jews by Nazi Germany was tantamount to eradication, as we shall see in chapter 7.

---

[38] Levine 1991.   [39] Gross 2001.

[40] Emphasis added; Grynberg 1993, quoted in Polonsky and Adamczyk-Garbowska 2001, xxvi.

[41] Burleigh 2000, 446–50.

As expected in the realm of realpolitik, Machiavelli places the state at the center of *The Prince*, for it begins: "All states and dominions which hold or have held sway over mankind are either republics or monarchies."[42] Turning to our contemporary examples, realpolitik helps us understand the genocidal impulse. But is there more in the ideational sphere than simply Hitler's often unintelligible rantings in *Mein Kampf*? The writings of Carl Schmitt help us bridge the gap between the "ordinary" politics of realpolitik, or prudent realpolitik, and the unimaginable happenings of the Holocaust. Schmitt, in his political theory, takes realpolitik and Machiavellian thought to its outer limits, although those annihilationist limits are to be found in Machiavelli's writings. Accordingly, he writes, "Men must either be caressed or else annihilated; they will revenge themselves for small injuries, but cannot do so for great ones; the injury therefore that we do to a man must be such that we need not fear his vengeance."[43] And presaging Schmitt's categorical distinction between friend and enemy, Machiavelli states that "A prince is further esteemed when he is a true friend or a true enemy, when, that is, he declares himself without reserve in favour of some one or against another. This policy is always more useful than remaining neutral."[44]

Although in Schmitt's best-known work, *The Concept of the Political*, no anti-Semitic statements are to be found (at least not in the earlier versions), nevertheless his theory, published immediately prior to Hitler's accession to power, constitutes, at bottom, a justification for genocide: Schmitt himself became a supporter of the 1935 Nuremberg racial laws[45] that began the process of dehumanizing the Jewish population as "a formula for the declaration of an internal enemy."[46]

Genocidal ideation

Not unlike Machiavelli, Schmitt begins his theory with an emphasis on the state. Accordingly, "The concept of the state presupposes the concept of the political"[47] and "The specific political distinction to which political actions and motives can be reduced is that between friend and enemy."[48] Further, and most important for our concerns here, "An enemy exists only when, at least potentially, one fighting collectivity of people confronts a similar collectivity. The enemy is solely the public enemy, because everything that has a relationship to such a collectivity

---

[42] Machiavelli 1950, 4 (*Prince*, 1).   [43] Ibid., 9 (*Prince*, 3).   [44] Ibid., 83 (*Prince*, 21).
[45] Bendersky 1983, 228.   [46] Schmitt [1932] 1996, 46.   [47] Ibid., 19.   [48] Ibid., 26.

of men, particularly to a whole nation, becomes public by virtue of such a relationship."[49]

Hitler did not stray far from this conceptualization. Accordingly, "politics is history in the making. History itself represents the progression of a people's struggle for survival."[50] Collectivities are the units to be categorized as friends or enemies. And, to be sure, such an intense focus has the virtue of recognizing "in concrete clarity" the enemy's identity.[51] According to Tracy Strong, for Schmitt, such clarity avoids the difficulties of bourgeois politics wherein solutions are the result of compromise; they are "in the end temporary, occasional, never decisive."[52] If necessary, war can be waged against the enemy to render decisive that which had been basically unresolved, or even at times otiose.

The book's dedication in itself is revealing. It is dedicated to Schmitt's friend, August Schaetz, who was killed in battle on the Western front during World War I. When we consider that Schmitt's concept of the political entails fault lines between enemies and friends, the dedication certainly cannot be ignored. Hitler himself intuitively understood this identification of politics with the friend–enemy distinction in the realpolitik mode. "With the Jew, there can be no negotiation, but only the decision: all or nothing! As for me, I have decided to go into politics."[53]

But beyond the presumed virtues of clarity, there is an even darker side to Schmitt's theorizing than merely the possible genocidal implications of the collective friend–enemy distinction. In elucidating his notion of clarity in recognizing the enemy, Schmitt refers to

> the fanatical hatred of Napoleon felt by the German barons Stein and Kleist ("Exterminate [the French], the Last Judgement will not ask you for your reasons") ... surpassed by Cromwell's enmity towards papist Spain. He says in his speech of September 17, 1656: "The first thing, therefore, that I shall speak to is *That* (sic) that is the first lesson of Nature: Being and Preservation ... The conservation of that, 'namely of our National Being,' is first to be viewed with respect to those who seek to undo it, and so make it *not to be*" ... "The Spaniard is your enemy," his "enmity is put into him by God." He is "the natural enemy, the providential enemy," and he who considers him to be an "accidental

---

[49] Ibid., 28.   [50] Weinberg 2003, 7.   [51] Schmitt [1932] 1996, 67.
[52] T. Strong 1996, xv.   [53] Quoted in Burrin 1994, 30.

enemy" is "not well acquainted with Scripture and the things of God," who says: " 'I will put enmity between your seed and her seed.'"[54]

Schmitt actually quotes Cromwell at greater length than is excerpted here. It is noteworthy that, of all English leaders of the recent past, the genocidal impulse is perhaps strongest in Cromwell, expressed not only in words against papist Spain, but in the vicious massacres at Drogheda and Wexford in 1649, as well as in the institution of the "plantation policy" in which Scottish Presbyterians were to replace Irish Catholics in northern Ireland. By 1703, the proportion of land held by Catholics in all of Ireland declined to 14 percent from a high of 59 percent in 1641.[55] The later response (or absence of it) by Westminster during the Irish potato famine of the middle of the nineteenth century, leading to an estimated 1 million Irish Catholic deaths, complemented the earlier Cromwellian policies of massacre and land expropriation.

The *existential* nature of such conflict is emphasized by Schmitt: "There exists no rational purpose, no norm no matter how true, no program no matter how exemplary, no social ideal no matter how beautiful, no legitimacy nor legality which could justify men in killing each other for this reason. *If such physical destruction of human life is not motivated by an existential threat to one's own way of life, then it cannot be justified.*"[56]

When collectivities are in a state of existential conflict in which one's way of life is threatened by the enemy, and the enemy does not even have to be "the private adversary whom one hates,"[57] then the justification for genocide is at hand. Even "good Jews," those who were liked personally by Nazis, were doomed to extinction in the Holocaust. It is no accident that, after 1933, Schmitt became the self-appointed ideologue of the Nazis, only to run afoul of SS ideologists in 1936. He would nevertheless keep his post at the University of Berlin until the war's end under Hermann Göring's protection.

Schmitt's theorizing clearly stemmed from the experience and legacy of World War I. Yet, although derivative of World War I, the principles enunciated by Schmitt can be understood as an application of realpolitik to a conflicted region. Machiavelli, writing in the uncertain period of wars among Italian city-states and invasions from without, suggests that war is of immense importance, "A PRINCE should therefore have no

---

[54] Gen. III: 15; emphasis in original, Schmitt [1932] 1996, 67–68.   [55] Hayton 1985, 216.
[56] Emphasis added; Schmitt [1932] 1996, 49.   [57] Ibid., 29.

other aim or thought, nor take up any other thing for his study, but war and its organization and discipline, for that is the only art that is necessary to one who commands."[58]

Machiavelli understood that, in order to achieve the required extent of commitment, courage, and ferocity, soldiers should be part of a citizen army, preferably a militia. He was bitterly opposed to the use of mercenaries, for according to Machiavelli "the ruin of Italy is now caused by nothing else but through her having relied for many years on mercenary arms."[59]

Certainly it is not fortuitous that the most rapidly executed genocide of the twentieth century, that of the Tutsi in 1994, was facilitated enormously by the machete-wielding Hutu of the Interahamwe, the extremist militia. Christopher Browning's description of the "Ordinary Men" of the Reserve Police Battalion 101 who committed mass murder of Jews in eastern Poland[60] would very likely conform to Machiavelli's image of the typical militia member. Similar observations apply to Kurdish irregulars drawn by the Ottomans from regions adjacent to areas of Armenian habitation, and to Ottoman conscripts who engaged in the large-scale murder of Armenian populations.

Most importantly, Machiavelli deemphasized the means a ruler uses to attain his ends. "In the actions of men, and especially of princes, from which there is no appeal, the end justifies the means. Let a prince therefore aim at conquering and maintaining the state, and the means will always be judged honourable and praised by every one."[61] Compare this statement with that of Hitler to Goebbels on June 16, 1941, shortly before the German invasion of the Soviet Union, "Right or wrong, we must win. It is the only way ... And once we have won, who is going to question our methods?"[62]

Yet Machiavelli did not advocate mass murder. His more extreme statements generally refer to the "foe" as a more personal enmity, instead of the collective "enemy" in Schmitt's writings.[63] Referring to Agathocles, king of Syracuse, Machiavelli states that "his barbarous cruelty and inhumanity, together with his countless atrocities, do not permit of his being named among the most famous men."[64] More generally, "victories are never so prosperous that the victor does not need to have some scruples, especially as to justice."[65] He would likely be

[58] Machiavelli 1950, 53 (*Prince*, 14).   [59] Ibid., 45 (*Prince*, 12).   [60] Browning 1992.
[61] Machiavelli 1950, 66 (*Prince*, 8).   [62] Goebbels 1983, 415.   [63] Schwab 1996, 10.
[64] Machiavelli 1950, 32 (*Prince*, 8).   [65] Ibid., 84 (*Prince*, 21).

shocked to discover that the realpolitik he advocated could under certain conditions be transformed into the facilitation of mass murder. What are those conditions? Clearly, a protracted period of conflict or war, contrary to Machiavelli's preferences, could establish the conditions for atrocity. As an article on Hitler in the *Frankfurter Zeitung* of January 26, 1928, put it,

> It is a matter of a manic idea of atavistic origin that pushes aside complicated reality and replaces it with a primitive fighting unit ... Naturally, Hitler is a dangerous fool ... But if one asks how the son of a petty Upper Austrian customs officer arrives at his craze, then one can only say one thing: he has taken war ideology perfectly literally and interpreted it in almost as primitive a way that one might be living in the era of the *Völkerwanderung* – the period of Barbarian invasions at the end of the Roman Empire.[66]

The domain of losses, risk, and loss compensation

The general question arises: why the increased probability and intensity (when it begins) of killing upon the diminution of state security and invocation of brute force realpolitik? A priori, there would appear to be no evident reason, other than Machiavelli's trenchant observation on the importance of property loss. His formidable reputation notwithstanding, Machiavelli would have had no access to scientific examination of this claim. In recent years, however, there has emerged a theory of decision making under risk and uncertainty that provides considerable empirical validation of the importance of loss aversion. Prospect theory was originated by the social psychologists Daniel Kahneman and Amos Tversky[67] to rebut certain claims of expected utility theory, principally in the field of economics. In 2002, Kahneman received the Nobel prize in economics for his contribution.

Two basic insights from the theory are relevant here and have been supported by substantial experimental evidence.[68] The first is the

---

[66] Quoted in Kershaw 1998, 302.   [67] Kahneman and Tversky 1979.

[68] In addition to the experimental evidence reviewed in Kahneman and Tversky 2000, applications to risk in international politics can be found in, among others, Farnham 1992, Levy 2000 and McDermott 1992, 1998. Critiques of prospect theory are found in O'Neill 2001 and Boettcher 1995, which has an experimental test of the theory applied to foreign policy decision making. In the domain of losses, 92 percent of the subjects were found to be risk-acceptant in military policy making (and 83 percent risk-averse in

asymmetry of losses and gains. "People are loss-averse in the sense that losses loom larger than the corresponding gains."[69] Put another way, "the response to losses is more extreme than the response to gains."[70] As a consequence of this loss aversion, people in the domain of losses[71] are *risk-acceptant*, in comparison with risk-averse behavior relative to the likelihood of gains.

The second insight concerns the importance of framing around a reference point. Losses and gains are defined for each person relative to some reference point unique to that individual. Identification of this reference point is called framing.[72] Accordingly, "After suffering losses political leaders have a tendency not to renormalize their reference point but instead to gamble in the hope of eliminating those losses and returning to the reference point, even at the risk of suffering a larger loss."[73]

Consistency of prospect theory with the tenets of realpolitik is found not only in the writings of Machiavelli, but in contemporary thinking as well. Randall Schweller, for example, considers that "states value what they possess more than what they covet," and that "rational states do not seek relative gains so much as avoid relative losses."[74] Although Schweller associates this loss aversion with neorealism's status quo bias, the reference point for the status quo in Nazi perceptions was not the geopolitical configuration of 1939, but that of 1914, as will soon become apparent in the discussion of Hitler's "war ideology." The unacceptability of the defeat of 1918 and its territorial losses, of course, was a basis of Nazi ideology.

It is no accident that both Machiavelli and Schmitt wrote their basic theories within the domain of losses, as in fact did Thucydides in his

---

the domain of gains), thus providing a significant confirmation of the theory for war-related decisions. This finding suggests a strong applicability of prospect theory to the onset of genocide within the war-related context found in all three cases considered here.

[69] Jervis 1992, 187.   [70] Tversky and Kahneman 1981, 454.

[71] The domain of losses is defined as that region in which all possible outcomes are inferior (or equal) to the reference point. Related to this concept is that of the endowment effect wherein an object acquires greater value after its possession than before the moment of acquisition (Kahneman et al. 1990). Further, "the main effect of endowment is not to enhance the appeal of the good one owns, only the pain of giving it up" (Kahneman et al. 1991, 197).

[72] Given our societal concerns here, the following definition of framing is appropriate: "Collective action frames are constructed in part as movement adherents negotiate a shared understanding of some problematic condition or situation they define as in need of change, make attributions regarding who or what is to blame, articulate an alternative set of arrangements, and urge others to act in concert to affect [sic] change" (Benford and Snow 2000, 615).

[73] Levy 2000, 203.   [74] Schweller 1996, 99.

lengthy meditations on the catastrophic Athenian defeat. Schmitt was "outraged" at the losses imposed on Germany by the victors at Versailles,[75] and later crises such as that of the Rhineland further deepened these concerns.[76] In reaction to these losses, Schmitt resonated strongly to the idea of *Lebensraum* articulated by the Nazis. The new German Reich could now (in 1939) set the law for itself within its "greater space (Grossraum)" and also "is able ... to reject the interference of powers that are alien to the space and do not belong to the folk."[77] Further, in 1941, he stated "the development leads to a new greater-space arrangement of the earth. New powers and new energies carry the new space revolution, and this time it is the German people to whom leadership is due."[78]

Schmitt also was aware of the Florentine and more generally Italian losses deeply felt by Machiavelli. "In actuality, Machiavelli was on the defensive as was also his country, Italy, which in the sixteenth century had been invaded by Germans, Frenchmen, Spaniards, and Turks."[79] One has only to examine the last chapter of *The Prince*, titled "Exhortation to liberate Italy from the Barbarians," to appreciate this sense of loss and despair. In the years before completion of *The Prince* in 1513–15,[80] Charles VIII of France conquered Florence (in 1494). Several years later, Fra Savanarolla staged his successful revolt and ultimately was deposed, and in 1512 the Florentine republic fell.[81]

US Supreme Court justice Oliver Wendell Holmes put it well when he stated: "It is in the nature of man's mind. A thing which you have enjoyed and used as your own for a long time, whether property or an opinion, takes root in your being and cannot be torn away without your resenting the act and trying to defend yourself, however you came by it."[82]

Yet the logic of the theory yields additional implications. A first implication concerning the possibility of compensatory behavior lies in the area of risk. Although actual losses or their possibility in the near future can yield risky behavior, neither the theory itself nor logic precludes the possibility of minimizing those risks. One can hedge against risky behavior by additional behavior that minimizes the risk, or at least diminishes it. The contextual logic of both risk acceptance and the imperative of realpolitik to protect the state suggests that, given any additional opportunity to minimize the primary risk already

---

[75] Schwab 1996, 5.   [76] Balakrishnan 2000, 83.   [77] Quoted in Weinreich 1999, 74.
[78] Quoted ibid., 124.   [79] Schmitt [1932] 1996, 66.   [80] De Grazia 1989, 23.
[81] Ibid., 15, 32.   [82] Holmes 1897, 477.

undertaken, decision-makers would at least consider it very seriously, and even seize the opportunity.

Risk minimization is typically found in anti-guerrilla warfare where civilians are often indistinguishable from combatants. Even if not actual combatants, sympathetic civilians still may transmit critical information to such people. A now well-known case is that of former US senator Bob Kerrey, accused of killing Vietnamese women and children to silence them after his Navy Seals group was discovered in the midst of its secret mission. Kerrey stated: "Standard operating procedure was to dispose of the people we made contact with. Kill the people we made contact with, or we have to abort the mission . . . It does not work to merely bind and gag people, because they're going to get away."[83] It is estimated that "24 people were killed. 13 were women and children and one old man."[84]

Even more to the point here and in anticipation of the later massacre of "dangerous" Jewish males presumably infected with Bolshevism in the opening stages of the conflict on the Eastern front,[85] an estimated 6,500 Belgian and French civilians were killed by invading German forces from August to October 1914.[86] Earlier, in 1870, as the French army was being defeated by the Prussian, the French leadership called for a *levée en masse* and guerrilla warfare conducted by *francs-tireurs* (free-shooters). Although Belgian civilians did not resist the Germans in 1914, an uprising along the lines of 1870 nevertheless was expected, and the German army behaved with unwarranted brutality toward Belgian civilians in the hope of preventing its outbreak.[87]

Yet, in all of these cases, the particular form of risk minimization was unnecessary. Jews in the Soviet Union and Belgian civilians were not uniformly hostile to the Germans. Certainly, as town dwellers and civilians without substantial military training, they would not have posed any military threat to the invading Germans, if treated with minimal decency.

Second, if people are exceedingly sensitive to losses, if the losses appear to be irreversible, then the best avenue of redress is to *compensate* for those *losses*. Here the quid pro quo of realpolitik nicely supplements

---

[83] Quoted in Vistica 2001, 55.   [84] Quoted ibid., 66.
[85] Shortly after the invasion of Russia, Hitler [1942] 2000, 29, remarked that: "The old Reich knew already how to act with firmness in the occupied areas. That's how attempts at sabotage to the railways in Belgium were punished by Count von der Goltz. He had all the villages burnt within a radius of several kilometres, after having had all the mayors shot, the men imprisoned and the women and children evacuated."
[86] Horne and Kramer 2001, 419.   [87] Strachan 2001b, 32.

the loss aversion emphasized by prospect theory. A seemingly irreversible loss in one area can be compensated for by gains in another. Indeed, the theory implies that loss aversion would be a powerful driving force behind this compensatory behavior.

If the potential compensation for losses and the risk minimization opportunity coincide, then there can be powerful incentives to engage in the compensation for losses and a simultaneous risk diminution. Genocide can provide just such a simultaneous opportunity. But before we examine the cases of genocide, it will be useful to consider the impact of realpolitik in the domain of threat alone without the actual experience of loss, Threat to state security itself is sufficiently important to warrant a separate examination of its potential consequences. Without the dimension of loss, however, the particular form of realpolitik is not likely to yield genocide. Later, realpolitik and loss will be combined in the analysis of our cases of genocide.

Altruistic punishment

Finally, we address the question raised by Michael Marrus noted in chapter 1: "For historians of the Holocaust, the greatest challenge has not been making sense of Hitler, but rather understanding why so many followed him down his murderous path."[88] Or, to put the question within the context of the actual killing, why were the perpetrators not deterred from the genocide even as defeat loomed unmistakably in the very near future? Surely there would be retribution from the victorious foe. Cooperation between leaders and actual perpetrators continued well beyond the time that one would expect a breakdown in cooperation between them, based on sheer self-interest of those doing the actual killing.

Experience of loss has an additional implication. The taking on of risk as a consequence of loss implies potential sacrifice. One can lose one's life in war that risk might entail, or commit atrocities that actually are extremely distasteful and can cause physical distress. Of course, the risk of retribution and the loss of one's own life can be the result of committing mass murder.

A field of experimental politics and economics has emerged that studies the development of cooperation under a variety of conditions.

---

[88] Marrus 1987, 46.

Most important for our purposes here is the body of literature stemming from the seminal contribution of Elinor Ostrom and her colleagues.[89] Generally, this literature concludes that cooperation or internal governance (in contrast to rules imposed from without) is most readily generated when sanctions are available.[90] As Ostrom and her colleagues put it, "Best of all the conditions we examined are covenants with an *internal* sword, freely chosen or made available as an institutional option."[91]

Most recently, Ernst Fehr and Simon Gächter[92] have introduced the concept of altruistic punishment to explain cooperation.[93] Following Fehr and Gächter, I define altruistic punishment as punishment inflicted on a defector from cooperation, which is costly to the punisher and without material gain. In a series of public goods experiments that pitted private return against public welfare requiring cooperation in a group project, cooperation was found to flourish when altruistic punishment was possible and to break down when it was ruled out.

Subjects were given the opportunity to invest in a group project with monies handed to them, or to keep the funds. Individually, if they chose to invest, they would receive less than if they kept the money, but collectively the group as a whole would receive more, if all invested. (This is reminiscent of the famous stag hunt in which an individual may gain by snagging a hare instead of participating in a group hunt; in such a hunt, the gain would be even greater for each participant if it is successful, but it will be more likely to fail if any participant drops out.) Subjects could punish others after information was provided as to how much each had invested. But each punishment of another subject was costly. Specifically, subjects who chose to punish were required to forfeit an amount equal to one-third of the monetary punishment imposed on a defector. Thus, the punishment is altruistic. Defectors – those who refused to cooperate – were punished even when material self-interest was sacrificed by cooperators. Participants who chose to punish defectors by withholding monies themselves had to sacrifice monetary rewards.

Punishment and non-punishment experimental conditions were compared. Where punishment was allowed, there occurred a significant

---

[89] Ostrom et al. 1992.
[90] Boyd and Richerson 1992; Sober and Wilson 1998; Boehm 1999; Fehr and Gächter 2000.
[91] Emphasis in original; Ostrom et al. 1992, 414.   [92] Fehr and Gächter 2002.
[93] Axelrod and Hamilton 1981; Axelrod 1984; Sober and Wilson 1998.

increase in investment in the public good, namely cooperation. Where punishment was forbidden, the average investment was much lower.

"Negative emotions towards the defectors are the proximate mechanics behind altruistic punishment."[94] Concerning altruistic punishment, Fehr remarks, "It's a very important force for establishing large-scale cooperation, every citizen is a little policeman in a sense. There are so many social norms that we follow almost unconsciously, and they are enforced by the moral outrage we expect if we were to violate them."[95] The greater the extent of deviation from cooperation by defectors, the more heavily they were punished by cooperators.[96] It was "punishment per se [that] provided the motivation, not some consequence anticipated by the player."[97] Instrumentality was not especially relevant.

Entirely consistent with these findings are those stemming from a related set of experiments. Two players are given an opportunity to split a sum of money: the first proposes a division; if the second player accepts, the game is over and the players receive their agreed-upon shares. If the second player rejects the offer, both receive nothing. Alan Sanfey and his colleagues describe the results of several studies: "Modal offers are typically around 50 percent of the total amount. Low offers (around 20 percent of the total) have about a 50 percent chance of being rejected. This latter, quite robust, experimental finding is particularly intriguing, demonstrating that circumstances exist in which people are motivated to actively turn down monetary reward."[98]

In other words, a modal cooperation of equal division is typically established. Defectors from that fair, cooperative division are often punished even at some cost to the punisher. Altruistic punishment has been robustly established. These findings stem from public goods experiments, but are readily generalizable to social groups seeking a basis for cooperation in the absence of a functioning external authority. Given an extreme, even life-threatening environment, such as massive economic failure followed by war, the particular form of altruistic punishment chosen can be severe.

Even as they were clearly losing their respective wars, Hitler proceeded mercilessly with his extermination campaign, Enver Paşa lent his approval to the Armenian genocide, and the Hutu extremists were rapidly eliminating the Rwandan Tutsi. Hitler would die by his own

---

[94] Fehr and Gächter 2002, 137. [95] Quoted in Angier 2002, F6.
[96] Fehr and Gächter 2000, 980. [97] Bowles and Gintis 2002, 126.
[98] Sanfey et al. 2003, 1755.

hand, Enver in battle attempting to unite Turkic peoples against the Soviets, and many of the Hutu *génocidaires* in the refugee camps of northern Congo.

Hitler's political testament written shortly before his suicide is revealing. He spoke of the German war as "the most glorious and valiant manifestation of a nation's will to existence,"[99] and ended: "Above all, I adjure the leaders of the nation and those under them ... to merciless opposition to the universal poisoner of all peoples, International Jewry."[100] Here, the connection between national unity in struggle and punishment of the "defector," even as one is about to die, is made manifest in the form of altruistic punishment. Equally to the point, he stated, "when man – not infrequently, it seems – renounces his own self-preservation instinct for the benefit of the species, he is still doing it the highest service. Because not infrequently it is this renunciation of the individual that grants life to the collective whole, and thus yet again to the individual."[101]

Having laid the theoretical foundations, we can now turn to their empirical examination in part III.

---

[99] Quoted in Kershaw 2000a, 822.   [100] Quoted in Burleigh 2000, 793.
[101] Quoted in Weinberg 2003, 7.

PART III

The theory applied

6

Threat of numbers, realpolitik, and ethnic cleansing

In this part, cynical and imprudent realpolitik are explored in their consequences for ethnic cleansing and genocide. Realpolitik alone as management of threats to the state (or preserving and strengthening the state) in whatever form will seldom, if ever, result in genocide. When constrained by loss, however, as suggested in the preceding chapter, the probability of genocide is vastly increased. Effectively, a single component of figure 5.1, the one with the most widespread political applicability, is now being examined, to be followed in the three succeeding chapters by an exploration of the entire model.

In this chapter, then, the consequences of realpolitik will be examined in three cases: the Irish famine of 1845–52, Polish ethnic cleansing policy of the interwar period, and ethnic cleansing in Bosnia with a genocidal incident embedded within it in 1995. I choose these cases because they are among the closest to genocide itself without reaching that level, thereby allowing for the possibility of one or two key variables distinguishing between ethnic cleansing and genocide. Certainly the accusation of genocide had been repeatedly leveled against the British as early as 1868[1] (see also chapter 17). At the local level, the Poles did engage in genocidal behavior during World War II, as at Jedwabne, discussed in chapter 1. And, to this day, Serbs have been accused of committing genocide in Bosnia. These cases are also among the most well-known instances of ethnic cleansing; they are richly illustrative of realpolitik, and in one instance, Srebrenica, realpolitik combined with loss.

As we saw at the outset of the preceding chapter, I will find it useful to distinguish between threat and loss. Threat is the fear of *potential loss*, while loss itself is the actual experience of the transfer of territory, population, or authority to another political entity, and/or military defeat or significant casualties in political violence. Concrete expectations of loss in the near term can yield outcomes similar to those of loss

---

[1] Mitchel 1868.

itself. If a particular ethnoreligious group for one reason or another is perceived to be threatening, then ethnic cleansing can be a consequence of attempts to blunt or remove the threat. If loss itself has been or is about to be experienced, attributable rightly or wrongly to that group, then genocide becomes a distinct possibility.

The British response (or absence of it) to the Irish famine, leading to approximately 1 million deaths, represents a reaction to the threat to continued British security posed by a burgeoning Roman Catholic Irish population. That threat was magnified enormously by the potential confluence of Irish rebellion with French invasion that actually occurred at the end of the eighteenth century, but was defeated by British arms. Somewhat earlier, a confluence of indigenous rebels and French military support actually resulted in the independence of the thirteen former American colonies. Ethnic cleansing occurred by allowing the famine to do its work or by encouraging emigration. Loss in Ireland was not experienced by the British prior to the famine, and genocide was not committed. However, a cynical realpolitik was functioning in the readiness of British officials to take advantage of the famine for purposes of strengthening the British state.

Another illustration is that of interwar Poland. Although only a partial ethnic cleansing occurred, largely of the much smaller ethnic German population, it was clear that the Poles planned an ethnic cleansing of Poland's Jewish population, if at all possible given worldwide restrictions on Jewish immigration (see chapter 11). The combined threat of a militarily resurgent Germany that clearly had irredentist claims on Polish territory, along with the steadily increasing arms production of the Soviet Union, and their own territorial claims, was decidedly threatening to the still relatively new Polish state. However, here again loss was not experienced nor was genocide. Although never put into practice, the threatened ethnic cleansing of Poland's Jewish population verged on an imprudent realpolitik – one that did not employ a reasoned scrutiny in recognizing the potential loyalty to the Polish state of the vast majority of its Jews. The experience of loss after the Nazi invasion led to the actual practice of genocidal behavior at the local level, as we saw in chapter 4.

Finally, ethnic cleansing in the former Yugoslavia included genocidal elements. As the Yugoslav state disintegrated, its inclusive security guarantees also disappeared, leaving individual successor states to fend for themselves. Serbia and Croatia found themselves in a security dilemma that led to competition for territory in Bosnia, an imprudent realpolitik, and the ethnic cleansing of Muslims, principally by Bosnian Serbs.[2] Demographic changes had been consequential in generating a Muslim plurality, displacing the Serbs from their formerly dominant position. The anticipation of and actual experience of losses by Bosnian Serb commanders were associated with genocidal acts, as at Srebrenica.

The Irish famine

Before illustrating the impact of threat and its evocation of a cynical realpolitik in the Irish famine of 1845–52, it is worthwhile to consider a metaphor. Recall the comment by Holocaust survivor Henryk Grynberg concerning the people of Dobre in Poland who benefited from elimination of the Jews. I will paraphrase, eliminating some material and substituting key members of the British cabinet for the people of Dobre, Irish for Jews, and country for town:

> The British cabinet members weren't monsters, and some of them sincerely sympathized with the Irish. But at bottom they were pleased. Even those who sympathized. *So many places had opened up in the country* ... They couldn't help taking a quiet pleasure in this. Even the best of them, who found it hard to admit this to themselves.[3]

The British government did not commit genocide, any more than did the Polish gentiles of Dobre, yet both gained considerably, at least in the short term, from the elimination of the respective victims. The famine led directly to deaths of approximately 1 million people during the famine itself, a generally acknowledged figure,[4] and an emigration process that led to the depopulation of Ireland by at least 4 million additional people between the famine and World War I.[5] In 1881, nearly 40 percent of Irish-born persons were not living in Ireland.[6]

Irish agriculture quickly rebounded from its previously moribund state. Productivity of farm workers steadily increased after 1851 and, most importantly, average farm size increased as well. Instead of the steady subdivision of farms and tenancies as before the famine, a consolidation of farmland took place. Between 1853 and 1902 the smallest farms of 1–5 acres actually decreased in number, while those over

---

[2] See Posen 1993 for the security dilemma applied to ethnic conflict.

[3] Emphasis added; after Grynberg 1993, quoted in Polonsky and Adamczyk-Garbowska 2001, xxvi.

[4] Kinealy 1994, 168.   [5] Guinnane 1997, 101.   [6] Ibid., 104.

30 acres increased.[7] Economies of scale now had a profound effect on Irish agricultural efficiency. The time from 1850 to the mid-1870s was "a period of great prosperity in Irish agriculture."[8] But, afterward, the seeds of bitterness and dissidence among the Irish planted during the famine would return from the United States and elsewhere to haunt the British, as will be detailed in chapter 17. For now, in order to understand the dimensions of this temporary gain for Britain, we need to examine Ireland at the time of the famine.

As of the last Irish census before the famine, that of 1841, the Irish population was estimated at 8,175,124,[9] approximately the same as that of England in 1800. In the four decades since the Act of Union in that year, the Irish population had grown by 50 percent. And the population growth was most rapid in the poorest, most heavily Roman Catholic sections of the country in the south and west. Overall, the Irish population was 40 percent of that of the United Kingdom as a whole.[10]

Relative to Britain, Ireland was underdeveloped and, in further contrast to Britain, increasingly so. According to Christine Kinealy, "The percentage of the labour force engaged in the industry declin[ed] from an estimated 43 percent in 1821 to 28 percent in 1841 ... Between 1821 and 1841, for example, the rural workforce within Ireland increased by an estimated 50 percent."[11] In Britain, on the other hand, the percentage of the workforce in industry had already exceeded that in agriculture. Great Britain was predominantly Protestant, with most adhering to the Protestant Church of England. Ireland was heavily Roman Catholic, with adherents of the Protestant Church of Ireland, the established church (until 1869), numbering no more than 12 percent and declining steadily in their relative share of the population.[12] And the Protestants as a whole were divided mainly between the official Church of Ireland and the Presbyterians situated primarily in the north, descended principally from Scottish settlers, encouraged to emigrate since the early seventeenth century.

Irish numbers began to weigh very heavily in the middle of the nineteenth century, for the rapid growth of the Irish population began to pose serious threats to the prevailing sociopolitical structure. Two movements are relevant. First, in the early nineteenth century, Daniel O'Connell and his followers successfully campaigned for Catholic emancipation, achieved in 1829.[13] But thereafter his campaign for repeal

---

[7] Ibid., 43.   [8] Ibid., 49.   [9] Tanner 2001, 240.   [10] Kinealy 1994, 9.
[11] Ibid., 9.   [12] Guinnane 1997, 67.   [13] Boyce 1985, 262.

of the Act of Union between Great Britain and Ireland deeply threatened the British. Created after the failure of the combined Irish uprisings and invasion of Ireland by the French in 1798, "the Union in British eyes had taken on the sanction of fundamental law."[14] It was presumed to be a bulwark of stability by British statesmen fearful of future French incursions and of willing Irish collaborators. It was precisely this security framework that was being challenged by Irish numbers.

O'Connell's demonstrations against the Act of Union were famous for their legions of Roman Catholic Irish supporters. In Boyce, one can see a portrait of one such massive demonstration held at Tara in 1843.[15] Another demonstration, that of June 8, 1843, in Kilkenny, was said to have attracted 300,000 supporters in a town that today boasts no more than 20,000 residents.[16] Shortly thereafter, O'Connell was imprisoned, but he was released after several months. Demonstrations of this magnitude must have been deeply upsetting to the British government.

Equally unsettling were demonstrations of a different kind directed against attempted reform of Irish agriculture. Irish landlords increasingly were ejecting their tenant farmers in favor of pastures in which to graze their sheep and cattle. The hovels in which the tenants lived were often destroyed shortly after forced evictions. A movement to reverse this process overtook Ireland in 1829–31, and in a sense was a socioeconomic precursor to the later attempts to repeal the Act of Union. The Terry Alt movement, as it was called (for idiosyncratic reasons), assembled hundreds of, and sometimes even more than 1,000, people at a single site to dig up the pastures that formerly had been used by tenant farmers. This process is described in the following manner:

> The size of the crowds was certainly one of their most arresting features. Though some involved only scores of people, most crowds numbered in the hundreds and not a few included more than a thousand. They were usually mixed in age and sex, comprising women and children as well as adult males ... In the typical case the diggers marched to their appointed work in military order, with spades and pitchforks hoisted on their shoulders, and with fifers or other musicians playing before them. Naturally, this ritual drew onlookers, who followed the marchers to the designated place and lustily cheered them on as they stripped and set to work. While some participants turned up the grass with their spades ... others broke the sods with their pitchforks ... It was a ritual to toss the

[14] Ibid. See also Foster 2001.   [15] Boyce 1985, 262.
[16] Rothe House exhibit, Kilkenny, Republic of Ireland.

> sods of grass into the air and at the same time to raise a cry, such as "*Hey*
> for O'Connell, and *hey* for Clare." Because the crowds were so large, it was
> possible to turn up a field of five or ten acres in an hour or less, and it was
> not unusual for one crowd to polish off several fields in a morning's work
> of protest, sport and conviviality. Small parties of police ... were no
> use ... Sizeable detachments of soldiers ... soon brought the turning
> up of pastures to an end.[17]

The O'Connell referred to here, of course, is the same O'Connell who
later led the movement for repeal.

Twenty-one members of the Terry Alt movement were condemned to
death and fifty-eight others were transported out of the British Isles, but
agrarian rebellion continued. In January 1831, William Blood, a land
agent for Lord Stradboke in County Clare, was ambushed and murdered. By May of that year, nineteen members of the landowning class
were murdered, presumably by Terry Alts. Agrarian rebellion did not
cease, but "effective armed resistance was defeated not by security forces
but the horrors of the potato famine."[18] These horrors – the massive
depopulation as the result of death and the desperate need to emigrate –
soon overshadowed and then displaced any serious efforts at rebellion.
Only a small and utterly ineffectual revolt occurred in 1848, easily put
down by the authorities.[19]

In 1846, the first serious famine year, the British government changed
from that of the Tory Sir Robert Peel to the Whig Lord John Russell.
Earlier, even in the midst of what appeared to be a "typical" small-scale
famine, Peel had made serious efforts to aid the affected population. He
established a temporary relief commission consisting of some of the
most competent members of the Irish administration. Peel also arranged
to buy large quantities of corn meal (maize) in the United States and
shipped it to Ireland for distribution to the most needy. Unfortunately,
the starving were never fully instructed in ways to cook the meal so that
ingested raw, as it often was, it led to bowel ailments and death.[20]
However, as the famine worsened in 1846–47, the new government
proved to be increasingly inadequate to the task. Further, as time passed,
a resentment grew of the Irish peasant of whom it was said by Sir Charles
Trevelyan, permanent secretary at the Treasury, "A fortnight planting, a
week or ten days digging and fourteen days turf cutting suffice for his
subsistence. During the rest of the year he is at leisure to follow his own

---

[17] Emphasis in original; Geraghty 1998, 290–91.   [18] Ibid., 291.   [19] Connolly 1995, 44.
[20] Kinealy 1994, 46.

inclinations."[21] Throughout the famine period, when starvation was rampant, large quantities of food were exported from Ireland to England.[22]

Encouragement of the Irish peasant to be more self-reliant as well as concerns about the economy became dominant themes of the time, especially after the fiscal crisis of 1847. And "after 1847, ideological and fiscal concerns, combined with a zealous determination to use the calamity to bring about long-term improvements in the economy of Ireland, took priority over the immediate needs of the distressed poor. The consequence was a breakdown in the provision of relief."[23] And, by 1849, even the £100,000 ($480,000 at that time) deemed to be required for famine relief was unavailable for this purpose.[24]

But these traditional explanations of Britain's inadequate response to the famine fail to answer certain critical questions. Why the inordinate concern for the work ethic of the Irish peasant and, more important, why after 1847 was the so-called Gregory Clause of the Poor Relief Bill instituted? This clause stipulated that tenants holding more than a quarter-acre of land were not eligible for public assistance.[25] Becoming law in June 1847, the worst of the famine years, it became the basis for mass evictions of hundreds of thousands that yielded not only death by starvation, but also by epidemic diseases of many sorts, made possible by the weakened constitutions of the malnourished.

Why were the rapid population increase, underdevelopment, and potential, though not actual dissidence of poor Irish Catholics so threatening to Britain? An answer is to be found in the earlier invasion of Ireland by the French and the attempted coalition of an external great power enemy and native rebels that earlier had proven so devastating to the British in the American Revolution. Even the external great power was the same in both cases – France. And while France was an ally of Britain during the Entente Cordiale of the 1830s and early 1840s, that condition would change radically precisely during the early stages of the famine.

The effort to "solve" the Irish Question through draconian measures can be fully understood only within the geopolitical security context of the period. Russell himself actually opposed ejecting the Irish tenants but came up against two of his cabinet members with Irish landholdings who opposed leniency. One of these, Lord Palmerston, the foreign

[21] Daly 1995, 132.   [22] Woodham-Smith 1962, 75.   [23] Kinealy 1994, 121.
[24] Ó Gráda 1999, 83.   [25] Donnelly 1995, 159.

secretary, was especially adamant. He also was the single most well-known and widely influential member of the cabinet. Some of his statements are revealing. On March 31, 1848, Palmerston recorded to the cabinet that "it was useless to disguise the truth that any great improvement in the social system of Ireland must be founded upon an extensive change in the present state of agrarian occupation, and that this change necessarily implies a long continued and systematic eject-ment of small-holders and of squatting cottiers."[26] The cabinet exhib-ited a "general shudder" when Lord Clanricarde (another landholder in Ireland) made similar pronouncements with an equal degree of ruth-lessness.[27] More directly on the matter of numbers, in Muriel Chamberlain's paraphrasing:

> On [Lord Palmerston's] estate there were about 6,000 persons "whom some of our Friends would call *my* Poor, & say that I ought to employ & support" but they had grown to such numbers "wholly without any consent, concurrence or Encouragement of mine". Now that their accus-tomed food had "vanished by a Dispensation of Providence," they were ten times more numerous than would be required for the profitable cultivation of the land and many times more numerous than the income from the land would enable him to employ. The only solution he could see was emigration.[28]

Palmerston suggested that the government should subsidize emigration by supplying money to landlords who would then send out emigrants. And when Palmerston sent his own tenants off to Canada in the summer and autumn of 1847, "the Canadians were shocked at the conditions of the immigrants, who arrived in a state of complete destitution."[29] Palmerston's behavior, as recounted in the Canadian press, was nothing less than scandalous.

   At the same time, Palmerston as foreign secretary was keenly aware of security threats that an economically more developed, less heavily Roman Catholic Ireland would have mitigated. His training included terms as a junior lord at the Admiralty in 1807, after which, in 1809, he became secretary at war for nearly twenty years. He was foreign minister in 1830–41 and 1846–51, and later prime minister in 1855–58 and 1859–65. Clearly, Palmerston was not only a central figure in Britain's foreign policy establishment, but on the domestic scene as well.

---

[26] Ibid., 163.   [27] Ibid.   [28] Chamberlain 1987, 65.   [29] Ridley 1970, 322.

The collapse of the Entente Cordiale between Britain and France came on Palmerston's watch as foreign minister. The issue centered on the proposed Bourbon spouses of heirs to the Spanish throne, supported by the French since the early 1840s. Palmerston strongly opposed these marriages specifically because of the virtual union between the Spanish and French governments that these betrothals implied, but more generally because "he regarded France, under whatever government, as the main enemy of England."[30] Palmerston also "particularly resented links between the French and the Irish rebels."[31]

Even before Palmerston's accession to the head of the foreign ministry, the Peel government was deeply anxious about this growth of French influence on the Iberian peninsula. Peel stated in 1844: "Let us be prepared for war ... They (the French) are much more likely to presume upon our weakness than to take offence at our strength."[32] The Duke of Wellington in 1845 studied the best ways to defend the British Isles against attack by the French. As he later remarked in 1848, the year of the Paris commune, "there can be no doubt now of the object of the disaffected in Ireland – to deprive the Queen of her Crown! And to establish a Republic. To obtain that object they are ready to arm and attack the City of Dublin. God send us a good deliverance."[33]

Palmerston, ever sensitive to these issues, stated in 1845 that: "The Channel is no longer a barrier. Steam navigation has rendered that which was before impassable by a military force nothing more than a river passable by a steam bridge."[34] A report by the Inspector General Fortification remarked on the greater precautions necessary for the south than for the north of Ireland in part because of the lesser reliability of this largely Roman Catholic population,[35] soon to be engulfed by the famine.

This period generally witnessed a greatly increased emphasis on British vulnerability culminating in the *Report of the Royal Commission on the Defence of the United Kingdom*, published in 1860. It said at one point:

> Having carefully weighed the foregoing considerations, we are led to the
> opinion that neither our fleet, our standing armies nor our volunteer

---

[30] Bullen 1974, 5. More generally, Palmerston subscribed to principles of realpolitik: "For him, mutual suspicion between states that were natural rivals was predestined" (Steele 1991, 309).

[31] Chamberlain 1987, 74.   [32] Quoted in Bullen 1974, 40.

[33] Quoted in Sloan 1997, 116.   [34] Quoted ibid., 115.   [35] Ibid.

forces, nor even the three combined, can be relied on as sufficient in themselves for the security of the kingdom against foreign invasion. We therefore proceed to consider that part of our instruction which directs our attention especially to fortifications.[36]

Faced with these weaknesses, Palmerston argued for strengthening national defenses, but even more generally "Palmerston was convinced that England's power was the result of her progress."[37]

If Britain were to successfully counter the French threat to its ascendance, then the British Isles, most vulnerable perhaps on the west coast of Ireland because of the possible coalition between the French and Irish Catholic rebels, had to "progress" as quickly as possible. Underdeveloped and partially seditious Ireland needed to be transformed quickly and thoroughly. The famine as a "Dispensation of Providence" could be used to further that end. According to G. R. Sloan, "The Act of Union which came into effect in 1800 did not immediately achieve the objectives that British policy-makers intended, but it began a process whereby at the end of the nineteenth century Ireland had been integrated into a defense system of the United Kingdom as a whole."[38]

The importance of Ireland, with its many estuaries and more than a few willing rebels, was not lost on the French. According to one French writer, "The independence of Ireland is necessary for the world. The French Revolution spread the seeds of liberty throughout the Continent of Europe. Perhaps the Irish Revolution will soon provide us with the liberty of the seas."[39] A more direct attack on the principal basis of British power cannot be envisioned; that attack would proceed through the region of greatest British vulnerability – Ireland. The British response to the famine, particularly the absence of effective relief and the wholesale eviction of peasants from their farms, stands squarely in the tradition of cynical realpolitik – that which ignores the consequences of state inaction for victimized populations, but emphasizes only the potential benefits of that inaction for the state.

Perhaps it was this very real concern with state security in the continued presence of perceived dissidence that led Cecil Woodham-Smith in a classic history of the famine to observe that:

[36] Ibid., 117.   [37] Bullen 1974, 54.   [38] Sloan 1997, 109.
[39] Quoted in Geraghty 1998, 260–61.

It is not characteristic of the English to behave as they have behaved in Ireland; as a nation, the English have proved themselves to be capable of generosity, tolerance and magnanimity, but not where Ireland is concerned. As Sydney Smith, the celebrated writer and wit wrote: "The moment the very name of Ireland is mentioned, the English seem to bid adieu to common feeling, common prudence and common sense, and to act with the barbarity of tyrants and the fatuity of idiots."[40]

Germans and Jews in Poland

The transition to a policy of ethnic cleansing of Poland's German and Jewish populations before World War II illustrates the consequences posed by a Germany rearming under Nazi rule and an equally hostile Soviet Union. State insecurity evoking the response of a realpolitik bordering on brute force-imprudence, but without the recent experience of loss (indeed, victory over the Soviets and an expanded territory were achieved by the Poles in 1920), characterizes the Polish condition during the interwar period. That the ethnic cleansing of Jews actually did not yet come about is attributable only to the start of World War II.

Overt threat to the new state of Poland began with the Locarno Pact of October 1925. Although hailed in the West as a milestone in the consolidation of peace, for it gained German recognition of the inviolability of Germany's western borders as prescribed in the Treaty of Versailles, in the East it evoked quite the opposite reaction. Instead of a direct international guarantee of Polish borders, Locarno obtained a French guarantee of these borders, but only within the framework of the Covenant of the League of Nations. In other words, in the event of hostile action against Poland, France could act only after the cumbersome League machinery had been put into motion, thereby delaying any international assistance until it was probably too late to do any good. Thus, the Franco-Polish alliance that had served as the principal bulwark of Polish territorial integrity since 1921 had been diluted almost to the point of uselessness. At least this was the conclusion reached by the Polish General Staff and communicated to the Polish ambassador in Paris in February 1926.[41]

Gustav Stresemann, the German foreign minister, repeatedly announced that Locarno did not limit Germany's right to obtain

---

[40] Woodham-Smith 1962, 411.   [41] Gieysztor et al. 1979, 566–67.

"corrections" to its eastern border.[42] Indeed, his personal antipathy to Poland was well known. In 1928, for example, at a meeting of the League Council, he shouted and pounded his fist in response to statements of the Polish foreign minister, August Zaleski, attacking the nationalist activities of the Upper Silesian *Volksbund*, then under Polish governance. As Harald von Riekhoff remarks, "in [Stresemann's] image the idea of Germans living under Polish rule entailed elements of perversion, while the reverse conformed to the natural order."[43]

Two additional factors were to compound the threat. The Soviet–German Neutrality Pact of April 1926 appeared to be explicitly directed against Poland.[44] German troops had occupied Poland during World War I and the Polish–Soviet war had ended only five years earlier. Hans von Seeckt, commander of the German army, was known to hate Poland and sought its destruction.[45] In order to avoid the limitations of the Treaty of Versailles, German troops actually began secretly training on Soviet soil; it would have been virtually impossible to conceal such military maneuvers from the Poles. In 1924 and 1925, the Soviets had proposed to the Germans an alliance that aimed at Poland's partition and a restoration of the 1914 borders.[46]

Second, in 1925, Germany began a tariff war with Poland that compounded its economic difficulties. An internal economic insecurity was thereby added to the military uncertainty, principally because half of Poland's trade was with Germany.[47]

In May 1926, Marshal Józef Piłsudski, hero of the Polish–Soviet war, overthrew the democratically elected government, significantly retaining only the minister of war and general inspector of the armed forces, after appointing trusted colleagues to civilian posts.[48] Initially, Piłsudski announced that the coup would have no revolutionary consequences for the polity or society,[49] which was largely true during the first years of his regime.

But despite Piłsudski's desire to avoid antagonizing ethnic minorities and thereby keep Poland's borders intact, majority–minority relations gradually deteriorated. In response to Ukrainian nationalist provocations, the infamous "pacification of Eastern Little Poland" occurred, in which the rural population was terrorized by the army as it was billeted

---

[42] Cienciala and Komarnicki 1984, 273.   [43] Von Riekhoff 1971, 265.
[44] Leslie et al. 1980, 158.   [45] Lukowski and Zawadzki 2001, 210.
[46] Von Riekhoff 1971, 265–66.   [47] Lukowski and Zawadzki 2001, 209.   [48] Ibid., 213.
[49] Gieysztor et al. 1979, 579.

locally and carried out its investigations of nationalist activity. Abandoned Orthodox churches were blown up and there occurred sporadic attempts to convert the Orthodox to Roman Catholicism. In 1934, a Polish version of the Nazi concentration camp (called an "isolation camp") was constructed to house Communists as well as members of the Ukrainian and Belorussian opposition to Polish rule.[50]

Relations with both Germany and the Soviet Union were tense, at times including crossborder violence. Typical of the period after 1930 was a speech delivered by the German minister of transport, Gottfried Treviranus, on the steps of the Reichstag building. The speech itself referred to the day, hopefully in the not too distant future, when all of the lost territories in the East would be reincorporated into the German Reich. The subsequent furor actually was intensified by Treviranus's efforts at clarification, which hinted that Germany's peaceful attempts at border revision stemmed solely from its then current absence of military power, the Reichswehr having been limited to a maximum of 100,000 by the Treaty of Versailles. Zaleski remarked that "from this the whole world had to conclude that Germany would make war on Poland if she had an adequate army."[51] The subsequent period was replete with border violations by Polish military aircraft and clashes between German and Polish border police.

Violent incidents also were common in relations between Poland and the Soviet Union. Most serious was the March 1928 assassination of Peter Voikov, the Soviet minister in Warsaw. Stalin himself commented on it in an article in *Pravda*. The Soviet government demanded an immediate investigation with Soviet participation (reminiscent of the assassination at Sarajevo and the aggressive Austro-Hungarian reaction to it in 1914). Military preparations began on both sides, leaving the French ambassador Jean Herbette to report to Aristide Briand that "the signs of preparation for a war are so numerous and open in the USSR that one cannot doubt the intentions of the Soviet government."[52] But cooler heads ultimately prevailed and hostilities were avoided.

Paradoxically, relations between Poland and Germany improved only after Hitler's rise to power, culminating in the nonaggression pact of January 1934. Hitler's plans did not include an initial foray against Poland; he preferred instead to consolidate his power in Germany and then Austria. Piłsudski was happy to be free of the virtually unrelenting pressure for border revision emanating from the previous German

[50] Ibid., 585–93.   [51] Quoted in Von Riekhoff 1971, 331.   [52] Quoted ibid., 291.

regime.[53] But as it rearmed and successfully militarized the Rhineland in defiance of the Treaty of Versailles, as well as adding Austria to its domains, Germany again began to loom as a serious threat. Soviet armaments build-up also was proceeding apace in response both to Germany's aggressive policies and to those of Japan in the Far East. Poland, literally caught in the middle, turned on its German and Jewish minorities that were assumed, rightly or wrongly, to be seditious.

Although cool at first to the Nazi message, after 1935 the German minority rapidly warmed to its appeal. At first, the Polish government did nothing to stem this tide. It was careful not to antagonize this minority in order to placate the rapidly growing power to the West. But despite these efforts by the Polish government, as early as 1936, eighty-six Germans in Katowice were convicted of having formed a pro-Nazi underground organization, which aimed at detaching Upper Silesia from Poland by means of an armed uprising.[54] Relations were further embittered by Polish efforts at land reform in the west that in the Germans' perception unfairly targeted them, as well as limitations on the entry of Germans into the professions.[55] As in the Irish case, emigration appeared to be the only solution. According to the German consul-general at Thorn writing to the Foreign Office in October 1938:

> In view of the severe pressure to which the German minority in Poland is subjected, for [sic] it finally sees no alternative but to emigrate to the Reich. These Germans maintain that, even if they themselves could endure the situation, their children would certainly have no chance of any start in life. The continual measures oppressive [sic] of the Polish administration as recently evinced in the expulsions from the frontier zone and in the closing of schools, etc., are sufficient evidence that it is impossible for the Germans to continue living here, and that they must leave the country if they are to survive. The prospects of waging a successful battle against the Polish authorities, without considerable active support from home, is so poor that the enormous emigration of earlier days and again of the past two years has seriously weakened the German community here.[56]

The Jews also were not to be spared, and in many respects their situation would worsen considerably because of the absence of emigration opportunities. Not only were the Jews to serve effectively as political sacrificial lambs to demonstrate Polish congruence with Nazi beliefs and thereby

---

[53] Leslie et al. 1980, 183.   [54] Polonsky 1972, 465.
[55] German Foreign Office 1940, 103–04.   [56] Ibid., 141.

appease the Germans, but the Jews also were indelibly identified with communism. According to an "order of the day" issued by the right-wing National Party prior to a demonstration outside Warsaw in 1936:

> The danger of the Judaeo-Communist conspiracy dispelled by the Polish victory of 1920 has increased seriously in the last few years and has made the menace of revolution hang over our country and over the other countries of Europe, particularly over those which have not yet succeeded in giving themselves a solid national regime. The victory of anarcho-Communist forces is particularly in the interest of the Jews, who are threatened by the tide of National movements, growing stronger every day.[57]

But it was not only political anti-Semitism that made this identification between Judaism and communism. According to a pastoral letter of February 1936 by Cardinal Hlond, the Roman Catholic primate of Poland, read from all the Catholic pulpits in Poland, "It is a fact that Jews oppose the Catholic Church, are steeped in free-thinking, and represent the avant-garde of the atheist movement, the Bolshevik move-ment, and subversive action. The Jews have a disastrous effect on morality and their publishing-houses dispense pornography. It is true that Jews commit fraud, usury, and are involved in trade in human beings."[58] To be sure, Jews were prominently active in the outlawed Polish Communist Party, but the vast majority of Jews did not support communism either in Poland or in the Soviet Union.

Polish governments tended to blur the distinction between hard-core Communist supporters of the Soviet Union who happened to be of Jewish origin, and others who, while socialist (e.g., Bundists; see chapter 14), nevertheless were politically loyal to the Polish state. Government offi-cials suspected that these Jewish socialists, like all others, were secretly subversive, if not openly so.[59] The imprudence of these officials in their realpolitik was manifest. Throughout this period, the Polish foreign minister, Józef Beck, regarded "the USSR as Poland's principal enemy."[60]

Economic measures taken against the Jews became increasingly harsh. After the onset of the Great Depression, a moratorium on the debts of peasants in 1933 was not extended to traders, principally Jews. They also were now almost entirely excluded from the timber trade, a field in

---

[57] Quoted in Polonsky 1972, 416–17.   [58] Quoted in Vital 1999, 767.   [59] Ibid., 785.
[60] Leslie et al. 1980, 203.

which Jews had once played the principal role. The tax burden on predominantly Jewish occupations was disproportionately high. Whereas Jews constituted 10 percent of the population, they were paying between 35 and 40 percent of all taxes. New restrictions were imposed on the entry of Jews into trade schools and universities. In 1938, fully one-half of Poland's Jews could not afford to pay a 5 złoty (then roughly 50 cents) communal tax. By the end of the decade, approximately one out of every three Jews was dependent on relief, largely financed by the American Jewish community. According to one astute Jewish leader in Lwów: "A year or two ago, 40 percent of our people applied for aid to the community, this year it is 50 percent., the next year or the year after that it will be 60 percent. We are waiting for death."[61]

By the late 1930s the Polish government had settled on a policy of ethnic cleansing its Jewish as well as its German population. The proportion of Jews in major Polish cities such as Warsaw, Łódź, Lwów, and Lublin was in excess of 30 percent and increasing.[62] Most of these Jews were impoverished. In June 1936, Prime Minister (also General) Sławoj-Składkowski told the Polish Sejm (national legislature) that economic conflict between Jews and Poles entailed a struggle for Poland's survival.[63] A leader of the principal political party, OZON (Camp of National Unity), General Stanisław Skwarczyński and 116 of his parliamentary colleagues declared in 1938 that "a radical reduction of the number of Jews in Poland by means of a massive emigration" was required.[64] A set of thirteen resolutions was adopted, indicating how reduction in the number of Jews was to be effected.[65]

As early as September 1934, Beck declared to the League of Nations that Poland was not required to safeguard the rights of its minorities. In 1936, the Polish delegate to the League's Economic Commission, upon Beck's instructions, claimed that the Jewish problem in Poland, especially its cities, required "rapid measures of relief," hopefully through large-scale emigration. Almost immediately thereafter, the Polish delegate to the League's Political Commission raised the same issue of Jewish emigration. The Polish government also strongly supported Zionist attempts to increase emigration to Palestine, but British measures restricting Jewish immigration thwarted these efforts.

---

[61] Quoted in Polonsky 1972, 470.   [62] Vital 1999, 765.   [63] Ibid., 771.
[64] Polonsky 1972, 466.   [65] Vital 1999, 771.

The following year, a group of Poles visited Paris with the suggestion that Madagascar, then a French colony, be designated a site for Jewish emigration. Other locations also were explored, but the flood of Jewish emigrants from Germany, Austria, and Czechoslovakia led to an increasingly hostile worldwide response to Jewish immigration, a theme that will be explored in chapter 11. By November 1938, the principal newspaper of the National Democratic Party stated the party's wish "To show the Jews the door"; in order to effect this outcome, "one should push them through by means of a 'surgical operation' [sic] which would deprive them legally of the means to live in Poland."[66]

Within one month of Piłsudski's death, in June 1935 a massacre of Jews took place in Grodno. The following year witnessed intermittent pogroms throughout Poland that continued until the war broke out.[67] Jewish university students were forced either to attend lectures seated in separate benches set aside for them or to stand, which the vast majority chose to do. Only the onset of World War II prevented legislation depriving Jews "legally of the means to live in Poland" from being passed in the Sejm.[68] Poland was on the verge of either ethnic cleansing its Jews and/or exclusion of its Jewish minority from public life.

Muslims in Bosnia

Threat of numbers also weighed heavily in the ethnic cleansing of Bosnia-Herzegovina between 1992 and 1995. Ethnic cleansing was committed by all major actors in Bosnia – Serbs, Croats, and Muslims – but the greater part of the ethnically cleansed population was victimized by the Serbs. As a consequence, the Bosnian Serbs will be emphasized in the following account. In contrast to the preceding cases, the Srebrenica massacre incorporates a clear genocidal element within the overall ethnic cleansing.

The demography of Bosnia-Herzegovina underwent a dramatic change in the decades preceding the Yugoslav wars. In 1961, Muslims constituted only 26 percent of the population of Bosnia-Herzegovina, with the Serbs comprising 43 percent. By 1991, virtually a complete reversal had occurred with the Muslims rising to 44 percent and the Serbs dropping to 31 percent.[69] Many Serbs had migrated from Bosnia to Belgrade or other locations inside Serbia proper. A differential birth

---

[66] Quoted in Polonsky 1972, 468.   [67] Dubnov 1973, 880–81.   [68] Vital 1999, 772.
[69] Woodward 1995, 33.

rate between Muslims and Serbs also favored the former. Thus, from a near majority in 1961 or at least a large plurality, the Serbs now were a distinct minority. One group's former dominance was exchanged for a secondary status. And all of this was in addition to the genocidal elimination of a large portion of the Bosnian Serb population by the fascist Croatian Ustaše (with some Bosnian Muslim collaboration) in alliance with Nazi Germany.

In Tito's Yugoslavia under single-party Communist rule, such a reversal of fortune, however dramatic, would not necessarily yield a commensurate diminution of influence. However, by the early 1990s, more than a decade after Tito's death, democratic reforms ensured that ballots would count very heavily in the power distribution. The desire for electoral victories and the resulting power gain stoked the nationalistic fires. Local politicians within the republics sought to maximize their own political positions in republican elections as well as the positions of the individual republics vis-à-vis the federal government and competing republics.[70] Indeed, ethnic cleansing, and its genocidal corollary, had its roots in a democratization process associated with the emergence of sovereignty in the new post-Cold War period. According to the Badinter Arbitration Commission and the European Community (EC) support of its ruling, international recognition of national sovereignty required a referendum of the residents of a given territory on their choice of a state.[71]

Military control was not sufficient; a vote was required. Thus, the only guarantee of eventual incorporation of a strategically or economically desired territory within the borders of a state was the conformity of the (ethnoreligious) identity of most of the residents of that territory with that of the incorporating state. Ethnic cleansing, therefore, became a preferred modus operandi to maximize the security of the emerging state. As Susan Woodward comments:

> States are more than communities of political identity. In addition to legitimacy and citizens, they require strategically defensible borders, economic assets sufficient to survive against external threats, and a monopoly on the use of force over territory claimed. The borders of the republics had never had to satisfy the needs of independent states. Once nationalists turned to state-building, there was an additional reason on many sides for contesting existing republican borders. While political

[70] Janjić 1995.   [71] Woodward 1995, 292.

rhetoric and propaganda continued to emphasize ethnic criteria, the actual goals of military activity would be driven by strategic objectives.[72]

Serbia, despite its domination of the Yugoslav National Army (JNA), had legitimate security concerns as the dissolution of the former Yugoslavia loomed on the horizon. The July 1991 accord at Brioni stipulated the withdrawal of all JNA units from Slovenia, thereby implying international recognition of that new state. As a consequence, Prime Minister József Antall of Hungary warned Serbia that it could not assume that its province of Vojvodina with its large Hungarian minority would continue to be part of Serbia. "We gave Vojvodina to Yugoslavia. If there is no more Yugoslavia, then we should get it back," declared Antall, referring to the 1920 Treaty of Trianon.[73] This verbal threat was supported by the earlier sale of at least 36,000 Kalashnikov rifles to the Republic of Croatia in 1990. Serbia, therefore, could legitimately feel threatened not only by the newly emerging states of the former Yugoslavia, but by neighboring existing states as well.

German domination of EC political decision making at this time raised perhaps even deeper security concerns for Serbia. The taking on of Croatian fascist Ustaše symbols by Franjo Tuđman, the Croatian leader,[74] as the Croatian state emerged, of course, was hardly reassuring to the Serbs. Memories of the mass murder of at least 500,000 Serbs by the fascist Croatian state in alliance with Nazi Germany during World War II were rekindled by Tuđman's behavior.

The recent German unification and German emergence as the clear economic, even political leader of the EC made matters far worse. After considerable lobbying by the Croatian and Slovenian leadership as well as by the Vatican, Hans-Dietrich Genscher, the German foreign minister, emerged as an unequivocal supporter of Croatian and Slovenian independence.[75] When the actual recognition, by Germany, of both new countries came on December 23, 1991[76] – with agreement of the remaining EC members, apparently bullied by the newly augmented Germany – the Western threat became palpable. With growing economic ties to Germany, the Slovenian and Croatian economies, already burgeoning relative to the remainder of Yugoslavia, and the presence of NATO nearby, the JNA and mainly its Serbian leadership would feel an imminent threat to the Yugoslav state.

---

[72] Ibid., 267.   [73] Quoted ibid., 219.   [74] Glenny 1996, 11–13.   [75] Ibid.
[76] Woodward 1995, 184.

Although politically Yugoslavia had traversed a "middle way" between East and West during the Cold War, nevertheless, by the mid-1980s the JNA's contingency plans (Rampart-91) were based on the assumption that invasion would most likely come from the West. NATO maneuvers in Southern Europe in 1985 and 1986 emphasized this threat, as did Slovenian and Croatian appeals to NATO for protection from the JNA during the early phases of Yugoslav dissolution.[77]

Bosnia was pivotal in that dissolution, for Serbia and Croatia, already at war at the time of the EC recognition of Bosnian independence on April 6, 1992, would vie for maximizing the security of their own states on Bosnian territory. Recall from chapter 2 the efforts of the Serbs to persuade the Bosnian Muslims to remain within the Federal Republic of Yugoslavia. Within a newly independent Bosnia, a Serbian minority would be subservient to a Muslim–Croat majority, which the Serbs (in both Bosnia and Serbia) feared might seek alliance with Croatia and perhaps even Germany.

Bosnia also was pivotal to the JNA. During the 1980s, 40–55 percent of the Bosnian economy was tied to military industries. "Sixty to 80 percent of the army's physical assets (armaments factories, supply routes, airfields, mines and basic raw materials, stockpiles, training schools, oil depots) were located in Bosnia-Herzegovina. On the eve of the war, 68 percent of the federal army's 140,000 troops were stationed in the republic. To the extent that the Yugoslav army was fighting a war for its own integrity and state, it could not easily be a neutral party in Bosnia-Herzegovina or abandon its own economic foundations."[78]

A two-tiered threat to the Serbs emerged from Serbian numerical weakness within Bosnia coupled with the looming presence of the newly united Germany at the head of the EC. The end result of the military clashes and ethnic cleansing was a near-equal division of Bosnia between the Federation of Bosnia-Herzegovina (the Bosnian Muslim–Croat Federation) holding 51 percent of the territory and the Republika Srpska (the Bosnian Serb Republic) occupying 49 percent with corresponding ethnic majorities within each. The two halves together formed the Republic of Bosnia-Herzegovina, but with rights of each half to affiliate with other political entities, if they so wished.[79]

Yet, as we know, there were genocidal elements to the ethnic cleansing, particularly on the part of the Serbs. And here, in contrast to the previous cases, loss was far more tangible for the Serbs than it was either

[77] Ibid., 72, 136.   [78] Ibid., 259.   [79] Burg and Shoup 1999, 367.

for the Poles or the British at the times of their respective efforts at or acquiescence in ethnic cleansing. This loss was not only that of the mass murder of Serbs during World War II, important as it was. Its significance was echoed in the building of Serbian concentration camps for Muslims such as Omarska in the Prijedor region at major sites of Serbian deportations and mass murder by the Ustaše during the early 1940s.[80] In addition, the head of Omarska, Dr. Milan Kovačević, was born in Jasenovac, the site of the most deadly and infamous of the Ustaše concentration camps. As noted earlier, Jasenovac for the Serbs has the same significance as does Auschwitz for the Jews.[81] But, in addition, there were anticipated significant territorial losses that likely influenced the mass murder at Srebrenica, one of the genuinely genocidal efforts on the part of the Serbs.

Ratko Mladić, a Bosnian Serb, was in charge of the genocidal behavior in Srebrenica. He had been commander of the Serb garrison at Knin, the most important city in the Serb-held Croatian *krajina*, and later became head of the Bosnian Serb army.[82] Thousands of Muslim men were killed after the Bosnian Serb army completed its conquest of Srebrenica on July 12, 1995.[83] Mladić was operating in the domain of losses in two senses. Like other Serb officers in the old JNA, he had lost his Partisan father in battle with the Croatian Ustaše. His worldview was not unlike that of many Nazis, such as Himmler (see chapter 8). According to Mladić, "Regardless of what we decide, the west will continue to implement its infernal plan. What is at stake is an attempt to disunite the Orthodox world, and even annihilate it."[84]

More important, perhaps, was the conclusion he must have reached that the Serb-held *krajina* in Croatia would soon be lost to a Croatian offensive. Mladić's task as commander of the Bosnian Serb army was to keep a corridor open to the *krajina* through Bosnia.[85] As the former commander of Knin, he would have been highly sensitive to this military requirement. Yet during the late spring and early summer it must have been obvious that the *krajina* would not be held. By early July, just prior to the Srebrenica massacres, the Croatian army had made significant gains, putting their artillery and troops within striking distance of Knin. As early as July 15, the *New York Times* was reporting the Croatian build-up.[86] It must have been obvious much earlier to a highly interested

---

[80] Judah 2000, 235–36.   [81] Ibid., 129, 236.   [82] Ibid., 230.
[83] Burg and Shoup 1999, 324–25.   [84] Quoted in Judah 2000, 231.
[85] Woodward 1995, 262.   [86] Burg and Shoup 1999, 342, 461.

Bosnian Serb military leader like Mladić. When the Croats launched their offensive on the *krajina* on August 4, the *krajina* Serb military put up little or no resistance. Hundreds of thousands of Serb refugees fled to Serb-held regions in Bosnia and Serbia.[87]

Reasons for the lack of *krajina* Serb resistance rested not only on the obvious massive Croatian buildup. US Army chief of staff, General Carl Vuono, is reported to have met ten times with senior Croatian officers prior to the attack.[88] But Slobodan Milošević himself had apparently signed on to an exchange of populations wherein Srebrenica would become Serb-held, while the *krajina* would fall to the Croats. The *krajina* Serbs had an arsenal of rockets that could have been used to shell Croatian cities in the event of a successful offensive. Indeed, they did just that, firing a rocket at the heart of Zagreb in the midst of May during the Croatian offensive on western Slavonia. A furious Milošević then seized many of the rockets from the *krajina* Serbs. Clearly, Serbia would be of no help to them.[89] According to Tim Judah:

> Thinking like this [population exchanges] was the green light for the conquest not only of Srebrenica but of Krajina too. Even if there were no formal meetings in which such forms of brutal population exchanges were mooted, the messages were clearly understood by all concerned. The disaster was that, while it was possible, if not highly likely, that the Croatian offensive on Krajina would drive out its population, no one had foreseen that Mladić would oversee the wholesale slaughter of thousands of Srebrenica's men after it duly fell in July.[90]

Being situated within the domain of losses, however, could lead Mladić to just such an outcome.

The discussion of realpolitik and ethnic cleansing, including a genocidal element is now complete. The following chapter empirically examines the expanded theory in which realpolitik is combined with loss in our three cases of genocide.

[87] Ibid., 331.   [88] Ibid., 339.   [89] Judah 2000, 301.   [90] Ibid.

7

Realpolitik and loss

The path is now open for an empirical examination of the full theoretical complement of realpolitik, loss, and their consequences for genocide, as suggested in chapter 5. Loss is the initial variable that sets the entire sequence in motion, ending in genocide. In each of the three cases of genocide studied here, first the domain of losses and state insecurity (suggesting the beginnings of brute force realpolitik) are explored, followed by risk acceptance, minimization, and loss compensation as indicated in figure 5.1. Examination of altruistic punishment will be left to the succeeding chapter.

The Holocaust

The domain of losses and state insecurity

Turning first to the most extensive genocide and one that is most surprising because of the utter absence of opposition, among most Jews, to either Germany or German culture prior to the Nazi period, World War I provides the key. Indeed, World War I is the reference point around which many, even most of the Nazi perceptions were framed. As we saw in chapter 6, territorial losses were not confined to former colonies and ethnically Polish territories in the East, but also encompassed the enormous losses of European territory occupied by Germany in 1918 prior to the Armistice.

The dimension of loss was magnified immeasurably by the appearance of refugees from the lost territories. A contraction of socio-economic space had been effected with visible consequences.[1] If, as did many Germans, one measures the territorial losses from June 1918 when

---

[1] As early as the middle of the nineteenth century, loss and migration were to be found in Central Europe. Defeat of Austria by Prussia in 1866 was to lead to political reforms that eventually resulted in an extraordinarily large Czech population in Vienna, Hitler's early political training ground. It is estimated that nearly half of Vienna's population in 1910

much of Eastern Europe and Ukraine and portions of France and Belgium were under German and Austro-Hungarian authority, then the contraction would appear to be immense.[2] While in the election of 1912 it had become apparent that anti-Semitic political parties had lost virtually all of their influence,[3] the same certainly could not be said of the post-World War I period.

Eastern territories lost to Poland gave rise to German-identified refugees, as did the Baltic states now governed by indigenous populations unwilling to continue experiencing German land ownership. Many of these Baltic Germans, including the Nazi ideologist Alfred Rosenberg, were to be rabid supporters of the Nazi cause. These migrations and expulsions continued until the start of World War II (see the preceding chapter).

At the same time, many Jews crossed into Germany fleeing the pogroms of Petlura and other Ukrainians, as well as White Russian nationalists. The image of both the German and the Jew on an equal footing as uprooted minorities must have been anathema to the traditional German,[4] indeed ubiquitous European Christian, view that the Jew was to be held in a subordinate position.

Certainly the defeat of Germany in World War I is important in understanding Nazi genocidal behavior during World War II; the singular perception of that defeat is crucial – for with his abdication, the kaiser blamed the Jews bitterly for Germany's defeat. This is the infamous "stab in the back" accusation, or as the kaiser put it in a letter to General August von Mackensen in December 2, 1919:

> The deepest, most disgusting shame ever perpetrated by a people in history, the Germans have done onto [sic] themselves. Egged on and misled by the tribe of Juda [sic] whom they hated, who were guests

---

was either from Bohemia or of Bohemian descent (Hamann 1999, 307). In 1943, Hitler remarked that "I've managed to get the Jews out of Vienna, now I also want to get the Czechs out of there" (ibid., 324). Significantly, the origins of the Nazi Party are to be found in anti-Czech agitation that led to the formation of the German Workers' Party (DAP) in 1903 that later become the National Socialist German Workers' Party (NSDAP) under Hitler's leadership (ibid., 259–60).

[2] Evans 2004, 52–53.   [3] Melson 1992, 119.

[4] According to Hitler on April 4, 1942: "Our upper classes, who've never bothered about the hundreds of thousands of German emigrants or their poverty, give way to a feeling of compassion regarding the fate of the Jews whom we claim the right to expel. Our compatriots forget too easily that the Jews have accomplices all over the world, and that no beings have greater powers of resistance as regards adaptation to climate. Jews can prosper anywhere, even in Lapland and Siberia" (Hitler [1942] 2000, 397).

among them! That was their thanks! Let no German ever forget this, nor rest until these parasites have been destroyed and exterminated [*vertilgt und ausgerottet*] from German soil! This poisonous mushroom on the German oak-tree![5]

Only in this way could many Germans understand their country's traumatic transition from near-European hegemon in the spring of 1918 to the truncated and militarily constrained pariah of the early 1920s.

In the hierarchical society of early twentieth-century Germany, such sentiments would have had considerable weight. Certainly, Hitler agreed completely. Speaking to the Czechoslovakian foreign minister Franzisek Chvalkovsky on January 21, 1939, Hitler stated "The Jews have not brought about the 9 November 1918 for nothing. This day will be avenged."[6] And in anticipation of the massive deportations to the East and a loss compensation that would not yet constitute genocide, Hitler summarized on October 25, 1941:

> From the rostrum of the Reichstag I prophesied to Jewry that, in the event of war's proving inevitable, the Jew would disappear from Europe. That race of criminals has on its conscience the two million dead of the first [sic] World War, and now already hundreds of thousands more. Let nobody tell me that all the same we can't park them in the marshy parts of Russia! Who's worrying about our troops? It's not a bad idea, by the way, that public rumour attributes to us a plan to exterminate the Jews. Terror is a salutary thing.[7]

Sentiments concerning Jewish responsibility for the outcome of World War I were rife throughout the Nazi hierarchy. Heinrich Himmler, the chief architect and implementer of the Nazi genocide, perhaps expressed them most clearly, also linking them to risk minimization. In a now-infamous speech to senior SS officers in Posen in October 1943, Himmler referred openly to the "evacuation of the Jews, the extermination of the Jewish people." Further: "*If the Jews were still lodged in the body of the German nation, we would probably have reached by now the stage of 1916–17.*"[8] According to Himmler, had the Jews not been removed from Germany, by whatever means, then defeat would have been imminent in 1943, as it was in 1916–17 when the Jews were present.

---

[5] Quoted in Röhl 1994, 210. [6] Quoted in Kershaw 2000a, 127.
[7] Hitler [1942] 2000, 87. [8] Emphasis added; quoted in Burleigh 2000, 660.

All of this despite the reality of 100,000 Jewish men under arms (80,000 having served in combat), 12,000 Jewish dead, at the front and 35,000 decorated for battlefield bravery. These statistics are out of all proportion to the roughly 500,000 Jewish citizens living in Germany in 1914.[9]

Equally consequential for later developments was the period immediately thereafter, called "the Great Disorder" by Gerald Feldman.[10] This was the period of massive inflation during which the dollar exchange rate of the paper mark in Berlin went from a yearly average of 4.28 in 1914 to 534,914 in 1923. The greatest rate of increase was in 1922–23.[11] Clearly, pensioners and those living on fixed incomes, either salaried or based on investments, had their financial lives ruined. The business climate also was devastated. One economist called it

> one of the outstanding episodes in the history of the twentieth century. Not only by reason of its magnitude but also by reason of its effects, it looms large on our horizon. It was the most colossal thing of its kind in history: and, next probably to the Great War itself, it must bear responsibility for many of the political and economic difficulties of our generation. It destroyed the wealth of the more solid elements in German society: and it left behind a moral and economic disequilibrium, apt breeding ground for the disasters which have followed. Hitler is the foster-child of the inflation.[12]

Additionally, the deep malaise was attributed to the economic and political mismanagement of the German Republic. The first major act of violence against a prominent Jew, the assassination of Foreign Minister Walter Rathenau in 1922, was not only an expression of the extraordinary difficulties of the time, but a harbinger of much worse things to come. The Great Depression, begun by the stock market crash of 1929, would bring back memories of "the Great Disorder." Now unemployment was rampant and the economy once again in shambles. Enormous and unimagined societal insecurity had appeared twice within less than a decade with, of course, enormous consequences as well. The November 1918 revolution in Bavaria, soon to be the hotbed of Nazism, occurred even before that which swept the Reich. It was a more radical revolution and one that happened to have several Jews among its leaders, including those with East European origins and Bolshevik connections. At the head stood Kurt Eisner, a Jewish journalist and left-wing

[9] Fischer 1998, 120.   [10] Feldman 1993.   [11] Ibid., 5.   [12] Robbins 1937, 5.

socialist who earlier had organized the "January strike" of 1916 in an attempt to initiate industrial unrest. As Kershaw put it, this revolution, albeit unsuccessful (Eisner was assassinated soon after its start) "developed in ways that were to leave a profound mark on Hitler."[13] The connection with Bolshevism was particularly important for, as Hitler himself said of Bolshevism and incidentally capitalism as well,[14] "the bearers of this [Bolshevik] system are also in both cases the same: Jews and only Jews!"[15]

By 1925, the German-Jewish population had grown to 565,000. But more important, at least for the Nazis, was its prominence. As of 1930, Jews owned approximately two-thirds of Germany's larger department and chain stores and almost half of Germany's textile firms. At least half of the German industry in Upper Silesia, including its largest steel manufacturer, was owned or managed by Jews. The two largest publishing houses (Ullstein and Mosse) were owned by Jews. In addition to prominence in journalism as well as the arts and sciences, more than half of the lawyers in Berlin were Jewish.[16]

As bad as the situation was in Germany before World War II, it was worse in Austria, especially Vienna, site of Hitler's early political education and a preferred location for Jewish immigrants from Galicia and elsewhere within the Austro-Hungarian Empire. Post-World War I Austria, of course, was a rump state vastly shrunken in size from its prewar imperial expanse. During World War II, a disproportionately large number of concentration camp guards and SS men were Austrian.

A common political framework greatly facilitated the migration from one part of the empire to another. Between 1860 and 1910, the Jewish population of Vienna rose from 6,200 to 175,300, roughly a quadrupling from 2.2 to 8.7 percent.[17] By the end of World War I, their number had increased beyond 10 percent both because of a somewhat larger number of Jews (200,000), and a smaller total Viennese population (1,865,000) as the result of the privation and immigration stemming from the war.[18]

---

[13] Kershaw 1998, 112.

[14] On June 25, 1941, Joseph Goebbels illustrated this presumed connection between Bolshevism and capitalism. "Sumner Welles [US undersecretary of state] has spoken on behalf of the USA. Totally subservient to Red Bolshevism. The old, so-familiar alliance between capitalism and Bolshevism has been resurrected in the foreign-policy field" (Goebbels 1983, 429).

[15] Quoted in Kershaw 2000a, 431.   [16] Sachar 2002, 242.

[17] Hamann 1999, 326.   [18] Sachar 2002, 179.

In 1912, almost half of the secondary school population was Jewish (47.4 percent). Nearly one-third of all university students in Vienna were Jewish; in 1913 Jews constituted more than 40 percent of all medical students in Vienna. In excess of 25 percent of the law students were Jewish. To gauge the rapidity of this demographic change, one has only to note that of 681 lawyers in Vienna in 1889 over half, 394, were Jewish. Two decades earlier, the number was 33. Wealthy Jews occupied newly constructed mansions in Vienna that were the envy of the aristocracy. Because of the tolerant reign of Franz Josef II, Austro-Hungarian Jews were protected, even rewarded with medals and titles by the grateful monarch.[19] By the mid-1930s, Jews constituted 62 percent of Vienna's lawyers and 47 percent of physicians. A minimum of 70 percent of the city's wholesale and retail businesses were in Jewish hands.[20]

In Germany, a sign of the times was a 1919 memorandum from the Reichsbank to the interior minister saying:

> Because of their shrewdness, their connections with one another and with third parties, and their skill in using loopholes in the regulations … to get around the legal requirements, a complete success against their mischief is unlikely to be achieved … unless it proves possible to keep these unwanted foreign guests, whose presence from a political as well as from a food and housing perspective is not exactly advantageous, out of Germany.[21]

In Germany, the rise of Jews to prominence threatened the traditional hierarchical dominance of Jews by Christians. It was not only prominent Jews that could be threatening to that hierarchy, but the rapid rise of the German-Jewish middle class could also have that consequence. According to Albert Lindemann, "Jews themselves in nineteenth-century Germany were predominantly of lower-middle-class origin, but their rapid upward mobility had only weak parallels in the Gentile lower-middle class, a development that threatened the self-image of many of its members."[22] This threat is to be found in the appellation *Judenrepublik* for the Weimar Republic, perhaps as an expression of traditional German anti-Semitism or perhaps also as a shocked recognition that a people that only a generation or two ago had been living on the sidelines of German political life and even had legal barriers to their

[19] Hamann 1999, 327–28.   [20] Sachar 2002, 179.
[21] Quoted in Feldman 1993, 201–02.   [22] Lindemann 1997, 116.

full participation were now full and perhaps even leading participants in the founding of the new German state. The rise to cultural and scientific prominence of world-renowned Jewish figures such as Albert Einstein and Sigmund Freud also could have appeared to be consistent with communist political revolution in the name of the revolutionary figure with Jewish origins – Karl Marx.

In Vienna in 1920, there occurred a concerted campaign against Vienna's Eastern Jews, many of them recently arrived, including physical violence. And in 1923, all Jews who had settled in Bavaria since 1914 were expelled, principally, of course, the Eastern Jewish refugees. Between November 5 and November 8, the twentieth-century's first German pogrom occurred. In Berlin's ghetto, Jews were robbed and beaten by a rampaging mob estimated to be approximately 10,000 in size.[23] Soon, German battlefield losses during World War II, beginning in August 1941, would signal that the horrific losses of World War I would be augmented by the unfolding of vicious combat on the Eastern front.[24]

Risk acceptance, minimization, and loss compensation

The onset of the Holocaust is generally dated from the appearance of the *Einsatzgruppen* in the East shortly after the invasion of the Soviet Union on June 22, 1941.[25] These mobile killing squads would later be supplemented and ultimately replaced by the extermination camps dotting the East European countryside. At the same time, despite expressions of Nazi hubris, the invasion of the Soviet Union was seen to be the riskiest military venture undertaken at that point by the Third Reich.

There are many indicators of Hitler's awareness of this gigantic risk. Even as operational plans for Barbarossa, as the invasion was code-named, were put into place in early 1941, Hitler was "unsure how things would go. He was distrustful of his own military leaders, uncertain about the strength of the Russians, and disappointed in the intransigence of the British."[26] Hitler also was likely aware of the need for a quick strategic victory. Not only was Britain undefeated, but Hitler was convinced, correctly as it turns out, that if the United States would not shortly be an active participant in the war then at least it would supply massive amounts of materiel should the war drag on into another year.[27]

---

[23] Aschheim 1982, 242–43. See also Wertheimer 1987.   [24] Mayer 1988; Burrin 1994.
[25] Hilberg 1985; Bartov 1992; Burleigh 2000; Kershaw 2000a.
[26] Kershaw 2000a, 344.   [27] Ibid., 388.

The Soviet Union as a potential adversary needed to be eliminated quickly, in order to avoid the linkage of its resources with those of the West.[28] According to prospect theory, "Crucial is the argument that people will run much higher risks to avoid losses than to make gains."[29]

Of course, the example of Napoleon and his catastrophic invasion of Russia weighed heavily on Hitler's mind, as it did on those of many of his military leaders. General Franz Halder, army chief of staff, noted in his diary as early as January 28, 1941, as Barbarossa was being planned that "Purpose is not clear ... Risk in the west must not be underestimated. It is possible that Italy might collapse after the loss of her colonies, and we get a southern front in Spain, Italy, and Greece. If we are then tied up in Russia, a bad situation will be made worse."[30] Hitler himself signaled his uncertainty and hesitancy by not moving his headquarters to East Prussia until thirty-six hours into the conflict, in contrast to his procedure in the earlier Western engagements.[31] According to Hitler, the invasion of Russia constituted "a risk," even a "big risk."[32]

Two additional interrelated factors were to increase the risk and thence the brutality. First, as a consequence of the failure to defeat Britain in 1940, a naval blockade prevented the arrival of grain and oilseeds. Fowl were being slaughtered because they consumed too much feed. The invasion of the Soviet Union would significantly disrupt essential food supplies from the East; as a consequence all available food would be transported to Germany, leaving Soviet citizens in major cities to starve. The Reich's food ministry even drafted plans to allow "x [sic] millions of people to starve."[33]

Second, because of the enormity of the Barbarossa task and its extraordinarily long supply lines, the army to a large extent would have to live off the land. Much of the food necessary for the army would be requisitioned by the German military, again entailing starvation for the local inhabitants. This condition was exacerbated by the necessity for a quick

---

[28] For Hitler's keen awareness of this possibility, see Goebbels 1983, 414. Saul Friedländer 1967, 313, concludes that "If Hitler had actually succeeded in smashing Russia swiftly, an Anglo-American victory using conventional weapons alone would have been hard to achieve. As we know from the history of the Normandy landing in 1944, Operation 'Overlord' would have been impossible if 174 German divisions had not been tied up in the East."

[29] Jervis 1992, 202.   [30] Halder 1988, 314.   [31] Warlimont 1964, 172.

[32] Quoted in Burrin 1994, 134. Reflecting the insecurity of the moment, Hitler said, "On 22 June, a door opened before us, and we didn't know what was behind it ... the heavy uncertainty took me by the throat" (quoted in Cooper 1990, 285).

[33] Gerlach 2000a, 214.

victory prior to a likely American intervention, as we saw, and requiring incursions deep into the Soviet Union to quickly eliminate all resistance, further extending the already vulnerable supply lines.[34]

Precisely because of the extreme risk, extreme brutality was seen to be necessary for a quick victory. Or as Michael Geyer put it: "On the front this war was fought with utter brutality from the very beginning, because victory had to be achieved quickly. Thus destruction became an end in itself in the hope that unleashing violence would eventually destroy the enemy. The military had little choice in this matter. If it wanted to win, it had to act quickly. If it wanted to do so against a defiant enemy, it had to escalate the use of force."[35]

Thus, at the outset, all male Jews, assumed to be Communists and political commissars were to be shot by the *Einsatzgruppen*.[36] Jews in any sort of leadership capacity were especially targeted. Yet even in Lithuania, for example, site of the most brutal and extensive killing, women and children were not yet subject to mass murder. According to Christoph Dieckmann, "When on 30 June 1941, the Lithuanian police chief of Alytus, a town in the south of Lithuania, offered to kill all of the Jews in the whole region with a squad of 1,050 Lithuanian police and partisans in a few days, it was rejected by the German side."[37] However, as the extent of Soviet opposition became apparent in July, the killing began to be extended to all Jews, including women and children. A summary of the German view at that time is given by Jürgen Matthäus: "Beginning in late July, as a result of the failure to win a quick victory over the Red Army, German obsession with security increased. The Reich was, as Hitler put it, forced 'to rule areas extending over 300 to 500 kilometers with a handful of people.' The army leadership compensated for that lack of manpower by an even more massive use of force."[38]

Earlier, in 1940, before US aid to the Allies began and when the Nazi state still appeared to be secure, Hitler spoke of the Jews as "stupid" and not nearly as powerful as he had first thought. Further, "On 25 April 1940, Goebbels noted, Hitler had said that, 'all things considered, the Jews are still very stupid.'"[39] On August 17, 1940, Goebbels, ever

---

[34] Ibid.   [35] Geyer 1986, 592.
[36] Burleigh 2000, 602. For evidence on the positive reception Jews accorded the Soviet occupation of eastern Poland in 1939, especially in contrast to the overtly anti-Semitic policies of the displaced Polish government, see Korzec and Szurek 1993.
[37] Dieckmann 2000, 245.   [38] Matthäus 2004, 278.   [39] Burrin 1994, 80.

slavishly following his *Führer*, noted exterminatory solutions ("liquidate them") suggested for "asocial elements," but not for the Jews, who were to have their own state in Madagascar.[40]

The nonexterminatory approach to the Jewish population at this time helps explain an apparent anomaly. During this period, in January 1940, the Germans allowed a Jewish welfare organization to be established named "Jewish Social Self-Help" (ŻSS, the acronym in Polish) headed by a Michael Weichert. It was the only Jewish institution that was allowed to function in the Generalgouvernement. As Weichert commented, "It simply wasn't logical. On the one hand they persecute Jews to the utmost, and on the other they discuss a central organization for social aid with them."[41]

In part, the answer resides in Nazi policy goals. American welfare organizations such as the Commission for Polish Relief and the American Red Cross were active in Poland at this time. They demanded that distribution of food, medicine, and clothing be handled by representatives of the local population, not the Germans. Because the Nazis desperately wanted to preserve US neutrality and also keep the door open to negotiations with the Western powers, they acceded to these American requests. As chapter 17 will make clear, while the United States remained neutral, genocide of the Jewish population could not proceed. Nor had the Jews at this time given any evidence of the international "power" that had, in the distorted Nazi view, led to the German defeat in World War I. From this perspective, too, the genocide was unwarranted.

Even as late as May 1941, following earlier policies instituted in Łódź, the Warsaw ghetto was encouraged to be economically productive. The so-called productionists among German planners had won out over "annihilationists," who wanted the ghetto residents to die by slow attrition. If necessary, the ghetto would be subsidized initially by the Germans in order to eventually achieve the goal of economic self-sufficiency.[42]

Consistent with this emphasis on instrumentality, in contrast to annihilation, in April 1941, the German authorities granted permission to Adam Czerniakow, chairman of the Warsaw *Judenrat* (Jewish Council), to open three synagogues. Funds were then solicited for the

---

[40] Goebbels 1983, 124–25.   [41] Quoted in Gutman 1982, 41.
[42] Browning 2004, 130–31.

renovation of the Great Synagogue. And on the next major Jewish holiday, Shavuot, on June 1, 1941, Czerniakow prayed there.[43]

But on June 30, 1941, Hitler confided to Mussolini his surprise at discovering the immense quantities of armaments held by the Soviets. By July 15 he indicated to the Japanese ambassador his concern about the "gigantic" supplies available to the Soviets and the fact that the Russians fought "like wild animals."[44] Goebbels in his diaries also reflected these deepening concerns about the future. On July 17, he noted "the enemy's extraordinarily strong resistance on all fronts." Within two days, he was describing the war as a war of survival between Bolshevism and Nazism. On July 26, Germany was described as fighting for its life.[45] On August 11, Halder noted that "the whole situation makes it increasingly plain that we have underestimated the Russian colossus."[46] Halder further indicated that instead of the expected 200 Soviet divisions, there were 360 and that, for every dozen divisions destroyed, another dozen replaced them. "Hitler, pondering the experience of the first six weeks of the war, concluded 'that one cannot beat the Russian with operational successes ... because he simply does not acknowledge defeat.'"[47] Clearly, Soviet resolve was preventing the quick victory that Nazi Germany needed, and male Jews were paying with their lives.

Events were making Nazi state security even more uncertain, and "The killing, though horrifying, was on nothing like the scale that it reached from August onwards."[48] On August 11, Prime Minister Winston Churchill of Great Britain and President Franklin Roosevelt of the United States issued the Atlantic Charter, as a consequence of their meeting at sea off the coast of Newfoundland. Although several provisions pertained only to the two signatories, at least three must have been of deep concern to the Nazi leadership: (1) no territorial changes would be made without the freely expressed wishes of the people concerned; (2) sovereignty rights and self-government would be restored to peoples forcibly deprived of them; (3) all countries that threatened or committed aggression would be disarmed.[49] This agreement was a further solidification of the developing Anglo-American alliance that had already witnessed the Lend–Lease Act of March 1941 and the sale of fifty American destroyers to Britain in return for 99-year leases on bases

---

[43] Kermisz 1979, 10.   [44] Burrin 1994, 136.   [45] Ibid., 137–38.   [46] Halder 1988, 506.
[47] Geyer 1986, 591.   [48] Kershaw 2000a, 467.   [49] Albrecht-Carrié 1958, 565.

in British possessions in the Atlantic. The greatly feared two-front war was becoming a reality for Hitler.

All of this was so upsetting to Hitler that, on August 18, much to Goebbels's surprise, Hitler raised the possibility of peace with Stalin.[50] Although the terms potentially to be offered to Stalin would likely have been unacceptable to him, nevertheless thoughts of peace on the Eastern front must have been generated by the growing fears of defeat at the hands of the combined Soviet and Anglo-American forces. Failing such a peace with Stalin, the war would grind on and "A rough estimate would show about 50,000 Jews killed up until mid-August, in nearly two months of activity. An impressive figure, ten times higher than the one for Jewish victims of the Polish campaign; but a modest figure compared to the total, ten times higher still, that would be achieved by the end of the year, in four more months."[51]

Significantly, August 15 is the date after which women and children were being killed en masse.[52] Risk minimization – the killing of male Jews and new stricter controls on Jews ordered on July 22, in response to Stalin's July 3 call for partisan activity against the German occupiers – had now been transformed into loss compensation. The Jews would now have to pay not only for the "stab in the back" of World War I and the consequent German loss, but also for German blood shed on the Eastern front and the likely imminent opening of other fronts. On August 26, Goebbels noted that "as long as Germany was fighting for her life, he would make sure the Jews neither profited from the war nor were spared by it."[53] And on January 30, 1942, Hitler stated that: "For the first time, other people will not be the only ones to spill their blood; this time, for the first time, the old Jewish law will be in effect: an eye for an eye, and a tooth for a tooth."[54]

An order to his troops from General Walter von Reichenau, commander of the Sixth Army, on October 10, 1941, concisely illustrates the combination of risk minimization and loss compensation effected after August 15:

> The essential goal of the campaign against the Jewish–Bolshevik system
> is the complete destruction of its power instruments and the eradication
> of the Asiatic influence on the European cultural sphere.

---

[50] Kershaw 2000a, 412.   [51] Burrin 1994, 113.   [52] Ibid., 110.   [53] Quoted ibid., 152.
[54] Quoted ibid.

Thereby the troops too have tasks, which go beyond the conventional unilateral soldierly tradition. In the East the soldier is not only a fighter according to the rules of warfare, but also a carrier of an inexorable racial conception *and the avenger of all the bestialities which have been committed against the Germans and related races.*

Therefore the soldier must have *complete* [sic] understanding for [sic] the *necessity of the harsh, but just atonement of Jewish subhumanity. This has the further goal of nipping in the bud rebellions in the rear of the Wehrmacht which, as experience shows, are always plotted by the Jews.*[55]

General Erich von Manstein, one of the most successful field commanders of the German army, on November 20, 1941, declared that:

Since 22 June the German *Volk* is in the midst of a battle for life and death against the Bolshevik system. This battle is conducted against the Soviet army not only in a conventional manner according to the rules of European warfare ... Jewry constitutes the mediator between the enemy in the rear and the still fighting remnants of the Red Army and the Red leadership. It has a stronger hold than in Europe on all key positions of the political leadership and administration, it occupies commerce and trade and further forms cells for all the disturbance and possible rebellions.

The Jewish–Bolshevik system must be eradicated once and for all. Never again may it interfere in our European living space. The German soldier is therefore not only charged with the task of destroying the power instrument of this system. He marches forth also as a carrier of a racial conception and as an avenger of all the atrocities which have been committed against him and the German people.

The soldier must show understanding for the harsh atonement of Judaism, the spiritual carrier of the Bolshevik terror.[56]

A companion statement from Field Marshal Wilhelm Keitel stated that "the fight against bolshevism [sic] demands in the first place also reckless and energetic action against the Jews, the main carrier of bolshevism [sic]."[57]

Arno Mayer was among the first to identify the pattern of war-related massacres.[58] The first such large-scale massacre occurred at Zhitomir, where the Wehrmacht for the first time encountered serious opposition. Many more Jews were killed there than in the surrounding towns. Soon

[55] Emphasis added; quoted in Bartov 1992, 129–30. [56] Quoted in Wistrich 2001, 95.
[57] Quoted in M. Gilbert 1999, vi. [58] Mayer 1988.

the massacres ended and the Jews were enclosed in ghettos. But, when effective opposition was again encountered in Kiev, the city surrendering only on September 19 after more than a full month of fierce resistance, the mass killing resumed. The final precipitants for these massacres were large explosions, apparently set by the retreating Soviets, which leveled portions of the city, killing many Germans. Leaders of *Einsatzkommando* 4a of *Einsatzgruppe* C notified their superiors in Berlin that "in retaliation for the arson in Kiev all Jews were arrested and that on September 29 and 30 a total of 33,771 Jews were executed."[59] Most of those murdered were women, children, and older people, most of the younger and middle-aged men away serving in the Red Army. This is the infamous Babi Yar atrocity that has been immortalized in the poetry of Yevgeni Yevtushenko and the music of Dimitri Shostokovich.

In 1941, as they entered Soviet territory, the *Einsatzgruppen* did not kill many Jews in the eastern Polish cities (under Soviet occupation since 1939) that happened not to offer major resistance. But as these killing squads approached the Ukrainian heartland and its stiffened resistance, the butchery began in earnest.[60] By now, the killings of Communists and Jews were being called "measures of atonement."[61] But in reality, according to Omer Bartov, "the army reverted to the crudest moral code of war, according to which everything which ensured one's survival was permitted (and thus considered moral), and everything even remotely suspect of threatening it must be destroyed (and was by definition immoral)."[62]

The whirlwind destruction of the majority of Hungarian Jewry in several months of mid-1944 with Wehrmacht support is explainable by the perceived necessity for risk minimization by the German forces. The sequence of deportations is important because it reflects the variability in military risk. Soviet forces were rapidly approaching northeastern Hungary as well as Carpatho-Ruthenia.[63] Von Reichenau's thinking indicated in the quote above is applicable here in reflecting on the perceived, though not actual, dangers to German forces posed by large concentrations of Jews in these regions. Thus, these two areas were the first to be rapidly "cleansed" of Jews, with Budapest and other regions to the west, with large Jewish concentrations but not directly in the invasion path, to be left for later disposition.

---

[59] Quoted ibid., 268.   [60] Ibid., 277.   [61] Manoschek 2000, 170.
[62] Bartov 1992, 70.   [63] Murray and Millett 2000, 449.

Even from within Jewish ghettos in Poland, one finds observations along these lines. One of the most astute commentators of the Warsaw ghetto, Emmanuel Ringelblum understood this element of risk minimization. Commenting on the episodic massacres of Jews (some of notables, others not) beginning on April 18, 1942, and lasting until the summer deportations, he states: "During his last visit, Himmler must have issued an order for massacres to be perpetrated to terrorize the Jewish populace. Probably this is in connection with the spring campaigns. They want their rear to be secure. They threw a little fright into the Jews, so the Jews would keep their heads down."[64]

Similarly, Chaim Kaplan notes that "in order to prepare for the coming events [an offensive] the Pawia [Gestapo political prison] is being filled with hundreds of prisoners, all Aryans ... The Aryans are put to death after a short period of arrest; the Jews are killed without even a pretense of arrest."[65]

After the deportations began, Ringelblum sees the mass murders as loss compensation. He tells a folktale followed by his judgments. "Once there was a landed gentleman who was living high. He kept borrowing money on interest from his banker Shlomo, until finally the Jew collected his debts by auctioning off the gentry's property. Foaming at the lips, the impoverished nobleman cursed the Jew who had made him poor. In revenge, he called his dog 'Shlomo' and beat it. The same thing, people say, is happening to the Germans. They are being defeated, their cities are being destroyed, so they take their revenge on the Jews by beating them three times a day."[66]

It matters not that the decision to murder Europe's Jews in December 1941 (with the Wannsee conference, planning the actual extermination process, taking place the following month) would in no way affect the air raids destroying Germany's cities. In the Nazi mind, the losses of World War I, those of the Russian front, and any underlying future losses as a result of the increasingly difficult war were to be laid at the Jews' doorstep.

---

[64] Ringelblum 1974, 262. Another interpretation is that these massacres were intended to destroy elements of the Jewish leadership in anticipation of the forthcoming mass deportations (Gutman 1982, 176–80). Yet the two interpretations are consistent. The Jews were by 1942 increasingly identified as the quintessential enemy, so that terrorizing them initially in the expectation of quelling enemy opposition soon shaded into loss compensation when the deportations began.

[65] Kaplan 1973, 318.   [66] Ringelblum 1974, 290–91.

But how did the order to destroy *all* of European Jewry come about? Thus far, into the autumn of 1941, only Soviet Jews presumably infected by the Bolshevik bacillus were being murdered en masse. Now the certain, not merely probable, opening up of new fronts and extreme dangers to the Nazi state eventuated. On November 29, 1941, Dr. Fritz Todt, minister for armaments and war production of the Nazi government, after returning to Berlin from the Russian front, reported to Hitler: "Given the arms and industrial supremacy of the Anglo-Saxon powers, we can no longer militarily win this war."[67] On November 30, General Franz Halder recorded in his diary, "The eastern army has a shortage of 340,000 men, i.e., 50 percent of the combat strength of its infantry. Company combat strength is 50–60 men ... In Germany we have only 33,000 men available. The bulk of the replacements are not yet broken in to the front-line routine and so have limited combat value. Trucks: Serviceability, at most 60 percent."[68]

On December 7, 1941, Japanese forces attacked the United States naval base at Pearl Harbor. True to the Axis alliance, Hitler declared war on the United States on December 11. On December 12, 1941, Hitler addressed a meeting of the most important sectional and regional leaders of the NSDAP. Goebbels's notes on the meeting are as follows:

> Regarding the Jewish question, the Führer is determined to clear the table. He warned the Jews that if they were to cause another world war, it would lead to their own destruction. Those were not empty words. Now the world war has come. The destruction of the Jews must be its necessary consequence. We cannot be sentimental about it. It is not for us to feel sympathy for the Jews. We should have sympathy rather with our own German people. *If the German people have to sacrifice 160,000 victims in yet another campaign in the east, then those responsible for this bloody conflict will have to pay for it with their lives.*[69]

Goebbels of course was referring to Hitler's Reichstag speech of January 30, 1939, in which he warned: "If the world of international financial Jewry, both in and outside of Europe, should succeed in plunging the nations into another *world war*, the result will not be the Bolshevization of the world and thus a victory for Judaism. The result will be the extermination of the Jewish race in Europe."[70]

---

[67] Quoted in M. Gilbert 1989, 265.   [68] Halder 1988, 571.
[69] Emphasis added; quoted in Gerlach 2000b, 122.
[70] Emphasis in original; quoted ibid.

Now a world war had come about, and the Jews would have to pay for German blood spilled in the war. Soon, speeches such as that of Hans Frank, the leader of the Generalgouvernement of Poland, on December 16, spoke of Hitler's "prophecy" and the efforts to realize its goals of the liquidation of European Jewry now that a world war had actually come to pass. Accordingly, "as far as the Jews are concerned, I would therefore be guided by the basic expectation that they are going to disappear. They have to be gotten rid of."[71] Additional evidence is found in Gerlach's comprehensive treatment that has been cited approvingly by historians such as Ian Kershaw and Michael Burleigh.

Despite the Germans' imperative need for rolling stock immediately after the successful Soviet counteroffensive defending Moscow began on December 5, 1941, transport thereafter was principally allocated to the mass murders.[72]

A grisly indicator of the importance of the December dates is the following change in the construction of large gas vans intended for the *Einsatzgruppen*. Whereas in early October, vans with the capacity of approximately thirty people were ordered, in December the killing capacity was raised twelve-fold, "a clear qualitative leap," according to Götz Aly.[73] Peter Longrich corroborates these facts. Accordingly, "In the fall of 1941 the decision for the immediate murder of all European Jews had not yet been taken. In the fall of 1941 the murder of hundreds of thousands, but not millions of human beings was being prepared."[74] As late as November 30, evidence exists for the absence of a generalized policy for the liquidation of Jews, whether confined in ghettos or not.[75]

Thus the Holocaust was a contingent event, one not predestined by the intensity of Nazi anti-Semitism, virulent as it was, but facilitated by the exigencies of a world war that threatened to destroy the Nazi state, with the Jews perceived by Hitler as leading the vanguard of that destruction. Each step in the decision-making process concerning the Jewish Question was dependent on critical war-related events. After the defeat of France in 1940, Madagascar, a French colony, was chosen as

---

[71] Quoted in Gerlach 2000b, 125. Also see Kershaw 2000b, 125–26.

[72] Braham 1981; 2000, 136.   [73] Aly 1999, 232.

[74] Quoted in Browning 2004, 373. Yet, despite a fundamental agreement with Longrich, for different reasons Browning argues for the last week in October 1941 as the "watershed" date for decisions initiating the Final Solution.

[75] Matthäus 2004, 305. Evidence exists in the form of Himmler's direct order on November 30 not to kill Berlin Jews transported to Riga.

the future "homeland" of the Jews.[76] When the undefeated British navy made such mass shipping impossible, an area at the fringe of the German empire near Lublin was chosen, to be later changed to an unnamed destination in the soon-to-be-conquered Soviet Union. This harsher decision was made in March 1941[77] at the same time as the Lend–Lease Agreement between the United States and Great Britain. Difficulties in the invasion of the USSR led to the killing of Jewish women and children after August 15. As these difficulties became increasingly apparent to the Germans, harsher measures including deportations of Jews from Western to Eastern Europe were carried out,[78] to be followed by the ultimate decision to commit genocide after the attack on Pearl Harbor and the first Russian land victory defending Moscow.

Even after the onset of the genocide, the rate of killing depended on state insecurity in the form of the potential for defeat of Nazi Germany and supporters such as Vichy France. As Isaac Levendel, a child survivor in Vichy France and winner of the Prix Franco-Européen for his memoir, observed: in early 1944 "as the situation became tougher for the Germans at the front, there were rumors of Jewish arrests closer to home. Soon they were happening all around us."[79]

An interesting sidelight on Hitler's changing policies is seen through the lens of his treatment of *Mischlinge* (part Jews) in the armed forces. Although at first willing to declare certain part Jews *deutschblütig*, or of equal status with those of German blood when they were deemed to be necessary, this policy began changing as the war worsened. Exemptions allowing *Mischlinge* to remain in the armed forces were given less frequently and even accomplished officers of part-Jewish ancestry were dismissed. As Bryan Rigg indicates: "The more Hitler realized that he could not change the war's outcome, the more irrational he became,

---

[76] Aly 1999, 109.
[77] Ibid., 255. Although Aly argues that population policies made this decision virtually inevitable, his position ignores the likely elation after victory had the Germans won the war in the East. Such euphoria undoubtedly would have led to less harsh measures since, in the Nazi view, the Jews would have been "defeated" as they were after the fall of France in 1940, and therefore far less dangerous.
[78] Browning 2004, 375–388. An additional motivation was the seizure of Jewish property to house incoming *Volksdeutsch* transported from the East.
[79] Levendel 1999, 89. Other students of the period such as Paul Webster 1991, 71, agree, stating that: "The closer Germany came to defeat, the more Vichy was prepared to support the Nazi cause, claiming that France was in the front line of the fight against Communism."

which had a catastrophic effect on the conduct of government."[80] Two dozen generals were released precisely when their expertise at the front was most desperately needed.

The dynamic approach adopted here helps explain an apparent anomaly. While there is clear evidence of virulent German anti-Semitism during the war even among "ordinary" Germans who behaved abominably toward Jews in the death marches from the concentration camps into Germany proper in 1944–45,[81] the evidence of earlier German anti-Semitism is variable. German anti-Semitic political parties had declined precipitously in their share of the Reichstag vote prior to World War I, achieving only 0.86 percent in 1912 compared with 3.70 percent in 1898.[82] Even after World War I and the rapid rise of anti-Semitism, reasons for joining the Nazi Party given by early members generally did not include anti-Semitism among the primary factors.[83] The economic boycott of Jewish businesses called by the Nazi leadership for April 1, 1933, shortly after its accession to power, was generally regarded as a public relations failure, even by the Nazis themselves.[84] Only after the events of World War II and the growing threat to the Nazi – by now identified as German – state did the German population behave in a deeply anti-Semitic manner. Thus one resolution of the apparent inconsistencies between Goldhagen's account and the many critics of his emphasis on "eliminationist anti-Semitism" can be found in the dynamics of the confrontation between Nazi Germany and its systemic environment.

The Armenians

The domain of losses and state insecurity

Turning to the case of the Ottoman Empire, we see that, despite the conclusion that "The decline of the Ottoman Empire was neither rapid nor continuous,"[85] by the end of the nineteenth century that decline was evident. As early as 1774 and the Peace of Kuchuk Kainardji, the Ottomans had lost not only territories in the Caucasus to the Russians in which the

---

[80] Rigg 2002, 233.   [81] Goldhagen 1996.   [82] Melson 1992, 119.

[83] According to Theodore Abel [1938] 1986, 161, in his survey of early Nazi Party members, "Sixty percent of the contributors make no reference whatsoever to indicate that they harbored anti-Semitic feelings." In his reanalysis of the "Abel" set of respondents, Peter Merkl 1975, 522, found that only 14.6 percent identified Jews as their chief objects of hostility.

[84] Gellately 2001, 27.   [85] Palmer 1992, 32.

Turks had long been dominant, but even control of Christian (principally Orthodox) communal life within the empire. The nineteenth century witnessed a virtually unmitigated series of disasters. Lost wars with Russia in 1829 and again in 1878 led to further shrinkage of the empire; this pattern of losses would continue into the early twentieth century.

Between 1750 and 1914, the area of the empire had been almost halved, from 3,470 to 1,790 square miles.[86] All of North Africa and virtually all of the Balkans were lost. Soon after, during World War I, Syria, Iraq and Palestine would also be lost.[87] The disastrous performance of the Ottoman army during the First Balkan War had nothing less than a traumatic effect on the Ottoman state leaders.[88] This is a virtually uninterrupted decline of the state, which if unimpeded would lead to state dissolution. In response, a coup was carried out by militant young officers on January 23, 1913, and was followed by efforts at state building initiated by the Committee of Union and Progress (CUP), loosely but somewhat erroneously identified as the Young Turk Movement. Their efforts at reform not only forced the abdication of Sultan Abdulhamit in 1909, but also set the stage for the Armenian genocide of 1915–16.

The Ottoman state at the start of the twentieth century was extra-ordinarily weak and insecure in several respects. Financially it was seriously indebted to the European powers; its non-Muslim religious institutions (with the exception of Jewish ones) were under the control of foreign powers. The empire had granted special legal rights as well as tariff concessions to foreign merchants residing within it, and the military was no match for modern European armies. Worst of all, perhaps, was its image of the "sick man of Europe" gained as the result of these debilities and its steady loss of dominion to the Russian Empire and independent successor states. World War I and its military con-frontations with the old foe Russia as well as Russia's allies would magnify this insecurity greatly. The confrontation itself emerged from Ottoman weakness, for it was dependence on the German ally that brought Turkey into the war to begin with. Germany's influence within the Ottoman Empire was considerable, not the least aspect being the army's virtually complete dependence on its German advisors and armaments suppliers. This close political and military relationship that would bring war and further dismemberment to the empire also would have unforeseen implications for the Armenian genocide of 1915–16.

---

[86] McCarthy 1997, 199.   [87] S. Shaw and Shaw 1977.   [88] Sicker 2001, 203–04.

Prior to that genocide, the Ottoman authorities were deeply concerned that the traditional dominance of Islam be retained.[89] Not only were the Christian communities under the protection of various European authorities, but the traditional political dominance of Muslims in the Balkans and areas of the Caucasus was undergoing challenge. Bosnia-Herzegovina, Bulgaria, and Armenia were cases in point but, in contrast to other cases where the Christian populations were localized and their challenges therefore could be seen to be contained, the Armenians were spread throughout the empire. Thus, if a challenge to the dominance of the Muslim Ottomans and their Kurdish agents occurred in eastern Anatolia, it could be quickly interpreted to be a more widespread challenge to the imperial authority, say in Constantinople, where Armenians were found in significant numbers. Armenian communities were found in all six of the Turkish provinces.[90]

At the end of the nineteenth century, there was a determined effort by the Ottoman authorities to revitalize Islam as the dominant religion. "The most widespread ideological force in the Ottoman Empire during Abdulhamit's years was Islamism, calling for a return to the fundamental values and traditions of the civilization of which the empire was the most modern manifestation."[91] After the Young Turk revolution of 1908, Islamization was now tied to state modernization and revitalization. The intimate connection between Islam and the Ottoman state was reborn in the new context of Turkish nationalism and state making. The truncated empire, shorn of most of its Christian subjects, could be seen as an Islamic redoubt consisting almost entirely of Muslim Turks and Arabs. Military opposition from Orthodox Christian Russia during World War I must have seemed doubly threatening in this context, for the Orthodox Armenians could have been the handmaidens of Russia in eliminating or even reversing the traditional political dominance of the Muslim Ottoman authorities.

Refugees in sufficiently large numbers are a potent indicator of the contraction of physical space. According to Kemal Karpat, "The quantitative indicators cited in various sources show that during this period [1856–1916] a total of about 7 million migrants from Crimea, the Caucasus, the Balkans, and the Mediterranean islands settled in Anatolia. These immigrants were overwhelmingly Muslim. By the end of the century the immigrants and their descendants constituted some

[89] Karpat 2001.   [90] S. Shaw and Shaw 1977, 201.   [91] Ibid., 259.

30 to 40 percent of the total population of Anatolia."[92] After the Balkan Wars, many Muslim refugees were settled in Armenian areas of eastern Anatolia. According to Fridjot Nansen, "The settlement of Muslim refugees in the Christian sections of Armenia was carefully prepared and promoted. After the Balkan defeat thousands of Turkish refugees from Thrace and Macedonia arrived in Anatolia full of anti-Christian hatred which was inflamed by the government."[93]

This anti-Christian hatred had its roots in the 1877–78 forced ejection of Muslims from their homes in the Balkans. Although this anti-Muslim violence stemmed from an earlier massacre of Bulgarians by the Ottomans (estimates vary from 4,000[94] to 15,000[95] killed), nevertheless, according to British ambassador Henry Layard:

> When the Russians crossed the Balkans last summer and, disarming the Mussulmans whom they had induced to submit by promises of justice and protection, had handed over their weapons to the Bulgarians, a scene of indiscriminate slaughter and devastation ensued, such as had not been known since the most barbarous times ... The Russian authorities have sanctioned and encouraged the destruction of Turkish property in all the towns and villages they have occupied, to the very gates of the capital. They have defiled the mosques, and turned them to vile uses; they have desecrated the Mussulman graves, broken up the tombstones, and turned the cemeteries into public gardens and places of amusement, compelling the unfortunate Mussulmans themselves to do the work.[96]

Refugees affect the economic and hierarchical relations among indigenous residents. Competition for living space, agricultural land, and jobs intensifies. Instead of resenting the Muslim refugees, the long-standing Muslim residents tended to sympathize with them, and to resent still more the living space and economic holdings of the Armenians, already perceived as an entrepreneurial, mercantile-oriented ethnie, despite the status of most Armenians as poor or mid-level peasants. Nevertheless, based on data drawn from various 1912 yearbooks,[97] Fatma Göçek concludes: "While Ottoman Muslim [Turkish] participation became limited to 15 percent in internal trade, 12 percent in industry and crafts, and 14 percent in the professions, the share of Ottoman minorities [Greeks and Armenians] expanded to comprise 66 percent of those

---

[92] Karpat 2001, 343.   [93] Quoted in Dadrian 1999, 145.
[94] S. Shaw and Shaw 1977, 162.   [95] M. Anderson 1966, 184.
[96] Quoted in Karpat 1985, 72–73.   [97] Issawi 1980, 14.

engaged in internal trade, 79 percent in industry and crafts, and 66 percent in the professions."[98]

In the 1877–78 war alone, approximately 250,000–300,000 Muslims were killed, mostly ethnic Turks, and roughly 1.5 million others had to seek refuge in the Ottoman Empire.[99] Constantinople alone received 200,000 Muslim refugees in 1878.[100] When the tsarist government stationed Cossack soldiers in Circassia in the north Caucasus beginning in 1863, Circassians began to migrate in large numbers to Ottoman domains.[101] Later, as a part of their Islamization campaign, the Ottomans actively encouraged Muslim migration. In 1905–06, the flow of Circassians increased substantially. Villages were built for their settlement, and the location was chosen "in order to assure there the numerical preponderance of the Muslims against any future territorial claims by non-Muslims."[102] The fact that the wealthier refugees went to large cities like Constantinople,[103] but poorer ones to rural areas such as eastern Anatolia (where the Armenians were concentrated), introduced an element of envy of the Armenians in the rural regions that also contributed to the later massacres and genocide.

The widely held public view of the Armenians as favored economically, of course, fed into the ideational justification for mass murder and, later, genocide. Refugees also have an impact on the prevailing hierarchical relations. To see the misery and forlorn status of Muslim refugees from newly independent Christian lands must have further reinforced the prevailing view that the "elevated" economic status of Christian Armenians was unjust. In a largely Muslim land, it was thought that the Muslim must be more favored; the Muslim refugee should be at least equal to the Christian Armenian, if not substantially superior. In the end, many of the holdings of slaughtered Armenians would be given to these refugees.

State insecurity was substantially increased by a renewed Russian interest in the Armenians of eastern Anatolia, largely as a result of the Muslim influx. After considerable Russian pressure in early 1914, a Russo-Turkish Convention was signed giving the Russians authority to supervise reforms in the governance of Armenian communities in that geopolitically sensitive region. Specifically, foreign inspector-generals were to be appointed, and community representatives of the

---

[98] Göçek 1996, 114.   [99] Karpat 1985, 75.   [100] Karpat 2002, 702.
[101] Ibid., 791.   [102] Ibid., 670.   [103] Ibid., 704.

Armenians and Muslims were to be elected, all under Russian influence.[104]
Once again, foreign intervention in the domestic affairs of the Ottoman
Empire had occurred, but this time at the hands of its chief enemy.

Risk acceptance, minimization, and loss compensation

With such a history of loss, the tendency toward risk taking is increased.
The entry into World War I on the side of the Central Powers was just
such a risk. The magnitude of the risk can be gauged by the extent of real
and potential opposition to the decision by the Ottoman leaders, Enver
Paşa, Djemal Paşa, and Talât Bey. Turkey offered the alliance to
Germany on July 22, 1914, but the offer was kept secret from the cabinet
as a whole.[105] The three Turkish leaders were convinced that neutrality
was not an option because of the prevailing sentiments for the partition
of Turkey among the European powers, Russia foremost among them.
All had staked out claims to spheres of influence within the Ottoman
Empire: France to Syria, Britain to Mesopotamia and the Gulf, Russia to
the Caucasus, and Germany to central Anatolia. In the event of partition
resulting from war or some other triggering mechanism, these spheres of
influence could be transformed into colonies.[106] Indeed, in the British
and French instances, this is precisely what happened at the end of the
war. Seeking protection, offers of alliance were first extended to the
Entente Powers – respectively Britain, Russia, and then France – but, for
a variety of idiosyncratic reasons, each of these offers was rejected.

Just as alliance with Germany was seen to be risky by a majority of the
government cabinet and the Committee of Union and Progress, even
more so was the decision to actually join the war effort. By the autumn of
1914, much had happened to thrust Turkey into the war itself, beyond
its earlier declaration of neutrality in August. The *Goeben* and *Breslau*,
two German cruisers, had escaped British pursuit and were now, with
German agreement, incorporated into the Turkish navy, virtually at its
head.[107] Relations with the Entente Powers had deteriorated even to the
point of the Turkish navy bombarding Russian bases on the Black Sea
that the Russians did not respond to in the hope of preserving Turkish
neutrality. Yet the cabinet was still divided as to the wisdom of formally
entering the war, especially in light of the perceived weakness of the

---

[104] Bodger 1984, 96.   [105] Strachan 2001a, 669.   [106] Ibid., 655.
[107] Sicker 2001, 208.

Turkish army. In order to contrive entry into the war, Enver Paşa had the government meet not with the cabinet, but with the more bellicose central committee of the Committee of Union and Progress. On October 30, war was declared, but only after a defensive agreement with Bulgaria had been signed that assured the security of the landward approach to the Dardanelles straits on the European side.[108]

Thus, the war was seen to be risky in the extreme, "The fact that Britain and France, as well as Russia, were at war with Turkey transformed the Ottoman Empire's strategic position. Its extended coastline, with its accessibility to naval power, its joint frontier with British-controlled Egypt, and the Government of India's interest in Mesopotamia meant that the entire perimeter lay under potential threat."[109]

Two events were to accentuate that risk immeasurably, and they were to occur in the period just prior to the onset of the deportations. First, upon the Ottoman declaration of war, the Russian army pushed across the border and, after fierce battles, including some Russian losses but a major Turkish defeat at Sarşkamiş in December 1914 and a Russian successful counteroffensive in January 1915, the Ottoman army scattered with over three-quarters of the men lost as they retreated. The way was now open for a Russian push into eastern Anatolia.[110]

It was precisely at this time (December 1914 or January 1915) that a document was prepared by the Committee of Union and Progress called "The Ten Commandments," presented below in a verbatim translation as given in the source:

1. Profiting by the Arts: 3 and 4 of Comite Union and Progress [In accordance with Articles 3 and 4 of the Committee of Union and Progress], close all Armenian Societies, and arrest all who worked against Government at any time among them and send them into the provinces such as Bagdad or Mosul, and wipe them out either on the road or there.
2. Collect arms.
3. Excite [Inflame] Moslem opinion by suitable and special means, in places as Van, Erzeroum, Adana, where as a point of fact the Armenians have already won the hatred of the Moslems, provoke organized massacres as the Russians did at Baku.

---

[108] Strachan 2001a, 677.   [109] Ibid., 689.   [110] S. Shaw and Shaw 1977, 315.

4. Leave all executive [executions] to the people in the provinces such as Erzeroum, Van, Mamuret ul Aziz, and Bitlis, and use Military disciplinary forces (i.e. Gendarmerie) ostensibly to stop massacres, while on the contrary in places as Adana, Sivas, Broussa, Ismidt and Smyrna actively help the Moslems with military force.
5. Apply measures to exterminate all males under 50, priests and teachers, leave girls and children to be Islamized.
6. Carry away the families of all who succeed in escaping and apply measures to cut them off from all connection with their native place.
7. On the ground[s] that Armenian officials may be spies, expel and drive them out absolutely from every Government department or post.
8. Kill off in an appropriate manner all Armenians in the Army – this to be left to the military to do.
9. All action to begin everywhere simultaneously, and thus leave no time for preparation of defensive measures.
10. Pay attention to the strictly confidential nature of these instructions, which may not go beyond two or three persons.[111]

The second extreme risk was posed by the Dardanelles campaign begun in February 1915. Because of difficulties in passing through the straits easily, the British-led Australian and New Zealand contingents began to land on April 25.[112] Extensive preparations for these landings were known to the Ottomans prior to that date, if only because of Liman von Sanders's (commander of the Turkish forces) correspondingly extensive military preparations on the Turkish side begun on March 25.[113] On April 24, the Interior Ministry authorized the arrest of the Armenian political and community leaders suspected of anti-government tendencies. In Constantinople alone, nearly 2,000 such leaders were arrested; eventually most were executed.[114] The following month, in late May, widespread deportations of Armenians were ordered. The genocide had begun.

Note the proximity of time and place of risk and genocidal response, much as in the case of the Holocaust. Constantinople, with its large (nearly 10 percent of the total)[115] Armenian population, lay close by the Dardanelles now under attack. The largest concentration of Armenians in the empire was found in eastern Anatolia, near the expected Russian

[111] Balakian 2003, 189–90.   [112] Hickey 1995, 109.   [113] Erickson 2001, 81.
[114] Dadrian 1997, 221.   [115] Karpat 1985, 188–89.

advances after the Ottoman defeat of January. Further, many of those defeats were attributed by the Turks to the Armenian volunteer movement fighting with the Russians, comprising Armenians from Russia, Persia, Europe, and the United States. Armenians from Turkey also were involved. Antranik, an Armenian hero of the Balkan Wars, was a leader of this movement; he was instrumental in inflicting a major defeat on much larger Turkish forces (a ratio of nearly 10 to 1) on April 18, 1915.[116] A successful uprising, later to be reversed, in the heavily Armenian city of Van in eastern Anatolia also began on April 15.[117] Note the beginning of the deportations from Constantinople on April 24.

As Kamuran Gürün put it, "In short, Armenians residing in the provinces bordering the area of military operations and in proximity to the Mediterranean Sea would be relocated."[118] The risk of state dissolution at the hands of powerful British and Russian forces was palpable. The genocide was perceived as a form of risk minimization and ultimately of loss compensation, should Britain and Russia win the war.

Contrary to many claims, however,[119] the vast majority of Armenians posed no threat to the Ottoman state. But the perception of them as Christians potentially allied to the Russians, especially in eastern Anatolia, must have added fuel to the genocidal fury, ultimately ending in full-fledged genocide.

An important issue here, as in the Holocaust and the Rwandan genocide, is the disjunction between intention and action. For example, there is evidence that the Turks sought to eliminate the Armenians as early as the end of the nineteenth century. After the Young Turk Revolution of 1908, this intention was made plain. In a speech prior to the Third Ittihad Convention in Salonika in 1910 by Talât, later one of the instigators of the genocide, he indicated the necessity for homogenization of the Ottoman Empire:

> You are aware that by the terms of the Constitution equality of Mussulman and Ghiaur [infidel, a derogatory label applied to non-Muslims] was affirmed by you and all know and feel that this is an unrealizable ideal. The Sheriat [*sharia*, the religious laws of Islam], our whole past history and the sentiment of hundreds of thousands of Mussulmans and even the sentiments of the Ghiaurs themselves ... present an impenetrable barrier to the establishment of real

[116] Dadrian 1999, 115. [117] Ibid., 116. [118] Gürün 1985, 207.
[119] S. Shaw and Shaw 1977; McCarthy 1997.

equality ... there can therefore be no question of equality until we have
succeeded in our task of Ottomanizing the Empire.[120]

Here we have a virtual "smoking gun" of genocidal intent (although
unclear as to the choice of ethnic cleansing or genocide) as in the
instance of Hitler's speeches and those of other Nazis even prior to
the start of World War II. Yet, after quoting the speech, Dadrian, the
historical doyen of the Armenian genocide, only some twenty pages
later, writes a chapter title referring to "The dysfunctional dynamics of
Armenian military successes and their lethal consequences for Ottoman
Armenians"[121] as the basis for the genocide. Intention has been galvanized into action by a series of events that make it seem imperative that
genocide be the Ottomans' instrument of choice. This was true of Nazi
decision making during World War II and, as we shall see, also of the
Rwandan genocide of 1994.

The Tutsi

The domain of losses and state insecurity

Here the domain of losses originated in a somewhat different manner
from the preceding cases, but in the end had similar consequences.
Instead of territorial losses at the outset, the initial losses were primarily
found in the status relations between Hutu and Tutsi. In place of the
combination of "Hutu supernatural powers with Tutsi military
powers"[122] in the early Rwandese state, and agriculturalists as well as
pastoralists of both origins living side by side, a gradual polarization set
in. Beginning in the middle of the eighteenth century, political power
was increasingly defined as a Tutsi prerogative, with the Hutu correspondingly degraded in status.

This process would be rapidly accelerated under Belgian colonial rule.
While there existed impoverished Tutsi or "petits Tutsi,"[123] and some
Hutu who could accumulate cattle and thereby rise in socioeconomic
status in the precolonial period, thus minimizing social differences, the
arrival of the Europeans rigidified the Hutu–Tutsi distinction. In particular, the Tutsi pastoralists were treated as "Hamites" having arrived

---

[120] Quoted in Dadrian 1999, 96.   [121] Ibid., 117.
[122] Mamdani 2001, 62. Mamdani recounts a historical narrative indicating the importance of a Hutu diviner in the formation of the Rwandan state.
[123] Ibid., 57.

from the Hamitic northeast carrying with them civilizational attributes that justified their rule over the indigenous Hutu. Seen as more "European" in appearance and presumed origins, the Tutsi were racialized into an elite class to be the handmaidens of Belgian colonial rule. With the revolution of 1959 entailing the emergence of the Hutu majority as the dominant political force, status relations between Hutu and Tutsi were reversed, at least in the political arena.[124] Yet the invasion of Rwanda by the Tutsi-led Rwandese Patriotic Front (RPF; initially based in Uganda) in October 1990 threatened to reverse these Hutu gains. Early RPF military successes led to the convening of the Arusha peace talks beginning in July 1992.

Four factors then led to an extraordinary evocation of the domain of losses. First, very early in the talks, it became clear that the presidential system that had favored Hutu power would be replaced by a parliamentary system combined with a council of ministers. Later in the talks, the strongest advocate of Hutu power, the Coalition pour la Défense de la République (CDR) was to be excluded from any transitional political institutions. At about the same time, it was decided that the number of seats in the new assembly and government ministries would favor the opposition to the Hutu-led government party, the Mouvement Révolutionnaire National pour la Démocratie et le Développement (MRNDD, formerly MRND).

Second, after the massacre of several hundred Tutsi, the RPF renewed its offensive in February 1993, and within two weeks had doubled the amount of territory under its control.[125] Only French intervention prevented the RPF from taking Kigali, the Rwandan capital. A consequence of this success was the agreement to allow 50 percent of the armed command of the RPF to be composed of Tutsi, despite the 10 percent representation of Tutsi in the population at large. Refugees abroad, including of course many Tutsi in Uganda and elsewhere in Africa, were to be allowed back in the country as envisioned by the earlier Dar-es-Salaam declaration on the Rwandan refugee problem.

Third, the assassination on October 30, 1993, of Melchior Ndadaye, the first Hutu president of Burundi by the Tutsi-dominated army began a series of killings of thousands of Hutu in that country. According to Bruce Jones, "The assassination and killings were rich material for the extremists in Rwanda, who used the events to lend credence to their

[124] Prunier 1995.   [125] Jones 1999, 141.

claims that the Tutsi of the RPF were returning to Rwanda to reestablish their historic dominance over the Hutu."[126]

Finally, as in our other two cases, the presence of refugees grievously accentuated the dimensions of loss. The refugees were of two types, both Hutu, but from different locations. First were Hutu from Burundi who fled the Tutsi-led massacres of 1972 and again in 1993.[127] In 1988, poor harvests led to near starvation in Burundi, leading to an additional refugee influx.[128] The latest of these, however, was to be the most consequential. After the assassination of President Ndadaye of Burundi in 1993, waves of violence spread that led to some 400,000 refugees from Burundi, mostly Hutu, crowding into Rwanda. Many of the *génocidaires* would be drawn from this group.[129] According to Gérard Prunier, "The psychological impact of the Hutu President's murder and of the arrival in Rwanda of hundreds of thousands of Hutu refugees spreading tales of terror and massacre at the hands of the Tutsi army of Burundi had enormous negative consequences on the already overcast Rwandese political weather."[130]

The assassination and refugee arrivals solidified the position of the extremist "Hutu-power" advocates. Supporters of a hardline approach suggesting virtually a "final solution" of the Tutsi now secured additional public support. Many of these Burundi Hutu participated in the genocide, even to the point of committing extraordinary torture and atrocity.[131]

After the RPF invasion of 1990, the number of refugees climbed from 80,000 in that year to 350,000 in 1992, and 950,000 after the February 1993 offensive.[132] Territories in Rwanda lost many Hutu as they fled before the advancing RPF forces, under the assumption that Hutu peasants themselves would be massacred. After earlier Hutu massacres of Tutsi, the RPF forces did take revenge on some Hutu communities.

An important complicating factor was a land shortage that predated the RPF offensive and consequent refugee inundation. At around mid-century, "the typical [Rwandan] peasant family lived on a hill which supported between 110 and 120 inhabitants per km^2; in 1970, that same family [had] to make a living on a hill which support[ed] between 280 and 290 people per km^2."[133] Thus, an average family saw its holdings more than halved in approximately twenty years. In the nineteenth

---

[126] Ibid., 144.   [127] Mamdani 2001, 204.   [128] Pottier 2002, 21.
[129] Newbury 1995, 16.   [130] Prunier 1995, 200.   [131] Mamdani 2001, 205.
[132] Ibid., 204.   [133] Pottier 2002, 20.

century, security for one's family had been achieved through "spreading the community" to distant places.[134] That kind of security was no longer available; palpable economic insecurity was compounded by the refugee influx. Some areas of the country experienced a population density in excess of 1,000 people per square mile.[135] Catharine and David Newbury single out the land shortage, and Hutu fears of returning Tutsi refugee demands for land to be returned to them, as a critical basis of the genocide.[136] The right of return of all Rwandan refugees (albeit limited; see below) of course significantly magnified the salience of this issue.

Timothy Longman shows that, within a single prefecture, in one village where socioeconomic disparities between local elites and the peasantry were emphasized by elite behavior, the killings were often committed by locals who were well acquainted with their victims.[137] In a neighboring village where such disparities were minimized, the *bourgmestre* (head of the commune) had to import outsiders to do the killing. Regionalism and perceived defection were additional complicating factors. In the south, many Hutu and Tutsi worked together, lived harmoniously with each other, and even intermarried. To the chagrin of Juvénal Habyarimana's northern elite, Hutu in the south were inclined toward power sharing with the RPF. As a consequence, many of these moderate Hutu were considered to be "traitors to the race" and along with the Tutsi "were subjected to the murderous wrath of the army and the militias of the old regime."[138]

The Arusha Accords of July 1993 threatened the "sociological majority" principle of the 1959 revolution,[139] namely that political power was to be held by the Hutu as the majority ethnicity in Rwanda. These agreements stipulated that the ruling MRNDD would be guaranteed only one-third of the parliamentary seats, thereby rendering it a minority party. Further, the RPF would receive a 40 percent share of the troops in a combined armed forces, in addition to the 50–50 split of the officers with the existing Hutu-led army.[140] The loss of political and military power would be accompanied by the right of return of all refugees to Rwanda. As these were mostly Tutsi, the political power base of the Tutsi in a multiparty system would be considerably enhanced at the polls. Despite the fact that only refugees who left the country ten years earlier

---

[134] Ibid., 29.   [135] Newbury 1995, 14.   [136] Newbury and Newbury 1999, 309.
[137] Longman 1995.   [138] Pottier 2002, 37.   [139] Prunier 1995, 161.
[140] Jones 2001, 93.

or less had the right to recoup lost properties,[141] the threat of numbers in an increasingly democratic system was substantial. By destroying the Tutsi demographic base, the MRNDD and its extremist allies might retain political power. The Arusha Accords and even a likely RPF victory in a renewed war might be nullified by the act of genocide.

Risk acceptance, minimization, and loss compensation

In the Rwandan case, risk took the form of essentially abrogating the Arusha Accords.[142] Although the CDR, the most extreme of the Hutu power advocates, did not participate in the talks, nevertheless its leadership was consulted on important matters before the agreement was signed in August 1993.[143] Once the CDR and other Hutu extremists became finally unalterably opposed to the accords, the risk consisted of defying them in the face of United Nations, Tanzanian, Ugandan, and of course RPF opposition, all of which had supported the Arusha peace process.

To minimize the consequences of this risky defiance, the genocide was executed. Should the RPF win the war, as there was no party committed to stopping it outside Rwanda, then at least the victory would be short-term. The risk of permanent domination by the Tutsi as had persisted for at least two centuries would be minimized by their demographic truncation. As democracy was making inroads even into central Africa (witness the then recent election of Ndadaye, the first Hutu president of Burundi), the massive decimation of the Tutsi would ensure a political future replete with Hutu-dominated governments. Additionally, augmented losses as the result of risky behavior – an increased number of refugees, military defeat at the hands of the RPF and short-term Tutsi domination – would be compensated for by the mass murder of enormous numbers of Tutsi. Risk minimization and loss compensation nicely complemented each other or, as Mahmood Mamdani recounts: "One recalls the more sober advice offered by a wise old Tutsi man to a young RPF fighter who had come to 'liberate' him in Ruhengeri in January 1991: 'You want power? You will get it. But here we will all die. Is it worth it to you?'"[144] Even more directly, the Hutu army chief of staff stated that "the RPF will rule over a desert," and a Hutu extremist

---

[141] Pottier 2002, 187.
[142] For more complete accounts of this process, see Jones 2001 and des Forges 1999.
[143] Jones 1999, 148.   [144] Mamdani 2001, 212.

party leader was quoted as saying: "Even if the RPF has won a military victory, it will not have the power. It has only bullets; we have the population."[145]

As Roméo Dallaire, military head of the United Nations Assistance Mission for Rwanda (UNAMIR), and a witness throughout the genocide, concludes: "As we crept further into May, more extremists in the government, including ministers, were encouraging the arming of the Hutu population and demanding more action at the roadblocks to weed out Tutsis and rebel infiltrators ... Reports were coming in of new massacres in towns around the country."[146] This intensification of the Rwandan genocide, even as the RPF was making rapid military advances, parallels Isaac Levendel's observation on the intensifying roundups of Jews in Vichy France in 1944 as the Germans were clearly going down to defeat, as we saw earlier in this chapter.

Here again, the genocidal intent was signaled well in advance of the events, as early as 1992, but again military matters were to have an inordinate effect on the outcome. Elsewhere, I suggested that the appearance (but not actuality) of unopposed genocide in Bosnia in 1992 may have influenced the intention of Habyarimana to plan the genocide.[147] Yet, after his death, the genocide was perpetrated, as we have seen, conditioned by the simultaneity of military failure and unacceptable international agreements. Only a salient series of intervening events can successfully transform intention into action, especially when such action requires that traditional moral restraints be shattered.

Conclusion

By combining elements of realpolitik and prospect theory, we more completely understand the transition from hatred and sporadic killing to the systematized mass murder associated with genocide. This transition depends heavily on the international setting and especially on its increasing threat to the potential perpetrator. Although ideological justification for the genocide clearly is necessary, it is not sufficient for the onset of genocide, since events in the immediate international environment are critical harbingers of the mass killing. A history of losses sets the entire process in motion in which the practice of realpolitik – politics without reference to any standard above politics – is invoked to protect the threatened state and minimize the risk, made far more

---

[145] I. Martin 1998, 159.   [146] Dallaire 2003, 363.   [147] M. Midlarsky 2000b, 39–42.

acceptable by the experience of loss. In this process, millions of people were doomed to extinction.

We cannot avoid concluding that, if Germany had been victorious in World War I, or indeed had defeated the Soviet Union on the Eastern front in 1941, the Holocaust in its final dimensions would not have occurred. Similarly, had the Ottoman Empire and Hutu-led Rwandan army been more successful in their military confrontations respectively with tsarist Russia and the RPF, the Armenian and Tutsi genocides also likely would not have occurred. This analysis has detailed the processes through which these losses were transformed into the commission of genocide. Because realpolitik and the principles underlying prospect theory are continuing elements of the human condition, we have no guarantees that genocide will not again occur in the future.

The following chapter examines the role of altruistic punishment in the implementation of genocide.

8

The need for unity and altruistic punishment

Let us now explore an additional consequence of loss. The taking on of risk as a result of loss implies potential sacrifice among significant elements of the population. Such processes typically occur at the societal level.

Turning to the societal context, as already noted in chapter 5, if there is a single question that penetrates to the heart of analyses undertaken here, it is this: "For historians of the Holocaust, the greatest challenge has not been making sense of Hitler, but rather understanding why so many followed him down his murderous path"[1] and sacrificed their own lives in the process. Hitler himself, as other genocidal leaders, could have been seen as a political crank and marginalized, even ignored altogether. Explaining why he enjoyed such a large following is one of the principal tasks of this book.

Without that following, two things could have happened. First, the German war effort might have faltered much earlier, as soon as the German army encountered serious resistance in the East, saving many hundreds of thousands if not millions of Jewish lives. Such a precipitous collapse, indeed, occurred during World War I even with the German army intact and occupying large swaths of European territory. Significant military and civilian sectors simply refused to continue the fighting.[2] Second, the SS and units of the Wehrmacht on the Eastern front might have been less willing to participate in the mass murder, especially as the war increasingly appeared to be a lost cause. The basis for an answer to this question of the extraordinary following enjoyed by Hitler will be provided by the perception of deep disunity in organic society.

In each of our three cases of genocide, a climate of disunity had prevailed for most of the period prior to the genocide itself. All had experienced serious divisions that in the view of many threatened the

---

[1] Marrus 1987, 46.   [2] De Gaulle 2002.

viability of the state. Later in this chapter, the theory of altruistic punishment will be applied as a means of understanding how that unity was to be effected through individual sacrifice. However, the role of altruistic punishment as a basis for cooperation in divided societies cannot be fully understood without first examining the historical desire for unity in our three genocidal states.

Germany

The German desire for unity had deep historical roots. It eventuated in Carl Schmitt's *The Concept of the Political*[3] that based virtually all of politics on the collective friend–enemy distinction. Essentially, a political justification for genocide was established.

The beginning of the Wilhelmine period witnessed the writings of Paul de Lagarde, a widely read social critic who was deeply pessimistic about Germany's future, despite the public euphoria in the immediate aftermath of the formation of imperial Germany. In 1880, he wrote, "I have no use for abstract truth. I want to bind and liberate my people."[4] Moreover, the unity of his people was paramount.

With the competing loyalties of north and south Germans, Protestants and Catholics, liberals and conservatives, as well as tensions between classes signified by the rapid rise of the Social Democrats, Lagarde emphasized the most critical problem facing the newly established Germany. Continuing divisiveness was, in many respects, the hallmark of the new Germany.

How then could the disunity and the increasing role of Jews as promoters of toxic ideologies such as capitalism be combated? In his *Deutsche Schriften* (German Writings), Lagarde argued that a *Führer* was required, a leader who could command the loyalty of all "true" Germans and who could also exterminate the Jews as the apostles of capitalism and disunity. He used the analogy of bacilli and trichinae to justify the mass killing of all enemies of German unity. Himmler's use of the word "bacterium" in his infamous Posen speech justifying the genocide (see pp. 180–81) obviously has a historical root in Lagarde's lexicon, and also serves as clear evidence of dehumanization of the presumed "enemy." It is not surprising that, in 1944, in the midst of the extermination campaign, the German army distributed an anthology of Lagarde's work that enunciated his sanctioning

---

[3] Schmitt [1932] 1996.   [4] Quoted in Stern 1974, 36.

of mass murder. As Fritz Stern comments, "Few men prophesied Hitler's work with such accuracy – and approval."[5]

Lagarde, Julius Langbehn, an advocate of the need for a "Germanic" art, and later Moeller van den Bruck effectively advocated the idea of national socialism in which German solidarity would be firmly established and would not necessarily be based on economic principles. But this desired unity was to be coupled with sacrifice. Two cases are especially relevant. In 1923, Leo Schlageter, a former member of the *Freikorps* who earlier had fought against the Russian Communists in the Baltic and the German Communists in the Ruhr, was executed by the French for attempted sabotage during their occupation of the Ruhr. He was immediately canonized as a hero of the German battle for unity in the face of enemies to both the East and West. He was especially prominent in Nazi martyrology.

The second instance is that of Moeller van den Bruck's suicide. Although not anti-Semitic as were Lagarde and Langbehn, he nevertheless wrote *Das Dritte Reich* (The Third Reich) as an expression of his extreme nationalism, emphasis on unity, and hatred of liberalism.[6] His suicide in 1925 was seen by both friend and foe as a "Germanic" suicide. His despair over Germany's future was said to have been the source of his suicide.[7] The Nazis later appropriated the name of his book for their new Germany. Although seemingly far less dramatic in the overt level of self-sacrifice, Himmler in his efforts to enhance German unity and cooperation follows this "Germanic" tradition. In the end, though, the nihilism that pervaded the Nazi Party was to find its ultimate expression in the suicides of Hitler, Himmler, Goering, and Goebbels, the most prominent architects of the Final Solution.

Interestingly, one of the first to think extensively about modern German nihilism was the political philosopher Leo Strauss, who was forced to flee Germany in the 1930s. In a lecture delivered in February 1941, Strauss, like Stern, saw the deep roots of German nihilism, with Nazism as only the most recent (in 1941) manifestation.[8] A moral life is inherently opposed to the idea of an open society, for in it all sorts of moral conceptions are allowed free rein. Pleasure seekers, those concerned only with the good life or economic satisfaction, are divorced from a singular moral conception that has the nation at its core. War on behalf of the nation, with its inevitable sacrifices, is a hallmark of this morality. According to Strauss, "What [the moral believers] hated, was

---

[5] Ibid., 63.   [6] Ibid., 261–2.   [7] Ibid., 266.   [8] Strauss 1999.

the very prospect of a world in which everyone would be happy and satisfied, in which everyone would have his little pleasure by day and his little pleasure by night, a world in which no great heart could beat and no great soul could breathe, a world without real, unmetaphoric, sacrifice, i.e. a world without blood, sweat, and tears."[9]

As early as 1880, the older Moltke, chief of the German General Staff, stated: "Permanent peace is a dream, and not even a beautiful one, and war is a law of God's order in the world, by which the noblest virtues of man, courage and self-denial, loyalty and self-sacrifice, even to the point of death, are developed. Without war the world would deteriorate into materialism."[10] Later, in 1932, just prior to the Nazi period, this idea would receive its apotheosis by Ernst Jünger: "What kind of minds are those who do not even know this much that no mind *can* be more profound and more knowing than that of *any* soldier who fell anywhere at the Somme or in Flanders? *This* is the standard of which we are in need."[11] And Jünger was no hypocrite. In 1944, when his son was killed in the Italian campaign, Jünger related to his friend General Speidel that his son had succeeded where he, Jünger, had failed. "This was his first day under fire – one he had keenly looked forward to. He always wished to follow in my path, and now, taking his very first step, he has gone further than ever I managed to do."[12] Nihilism is evident when death in the service of a goal, often political, is not to be avoided, but is to be valued, even cherished.[13]

In addition to ideological and societal calls for German unity, the demands of economic growth after World War I also required it. Not only was economic growth needed to compete with other European powers and the United States, but the Nazis understood that their continued tenure in power rested, in part, on German consumer satisfaction.[14] And the path to rapid economic growth was seen as a rationalization of industry along American lines, specifically with Henry Ford's assembly-line innovations as a model. An analysis of German economic efforts by Robert Brady just prior to the Nazi accession to power suggested that:

---

[9] Ibid., 360.   [10] Quoted ibid., 377.
[11] Emphases in original; quoted ibid., 369. See Jünger 1975.   [12] Keates 2004.
[13] Or as Saul Bellow 1982, 291, put it, "the first axiom of nihilism – the highest values losing their value."
[14] Schivelbusch 2003, 285.

> Rationalization will be retarded in Germany as long as national, political, social, and other barriers stand in the way of technological and economic forces ... There are definite limits set to rationalization and economic planning so long as Germany remains a house divided against itself – so long as Catholic Bavaria is pitted against Protestant Prussia, the right against the left, the industrialists against the agriculturists, the urban against the rural districts, the cartels against consumers, the states against the Reich.[15]

Thus, from a practical standpoint, German unity was absolutely required if the Nazis were to continue to govern and then successfully defeat their enemies on the battlefield. For these reasons, the spirit of 1914 was continually invoked as the one moment in recent German history when all of the divisions mentioned by Lagarde and Brady disappeared, and were replaced by a German people united against a common enemy. The nation rose as one to the challenge of the new war. And according to Wolfgang Schivelbusch: "To call upon the unity of the nation in the form of folk community was henceforth identical with reviving the spirit of 1914."[16]

The Ottoman Empire

Unity was also a principal concern of the Ottoman Empire, especially after the disastrous defeat by Russia in the Russo-Turkish War of 1877–78. According to Kemal Karpat, "over 300 thousand Muslims were massacred and one million uprooted in the Balkans and Caucasus, and the Balkan provinces of Serbia, Romania, Montenegro (which became independent), and Bulgaria (which became autonomous) were lost. The Berlin Treaty of 1878 sealed the Ottoman defeat and, contrary to its claim that it would settle the national question in the Balkans, generated a series of new ethnic–national–religious conflicts, which had been markedly absent during four centuries of Ottoman rule, and which culminated in the creation of a group of ethnic national states, including Turkey."[17]

The fundamental issue facing the Ottomans, particularly Abdulhamit II, was how to integrate these Muslim refugees along with Turks and Arabs (Sunnis and Shiites) into a cohesive political entity. Islam was the vehicle chosen to accomplish this task. Whereas prior to the nineteenth

[15] Quoted ibid., 283–84.   [16] Ibid., 222–23.   [17] Karpat 2001, 413–14.

century the Ottoman Empire had an approximate demographic equality between Muslims and non-Muslims (mainly Christian), that had been altered radically. Now Muslims were the clear majority and their religion was to be the principal unifier.

Mosques were repaired and restored. In addition to being encouraged to celebrate Islamic holidays, Muslims were offered lessons on Islam and the Arabic language through secular schools. Arabic was almost raised to equality with Ottoman Turkish as an official language, but, at the last moment, the sultan was dissuaded from this policy.[18]

Many of the Muslim migrants were encouraged to settle in areas with sizeable Christian populations such as eastern Anatolia with its large numbers of Armenians.[19] In this fashion, the incipient nationalisms of Christian groups would be blunted by the growing Muslim populations in these regions. Between 1862 and 1882, Muslim migrants from Russia and the Balkans increased the Ottoman Muslim population by 40 percent.[20]

The emphasis on Islam had an additional advantage. Because most of the nonagricultural economy was in the hands of Christians – Greeks or Armenians[21] – this strategy also managed to reinforce not only a religious, but also an economic cleavage between these Christian communities and Turkish as well as Kurdish Muslims. When calls for action came against the Christian communities in the form of genocide for the Armenians and exile for the Greeks, the Ottoman leaders could rely on the Turkish and Kurdish peasantry who were united against and hostile to the Christians. There were at least two sources of unity – Islam and intense class-based hostility – for the Ottoman leaders to draw upon.

Additionally, as early as 1873, the concept of *vatan* (fatherland, homeland) was gaining ascendancy within the Ottoman Empire. In Namik Kemal's thinking, the *vatan* was necessarily Muslim or, even more precisely, Turkish, clearly excluding all non-Muslim Ottomans. In Kemal's play of that year, the hero Islam bey (sic) tells his love:

> The state has declared war. The enemy is trying to trample under its feet the bones of our martyrs on the frontier (*serhat*, which has a powerful mystical connotation of martyrdom ...). How can I stay in comfort at home when the fatherland is in danger ... Fatherland! Fatherland! I shout that the fatherland is in danger, don't you hear me? God created me, the fatherland reared me. God nurtured me for the fatherland ... I feel the bounty of the fatherland in my bones. My body (is part) of the

---

[18] S. Shaw and Shaw 1977, 259–60.   [19] Karpat 2002, 64.   [20] Karpat 2001, 97.
[21] Issawi 1980.

fatherland's earth, my breath (is part) of the fatherland's air. Why was I born if I was not to die for the fatherland?[22]

Sacrifice for the Ottoman Empire clearly was the theme of Islam bey's declaration. Elsewhere, he decries the widespread absence of such support for the empire:

> When in need of defense, it has to be defended by forcing (whipping) the children of the fatherland ... to go to the frontier to fight. The fatherland is everybody's real mother, and yet many people try to exploit it in its good and bad days and aren't willing to shed even two drops of tear [sic] for it. The fatherland is nurturing forty million people and, yet now it has not found even forty souls to volunteer to die for it. In the past, this fatherland kept alive with its sword several states while now it is preserved with the help of a few other states (the English and French, who supported the Ottomans against Russia).[23]

Although a poet and playwright, Kemal became one of the architects of the constitution of 1876. His play concludes with a chorus:

> Wounds are medals on the brave's body;
> The grave (martyrdom) is the soldier's highest rank;
> The earth is the same, above and underneath;
> March, you brave ones, to defend the fatherland.[24]

Karpat concludes his analysis of Kemal with the comment: "In the ultimate analysis, the fatherland for Namik Kemal was the territory of the state (*devlet*) and the nation (*millet*) was the community of Ottoman Muslims, led by Turks or by those closely identified with Ottoman history."[25] As the Turks were the ascendant group by virtue of their numbers and their loyalty, it was not surprising that they became the most powerful force within the Ottoman Empire.

It was Kemal who would presage the transition from Ottomanism to Turkism as the basis of governance. Later, around 1890, Sultan Abdulhamit commented, "In fact the Turks constitute the real strength of the state. As long as the Turks survive, the rest will (follow) and *sacrifice themselves* for the dynasty as part of their absolute (religious) obligation. This is the reason for which the Sublime Sultanate should place on a higher level the national fate (*kadr-i millet*) but also respect the Arabs, with whom we share the language of our faith."[26]

---

[22] Quoted in Karpat 2001, 331.   [23] Quoted ibid., 332.   [24] Quoted ibid., 334.
[25] Ibid.   [26] Emphasis added; quoted ibid., 336.

When Arab nationalism proved to be more resilient than expected, and the Albanians, despite the presence of a Muslim majority, declared independence in 1912, Turkism became ascendant. The Committee for Union and Progress (also somewhat erroneously identified as the Young Turks) would transform the empire into a Turkish state "imperial in form and national in content."[27] There would be little room for non-Muslim or non-Turkish nationalism in the new empire.

Rwanda

As in Germany and the Ottoman Empire, Rwanda also had deep concerns about the absence of unity, even within the majority Hutu population. First, in contrast to Germany, where Jews were less than 1 percent of the population, and the Ottoman Empire, where Armenians were no more than 3 percent, the Tutsi in Rwanda were a substantially larger minority. At the time of the genocide, they numbered at least 10 percent (taking into account Tutsi registration as Hutu to avoid discrimination) of the total including both Hutu and Twa (no more than 1 percent).[28] Such a sizable proportion of the population had strong implications for governance in an emerging multiparty system. But in addition to this increasingly fundamental divide, the Hutu themselves were divided between northerners and those from central and southern Rwanda.

The northern Hutu, known as Kiga, formed a distinctive subculture that was brought under the aegis of the Tutsi monarchy only in the twentieth century with German and, later, Belgian help.[29] In contrast to the south, especially in the region of Butare, there was little intermarriage between Hutu and Tutsi in the north. Indeed, the northerners viewed the southerners as "other" because of the close ties between the Hutu and the Tutsi.[30] It was the perception of the southerners as "other" that most probably inspired the northern-dominated government to unleash especially severe genocidal action in the south of Rwanda. Many of the murdered Hutu moderates would be from this region.

Hutu from central and southern Rwanda actually dominated the government until the 1973 coup by Juvénal Habyarimana. It was not until attacks on the Tutsi, which some attributed to southerners, that northerners effectively took over governmental control. Others laid responsibility for the attacks on northerners hoping to generate instability and thereby justify the coup d'état. In either event, "the tactic was

---

[27] Ibid., 370.   [28] Des Forges 1999, 15.   [29] Lemarchand 1995, 8.   [30] Pottier 2002, 35.

clear: seek to resolve differences among Hutu at the expense of the Tutsi."[31]

From the outset, the search for unity among Hutu would involve the murder of Tutsi. At the same time, Hutu moderates who opposed this tactic were hated passionately. In one 1993 song, the popular singer Simon Bikindi targeted the Hutu of Butare:

> Let us start in the region of Butare where they like feudalism (the reign of the Tutsi), who would blame me for that? I hate them and I don't apologize for that. I hate them and I don't apologize for that. Lucky for us that they are few in number ... Those who have ears, let them hear![32]

The Hutu extremist newspaper *Kangura* stated: "Your unity, your mutual understanding, your solidarity are the certain weapons of your victory ... You understand that when the majority people is divided, (then) the minority becomes the majority."[33]

An ideology of hatred began to build on the presumed Hamitic and therefore alien origin of the Tutsi, but with strong emphasis on Tutsi unity that needed a strong Hutu counterpart. Using the term *inyenzi* (cockroach) to describe the Tutsi, in March 1993 *Kangura* published an article titled "A Cockroach Cannot Give Birth to a Butterfly." This article, characterizing the Tutsi as evil and dehumanizing them, included the following:

> We began by saying that a cockroach cannot give birth to a butterfly. It is true. A cockroach gives birth to another cockroach ... The history of Rwanda shows us clearly that a Tutsi stays always exactly the same, that he has never changed. The malice, the evil are just as we knew them in the history of our country. We are not wrong in saying that a cockroach gives birth to another cockroach. Who could tell the difference between the Inyenzi who attacked in October 1990 and those of the 1960s. They are all linked ... their evilness is the same. The unspeakable crimes of the Inyenzi of today ... recall those of their elders: killing, pillaging, raping girls and women, etc.[34]

With such an unchanging and united enemy, the Hutu were called on to be tightly organized in response. This press for a vigorous Hutu response went beyond the pattern already established of Tutsi exclusion. Although Habyarimana in 1973 actually included a Tutsi in his cabinet, the barriers to Tutsi participation in the real organs of power, the army

---

[31] Des Forges 1999, 41.   [32] Quoted ibid., 83.   [33] Quoted ibid., 82.
[34] Quoted ibid., 73–74.

and local government, were virtually impenetrable. There was actually one Tutsi officer in the army, but army members were forbidden by regulation to marry Tutsi women. Although defined as an ethnic minority, Tutsi were effectively denied group recognition and were completely excluded from power at the local level. Tutsi in neighboring countries, many of them refugees or descendants of refugees, were denied Rwandan rights of any kind.[35] The events of 1990 and thereafter would demand an exclusion well beyond this customary discrimination.

Yet another potential dimension of conflict was social class. Increased population density made existing landholdings smaller and even gave rise to landlessness, a deadly condition in a largely agrarian economy.[36] In 1984, 57 percent of rural households had less than one hectare to farm, and, of these, 25 percent had less than half a hectare.[37] Between 1984 and 1989, average farm holdings shrank by 12 percent. And the shrinkage occurred during only a five-year period, suggesting the exponential decline of holdings size under a condition of unremitting population growth.[38] Peasants are the first to shrewdly observe such processes and to predict their likely unhappy outcomes in the foreseeable future.[39] A USAID-commissioned study concluded that: "Disputes over land are reported to have been a major motivation for Rwandans to denounce neighbors during the ethnic conflicts of 1994."[40]

When such increasing scarcities intersect with regional political divisions, the result can be local massacre. In comparing two Rwandan communities, Kirinda and Biguhu, Timothy Longman found just such a relationship.[41] In the former community, located in central Rwanda, a cohesive elite was loyal to President Habyarimana's party consisting of northerners, while the peasantry on the whole supported the opposition. Despite the absence of Tutsi in either the economic or political elite, Habyarimana's supporters sought to deflect hostile sentiments of the peasantry onto the region's Tutsi minority, descendants of the pre-1959 elite. A mob was organized that murdered a significant portion of the local Tutsi community. In Biguhu, on the other hand, a local elite developed without significant ties to the northerners. The local peasantry was the focus of efforts to improve the status of the community. As a

[35] Mamdani 2001, 141.   [36] Pottier 2002, 184.   [37] Mamdani 2001, 197.
[38] M. Midlarsky 1999.   [39] M. Midlarsky 1988b.   [40] Quoted in Mamdani 2001, 197.
[41] Longman 1995.

consequence, few, if any, of the local elite participated in the genocide. External perpetrators had to be imported, in the absence of local participation.

Here, as in our other cases, sacrifice was required in the name of Hutu unity and power. Or as Mamdani puts it: "Faced with a military defeat that seemed to sound the very death knell of Hutu Power, the *génocidaires* chose to embrace death itself as an alternative to life without power."[42]

The search for unity establishes a powerful substratum upon which genocidal thinking can be built. If unity is to be imperiled by the presence of "alien" societal elements, and there exists evidence, either real or phantasmal, for the influence of these people on the genesis of loss, then genocide can emerge as a serious policy option. Succeeding chapters explore this and other consequences of the perception of disunity.

Partly because of the reluctance of the Turkish government and even many Turkish scholars to acknowledge that a genocide of the Armenians occurred, information on the lives and motivations of the perpetrators is limited. The same limitation is true of Rwanda, but for a different reason. Here, the genocide is ten years old as of this writing, and detailed information on the lives and motivations of the organizers of the genocide has yet to appear.[43] The first biography of Himmler in English appeared twenty-six years after his suicide,[44] and a more detailed and extensive one[45] not until twenty years after that. It may take many more years before reliable personal data on Rwandan central perpetrators becomes available. Consequently, I could only explore the moral dimension and inclinations toward cooperation satisfactorily in the case of Heinrich Himmler, the chief architect of the Final Solution. The others must await further research.

---

[42] Mamdani 2001, 215.

[43] Recently, Jean Hatzfeld has written a book based on the narratives of perpetrators in one commune of Rwanda, that of Nyamata. With only one exception, the ten perpetrators interviewed were ordinary farmers or laborers and not involved as prime movers. The exception, Joseph-Désiré Bitero, was the only one who was involved in preparations for the genocide several months before its onset ("Á ce titre, il est le seul de la bande à avoir été impliqué dans la préparation du génocide plusieurs mois avant que celui-ci commence"): Hatzfeld 2003, 304–05.

[44] B. Smith 1971.   [45] Padfield 1991.

Himmler and the necessity for cooperation

We now explore the nexus between Nazi leadership in the form of Heinrich Himmler and putative followers. It focuses on factors that could have motivated a thoroughly violence-averse individual to authorize the commission of mass murder on a truly horrendous scale. How do we reconcile such an apparent disjunction between personal preferences and collective behavior? An answer is to be found in the role of altruistic punishment as a strategy to maximize societal cooperation.

Materials from Himmler's life history are used to support the basic propositions. The relevance of altruistic punishment is compared with related but still very different concepts such as Saul Friedländer's "redemptive anti-Semitism"[46] and Robert Jay Lifton's "killing to heal."[47] The basic explanatory strength of altruistic punishment is found in its unique capacity to link the individual behaviors of leaders and collective behaviors of followers. This dynamic linkage is to be preferred over the essentially static "banality of evil" characterization by Hannah Arendt[48] of bureaucratic murderers like Adolf Eichmann, and even higher-level functionaries such as Heinrich Himmler.

Himmler as moralist

One of the most arresting speeches in German history and perhaps in all of human affairs is that given by Heinrich Himmler, Reichsführer-SS, to a meeting of senior SS officers, among others, in Posen on October 4, 1943. In it he spoke of the "evacuation of the Jews, the extermination of the Jewish people." That reference in itself, appalling as it is, does not necessarily give rise to utter amazement and consternation. After all, the Holocaust, though exceptional in its magnitude and absence of identifiable Jewish provocation, was not the first genocide of the twentieth century, nor would it be the last. It is the inverted moral calculus that is stunning in its impact. Himmler states:

> Most of you men know what it is like to see 100 corpses side by side, or
> 500 or 1,000. To have stood fast through this and – except for cases of
> human weakness – to have stayed decent that has made us hard ... We
> had the moral right, we had the duty towards our people, to destroy this

---

[46] Friedländer 1997.   [47] Lifton 1986.
[48] Arendt 1964. For a refutation of the "banality of evil" hypothesis, see Lozowick 2002, esp. 268–80.

people that wanted to destroy us. But we do not have the right to enrich ourselves by so much as a fur, as a watch, by one Mark or a cigarette or anything else. We have exterminated a bacterium because we do not want in the end to be infected by the bacterium and die of it. I will not see so much as a small area of sepsis appear here or gain a hold. Wherever it may form, we will cauterise it. All in all, however, we can say that we have carried out this most difficult of tasks in a spirit of love for our people. And we have suffered no harm in our inner being, our soul, our character.[49]

In Himmler's view, this was a "glorious page in our history that has never been written and is never to be written."[50]

Two days later, he amplified the moral theme before a high-level gathering of Reichsleiters and Gauleiters. "The entire property that we confiscated from the Jews – it runs to infinite value – has been passed over to the Reich Economics Minister down to the last Pfennig. I have taken the view: we have the duty to our *Volk*, to our race, if we want to win the war – we have the duty to our Führer, who now for once in two thousand years has been granted our *Volk*, not to be petty here but to be thoroughgoing. But we have not the right to take even one Pfennig from the confiscated Jewish property. I established from the beginning that SS men, even if they only take one Mark, are dead. In the last few days on that account I have signed several – I can say it calmly, it was about a dozen – death sentences. Here one has to be hard lest the whole suffer by it."[51]

SS sadists occasionally were punished. When questioned as to the appropriate response to the unauthorized killing of Jews, Himmler responded: "If the motive is purely political there should be no punishment unless such is necessary for the maintenance of discipline. If the motive is selfish, sadistic or sexual, judicial punishment should be imposed for murder or manslaughter as the case may be."[52] When corruption was combined with sadism, "Himmler let the hounds of justice loose."[53]

As the Himmler biographer Richard Breitman comments: "The architect of mass murder remained in his own eyes a moralist to the end."[54] Further, according to Yehuda Bauer, within the framework of the SS ethos, Himmler "changed the biblical 'thou shalt not murder' into a

---

[49] Quoted in Burleigh 2000, 660–61.   [50] Quoted in Kershaw 2000a, 487.
[51] Quoted in Padfield 1991, 469.   [52] Quoted in Höhne 1970, 383.   [53] Ibid.
[54] Breitman 1991, 243.

Nazi 'thou shalt murder' . . . a positive commandment. In other words, he did not deviate from accepted moral precepts but stood them on their head without changing the traditional framework in which people accepted them."[55] Clearly, Himmler's morality was not that typically associated with altruism,[56] nor did it conform to the canons of moral philosophy.[57]

The existence of this moral inversion, however, does not help explain its genesis. How could the not-unintelligent Himmler, and educated, even sophisticated SS officers, two-thirds with university degrees and nearly a third with doctorates, most frequently in law,[58] descend to this moral purgatory?

Preceding answers have centered on the peculiarities of Himmler's psyche. The existence of his youthful diaries and the many speeches he delivered provide a useful database for such inductive theorizing. Following Peter Loewenberg, Peter Padfield in his extensive biography of Himmler interprets many of his actions to be a consequence of a personality riven by emotional withdrawal and narcissism.[59] Both Bradley Smith and Richard Breitman follow more orthodox historiographic paths and attribute Himmler's behavior to the unique intersection of family circumstances and historical trajectories.[60] Neither of these idiographic approaches is sufficient, for they do not help explain the general acceptance of Himmler's actions by a large proportion of Nazi Germany's leaders. We now know that the Wehrmacht was deeply complicit in the Holocaust, especially in the East.[61] In early May 1944, at a gathering of generals and members of Hitler's headquarters staff, Himmler openly spoke of the mass murder of Jewish women and children as well as the men. A recording of the speech reveals that these remarks were greeted with applause.[62]

Morality, especially at the front, was relative. Viewing Judeo-communism as the *bête noire* of the Nazis, the German troops could believe that "No matter the scale of the *Wehrmacht*'s atrocities, the enemy's, by definition, were greater. Thus as long as the morality of one's actions was gauged in relation to the enemy's, there could not be any absolute moral limit. Personal moral outrage, instead of tempering one's conduct, rather

---

[55] Bauer 1994, 116.   [56] E. Midlarsky 1968, E. Midlarsky and Kahana 1994.
[57] Neiman 2002.   [58] Herbert 2000a, 26.   [59] Loewenberg 1971; Padfield 1991.
[60] B. Smith 1971; Breitman 1991.
[61] Bartov 1992; Hamburg Institute for Social Research 1999.   [62] Padfield 1991, 484.

enhanced it, by being directed at those perceived as the cause of all enormities."[63]

Defection and cooperation

Although Communists, Social Democrats, Roma, homosexuals, and other "asocials" were despised and in many cases subject to mass murder, the Jews occupied a singular position at the head of the group. Their defection was seen to be particularly egregious because of the infamous "stab in the back" popularized by Kaiser Wilhelm II upon his abdication at the end of World War I (see chapter 7).

Here we have the image of the classic defector. Residing in the midst of a mutually cooperating society, the Jews are assumed to take advantage of their "hosts" in ways that ultimately lead to the German defeat in World War I. To their great misfortune, further events would reinforce this illusion of the Jews as defectors. The November 1918 revolution in Bavaria, soon to be the hotbed of Nazism, occurred even before that which swept the Reich. It was a more radical revolution and one that happened to have several Jews among its leaders including those with East European origins and Bolshevik connections. At the head stood Kurt Eisner, a Jewish journalist and left-wing socialist who earlier had organized the "January strike" of 1916 in an attempt to initiate industrial unrest. The vast majority of revolutionaries, however, were not Jewish.

Later, in 1919, the revolution was to be further radicalized by three Jewish emissaries from the Soviet Union – Lewien, Levine-Niessen, and Axelrod. Before their soviet republic was quashed, one of the final acts of the revolutionaries was to execute a number of hostages. Among them were seven members of the Thule society, a conservative aristocratic society that gave rise to a German Workers' Party, later to become the NSDAP (Nazi Party) under Hitler's leadership.[64] Four of the murdered Thule society members were nobles. The nobility was very dear to the hearts of the Himmler family. Heinrich himself was the namesake of Prince Heinrich of the Bavarian house of Wittelsbad and a student of Professor Himmler, Heinrich's father. The prince's death from wounds suffered at the front was deeply felt by the Himmlers. According to Padfield, "It's against this background that Heinrich Himmler's views were formed."[65]

---

[63] Bartov 1994, 47.   [64] Kershaw 1998, 135–36.   [65] Padfield 1991, 36.

Himmler's notes on a book read in the spring of 1924 state: "A new frightful insight into the workshop of the enemy. Bitterness seizes one when one reads all this. *What have we done to these people that we should not live. And now with a vengeance. We want to be German and will always fight for this against every enemy.* What kind of enemies of belief and of the Christian religion of love are these people indeed."[66]

In a classic description of the hidden defector, Himmler, in the wake of the Röhm purge or "night of the long knives" in the summer of 1934, states: "That the Jews and our other enemies would not proceed against us with direct attacks must have been clear to each of you – even those who have no knowledge of them. The attack of the Jews and all secret enemies occurs, as it has for centuries, via seeds of discord, via lies, calumny, via shameless intrigue."[67] Even in their language, the Jews were seen as defectors. After reading a nineteenth-century book about Yiddish, Himmler comments, "One sees that Yiddish is a form of middle high German ... Shame to our beautiful language."[68]

While Jews were being identified as defectors, the necessity for coop-eration was emphasized in German society. As early as the formation of the Reichswehr after World War I by General Hans von Seeckt, the necessity for societal cooperation was recognized. In his reform of the military, von Seeckt set out to eliminate from the army many of the class barriers that had served as social fault lines and were thought to have contributed to the revolutionary ethos of 1918–19. In the manual authorized initially by von Seeckt, leaders were enjoined to "live with their troops and share with them their dangers and deprivations, their joys and sorrows."[69] This new spirit of cooperation was to be effected later during World War II, as exemplified by one incident recounted by Major General F. W. von Mellethin. While in Venice dining at a hotel, Italians were surprised to find von Mellethin's driver seated at the same table. Von Mellethin explained: "While normally officers and other ranks took their meals separately, it was a matter of course for us to eat together like this when an officer and a private were all on their own. In contrast to 1918 the inner knowledge that officers and enlisted men belonged together was never shaken, and even in 1945 there were no signs of rot in the German Army."[70]

---

[66] Emphasis added; quoted ibid., 70.   [67] Quoted ibid., 163.
[68] Quoted in B. Smith 1971, 143.   [69] Quoted in Condell and Zabecki 2001, 5.
[70] Quoted ibid., 6.

Cooperation within German society was a principal Nazi goal. Sebastian Haffner lists it as one of the genuine achievements of the Nazi period, what Hitler called the "socialization of people."[71] Younger-age school children belonged to the Jungvolk, while adolescents found a home in the Hitler Youth. Military sports were common in the SA (paramilitary assault divisions) or SS. Women were active in the German Women's League. These activities gave rise to an "undeniable sense of security, comradeship and happiness which flourish in such communities."[72]

And these efforts at cooperation were successful, even in the genocidal impulse among the German civilian population, not to mention the military, and even after the full extent of the genocide had been revealed. In October 1945, a survey of the German population in the American zone of occupation revealed that fully 20 percent of the respondents supported Hitler's treatment of the Jews, and another 19 percent "were generally in favor but felt that he had gone too far."[73] As late as 1947, 55 percent of the population believed that "National Socialism was a good idea badly carried out."[74] And we know that these attitudes were not characteristic of Germans in 1933 at the start of the Nazi regime (e.g., the failed Nazi-sponsored April 1 boycott of Jewish businesses). Victor Klemperer, an acute observer of the wartime German scene, indicated that, in the last year of the war, Germans were increasingly likely to vent their hostilities directly at Jews and were openly supportive of the Nazi policies toward them.[75]

Himmler himself was extremely sensitive to the imperative need for cooperation in the face of governmental collapse. An early expression of this societal orientation was found in his fraternity (*Bund*) activities. "The traditional *Kameradschaft* of the *Bund* had a deep appeal for him, and he took his responsibilities to his fraternity brothers very seriously. He visited sick Apolloneans [fraternity brothers] and sought out

---

[71] Haffner 1979, 37.

[72] Ibid., 39. Indeed, Haffner himself experienced these feelings despite his strong anti-Nazi sentiments, which led to his emigration before the war. Writing in his posthumously published memoir, Haffner recorded his reaction to the required attendance at an ideological indoctrinataion camp for soon-to-be-certified lawyers. Although put off by the SA leaders, Haffner soon succumbed to what he called "the trap of comradeship." At the end of the camp session, he comments, "'We' had become a collective entity, and with all the intellectual cowardice and dishonesty of a collective being we instinctively ignored or belittled anything that could disturb our collective self-satisfaction. A German Reich in microcosm" (Haffner 2002, 283, 288).

[73] Kulka 2000, 279.   [74] Ibid.   [75] Heim 2000, 324.

members and alumni wherever he went. The parallel between the
Kameradschaft of the *Bund* and the esprit de corps of a military unit
pleased him. In the *Bund* he found an expression of the 'genuine German
spirit.'"[76]

At around the same time, Himmler notes in his diary a visit to a
destitute old woman. "24 November: . . . Visit to Frau Kernburger. The
poor old woman. This is true misery. She is almost too weak from
hunger and exhaustion to walk . . . People are as hard and pitiless as
they can be . . . I fetched rolls for her and added a small cake which I put
down without her noticing."[77] His social instincts, at least among
"cooperators," were very strong. They would be manifested still further
in his cooperative behavior with Nazi leaders ("der *treue* [loyal]
Heinrich") and his successful leadership of the SS and Gestapo.

Clearly, Himmler understood the Jews to be defectors *par excellence.*
But how strongly did Himmler react to the appearance of defection from
the rules of cooperating society? Recall that one of the experimental
findings emphasized that the greater the amount of defection from
average levels of cooperation, the greater the extent of punishment
visited upon the defector.[78] Not only would the Jews have to be extraordinary defectors in Himmler's view, but he himself would have to be
sensitive to defection. In Himmler's case, strong sensitivity of this type is
indeed in evidence.

An incident reveals the extent of Himmler's reaction to any form of
defection from accepted norms of cooperative behavior. It occurred in
September 1916, as food shortages were making themselves felt in
wartime Germany. A clipping from a local newspaper kept by
Himmler denounced the hoarding behavior of a woman known to
him. She had complained to the Himmler family about the food restrictions in Germany that she was circumventing by her hoarding behavior
in Passau. Food she collected there was being sent home. Bradley Smith
concluded from this incident "that the Himmlers – perhaps Heinrich
himself – were directly involved in the denunciation of the hoarders. The
boy's wealth of information on the incident certainly suggests that he
played some part in its exposure."[79]

But the commission of systematic mass murder was actually against
Himmler's personal temperament. Unless judged to be absolutely necessary, Himmler found murder to be distasteful. For example, his written

[76] B. Smith 1971, 112.   [77] Quoted in Padfield 1991, 10–11.
[78] Fehr and Gächter 2000, 980.   [79] B. Smith 1971, 43.

commentary on a volume on human torture suggested that it was a horrifying work and a "frightening book about the beast in men which manifests itself in every century and in every state."[80] The subject of killing seems to have caused him physical distress.[81] Attending one execution of 200 Jews in Minsk, Himmler was barely prevented from physically collapsing.[82] While his fondness for children was widely noted, he readily gave time to widows and war orphans saying that, "Compared with their sacrifice, the half-hour which I sacrifice to them is such a small matter. I would be ashamed if I failed to listen to them or give them the feeling there was somebody to whom they could turn."[83] Yet he ordered and supervised the murder of millions, most frequently under barbaric conditions. A series of Himmler's statements strongly suggests the notion of altruistic punishment.

As early as 1924 when he worked hard to disseminate *völkisch* propaganda, delivering speeches in small towns and writing short articles for rural newspapers, he noted in his diary on February 24, "This service to the people is bitterly hard and full of heartaches."[84] Later, in September 1937, in a speech to the German army General Staff, he spoke of the difficulties in staffing the camps in the hands of the Death's Head Battalions. "It is ... necessary to have a relatively high number of these supervisory troops, – there are at present 3,500 in Germany, – because there is no service as debilitating and as exhausting as the supervision of these bums and criminals."[85] The editors of this document sought to disparage Himmler's comment by heading the section in which it appears, "Himmler Pities Prison Guards,"[86] but this statement is consistent with many others suggesting the concept of self-sacrifice for the good of the *Volk*. When Himmler spoke to the generals on June 21, 1944, he stated that "It was the most dreadful assignment and most awful commission that an organization could ever receive: the commission to solve the Jewish question."[87] Or, on May 5, 1944, "Please understand how difficult it was for me to perform this soldierly command, which I followed and performed out of obedience and the fullest conviction."[88] And finally, in his infamous speech in Posen, he spoke of the "difficulties" of committing mass murder and remaining decent, as we saw.

[80] Quoted ibid., 165.   [81] Padfield 1991, 373.   [82] Höhne 1970, 366.
[83] Quoted in Padfield 1991, 394–95.   [84] Quoted in B. Smith 1971, 137.
[85] Himmler 1938, 13.   [86] Ibid., 12.   [87] Quoted in Fleming 1984, 54.
[88] Quoted ibid., 53–54.

That Himmler personally extended himself there can be little doubt. But on behalf of whom and in the name of which process was he acting? Clearly, the German *Volk* was to be the recipient of his altruistic endeavors. By eliminating the Jews as the prime source of the 1918 defeat, Himmler was opening the possibilities for victory in the second round. Or, as he put it in his Posen speech of October 4, 1943, and is worth repeating, "If the Jews were still lodged in the body of the German nation, we would probably have reached by now the stage of 1916–17."[89] In early May 1944, he told a gathering of generals and members of Hitler's headquarters staff, "Of this you can be sure, had we not eliminated the Jews from Germany we would not have been able to endure the bombing despite the decency of the German *Volk*. That is my conviction."[90] Later, on July 26, 1944, he stated, "The war is precisely as surely to be won as the world war was in November 1918, January 1919, if only we had had a firm leadership then, a loyalty pervading the whole *Volk* up to the top, and good nerves . . . We are in the fortunate position that we have no more Jews within, so the scum of all revolts has been eradicated in the mass of the people."[91]

This latter quote reveals both the purpose and the principal base of the altruistic punishment. Himmler had devoted himself with super-human energy to the achievement of cooperation within Germany by eliminating the main group of earlier assumed defectors, the Jews. And without the perennially defecting Jews, the bedrock of German cooperation, loyalty, could now be established. *Treue* or loyalty was Himmler's main concern. Earlier in his life, he commented, upon reading Werner Jansen's *Das Buch Treue* (*The Book of Loyalty*), "One of the most wonderful German books that I have read. The German loyalty [*Treue*] problem . . . wonderfully presented."[92] According to Smith:

> A . . . direct connection between his early ideas and his later activities is to be found in his concept of *Treue* or loyalty. Praise of company or party loyalty is common in organizations, but *völkisch* writers and speakers in the early 1920s elevated it to the paramount position in their value system. Loyalty became the bedrock of the *völkisch* faith . . . The slogan of the *SS, Meine Ehre heisst Treue* [my honor demands loyalty], marked the institutionalization of this concept inside the Nazi system.[93]

---

[89] Quoted in Burleigh 2000, 660.   [90] Quoted in Padfield 1991, 424.
[91] Quoted ibid., 519.   [92] Quoted in B. Smith 1971, 142.   [93] Ibid., 171.

To Felix Kersten, Himmler's personal physician who complained of the extent and personal cost of the killing even to perpetrators, Himmler remarked, "You oughtn't to look at things from such a limited and egotistical point of view; you have to consider the Germanic world as a whole ... a man has to sacrifice himself."[94] Throughout the invasion of Russia, Himmler exhorted his *Einsatzgruppe* minions to fulfill their "heavy task."[95]

Perhaps most indicative of prevailing sentiment about killing among the military is a pep talk given to Wehrmacht troops in Russia by a Captain Wesreidau in autumn 1943, after the major German defeats at Stalingrad and Kursk, and German troops in full retreat. I quote it at length because it so clearly reveals the relationships existing among the search for unity, risk, inverted morality, and altruistic punishment, especially the need for sacrifice:

> We are now embarked on a risky enterprise, with no assurance of safety. We are advancing an idea of unity which is neither rich nor easily digestible, but the vast majority of the German people accept [sic] it and adhere to it, forging and forming it in an admirable collective effort. This is where we are now risking everything. We are trying, taking due account of the attitudes of society, to change the face of the world, hoping to revive the ancient virtues buried under the layers of filth bequeathed to us by our forebears. We can expect no reward for this effort. We are loathed everywhere: if we should lose tomorrow those of us still alive after so much suffering will be judged without justice. We shall be accused of an infinity of murder, as if everywhere, and at all times, men at war did not behave in the same way. Those who have an interest in putting an end to our ideals will ridicule everything we believe in. We shall be spared nothing. Even the tombs of our heroes will be destroyed, only preserving – as a gesture of respect toward the dead – a few which contain figures of doubtful heroism, who were never fully committed to our cause. With our deaths, all the prodigies of heroism which our daily circumstances require of us, and the memory of our comrades, dead and alive, and our communion of spirits, our fears and our hopes, will vanish, and our history will never be told. *Future generations will speak only of an idiotic, unqualified sacrifice ...*
>
> We shall be suffering not only in the interests of ultimate victory, but in the interests of daily victory against those who hurl themselves at us without respite, and whose only thought is to exterminate us, without any

---

[94] Quoted in Höhne 1970, 365.   [95] Quoted ibid.

understanding of what is at stake. You can feel certain of me, in return, and certain that I will not expose you to any unnecessary dangers.

I would burn and destroy entire villages if by so doing I could prevent even one of us from dying of hunger. Here, deep in the wilds of the steppe, we shall be all the more aware of our unity. We are surrounded by hatred and death, and in these circumstances we shall daily oppose our perfect cohesion to the indiscipline and disorder of our enemies. *Our group must be as one, and our thoughts must be identical. Your duty lies in your efforts to achieve that goal, and if we do achieve it, and maintain it, we shall be victors even in death.*[96]

Guy Sajer comments: "Our conversations with Captain Wesreidau made a deep impression on us."[97] But according to Omer Bartov, "The more it became clear that the war would not lead to the promised victory, the more powerful became the faith in the mythical *Endsieg* [final victory], whose essence was a belief in the need to keep on destroying the present until eventually the ideal future emerged from the debris."[98] Needless to say, Captain Wesreidau died in battle. To quote Christopher Taylor's paraphrase of Benedict Anderson: "Fatality becomes transformed into continuity."[99]

Conclusion

In his article advocating a particularistic interpretation of Heinrich Himmler, Peter Loewenberg quotes the German historian Helmut Heiber: "Who was the true Heinrich Himmler? The petty schoolmaster who distributes report cards to his students? Or the writing-desk murderer whose total balance is just short of ten million people? Or the man of honor who controls millions of marks, yet deducts 150 marks for a wristwatch from his salary?"[100]

Clearly, the listing of polar opposites suggested by Heiber leads directly to the hypothesis of a split personality. Yet when one is faced with a more coherent, essentially simpler explanation of Heinrich Himmler, the interpretation of a split personality is unnecessary. Occam's razor demands the more parsimonious and general explanation that not only explains Himmler's behavior but also that of other

---

[96] Emphasis added; quoted in Sajer 1971, 217–18.
[97] Ibid., 218, son of a German father and French mother.   [98] Bartov 1994, 49.
[99] Taylor 1999, 152; and B. Anderson 1991, 11.
[100] Heiber 1968, 8; Loewenberg 1971, 612.

perpetrators not easily pigeonholed into this psychological category. Instead of unique personality traits peculiar to Himmler, we can understand his behavior as a consequence of his altruistic punishment chosen to maximize cooperation in the near-anarchic setting of Germany during the interwar period and then during the war itself. The increasing anarchy and threat of defeat in the war made the punishment incomparably harsher when compared with the concentration camps of the 1930s that had no extermination function. Before the war, altruistic punishment may be invoked as an explanation of brutal behavior toward defectors, mainly political, but the mass murders of the war years evolved under much harsher conditions that justified, to the Nazis, much harsher punishment of this large concentration of Jewish defectors. This is not to say that sheer sadism, looting, the settling of old scores, and other reasons were not factors in the frequently brutal mass murders of World War II. But to ignore the role of altruistic punishment, especially among leaders such as Himmler, is to omit a crucial variable in helping to understand the onset of mass murder and its abetting by large numbers of perpetrators and bystanders.

Among historians of the Holocaust, perhaps Friedländer's concept of "redemptive anti-Semitism"[101] is closest to that of altruistic punishment. In order to save the world, one must go to great lengths to destroy its ultimate parasites, the Jews. Hitler, in his anti-Semitic apotheosis, stated: "If, with the help of the Marxian creed, the Jew conquers the nations of this world, his crown will become the funeral wreath of humanity, and once again this planet, empty of mankind, will move through the ether as it did thousands of years ago ... Therefore, I believe today that I am acting in the sense of the Almighty Creator: *By warding off the Jews I am fighting for the Lord's work.*"[102]

Even closer in conception is Lifton's idea of "killing to heal." Here, the world requires the cleansing, even the mass murder of people, to be truly healed. Lifton initially used this concept to explain the behavior of Nazi doctors in extermination camps,[103] but then extended it to the nuclear genocidal mentality,[104] and to an obscure but deadly Japanese sect.[105] In discussing the genocidal ideology of the SS, Lifton and Markusen aver: "One must, that is, make sacrifices – or, as some SS officers put it, 'overcome' oneself – for the sake of the higher therapeutic purpose.

---

[101] Friedländer 1997.   [102] Emphasis in original; Hitler 1939, 84.   [103] Lifton 1986.
[104] Lifton and Markusen 1990.   [105] Lifton 2000.

One has taken one's place in an ideological narrative within which the murderers are virtuous, the victims evil, and the killing necessary."[106]

Here, the conceptualization comes very close to that of altruistic punishment, but with one crucial exception. Redemptive anti-Semitism and killing to heal are put forward in an effort to understand the lethal individual behavior of virulent anti-Semites. Although not explicitly suggesting self-sacrifice, it can be implied, as we just saw. But altruistic punishment not only straightforwardly suggests the denial of self for purposes of punishing the "other," it also is critically linked with cooperation. Not only is the experimental evidence clear on this point, but in the Holocaust the apparently selfless behavior on behalf of the *Volk* by the SS provided a model for others to emulate in enhanced cooperation.

Himmler and the SS comprised the quintessential cooperating community – only SS men were shot instantly when captured by the Soviets because the SS prisoners would never reveal any information – that had as its major purpose the extinction of the defecting group that in their view could undermine the new era of German "comradeship."

As the war progressed, the Germans evinced not only an increased anti-Semitism but also a steely resolve to oppose the Allies no matter the cost. The costly punishment of the defector became emblematic of the entire German war effort as World War II came to a close in 1944–45. The whirlwind destruction of the greater part of Hungarian Jewry[107] in but a few months in 1944 even at the cost of using much needed men and transport is explicable in this light. So is the unrelenting destruction of conspirators and their associates after the failed assassination attempt of July 20.

At this time, it is difficult to estimate the extent to which these conclusions apply to leaders of the Committee of Union and Progress (CUP) in the Ottoman Empire or *génocidaires* in Rwanda. Yet the embrace of death by both groups suggest the applicability of the concept of altruistic punishment. Certainly, as in Germany, the search for unity, the development of extremist ideologies ("Turkism" and "Hamitic origin") established the moral framework within which the killings were justified. Clearly too, the Armenians and Tutsi, viewed respectively by the CUP Turks and Hutu extremists as joined in battle against them, were defectors amply deserving of the most severe punishment. Indeed, after the successful nineteenth-century efforts of Armenians to influence

---

[106] Lifton and Markusen 1990, 58.   [107] Braham 2000, 252–53.

West European powers to intervene in Ottoman affairs on their behalf, and the rise of nationalist groups such as the Dashnaks and Hunchakists, the Armenians became prototypical "defectors" in the Turkish view.

The trials of Ittihad leaders after World War I leading to death sentences in absentia,[108] aborted only by the Kemalist resurgence and the death by assassination of Talât, suggest the risk of death undertaken by the CUP leaders in their costly punishment of Armenian "defectors." Similarly, the rapid mass murder of the "alien Hamitic" Tutsi and forced exile of Hutu *génocidaires* in neighboring countries, battles with and death at the hands of the Rwandese Patriotic Front in Congo and ongoing trials of the leading Rwanda murderers also suggest the applicability of altruistic punishment as an explanation. And, in all three cases, widespread societal cooperation in the mass murders was a distinguishing feature.

Finally, does the "altruistic" motive in costly punishment somehow absolve Himmler, his minions, and others of the evil that typically has been associated with their monstrous crimes? Of course not, simply because the intention, however laudable, should have no bearing on judgment of the outcome. Unless perpetrators are genuinely deranged, are psychologically disconnected from their surroundings, or are coerced with deadly force, judgments are to be based on actions, not motivations.[109] However noble the intent, whether it is to rid the world of "pestilential" Jews, satanic "infidels," or some other "offenders" as seen in the eyes of the beholder, the judgment of evil is always warranted by the premeditated murder of innocent and helpless men, women, and children. Without such a firm disjunction between motivation and action, we enter a labyrinth of moral relativism that is truly frightening in its import.

Our focus now shifts from the three cases of genocide to perpetrating states that collaborated with the Germans in murdering their own Jewish citizenry. These countries are Italy, Vichy France, and Romania.

---

[108] Dadrian 1997, 331.
[109] Neiman 2002. For evil as an intrinsic motivation of the Holocaust, see Lang 1999.

9

Perpetrating states

Contraction of socioeconomic space as part of the domain of losses can help us understand not only the onset of genocide in certain instances, but even the extent of collaboration with the initiators as a form of cynical or brute force realpolitik. In the following analysis, states to be examined are those with indigenous governments unfettered by military occupation and having some freedom of policy choice. Perpetrators are states that openly collaborated with the Nazis in victimizing their own Jewish citizenry. Exceptions are states that did not do so and will be examined in chapter 16. I choose these cases because only here can we observe either (1) the indigenous genocidal impulse, (2) willingness to comply with German genocidal policies, or (3) the ability to resist German pressures for Jewish deportation. These instances stand in contrast to cases of direct occupation or absolute dependence on the genocidal state that preordain the policy outcome.

All European states in the Nazi orbit[1] were examined for the extent of their decision-making autonomy in regard to their own citizenry. All countries directly occupied by German forces ultimately dedicated to the slaughter were excluded. These include Czechoslovakia (occupied from March 1939), Poland (September 1939), Norway (April 1940), Belgium, the Netherlands, and Luxembourg (May 1940), Greece and Yugoslavia (April 1941), the Soviet Union (June 1941; partial occupation), Denmark (August 1943), Albania (September 1943), and Hungary (March 1944).

Although Hungary was an ally of Germany with considerable domestic autonomy that even protected Hungarian Jews stranded in Germany during the war in addition to Jewish citizens within Hungary itself, that policy was reversed after the German occupation.[2] Hungary will be examined separately in a later chapter (12). The Danes, with Swedish help, did rescue almost the entire Jewish community of Denmark, but

---

[1] Hilberg 1985, 544; Fein 1979, 40–41; Murray and Millett 2000.   [2] Braham 1981, 255.

not as a consequence of policy choices made by Danish governmental leaders, who had already been removed from office by the German occupying forces.[3]

Successor states such as Slovakia and Croatia explicitly created by the Nazis in their subjugation respectively of Czechoslovakia and Yugoslavia were also excluded. Not only were these states thoroughly dependent on their creator, Nazi Germany, but their fictive independence was emphasized by United States non-recognition, before US entry into the war.[4] In contrast, the United States did recognize Vichy France as a sovereign entity.[5] All genuinely neutral states also were excluded.

These exclusions leave the small set of European German allies, *Italy* and *Romania*, plus the formally neutral but militarily constrained *Vichy France*,[6] which were all allowed substantial leeway in their domestic policies by the Germans in order to maintain their support for the war.

Italy: a genocidal trajectory

Although the entirety of Jewish genocidal victimization in Italy occurred after German occupation, Italy nevertheless deserves comment because its later behavior, just prior to German occupation, is suggestive of the central importance of loss. Because of Italy's status as Germany's principal European great power ally, it was, like Finland, allowed substantial freedom in its domestic policies. Yet there were pressures that were repeatedly placed on the Italian government to release Jews for deportation by the Germans. One of these sources of pressure emanated from the presence of Jews in Italian-administered areas of the former Yugoslavia. Appalled by the deadly brutality of the Croatian fascist Ustaše toward Serbs and Jews, Italian military forces interceded to protect as many as they could from the Ustaše, and then later from the Germans intent on Jewish deportation. A second focus of German pressure was the relatively large concentration of free Jews in Italian-occupied France in the area of Nice.

It has been suggested that this early experience in protecting endangered populations under Italian rule beginning in 1941 led to

---

[3] Goldberger 1987.
[4] *Keesing's Contemporary Archives; Foreign Relations of the United States 1940–1942.*
[5] Burrin 1996, 77.
[6] As exceptions, Bulgaria and Finland will be examined separately in chapter 16.

their continued refusal to allow German deportation of Jews throughout Mussolini's tenure in office prior to German occupation.[7] Perhaps this fact more than any other led to a positive view among scholars of Italy's record during the Holocaust.[8]

This relatively benign situation, however, changed after the experience of territorial loss, first in North Africa and then in Sicily. On May 13, 1943, the Axis forces surrendered in Tunis, leading to a reported loss of morale among Italian troops in Yugoslavia.[9] On July 10, the Allies invaded Sicily, making rapid advances on all fronts. By July 15, Guido Lospinoso, an Italian police officer charged with Jewish affairs in Italian-occupied France, was ordered by his superiors in Rome to deport 1,000–1,200 Jews. According to Susan Zuccotti, "Such a direct and unequivocal order could not have been issued without Mussolini's approval, and Lospinoso would not have been able to evade it. The Jews concerned were saved only by Mussolini's fall a few days later."[10]

Prior to this time, Mussolini had wavered on all German requests for deportation, ultimately declining to deport the Jews. Now, in the midst of experiencing the loss of nearly 10 percent of core Italian territory in Sicily, his position was unequivocal in favor of deportation, an action directly contrary to his earlier behavior. State weakness, signaled by the loss of Sicily and an expected immediate Allied invasion of the Italian peninsula, apparently proved decisive. German military support would be required to salvage his regime and so the Germans had to be propitiated by deporting the foreign Jews.

Given the extent of Italian state weakness, had Mussolini stayed in office it is quite likely that he would have extended the deportation to Italian Jews as well, especially in light of his agreement with Jewish deportation in his later tenure as leader of the rump northern Italian state under German occupation.[11] Among these Italian Jews was the young Primo Levi, a future Nobel laureate, and a suspected suicide many years after his Auschwitz experience.

Vichy France

Shortly after formation of the Vichy regime in August 1940, it repealed the *loi Marchandeau* (Marchandeau law), which had outlawed any attack in the press on a specific group of people on account of race or

---

[7] Carpi 1977, 505; Steinberg 1990, 133.   [8] Steinberg 1990, 132.   [9] Ibid., 138.
[10] Zuccotti 2000, 132.   [11] Ibid., 291–92.

religion and designed to arouse hatred against them.[12] Repeal of this law opened the floodgates to much anti-Semitic writing in the press. In October, a series of laws directed specifically at Jews was enacted. On October 3, the *Statut des juifs* defined who was Jewish according to the state, and then proceeded to exclude Jews from "top positions in the public service, from the officer corps and from the ranks of noncommissioned officers, and from professions that influence public opinion: teaching, the press, radio, film, and theater."[13] As Michael Marrus and Robert Paxton comment, "Without any possible doubt, Vichy had begun its own antisemitic career before the first German text appeared, and without direct German order."[14]

But this tawdry beginning was not to be the end of it. When the deportations to the East began in the summer of 1942, the Vichy police cooperated fully, indeed as the Germans requested. The Germans simply did not have the manpower to carry out the required administrative functions, including those involving Jews, throughout all of France. Vichy was created, in part, to serve these functions, while maintaining political neutrality in the war. According to Heinz Röthke, the SS lieutenant in charge of Jewish affairs within the German police hierarchy in France, "The entire operation in the southern French territory was much more dependent on the French police than in the formerly occupied territory. The German strike force there could only exercise a weak supervision over the operation."[15]

As early as February 1942, before the start of the deportations, the German consul in Vichy understood that "the French government would be happy to get rid of the Jews somehow, without attracting too much attention."[16] Vichy French neutrality was not a mere fictive creation of the Nazi regime. On all matters of internal administration, negotiations were required between the Germans in the occupied zone and the Vichy authorities. Yet, in the matter of the deportations, the Germans could rely on a rival homegrown anti-Semitism to effect the required cooperation. Little if any "arm-twisting" was required.

The extent to which Vichy cooperation was required may be gleaned from the following statistics. Under conditions of full cooperation from Vichy, in the summer and autumn of 1942 when the deportations began, approximately 42,000 Jews were sent to their deaths. Roughly one-third of this number was sent at Vichy's initiative from the unoccupied zone.

[12] Marrus and Paxton 1995, 3. [13] Ibid. [14] Ibid., 7; see also Curtis 2002.
[15] Quoted in Levendel 1999, 236; Marrus and Paxton 1995, 202. [16] Burrin 1996, 156.

In 1943, after forced labor of European youth required, in the end, 750,000 French males in Germany and a consequent diminution of French enthusiasm for cooperation with the Germans, only 22,000 Jews were deported. And in 1944, after the Germans were left more to their own devices, 12,500 were deported.

Alois Brünner, an SS captain with a formidable reputation for efficiency in his earlier successful actions in deporting Jews from Vienna and Salonika, Greece, failed entirely in late 1943 without the support of the French police. After the Italian war effort collapsed in the summer of 1943, Brünner was sent to the Italian zone of occupation in the Côte d'Azur to arrest and deport the Jews that previously had enjoyed the protection of the Italian authorities. Left with only the support of his German staff, only 1,900 Jews of the estimated 25,000 in the region were found and deported.[17] Inescapably, one arrives at the conclusion that (1) there was considerable initial enthusiasm for the deportations on the part of the Vichy government, and (2) the Germans absolutely required the cooperation of that government.

Why should this have been the case? One answer is to be found in an acute contraction of socioeconomic space, much as we saw in the histories of the Ottoman Empire, Germany, and Rwanda prior to their genocidal activities. Three-fifths of France was occupied by the Germans, and the remaining two-fifths was limited as to political maneuverability (required neutrality), size of the armed forces, and availability of resources for the German war effort. This was a major contraction from France's former status as a European great power, one that only twenty-two years before had, with the other victors, dictated the Peace of Versailles to the defeated Germans. Indeed, the preceding outbreak of anti-Semitism in France occurred after the first French contraction upon the defeat of 1871 and the loss of Alsace-Lorraine to the new united imperial Germany. French Jews fled these territories and according to Paul Webster, "There was a flood [in the print media] of what were to become familiar caricatures of hook-nosed, repulsively ugly, rapacious Jews barely able to make themselves understood through thick German accents – images that were copied by Pétain's propaganda services."[18]

As noted earlier regarding the three outright genocidal states, refugees are a significant indicator of socioeconomic contraction and a strong provocation in their own right. Here, in the case of Vichy, they perform

---

[17] Webster 1991, 170–71.   [18] Ibid., 10.

a similar function. Almost immediately after constitution of the Vichy regime, Germany was dumping its unwanted Jews across the demarcation line into the unoccupied zone, even over fierce French objections. Prior to at least mid-1941, it was German policy to encourage emigration of Jews to whatever state would have them. Here was a golden opportunity for this policy to be effected. Only the most intense French protests prevented over 270,000 Jews from being transported into Vichy France. Some trains containing Jews were simply sent back to the occupied zone by the French authorities. On their own, many French Jews fled the occupied zone for what was perceived to be the relative safety of Vichy.

In the interwar period, Jews were prominent in politics, with Léon Blum as premier leading the Popular Front coalition of 1936, and in industry with Henri Citroën establishing a leading car company, and Bloch heading an aviation manufacturer that later, after the war, was to become Dassault, Europe's largest contemporary exporter of combat aircraft. All of the ills plaguing French society during the 1930s – and there were many: the parliamentary disorder, a declining birthrate, and economic decline – would be attributed to the Jewish presence.

Even before the establishment of the Vichy regime, France had experienced large-scale immigration and refugee arrival. Now, with the contraction of socioeconomic space – territorially, economically, and in a radically diminished international stature – foreigners, especially Jews, could be convenient targets. For this reason, the Vichy French insisted on filling the early German deportation requirements with foreign or recently naturalized Jews. Initially, the Germans went along with this French preference but, later, many French-born Jews also went to their deaths with their foreign-born coreligionists. By mid-1942, the Germans had no interest in distinguishing between native or foreign Jew; all were targeted for extinction. Nevertheless, to placate the French, whose cooperation they required, the earliest transports contained few French Jews. Only later, when the internment camps containing the foreign Jews (built by Vichy) had been emptied and deportation quotas still had to be filled, were French Jews routinely included in the transports to the East.

Marrus and Paxton compare Vichy policy toward its Jews with those of other defeated countries – Hungary in 1919 (see chapter 12) and Romania in the loss of one-third of its territory to Hungary and Russia in 1940.[19] During the same year, France lost three-fifths of its territory to

---

[19] Marrus and Paxton 1995, 360–64.

German occupation. In our lexicon here, they could be said to experience socioeconomic contractions. All three had indigenous anti-Jewish legislation and to varying extents cooperated with the Germans in the deportations of Jews. Prior to the implementation of Nazi genocidal policy, nationals of these countries murdered Jews locally in hastily arranged pogroms (especially Romania) or, in the case of France, interned them in camps in which some 2,000 died – the first victims of the Holocaust – killed actually on French soil. In Romania, General Antonescu enacted a myriad of anti-Semitic ordinances shortly after inheriting the shrunken state from his predecessor, King Carol. Later, the viciously anti-Semitic Romanian Iron Guard staged atrocities of such a barbaric nature that members of the SS actually had to intervene to rescue Jews already targeted for extermination by them, but in a "humane" manner.

Even in comparison with the anti-Semitic legislation of Hungary during the interwar period, Vichy France comes off second-best. The definition of Jewishness adopted by the Hungarian government was actually more liberal than that of Vichy, thereby allowing more people to escape the consequences of the anti-Jewish legislation. Nevertheless, all three countries behaved in a very similar manner after experiencing territorial contraction, attempting to save at least some of their native Jews, but instigating anti-Jewish legislation, as well as cooperating in the Final Solution. Vichy France may actually have been the worst of the three, for as Marrus and Paxton tell us:

> When the Germans began their systematic deportation and extermination of Jews in 1942, Vichy's rival antisemitism offered them more substantial help than they received anywhere else in western Europe, and more even than they received from such allies as Hungary and Romania.[20]

Contraction of socioeconomic space helps explain not only the extreme Vichy anti-Semitic response, but also those of Hungary and Romania. Increasing state insecurity can help us understand the intensification of anti-Semitic sentiment as the war proceeded. By early 1944, it was clear that an Allied invasion was imminent. And, instead of diminishing their anti-Semitic activity, it actually increased, as suggested by the theory of state insecurity. According to Marrus and Paxton, "The anxieties of the summer of 1944 did not diminish anti-Jewish feeling among Vichy

[20] Ibid., 369.

leaders but, if anything, sharpened it."[21] Levendel records that "As the situation became tougher for the Germans at the front, there were rumors of Jewish arrests closer to home. Soon they were happening all around us."[22] And Webster suggests that "The closer Germany came to defeat, the more Vichy was prepared to support the Nazi cause, claiming that France was in the front line of the fight against Communism."[23]

The precedent of sending foreign-born Jews to their deaths (including those whose status as naturalized citizens had been nullified by Vichy law) undoubtedly made it easier for some of the French-born to be deported as well. From the start, the Vichy leaders attempted to avoid deporting French Jews "for reasons of public opinion, prestige and sovereignty."[24]

At the same time, foreign-born Jews were deliberately offered up to the Germans, including many to be rounded up in the unoccupied zone by the French police and herded into the occupied zone as substitutes. This was the basis of the first massive roundup of Jews in La Grande Rafle of July 16 and 17, 1942, in which approximately 9,000 Jews were kept in the Vélodrome d'Hiver, an indoor bicycle stadium, in vile conditions for five days prior to deportation. Over 4,000 children were included, the vast majority of whom never returned from Auschwitz.[25] Initially the Germans did not request that children under the age of sixteen be included, but the Vichy officials, especially Pierre Laval, did not want the responsibility of those soon-to-be orphans, and so offered actually more than were requested by the Germans. It was Laval, the French prime minister, who directly proposed that children younger than sixteen years old be included in the deportation.[26] Most of the children were born in France and therefore were French citizens. In the end, many French Jews, including some of the most prominent, and even supposed "friends" of Pétain, were sent to their deaths in Auschwitz.

Although Laval was prominent in the anti-Jewish activities of the Vichy regime and was executed after the war for his efforts, it was Maréchal Philippe Pétain, hero of Verdun in World War I and invested with the legal authority of the Vichy government, who made state policy. And here we confront the same phenomenon that saw a deep complicity of the German military in the Armenian genocide, as well as the central role of the French military in the Dreyfus affair around the turn of the twentieth

[21] Ibid., 339.   [22] Levendel 1999, 89.   [23] Webster 1991, 71.
[24] Burrin 1996, 157.   [25] Webster 1991, 115.   [26] Ibid., 113.

century (a Jewish officer, Alfred Dreyfus, was falsely accused of treason, and imprisoned until ultimately exonerated): a far greater susceptibility of the military to the dictates of realpolitik. After all, military officers are responsible for the physical protection of the state and, to this extent, Pétain could assert in his farewell address at the end of the war in France, "While it is true that de Gaulle has bravely raised France's sword, history will not forget that I patiently held the French people's shield." This "shield" of a brute force realpolitik could be raised to protect the insecure and dependent Vichy French state but, as in the case of the German military in Turkey and perversely misguided French officers at the turn of the twentieth century, helpless minorities were chosen to be sacrificed for this purpose. Jews, instead of French Christians, were to be sacrificed on the altar of Nazi preferences, and mostly foreign-born Jews in place of French Jews. The "shield" of at least a partial genocide was intended to protect Vichy from potentially harsh German demands to be made on the larger French Christian population.

That many of Pétain's closest prewar associates were Jewish made no difference to their fate. Jacques Heilbronner, head of the Jewish Consistory, had been a close friend of Pétain. As an officer on the French General Staff, he had strongly supported Pétain's elevation to lead the French army. In a letter of appeal, Heilbronner affirmed that the Maréchal "always shown me so much kindness and confident affection."[27] In 1943, Heilbronner and his family were gassed in Auschwitz.

Romania

Romania presents a mirror image of Hungary and in doing so further confirms the importance of truncation as a key stimulant to domestic anti-Semitism leading ultimately to the perpetration of mass murder. While Hungary was truncated after World War I and for the first time since 1867 promulgated anti-Semitic legislation, Romania was expanded at that time and for the first time ceased its earlier anti-Jewish campaigns. Later, just prior to its entry into the war, however, when it too experienced territorial and population losses, Romania passed its first anti-Semitic legislation of the interwar period.

After World War I and the dismemberment of Austria-Hungary (complete) and imperial Russia (partial), Romania was one of the states that gained most from this process of changing borders. As of 1920, the territory

---

[27] Quoted ibid., 101.

of Romania doubled, as it absorbed Transylvania, Bessarabia, Bukovina, and Cişana; in the process, Romania was transformed from a relatively homogenous state to one with 28 percent of its population composed of non-Romanian minorities. They included Magyar, German, Jewish, Ukrainian, Bulgarian, and Turko-Tatar minorities.[28] The addition of these territories to Romania served to accentuate the prominence and visibility of Jews. As in Hungary, neither the feudal aristocracy nor the peasantry was prepared to engage in economic development. This was left to the Jews as an entrepreneurial middle class. Thus,

> By the middle of the interwar era, Jews controlled the bulk of the private capital in the export, transportation, insurance, textile, leather, electrotechnical, chemical, housing, printing, and publishing industries. Though their access to the universities was restricted by statutory limitations and extralegal violence, they were also strongly represented in the legal, medical, dental, journalistic, and banking professions. Though only 4.2 percent of the total population, they constituted 30.1, 27, and 23.6 percent, respectively, of the town populations of Bukovina, Bessarabia and Moldavia, and 14.3 percent of the entire country's urban population. In such cities as Chişinău (Kishinev) and Cernăuşti ... where the Jews accounted for 52.6 and 44.9 percent of the population, most store signs were in Hebrew letters.[29]

Even in Regat (historic) Romania, the Jewish population of Iaşi, the largest city in Moldavia, was 42 percent.[30] As in Hungary, the Jews were disproportionately visible economically and socially. "In the textile industry 80 percent of the engineers were Jews, in the Army Medical Corps 1,960 doctors were Jewish, 460 belonged to other minority groups, and only 1,400 were Romanian; 70 percent of journalists were Jews; and in the universities, where, in 1925, 27 percent of the student body had been of foreign origin, the proportion in 1934 had risen to 43 percent."[31]

The sense of foreign, especially Jewish, domination was palpable. According to a poet of the Iron Guard, the premier Romanian fascist organization,

> You've come with foreign laws
> To steal my stock, my song, my poverty;
> Out of my sweat you've built your property,
> And taken from our children for your whores.[32]

---

[28] Jelavich 1983, 122–24.   [29] Ibid., 160.   [30] Boia 2001, 173.
[31] Weber 1965, 529.   [32] Quoted ibid.

The "foreign laws" mentioned by the poet most likely were elements of the 1923 constitution promulgated at the behest of Allied Powers, granting Jews citizenship rights equal to those of other Romanians.[33]

The boundaries of this expanded state were guaranteed by the Little Entente: Czechoslovakia, Romania, and Yugoslavia in association with France as the great power protector of them all. Hungary (as part of Austria-Hungary) and Bulgaria as Central Power allies during World War I were the targets of this alliance, lest they adopt revanchist policies to regain their lost territories.

According to Radu Ioanid, "The period between 1923 and 1938 represented a golden age of human rights in Romania."[34] But the rise of anti-Semitic movements such as the Christian National Defense League and the Iron Guard clouded the horizons. Nevertheless, no anti-Semitic legislation was proposed until the actual takeover of Romanian territory, first by the Soviet Union (Bessarabia and northern Bukovina, June 1940), then by Hungary (northern Transylvania, August 1940), and finally by Bulgaria (southern Dobruja, September 1940).[35] Just as Hungary earlier was forced by the victorious Allies to cede territory at the Trianon Palace in 1920, in 1940 Romania was forced to cede territory by the allied Soviet and Nazi governments, united now in their eastern policies by the Soviet–Nazi pact of June 1939. When the Romanians consulted the Germans upon the receipt of Soviet territorial demands, they were advised to acquiesce.[36] Germany also was instrumental in effecting the losses to Hungary and Bulgaria.

These cessions "caused enormous public indignation, especially the surrender of the Transylvanian lands."[37] As a contemporary Romanian historian, Iosif Drăgan, put it without embellishment, "With the support of the Soviet army, Party activists were brought in, under new, Romanized names, people like Ana Rabinovici-Pauker, Leonte Răutu (Rotmann), Mihail Roller, Silviu Brucan, Teoharia Georgescu, Lászlo Lukács (Vasile Luca) and the Bulgarian Borilă, etc. [...] The leadership of the Party was monopolized by these allogenic elements."[38]

Now the Romanian truncation to the boundaries of the old kingdom (Regat) existing prior to World War I would yield anti-Semitic legislation. The law of August 8, 1940, defined Jews racially in even more draconian fashion then did the Nazis. Another law forbade marriage

---

[33] Nagy-Talavera 2001, 357.   [34] Ioanid 2000, 12.   [35] Jelavich 1983, 226.
[36] Ibid., 225.   [37] Ibid., 226.   [38] Quoted in Boia 2001, 172.

between Jews and gentiles while directly citing the 1935 Nuremberg laws as precedent.[39] Further legislation restricted Jewish access to education and entry into both the medical and military professions. Economic legislation severely limited Jewish business activity and further restricted Jewish life circumstances. Jewish rural property was nationalized and Jewish civil servants were purged.

Prior to the invasion of the Soviet Union, the worst period for Romanian Jewry was that just before and during the Iron Guard government of September 6, 1940–January 21, 1941. It came to power as the result of the foreign policy reverses suffered by King Carol II, especially the loss of significant territories, and his subsequent forced resignation. Even before the accession of the Iron Guard, as the Romanians were withdrawing from territories ceded to its neighboring acquisitors, massacres of Jews occurred. Bessarabia and northern Bukovina, ceded to the Soviet Union, were scenes of some of the worst atrocities.

The massacres were fueled by the rumor and, in some cases, the actuality of Jewish positive responses to the Soviet entry. After twenty-two years of anti-Semitic and corrupt rule by the Romanian authorities, many of the Jews in Bessarabia and northern Bukovina welcomed the Soviets as liberators.[40] Although most Jews would come to see the advent of Stalinism as more of a curse than a blessing,[41] nevertheless the atrocities against Jews by Romanian soldiers and peasants would continue during the summer of 1940. Between June 1940 and May 1941, more than 600 Jews were killed in Romania.[42] The massacres would later be vastly expanded during the return of the Romanians a year later at the start of the German march to the East in June.

The uniquely Romanian nativist fascist Iron Guard ideology operating since the end of the 1920s had much to do with setting the stage for these massacres. Once the Guard achieved control, sporadic murderous rampages against Jews continued until the Guard was ousted from power in January 1941. But the die had been cast. When the Romanians joined the Germans in Operation Barbarossa after June 22, 1941, depredations against the Jews began on a massive scale.

Iaşi was the location of the first large-scale massacre of the Romanian Holocaust. In addition to its anti-Semitic traditions of over a century, because of its proximity to the Soviet frontier, "it became the focus of many of the anti-Semitic measures that accompanied plans to join

---

[39] Ioanid 2000, 20–22.   [40] Nagy-Talavera 2001, 461–62.
[41] Ioanid 2000, 39.   [42] Ibid., 61.

Germany's invasion of the USSR."[43] The terms "Jew" and "Communist"
were virtually interchangeable, as in the order by Ion Antonescu, the
Romanian head of state, to compile lists of "all Jews, Communist agents,
or sympathizers in each region."[44] Worse was Order No. 4147, issued at
about the same time, which demanded the expulsion of all Jews between
the ages of eighteen and sixty from northeastern Moldavia (the Iaşi
region) in expectation of fighting there. The presence of large numbers
of Jews in the region was anathema to both the German and Romanian
officials. Fully half of Iaşi's population of 100,000 was Jewish. In cooperation with the German Gestapo and the SD (the intelligence arm of the
SS), the Romanian Secretariat of the Secret Intelligence Service (SSI)
prepared the expulsions. At the same time, former Iron Guardists (also
called legionaries because of the virtually equivalent organizational
name of Legion of the Archangel St. Michael) were informed of the
impending expulsions and likelihood of a pogrom.

A raid against Iaşi by the Soviet air force provided the spark for the
pogrom. Damage was minor but rumors spread that the entire Jewish
population of Iaşi was in league with the Red Army. Further rumors of
Iaşi natives flying Soviet aircraft fanned the flames still further. On
June 20th, four days after the beginning of Operation Barbarossa, the
pogrom began in earnest. It lasted over a week, until June 29. Although it
is difficult to gain accurate estimates of the number of Jews killed, the
minimum is probably about 900, with a more forthright testimony from
a witness estimating the number of dead at 3,000–4,000.[45]

But worse was yet to come. Several thousand Jews had been interned
in police stations and special camps as "dangers" to Romanian security.
At the end of June, these Jews were loaded onto death trains to be
transported out of the region. The cars were decorated with signs stating
that inside were "Communist Jews" or "killers of German and
Romanian soldiers." Several destinations were chosen and ultimately
few survived the densely packed, poorly ventilated cars. No food or
water was allowed. Jews, who frantically jumped from train cars to
drink at a river crossing were shot or forcibly drowned. Those who
survived were forced to hand over their valuables in a pattern of vor-
acious looting that would be characteristic of the entire Holocaust, and
of other genocides as well. Of 2,530 Jews who were transported in the
first train, some 1,400 died. Of 1,902 Jews who boarded the second train,
1,194 died.

---

[43] Ibid., 63.   [44] Ibid., 64.   [45] Ibid., 77.

Iași was only the first of many massacres of Jews that were to take place in nearby Bessarabia and Bukovina, territories that had been transferred to Soviet control in 1940, but were now under German and Romanian authority. Mihai Antonescu, a relative of Ion Antonescu and deputy premier, supported the forced "migration" of Jews from Bessarabia and Bukovina. This attitude of "blame" for the loss of these territories in 1940 was to characterize much of Romanian Jewish policy. Frequent massacres occurred immediately after the German invasion. During July alone, Raul Hilberg estimates that more than 10,000 Jews were murdered by the Romanian and German military, as well as the native Ukrainian peasantry.[46] These massacres were to be followed by mass deportations to work camps in Ukraine and ultimately death camps in Poland. At first, the Germans resisted the massive relocation of Jews from northern Bessarabia into German military-controlled districts. The number of Jews in each of these attempted transports was in the tens of thousands. The Germans conjured up the specter of more than a half million Jews to be added to the many indigenous Ukrainian Jews now being murdered by *Einsatzgruppe D* with only 600 men. Consequently, the German legation informed Mihai Antonescu that the Jews were to be eliminated in "a slow and systematic manner."[47]

Jews were now interned in transit camps throughout Bessarabia. In October, deportations to Ukraine began. During the first months of the war, it is estimated that at least 65,000 Jews from Bessarabia and Bukovina were killed in mass murders, in the transit camps and during deportation.[48] If we add the number of Jews deported who died in southwestern Ukraine (called Transnistria by the Romanians), the number reaches approximately 130,000. If we add to this the number of native Ukrainian Jews in Odessa and elsewhere killed by the Romanian and German authorities, the number reaches approximately 250,000 murdered under Romanian jurisdiction. According to Raul Hilberg, "no country, besides Germany, was involved in massacres of Jews on such a scale."[49]

This chapter completes the direct empirical examination of the theory detailed in chapter 5. The inquiry included Germany, Austria, the Ottoman Empire, and Rwanda among the genocidal states. Italy, Vichy France, and Romania, allies of Germany during World War II, were included among the perpetrating states collaborating in the

---

[46] Hilberg 1985, 771. [47] Quoted in Ioanid 2000, 121.
[48] Ibid., 172–73. [49] Hilberg 1985, 759.

Holocaust. Later, in chapter 16, the noncollaborating behavior of Bulgaria and Finland, also allies of Germany, will provide a stark contrast. Interestingly, when the single politicide, Cambodia, is examined in chapter 15, genocide of the Vietnamese within the overall politicide will follow the contours suggested in the theoretical framework put forward here, and confirmed in the genocidal and perpetrating state behavior. We turn now to an assessment of victim vulnerability, identifying factors that increase the magnitude of the killing, once begun.

PART IV

Victim vulnerability: explaining magnitude
and manner of dying

10

Raison d'état, raison d'église

The etiologies of the onset and magnitude of genocide are not necessarily distinct processes. Variables like realpolitik and the contraction of socioeconomic space associated with loss can influence both facets of genocide. But in this part of the book, emphasizing the magnitude of the killing, we are not dealing with temporally based processes, as in the transformation of massacre to genocide detailed in figure 5.1. The onset of genocide is not a dichotomous variable; it has strong elements of continuous build-up over time until the decision to commit genocide is reached. The magnitude of the killing, on the other hand, can be influenced simultaneously by several factors, each of them acting for the most part independently of others.

To understand the magnitude of the killing, once again we begin with variables derived from the international context, namely realpolitik in two forms, cynical and brute force. Here, decisions by political elites in countries external to the killing sites can be critical in explaining magnitude. At the same time, as in altruistic punishment within the German military and society, we will turn to the societal context to understand behavior within besieged Jewish communities. Later chapters in this part will focus not only on altruistic punishment within East European ghettos, but also on inequality yielded by the contraction process and consequent failures of mutual identification that inflated the magnitude of the killing. Altruistic punishment and failures of mutual identification can also have an impact on the *manner* of dying, a factor of immense importance to those who looked forward to the future status of Jewish communities after the war.

Accordingly, the first two chapters in this part extend the net of participants beyond the genocidal and perpetrating states. Policies of Germany during World War I along with other European great powers are explored in regard to the Armenian genocide, to be followed by policies of the Vatican in relation to the Nazis prior to and during World War I, and of France in its association with the Rwandan state in 1994. Failures of the United Nations to thwart or at least limit the magnitude of the killing in Rwanda also are highlighted. The succeeding chapter examines immigration policies of the United States, Great Britain, and other Western democracies as the increasingly virulent anti-Semitic policies of the Nazis unfolded.

In examining the consequences of cynical realpolitik, I begin with the Armenians during World War I, because here, in some contrast to the Holocaust, both the onset and magnitude of the killing were influenced by Germany as the external permitting agent. This case also is exemplary in demonstrating the murderous impact of strong external support, or at least a permissive context for genocidal behavior.

The Armenians

Consider the genocide of Armenians by the Ottomans during World War I and immediately thereafter. There are essentially two phases of cynical realpolitik affecting the Armenian genocide. The first consists of the policies surrounding great powers prior to and during the massacre of Armenians in 1894–96. This precursor of the later genocide led to the deaths of approximately 200,000 Armenians.

Russia was easily the most important early great power referent for the Ottoman rulers, as they had experienced a long series of defeats at Russian hands. Beginning with the Peace of Kuchuk Kainardji in 1774, the Ottomans lost to the Russians not only territories in the Caucasus in which the Turks had long been dominant, but even control of Christian (principally Orthodox) communal life within the empire. The nineteenth century witnessed a virtually unmitigated series of disasters for the Ottomans.[1] Lost wars with Russia in 1829 and again in 1878 led to further shrinkage of the empire; this pattern of losses would continue into the early twentieth century.

The images of Constantinople and the Dardanelles straits under eventual Russian rule still shimmered in their eyes. As the Russians were Orthodox Christians, one would expect a continuation of the traditional Russian policy of protecting Armenian (Orthodox) communities in the Ottoman Empire. Instead, a role reversal occurred in which "The Armenian policy of Tsarist Russia gradually stiffened, assuming a harsh and uncompromising stance in the last two decades of the 19th century." Indeed, Vahakn Dadrian calls this reversal "the crux of the Armenian disaster."[2] What were the bases of Russian realpolitik at this time?

---

[1] S. Shaw and Shaw 1977.   [2] Dadrian 1997, 70.

Russian policies were deeply influenced by what they viewed as the disappointments of the Balkans. After decades of diplomatic intervention on behalf of Christian nationalities in the Balkans, the Russians felt that they came up empty-handed. Not only were these newly independent countries not firmly allied with tsarist Russia, but in some instances they actually thwarted its interests. Russia had come up against the hard rock of late nineteenth-century European nationalism, particularly strong in Bulgaria, which would not in any way be subservient to Russian interests.

Armenian groups at the time were active in seeking autonomy along lines similar to those originally granted to Bulgaria. But according to Nikolaus Giers, Russian foreign minister in the 1882–95 period, "Russia has no reason at all to desire the formation of a second Bulgaria. The emergence of an autonomous Armenian principality would then entail the danger for Russia that the Russian Armenians will aspire to become part of it."[3]

Russian policy was increasingly centered on the preservation of Ottoman boundaries, especially in Anatolia, where the vast majority of Armenians resided. The tsarist empire was subject to the same sorts of nationalist pressures as the Ottoman. Any disintegration of the latter into independent states clearly would affect the former. Tsarist Russia, the seat of European autocratic reaction, would in no way countenance devolution of its authority, and so, without enthusiasm, but with a firm hand, the Ottomans were supported in their increasingly anti-Armenian policies. Even during the massacres, the Russian foreign minister, Prince Alexis Lobanof-Rostowski declared his firm opposition to the formation of "another Bulgaria" in eastern Anatolia, site of the greatest Armenian population density. A contemporary Turkish historian suggested that "Abdul Hamit was able to push forth his Armenian policy thanks to the underhanded [el altindan] support of the Tsar."[4] Later, in the years immediately preceding World War I, partly as a consequence of the massacres and the continued influx of Muslims into the Ottoman Empire, the Russians reversed themselves, and once again sought to assume a protective role vis-à-vis the Armenians.[5]

[3] Quoted ibid., 72.
[4] Quoted ibid., 74. Later Russian policy supporting the status quo in the Ottoman Empire is outlined in Bodger 1984.
[5] Ibid., 96.

Germany clearly is the most important great power influencing Ottoman policy during the later genocide, for Germany at the turn of the century was emerging as the Ottomans' most important ally. Already during the period of the massacres, the outlines of German policy concerning the Armenians were decisively formed. In November 1898, a policy brief was put forward by the German foreign ministry that became the basis not only for German official reaction to the massacres, but also for the later genocide. Essentially, it stated that the Armenians were crafty and seditious and had grievously provoked the Ottoman authorities. Further, Germany had little if any reason to intervene on behalf of the Armenians, especially given the business interests of many German firms in the Ottoman Empire, which might be endangered by German intervention. Very early in the day, cynical realpolitik had become the basis of German policy on the Armenian Question. Only two years after the end of the 1896 massacres, with great pomp and circumstance, Wilhelm II visited Turkey, was greeted lavishly by Sultan Abdulhamit II, and the upward trajectory of Turko-German collaboration was firmly established.[6]

Yet this open expression of support by the kaiser came after the massacres had occurred. How could the Ottomans believe that they could massacre 200,000 people, often in the most brutal fashion, without repercussions from interested great powers such as Great Britain and France? The two powers had pressed for Ottoman action on reforms of the Armenian condition, incorporated in the Treaty of Paris of 1856, and reiterated frequently thereafter.[7] Indeed, the British and French did protest, and the British contemplated sending their fleet into the Aegean sea and possibly even through the Dardanelles straits. But, in the end, no military intervention occurred.

The answer to the question of Ottoman impunity is to be found in the emerging German presence in Turkey *prior* to the massacres. Militarily, between 1885 and 1888, huge Krupp cannon were put into place guarding the Dardanelles straits and the Çatalca defense line north of Constantinople. Upon request, Helmuth von Moltke, the chief of the German General Staff, sent some of his best officers to reform the army, including General von der Goltz of later fame as commander of the Ottoman forces in Arabia during World War I.[8] In 1888, the traditional predominance of Britain and France in the Ottoman economy was

---

[6] See Dadrian 1997, 93–97, and Trumpener 1984.
[7] See M. Anderson 1966, 204 and 253–59.   [8] S. Shaw and Shaw 1977, 245.

challenged by the Deutsche Bank's participation in the construction and ultimate operation of what was to become the Berlin–Baghdad railway.[9] Clearly, Germany, whose power was so vividly demonstrated militarily in the humiliating defeat of France in 1871, diplomatically in the triumph of Otto von Bismarck as the "honest broker" at the Congress of Berlin in 1878, and economically in the extraordinarily rapid expansion of the German economy toward the century's end, was to be relied upon in place of the Western powers. That the Germans asked few if any questions about the ghastly treatment of Christian minorities such as the Armenians was a clear bonus.

The Ottoman Empire was now heavily dependent on its only close ally, Germany; the Ottoman leadership could not ignore the potential reaction of their sole military ally commanding their troops and supplying their arms. As early as September 1913 when negotiations were again ongoing for Armenian reforms, the German ambassador to the Porte, Hans Wangenheim, indicated that Germany would agree to the terms of the proposed reform agreement only if the Ottoman Empire itself agreed.[10]

During the 1909–13 period, Enver Paşa, later war minister during World War I, twice served as a military attaché in Berlin. Kaiser Wilhelm II made particular efforts to cultivate a special relationship with him. During his tenure as war minister, Enver Paşa essentially became a co-conspirator with Talât Bey, a leader of the Young Turks, and other governmental figures. Indeed, the genocide could not have been carried out without the participation, even leadership, of the War Ministry. Deeply entangled with the Young Turk leadership, especially with the War Ministry, was the German Military Mission, which at the height of wartime operations had 700–800 officers and 12,000 troops. Among its officers were to be found a Prussian field marshal, Count von der Goltz, two generals who later became marshals, Liman von Sanders and Erich von Falkenhayn, and three admirals, Usedom, Souchon, and Martens.[11]

From the start, the Germans seemed to have encouraged the formation of an ethnically pure Turkish Anatolia. Von der Goltz, in particular, argued in the immediate aftermath of the 1894–96 massacres that Turkey's future lay not in the European portion of the empire, but in the Asiatic Turkish–Arabian portion. Islam would be the cement that unified this Anatolian–Arabian empire; of course, remaining Christians like the Armenians would have little place in such a reconfigured state.[12]

---

[9] Ibid., 227.   [10] Dadrian 1997, 249.   [11] Ibid., 251. See Strachan 2001a, 644–93.
[12] See Karpat 2001, esp. 321–52.

Dadrian concludes that "The ideological rudiments of the Turkish scheme to divest Turkey of its indigenous Armenian population in this respect bear a German imprint."[13] At the very least, according to Paul Rohrbach, an advocate of German imperial expansion in the Middle East, Armenians could be relocated from their ancient homeland in eastern Anatolia to areas along the new Baghdad railway system. Here is the core of the later forced evacuation of Armenians from Anatolia to Mesopotamia, where so many were either shot to death en route, or died of thirst and starvation in the Mesopotamian desert.[14]

Such ideas did not emerge *sui generis* in the German mind. A prior German colonial experience may have been a "successful" prototype for Rohrbach's suggestion; he had been head of the South-West African Settlement Commission. In his *German World Politics*, published in 1912, Rohrbach advocated the extermination or expulsion of native inhabitants to make way for the white race.[15] It was an easy matter to alter the model slightly to fit Turkish requirements.

In German South-West Africa, genocidal behavior had already occurred, as we saw in chapter 2. Thus, we see an unbroken chain of colonial military policy in South-West Africa affecting the Armenian genocide not only in annihilationist intent, but also in actual method of implementation – death from thirst and starvation in the desert. This method was even extended later into the Holocaust in areas where practical (not many), as we shall see in the following section.

Were German officers actually involved in the planning and implementation of the deportations? Documentary evidence exists in two forms, both indicating extreme complicity. The first was unearthed by the British high commissioner's office; in it, Bronsart von Schellendorf, chief of staff at the Ottoman High Command, ordered deportation of the Armenians with special attention to the Armenian labor battalions, to prevent them from interfering with the remaining deportations. Further, General Bronsart instructed Count von Schulenburg, newly installed consul at Erzerum, not to intercede on behalf of the Armenians, as was done by his predecessor in that position. Bronsart's order referred to "'the Armenian people' (*Ermeni ahalinin*), whose deportation has been 'determined upon' (*mukkarrerdir*), [and had] the additional specific purpose, namely targeting 'the Armenians in the

---

[13] Dadrian 1997, 254.   [14] Ibid.   [15] Jonassohn and Björnson 1998, 69.

labor battalions' who, for security reasons, were to be subjected to 'severe' treatment."[16]

The second document, signed by Lieutenant Colonel Böttrich, chief of the Ottoman General Staff's railway department, and dated October 17, 1915, "stated that the deportation of the railway employees was an integral part of the general deportation policy of the Ottoman government. No further reason for the order was given. All the Armenian employees, with no exemption for those living in Constantinople, were to be deported."[17]

Henry Morgenthau, American ambassador to the Ottoman Empire, had many conversations with German officers who either concurred with the deportation and extermination of the Armenians, or expressed a studied lack of concern. The German naval attaché, Hans Humann, a very close friend of Enver Paşa, confided, "I have lived in Turkey the larger part of my life, and I know the Armenians. I also know that both Armenians and Turks cannot live together in this country. One of these races has got to go. And I don't blame the Turks for what they are doing to the Armenians. I think that they are entirely justified. The weaker nation must succumb."[18] Also typical of attitudes of German officers is that of Rear Admiral Wilhelm Souchon. He stated in August 1915: "It will be salvation for Turkey when it has done away with the last Armenian; it will be rid then of subversive bloodsuckers."[19]

Bronsart, signatory of one of the two documents implicating German officers in the genocide, quite explicitly compares Armenians with Jews, and, specifically, Polish Jews, foreshadowing widespread attitudes in Germany prior to and during the Holocaust. "Namely, the Armenian is just like the Jew, a parasite outside the confines of his homeland, sucking off the marrow of the people of the host country. Year after year they abandon their native land – just like the Polish Jews who migrate to Germany – to engage in usurious activities. Hence the hatred which, in a medieval form, has unleashed itself against them as an unpleasant people, entailing their murder."[20]

Yet, one must be careful to pinpoint the particular Germans who were most complicit in the genocide, and these turn out to be military officers. German civilians, especially those involved in building the Berlin–Baghdad railway were, for understandable reasons, opposed to

---

[16] Quoted in Dadrian 1997, 257.   [17] Quoted in Kaiser 1999, 82.
[18] Quoted in Morgenthau 1918, 375.   [19] Quoted in Dinkel 1991, 116.
[20] Quoted in Dadrian 1997, 259.

the deportations.[21] Approximately 880 skilled Armenians were employed by the railway company and an additional large number of Armenian workers were to be found on construction sites in the Taurus and Amanus mountains. A delegate of the Deutsche Bank, Franz J. Günther, headed the railway office, and his considerable efforts were critical in at least delaying deportation of the railway workers, though not preventing their ultimate annihilation. Günther saw quite clearly that these workers were essential to the railway's completion, hence to the recouping of and profit on the Deutsche Bank's investment. He also was motivated by humanitarian concerns. Railway stations had become detention camps all along the railway lines. Some of the camps were enormous by standards of the day. At the end of October 1915, some 40,000 Armenians were found in Katna; soon they would be transported to Ras-ul-Ain where many thousands would die from exhaustion, epidemic diseases, and the brutality of the Ottoman forces.

Because of the centrality of the Baghdad railway in this deportation process, civilians like Günther could not help being intimately aware of the brutalities and ultimate genocide then taking place. That the railway staff, many of them Armenian, were collecting evidence on the deportations also likely increased their vulnerability.[22] In addition to Günther, Engineer Winkler, responsible for railway construction in the province of Adana, site of extensive deportations, also tried to protect his workers, in vain. He was told that they would be replaced by Muslims, whatever their qualifications. Some German consuls reported the ongoing deportations, asking their government to intercede. The German government refused, avoided any interference in Ottoman affairs, and asked that reports be prepared to show how the Armenians were seditious, hence justifying the Ottoman severity. The German press was instructed to publish denials of the rumored atrocities.[23]

How do we interpret this disjunction between civilian and military responses, including the military-dominated government in Berlin?

[21] Trumpener 1968 records the activities on behalf of the Armenians of many German political figures as well as private citizens. For a history of German involvement in the building of the Berlin–Baghdad railway, see McMurray 2001.

[22] Kaiser 1999, 77.

[23] Ibid., 68. For some of the Turkish military orders expelling the Armenians from Anatolia, see Gürün 1985, 204–10. For an entirely different interpretation of these military orders and one consistent with Turkish genocidal intent, see Dadrian 1999, 123–31.

Confronted with an unexpectedly long war on three fronts (Western, Eastern, and Southern), the demands of cynical realpolitik *in extremis* impressed themselves far more on the military planners than on their civilian counterparts. Men like Günther and Winkler were still concerned with the quintessentially peacetime motives of construction and profit maximization. In such an instrumental atmosphere, humanitarian considerations could be allowed to emerge. Military planners, however, were exposed to an entirely different decision calculus. The goal of the officer in wartime is not the construction of public works or other such utilitarian enterprises. Instead, the purpose is the destruction of enemy forces by whatever means necessary, either in their surrender or annihilation on the battlefield.[24] In extreme cases, a mostly civilian population can be destroyed, as in Melos in the Peloponnesian War, the Herero in South-West Africa, or the Armenians during World War I.

Certainly the hierarchical feudal traditions of the Prussian officer corps dominating the German army had much to do with its willingness to support mass deportations of civilian populations. Racism was endemic within that corps; Jews were forbidden to be officers in the Prussian army. Slavs and native Balts were looked down upon as decidedly inferior beings. Indeed, the earlier eastward expansion of the Germans resulted in the conquest and ultimate disappearance of the native Baltic Prussians and Livonians. A combination of genocide and forced assimilation served as a harbinger of the modern Prussian state. To be sure, later there was strong opposition among the Prussian officers to Hitler's early leadership, but this was more a hierarchical nativist reaction to the "Austrian corporal" than a disavowal of his rabid anti-Semitism.

In the Armenian case, both the onset and magnitude of genocide were facilitated by the Germans. It is likely that the precursors of the World War I genocides, the 1894–96 massacres followed by the smaller but not insignificant 1909 Adana massacre (approximately 25,000 dead),[25] enabled the later onset of the 1915–16 genocide. Neither of the two earlier discrete episodes was halted by any of the European powers, although they had earlier committed themselves to Armenian protection. Thus, in the context of war and the strong support of Germany, the

---

[24] The relationship between total war and the Armenian genocide is treated in Reid 1992. The more general relationship between genocide and total war is examined in Markusen 1987 and in M. Shaw 2003.

[25] Dadrian 1997, 182–83.

onset of genocide in 1915–16 could proceed initially at a high level of magnitude against Armenian males, to be followed quickly by the deportation of entire villages and communities.

The Holocaust

We find the German permission of genocide in 1915–16 rooted in a cynical realpolitik stemming from the increasing domination of the military within German policy-making circles. But which agency, if any, played a similar role in establishing a permissive context for the Holocaust in 1941–45? Might not the virulence of Nazi ideology have been sufficient to establish such an "eliminationist" climate as claimed by Goldhagen? Certainly Nazi ideology was important, if not crucial, in understanding the mass murder of Jews during that period. Yet I claim that its existence was not sufficient for understanding the onset of that genocide. An external permissive element was necessary, also rooted in a cynical realpolitik. I refer here to Vatican policies beginning in the early 1930s and ending shortly after the Allied victory in World War II. These policies center on the person of Eugenio Pacelli.

There were four elements to the realpolitik of Eugenio Pacelli, papal nuncio in Munich between 1917 and 1930, cardinal secretary of state between 1930 and 1939, and Pope Pius XII thereafter until his death in 1958. These elements are: (1) a virulent anti-communism that demanded the subordination even of national Catholic interests for purposes of defeating the larger threat to the Church of Soviet-inspired communism, (2) expansion of Catholic belief especially among Eastern Orthodox "schismatics," (3) expansion of the Holy See's international political influence, and (4) physical preservation of the Vatican as the institutional seat of Roman Catholicism. Each of these elements would be heavily influenced by three stages in Pacelli's international career. In the first of them, he cultivated an extreme hatred and fear of communism that would deeply influence his political worldview. In Munich, in 1919, he witnessed firsthand the abortive Communist coup that, had it succeeded, would have ushered in a period of extreme difficulty for the Roman Catholic Church. That many of the revolutionaries were Jews would establish a strong connection in Pacelli's mind between Jews and communism that would bode ill for his later policies during the Holocaust. Indeed, in a typewritten letter signed by Pacelli describing the meeting between representatives of the nunciature and the revolutionaries, he used anti-Semitic stereotypes to describe the

Russian-Jewish leader as "Pale, dirty, . . . vulgar, repulsive, with a face that is both intelligent and sly."[26]

As cardinal secretary of state, Pacelli had the opportunity to formulate Vatican foreign policy. In that position he was decisive in silencing the German Catholic Center Party that could have provided the only coherent opposition to the Nazi Party. Hitler and the Nazis were seen by Pacelli to be the only effective bulwark against the western expansion of communism from its Soviet base. As the price for Hitler's concordat with the Catholic Church, he demanded the cessation of *all* political activity by the Church. Hitler understood that only the Catholic Center Party in the Reichstag had the potential support of roughly 27 million German Catholics. Between 1919 and 1933, five Catholic Center Party members served as chancellors in ten ruling cabinets of the Weimar Republic. The Center Party typically was second only to the Social Democrats in electoral popularity. Shortly after the July 1932 elections, before Hitler assumed power and well before the concordat, the German Catholic hierarchy denounced the Nazis once again. In a bishops' conference in August, the minutes stated that "All diocesan authorities have banned membership in this party." The official program of the Nazis was said to contain "false doctrine" and was "hostile to the faith."[27] Only by undermining the capacity of the Center Party to politically mobilize this anti-Nazi sentiment could Hitler ensure success of his totalitarian program.

Left to its own devices, the Center Party would have remained committed to a pluralist democracy, as it had pledged at the beginning of the Weimar Republic. The last functioning chancellor of the republic, Heinrich Brüning, a leader of the party and a devout Catholic, was loyal to parliamentary democracy and utterly opposed to concordats with totalitarian regimes. As chancellor, he also had been opposed to Pacelli's notion of a concordat that had centralized papal ecclesiastical authority, instead of local needs and desires at the core of German Catholic decision making. After Hitler's accession to power, Brüning desperately argued against the concordat that would have depoliticized German Catholicism. His opponent now was the leader of the Center Party, Ludwig Kaas, a Jesuit priest and an intimate of Pacelli, increasingly under his influence. Kaas argued that a concordat with Hitler would better serve the German Catholic Church than would its continuance as the basis of a political minority opposed to Nazism.

[26] Quoted in Cornwell 1999, 75.   [27] Quoted in Scholder 1987, 159.

Indeed, well before the concordat was signed, Kaas was influential in generating support in the Center Party for the Enabling Act of March 23, 1933, which delegated to Hitler virtually dictatorial powers. Goebbels's newspaper, *Der Angriff*, mentioned openly that Kaas held the Center Party's approval of the Enabling Act contingent "upon the willingness of the Reich government to negotiate with the Holy See for a Reich concordat, and to respect the rights of the church."[28] All members of the party eventually voted for the Enabling Act. Even earlier in January, Kaas sent a letter to Chancellor Kurt von Schleicher, with a copy to President Paul von Hindenburg, suggesting that, since von Schleicher did not have parliamentary backing, he should be dismissed and his place assumed by Hitler, who controlled the largest party in the Reichstag.[29] These positions, of course, accorded with Pacelli's views.

The working relationship between Kaas and Pacelli had begun as early as 1920, in the negotiations over the concordat with Bavaria.[30] It would end only after Kaas's death in Rome in 1952, after he left Germany in April 1933 to become one of the pope's most trusted advisors in the curia.[31] Given this long history of close cooperation over the interests of the Catholic Church, it is virtually inconceivable that a Reich concordat would not have been a topic of discussion at the negotiations leading to passage of the Enabling Act.[32] Concerning Pacelli, Brüning wrote, "All successes [Pacelli believed] could only be attained by papal diplomacy.

---

[28] Quoted ibid., 246. Scholder also records the recollection of Fritz Günther von Tschirsky, an associate of Franz von Papen in the Vice Chancellery, to the effect that negotiations of this type occurred between Hitler and Kaas prior to the decisive Reichstag session of March 23. Center Party members were also suspicious that such conversations were ongoing. Even from the Protestant side, there is strong evidence for such an arrangement being discussed as early as March. See ibid., 246–47. Ernst von Weizsäcker, the German ambassador to the Vatican and Ribbentrop's former under-secretary at the Foreign Office, described Pope Pius XII as a "*realist*" (emphasis in original). See Chadwick 1989, 1266. For a different view of Weizsäcker's motives, see Friedländer 1966, XX–XXII. Other views of the pope are to be found in Cargas 1998, Morley 1980, Conway 1968, and Chadwick 1986.

[29] Schwab 1996, 16.   [30] Helmreich 1979, 105.   [31] Ibid., 240.

[32] Heinz Hürten 1992, 233–34, argues that there was no connection between the concordat and the Enabling Act. But his evidence and interpretations appear to be inaccurate. He cites, for example, a letter written by Kaas to the German ambassador to the Vatican, Diego von Bergen, suggesting that Kaas had no knowledge of the negotiation until he met Vice Chancellor von Papen on the train. Yet in that same letter according to Scholder (1987, 247), Kaas states: "Immediately after the passing of the Enabling Act, in the acceptance of which I had played a positive role on the basis of certain guarantees given to me by the Reich Chancellor (guarantees of a general political as well as a cultural political nature), on 24 March I traveled to Rome. Apart from having a holiday,

The system of concordats led him and the Vatican to despise democracy and the parliamentary system … Rigid governments, rigid centralization, and rigid treaties were supposed to introduce an era of stable order, an era of peace and quiet."[33]

Thus, at a simple stroke on July 20, 1933, the Reich concordat was signed, the Center Party was disbanded for good, and Hitler expressed the chilling opinion that the concordat would be "especially significant in the urgent struggle against international Jewry."[34] For the sake of erecting a central European bulwark against communism, Pacelli effectively silenced the only potential large-scale opposition to Hitler's violently anti-Semitic program.

Expansion of ecclesiastic Roman Catholicism always had been a goal of the Vatican, never more than under Pius XII. And in the German invasion and conquest of Yugoslavia in 1941, just such an opportunity was presented. The Nazi puppet-state of Croatia was carved out of Yugoslavia, with Ante Pavelić, the leader of the Croat fascist movement, the Ustaše, at its head. The Vatican was eager for the Catholic state of Croatia to succeed. Instead of the nominally secular state of Yugoslavia, increasingly under Orthodox Serbian control, a state ruled by Catholics had come into existence and with the head of the Croatian church, Bishop Alojzije Stepinac, in an influential role.

When the massacres of both Serbs and Jews began, would the Vatican respond? Almost as soon as "Croatia," including also Slovenia, Bosnia-Herzegovina, and portions of Dalmatia, was removed from Yugoslavia, the persecution began. In April 1941, all publications employing the Cyrillic alphabet, used principally by Serbs, were banned. At the same

in order to develop the views I put forward in the Reichstag on 23 March I wanted to explain the situation created by the Reich Chancellor's declaration and to investigate the possibilities for a comprehensive understanding between church and state." As Scholder (ibid., 247–48) remarks, "those who dispute a link between acceptance of the Enabling Act and the conclusion of the Reich concordat definitely seem unconvincing." It simply stretches the bounds of credulity to believe that Kaas was unaware of any such connection between these two signal events. Having written to von Schleicher and von Papen in January effectively nominating Hitler for the chancellorship (see p. 222), having at his disposal the second largest bloc of available non-Nazi votes needed for passage of the Enabling Act, having worked on concordats such as those with Bavaria and Prussia since 1920, and being an intimate of Pacelli with his desire for ordered church–state relations, Kaas was simply too thoroughly enmeshed in these proceedings not to have investigated at the earliest possible moment the potential for "a comprehensive understanding between church and state." For the text of the letter from Kaas to Bergen, see Kupper 1969, 495–98.

[33] Quoted in Cornwell 1999, 124.   [34] Scholder 1987, 404.

time, the "Aryanization" of professions, bureaucracies, and Jewish capital was begun. Although the fate of the Jews was not yet fully decided,
intimations of genocide against the Serbs already existed. Serb villages
were raided and hundreds massacred, in one case (Glina) inside a
Serbian Orthodox church. This practice foreshadowed the later
German massing of Jews inside their wooden synagogues in Poland
and then setting fire to the buildings, as the congregants inside burned
alive.

Four days after the Glina massacre, Pavelić had a "devotional" meeting with Pope Pius XII in the Vatican; at the same time, the Holy See
granted de facto recognition to the newly created Nazi puppet
Independent State of Croatia. As John Cornwell indicates, there is no
evidence that the pope was aware of these massacres at that time.[35] Yet,
he must have known that Pavelić was a totalitarian dictator, appointed
by Hitler to oversee the Catholicization and "Aryanization" of Croatia.
Racist and anti-Semitic laws had already been passed, and enforced
conversion from Orthodox Christianity to Roman Catholicism was
already underway. He could also have been aware of the exclusion of
the Orthodox Serb intelligentsia – priests, teachers, and even rich artisans and tradesmen – from the possibility of conversion, suggesting
their future annihilation in the new Croatia.

By early June, massacres of Serbs on a larger scale had begun. Even the
German general plenipotentiary assigned to Croatia stated that, according to reliable reports received by him, "the Ustasha [Croatian fascists;
sic] have gone raging mad."[36] The Germans were embarrassed as they
watched helplessly "the blind, bloody fury of the Ustasha [sic]." Priests,
principally Franciscans, played a major role in the massacres. One,
Father Bozidar Bralow, known for routinely carrying a machine gun,
was seen dancing around the bodies of 180 massacred Serbs.

That the Vatican was aware of these depredations against Serbs and
Jews cannot be doubted. Undersecretary of State Monsignor Giovanni
Battista Montini (later Pope Paul VI) was heavily involved with day-to-day
matters concerning Croatia and Poland. Late in 1941, he heard of the
Ustaša atrocities; Pope Pius was also by then aware of these events, because
he received daily reports from Montini. His colleague, Monsignor
Domenico Tardini, interviewed Pavelić's representative to the pope.
Tardini reportedly told him that "Croatia is a young state ... Youngsters
often err because of their age. It is therefore not surprising that Croatia has

---

[35] Cornwell 1999, 252.   [36] Quoted ibid., 254.

also erred."[37] This indulgence toward Ustaša excesses would characterize Vatican policy concerning Croatia even to the end of the war, after 487,000 Orthodox Serbs, 30,000 Jews, and 27,000 Roma were murdered, mostly in Ustaša death camps or in German gas chambers.[38] Shortly after the Wannsee conference formalized the beginning of the industrialized mass murder of Jews, the World Jewish Congress and the Swiss Israelite community sent a cry for help to the Vatican via Monsignor Filippe Bernadini, the apostolic nuncio in Berne. Dated March 17, 1942, representatives of the two agencies documented persecution of Jews in Germany, France, Romania, Slovakia, Hungary, and Croatia. The document requested that the pope use his influence in the latter three countries, which had strong ties between their governments and the Roman Catholic Church.

Regarding Croatia, the document reads, "Several thousand families were either deported to desert islands on the Dalmatian coast or incarcerated in concentration camps ... all the *male* Jews were sent to labor camps where they were assigned to drainage or sanitation work and where they perished in great number ... At the same time, their wives and children were sent to another camp where they, too, are enduring dire privations."[39] Gerhart Riegner, a signatory of the document, revealed in his 1998 memoirs that this document was excluded by the Vatican from the eleven volumes of released wartime documents, suggesting an extreme sensitivity concerning the Vatican's behavior during World War II. Later, in August 1942, Riegner was the first to directly inform the Allied Powers of the full extent of Nazi genocidal intentions.[40]

The Vatican's penchant for ecclesiastical expansion during World War II went so far as to forbid the postwar reunification of many Jewish families with children sheltered from the Holocaust in Catholic institutions. A Vatican directive containing Pius XII's approval forbade the return of hidden children to their Jewish parents if the children had been baptized, typically without their parents' consent, or with a formal permission, but one not genuinely granted under the extraordinary duress of the moment.[41] To this day, there are Holocaust survivors

---

[37] Quoted in Phayer 2000, 37.   [38] Cornwell 1999, 253.
[39] Emphasis in original; quoted ibid., 258.
[40] See Riegner 1998, and his obituary by D. Martin 2001.
[41] Sciolino and Horowitz 2005.

who resent the length of time (nearly twelve years in one instance) required to rejoin their Jewish families.[42]

Contrast this behavior by the pope, his silence on the Holocaust, and marginal private help to individual Croatian Jews with the behavior of Italian forces stationed on Yugoslav territory. Beginning with the earliest massacres in the spring of 1941, individual young officers intervened on behalf of threatened individuals. By July 1, 1943, before the entry of German troops, Italians had rescued 33,464 civilians in their Yugoslav sphere of influence, of whom 2,118 were Jews.[43] All this was done in the highly constrained circumstance of Italy as Germany's ally in the war. As Jonathan Steinberg comments, "A long process which began with the spontaneous reaction of individual young officers in the spring of 1941 who could not stand by and watch Croatian butchers hack down Serbian and Jewish men, women and children ended in July 1943 with a kind of national conspiracy to frustrate the much greater and more systematic brutality of the Nazi state ... It rested on certain assumptions about what being Italian meant."[44]

But there was an even more general purpose to the pope's silence before and during the Holocaust. As early as the seizure of Prague and before the invasion of Poland by Germany, Pacelli had hoped to be the "honest broker" and settle the rapidly emerging crisis between Hitler's Germany and the Allied Powers.[45] If, under his auspices, the crisis could be ended without war, the Vatican's influence would be greatly enhanced. This vain hope would continue throughout the war. Virtually all of Pacelli's actions would be taken with the following consideration in mind: would anything he did compromise the Vatican's neutrality so that it would be unable to convene a peace conference and thereby immeasurably extend the Vatican's influence? Given his Germanophile tendencies and knowledge of German history, he must have been aware of Germany's vastly increased prestige after the Congress of Berlin in 1878 that brokered the peace between Russia and the Ottoman Empire, with Otto von Bismarck as the "honest broker." Indeed, given its wideranging consequences for Eastern Europe, hence for the onset of World War I, the Congress of Berlin ranks as the single most important such event in the half-century prior to that war. International prestige, such as that conferred by convening such a conference, could reverse the declining worldwide influence of the

---

[42] Greenberg 2005, 3.   [43] Steinberg 1990, 132.   [44] Ibid., 133.
[45] Cornwell 1999, 222.

Roman Catholic Church in the face of communism's advance and the rise of other secular "isms." As Michael Phayer put it,

> Years after the end of the war, Robert Leiber, the German Jesuit who was one of Pius's closest confidants, made clear the connection between the Pope's silence about the Holocaust and his diplomacy. The reason that Pius XII did not speak out about the murder of the Jews, Leiber confided to the Dutch historian Ger van Roon, was that he wanted to play the peacemaker during the war. To safeguard his credentials for such a role, the Holy See had to preserve Vatican City's status as an independent state and neutral government. Pius's role model in this respect was Pope Benedict XV, whose efforts to negotiate a European peace during World War I had impressed a younger Eugenio Pacelli.[46]

Thus, in addition to Bismarck's role in furthering German influence through peacemaking, Pius XII actually had a papal model for such efforts. That they were unsuccessful in the case of Benedict XV would not deter Pius, because of the perceived greater need for the reversal of Catholicism's decline after the carnage of World War I and the rise of communism.

Finally, in order to play this international role, Vatican City and Rome itself needed to be intact, and the Vatican thoroughly neutral. By refusing to speak out publicly against the Holocaust, this neutrality would be enhanced, so that none of the Axis Powers or their collaborators would feel discomfited. However, as Guenter Lewy commented: "A public denunciation of the mass murders by Pius XII, broadcast widely over the Vatican radio and read from the pulpits by his bishops, would have revealed to Jews and Christians alike what deportation to the East entailed. The pope would have been believed, whereas the broadcasts of the Allies were often shrugged off as war propaganda. Many of the deportees, who accepted the assurances of the Germans that they were merely being resettled, might thus have been warned and given an impetus to escape. Many more Christians might have helped and sheltered Jews, and many more lives might have been saved."[47]

Here, in contrast to the Armenian case, we have a disjunction between onset and magnitude. Clearly, the magnitude of the killing would have been affected by an open declaration by the pope. Jews might have believed the pope and fled for their lives, or resisted strongly. Roman Catholics

---

[46] Phayer 2000, 57.   [47] Lewy 1964, 303.

would have been far more likely to help Jews targeted for annihilation, even if only to care for newly orphaned children. But the onset of the Holocaust occurred in the context of Operation Barbarossa, the invasion of the Soviet Union, which seemingly would be unaffected by any activities, declarations or otherwise, by the papacy far to the west.

Yet, in one sense, the onset of the Holocaust was affected by Eugenio Pacelli, then papal secretary of state, especially in his political activities, first through Ludwig Kaas in supporting Hitler's accession to the chancellorship and then support for the Enabling Act giving Hitler virtually dictatorial powers. The consequences were political silencing of the Catholic Center Party, and finally the concordat itself, which provided the first external legitimation of Nazi rule. Hitler's comment upon signing the concordat that it was "especially significant in the urgent struggle against international Jewry," quoted earlier, suggests the concordat's importance in facilitating onset of the Holocaust. The counterfactual positioning of the Center Party and the Roman Catholic Church as domestic opponents of Nazism might have given Hitler pause prior to his later homicidal onslaught against the Jews. As the preceding quote reveals, in Hitler's view, one major obstacle to this onslaught had been removed.

The Tutsi

Turning now to the case of Rwanda, in which approximately 800,000 Tutsi and Hutu moderates were murdered over six weeks in 1994, we have an instance more like that of the Ottoman Empire during World War I. Instead of Germany as the principal agent of the permissive context, France, another European power, played that role.

In order to fully understand French policy during that period, one must see two sides of the same coin representing that policy. First, there were strongly positive elements to the relationship between France and governing elites not only in Rwanda but also throughout Francophone Africa. According to Gérard Prunier, "There is a high degree of symbiosis between French and francophone African political élites. It is a mixture of many things: old memories, shared material interests, delusions of grandeur, gossip, sexual peccadilloes – in short a common culture for which there is no equivalent among ex-colonial powers with the possible and partial exception of Portugal."[48]

---

[48] Prunier 1995, 103–04.

More to the point, and in accordance with the realpolitik model, Rwanda, precisely because of its Francophone status and widespread Roman Catholicism, was in the process of inclusion in the French-dominated African "community." It would be the first such country not to have experienced French colonial role. On the negative side, there was potential opposition stemming from Anglophone African states, especially Uganda, home base of the Rwandese Patriotic Front (RPF), the Tutsi rebel organization that invaded Rwanda in 1990. According to Prunier, the French were reacting to the "Anglo-Saxon" threat:

> The notion of "Anglo-Saxon" is hazy yet it also has a deadly clarity. Anybody who speaks English can be "Anglo-Saxon," and indeed northern Europeans such as the Scandinavians and the Dutch are honorary "Anglo-Saxons" because they tend to speak English so well. Of course "Anglo-Saxons" are usually white, but not always. President Yoweri Museveni [of Uganda] ... was definitely an incarnation of the "Anglo-Saxon" menace in its truest form: because an "Anglo-Saxon" is an English-speaker who threatens the French.[49]

The confrontation between the heirs of "les Anglais" and the French in Africa has been dubbed the "Fashoda syndrome" by Prunier, after the 1898 confrontation between English and French troops in southern Sudan. He asserts that this syndrome is the main reason why France intervened so quickly and so deeply in the Rwanda crisis.

In agreeing with this view, former French minister of defense, François Leotard, told members of the French Assembly that "The President of the Republic [Mitterrand] was the person who in his comments seemed to define best the balance of power between the Anglo-Saxons and the French in this part of the world, and to do so with greatest precision and sense of strategy and history."[50]

Not only was this thinking symptomatic of the Fashoda syndrome, but the very idea of a balance of power between the Anglo-Saxons and France is redolent of realpolitik. After all, was it not, according to Thucydides, the growth in Athenian power thereby destroying the

---

[49] Ibid., 104.

[50] Quoted in Des Forges 1999, 117. That the French were not unrealistic in their assessments is suggested by the fact that Paul Kagame, leader of the RPF, received training in military tactics and intelligence methods at the Kansas-based Tactical Command and General Staff College of the US Army. As a consequence, he was called "America's Man in the Great Lakes." See Madsen 1999, 104–05.

balance with the Spartans that led to the Peloponnesian War and its genocidal consequence? Additionally, Rwanda was seen by French policy-makers to be geopolitically pivotal in affecting events in Zaire, another French-speaking former Belgian colony in the French–African political orbit. Given its size, mineral wealth, and serious internal weakness, Zaire would have made a valuable and fairly easily acquired addition.[51]

Beginning in 1990, the French military mission maintained between 600 and 1,100 troops in Rwanda. At the time of the French arrival, the Rwandan army consisted of as few as 3,000 men, of whom only about 2,000 actually knew how to fight, so that the French addition was not inconsiderable. According to both French and Tanzanian military intelligence sources, the RPF offensive stopped short of the Rwandan capital, Kigali, in February 1993 only because of the presence of French troops in the vicinity.[52] A Nigerian colonel serving in the international military observer group apparently accused French troops of bombarding RPF positions in Ruhengiri.[53]

Equally as, if not more important for understanding the genocide, is the French military aid and troop training supplied to the Rwandan army. Arms and ammunitions had been continually supplied but, after February 1993, up to twenty tons of materiel per day were sent.[54]

As early as February 1992, the Rwandan Ministry of Foreign Affairs formally asked approval for naming a Lieutenant Colonel Chollet, head of the French military assistance mission, to be military advisor to President Habyarimana. Although this appointment was aborted largely because of negative publicity as the result of a news leak, in April, Lieutenant Colonel Jean-Jacques Mourin was named adjunct to the French military attaché in Kigali and fulfilled essentially the same role that had been proposed for Chollet. In addition, "French soldiers on the ground were assisting in combat, in interrogating military prisoners, and in enforcing control measures on the civilian population."[55]

Further, there is evidence that the French actually helped train the Interahamwe, the Hutu extremist militia. One former militia member claimed that "French militaries [sic] taught us how to capture our victims and tie them up ... the French taught the interahamwe to throw knives and assemble rifles. The French trained us ... for a total

---

[51] For regional perspectives on the Rwandan genocide, see Jones 1999 and Gnamo 1999.
[52] See Callamard 1999, 160.   [53] Ibid., 166.   [54] Des Forges 1999, 20.   [55] Ibid., 68.

of 4 months between February 1991 and January 1992."[56] He further alleged that French soldiers were present when the Presidential Guard committed a large number of massacres. A member of the International Enquiry Commission claimed that French trainers were present in a military camp where hundreds of civilians were brought and killed.

From the start of the French military presence in Rwanda, there was an awareness of genocidal intent. A Colonel Rwagafilita, a close associate of President Juvénal Habyarimana, told a French general directing French military cooperation in Rwanda that the Tutsi "are very few in number, we will liquidate them."[57]

Propagandists had given ample warnings of the possibility of genocide that the French could hardly ignore. As early as November 1992, Léon Mugesera gave a speech before a meeting of the leading political party, the Mouvement Révolutionaire National pour la Démocratie et le Développement (MRNDD), outlining the justification for genocide. In the face of Tutsi hostility and the purported objective of Hutu extermination, the Hutu were to "rise up" in self-defense. He said that the Tutsi must be made to recognize that "your home is in Ethiopia, that we are going to send you back there quickly, by the Nyabarongo."[58] The Nyabarongo river is mentioned as a clear reference to earlier massacres of the Tutsi and deposition of their bodies in that river to float in the direction of Ethiopia.

In April 1993, a new radio station, the Radio Télévision Libre des Mille Collines (RTLM) was incorporated with the express purpose of establishing a hardline Hutu stance against the Tutsi. One of the chief financial supporters of the project was related through marriage to President Habyarimana. The RTLM was basically hate radio carrying a message of virtual Tutsi extermination, especially as the genocide itself was approaching.[59] Essentially, the theme of self-defense against the pernicious Tutsi was the justification for the coming violent actions.

There were warnings, as well, from United Nations-affiliated personnel that implicate not only the French, who must have been aware of these signals of genocide, but the larger international community as well.[60] For example, in November 1993, Lieutenant Marc Nees, an intelligence officer with the Belgian paratroopers attached to the United Nations Assistance Mission in Rwanda (UNAMIR), reported that persons attending a meeting chaired by Habyarimana had decided

[56] Quoted in Callamard 1999, 181. [57] Quoted in Des Forges 1999, 121. [58] Quoted ibid., 71. [59] Chalk 1999. [60] See Melvern 2000 and Power 2001.

"to distribute grenades, machetes and other weapons to the Interahamwe and to CDR [Coalition for the Defense of the Republic] young people. The objective is to kill Tutsi and other Rwandans who are in the cities and who do not support them (i.e. the Interahamwe and CDR). The distribution of the weapons has already begun."[61] At the time, the number of machetes imported into the country was sufficient to equip every third Hutu male.[62]

In December 1993, Canadian general Roméo Dallaire, military head of UNAMIR, received messages from senior officers of the Rwandan armed forces that, after killings at Kirambo, Mutura, and Ngenda, "more massacres of the same kind are being prepared and are supposed to spread throughout the country, beginning with the regions that have a great concentration of Tutsi."[63] General Dallaire sought additional discretion in action from his UN superiors, but did not receive it. Shortly after the massacres in Kigali began on April 6, the rapid withdrawal of foreign nationals and stated opposition to the UNAMIR presence by France, the United States, and other powers on the Security Council led Dallaire to conclude that April 12 was "the day the world moved from disinterest in Rwanda to the abandonment of Rwandans to their fate."[64] That information was immediately made available to the Rwandan government because its representative on the Security Council (a rotating seat), inappropriately, was not asked to leave the room.[65] Shortly thereafter, the leader of the Rwandan army, a moderate, and his aides, as well as other administrative personnel opposed to the genocide, primarily regional, were removed from office by the Hutu extremist leadership,[66] and the killing spread rapidly from Kigali to other cities and regions.[67]

A report of Belgian intelligence, also in December, stated that: "The Interahamwe are armed to the teeth and on alert. Many of them have been trained at the military camp in Bugesera. Each of them has ammunition, grenades, mines and knives. They have been trained to use guns that are stockpiled with their respective chiefs. They are all just waiting for the right moment to act."[68] Officials in France, Belgium, the United States, and the United Nations were well aware of the possibility of mass killing, yet did little if anything to stop it. Actually, France was in the best

---

[61] Quoted in Des Forges 1999, 143.   [62] Ibid., 127.   [63] Quoted ibid., 145.
[64] Dallaire 2003, 291.   [65] Power 2002a, 367–69.
[66] Dallaire 2003, 292; Des Forges, personal communication, May 8, 2004.
[67] Des Forges 1999, 263.   [68] Quoted ibid., 146.

position to do so, but did not. Indeed, when President Mitterrand, the intimate of President Habyarimana and architect of France's realpolitik policy in central Africa, was asked by a journalist about the genocide, he answered: "The genocide or the genocides? I don't know what one should say!,"[69] as if there existed a symmetry between Hutu and Tutsi behaviors during that period. One might just as well have argued that the German mass murder of Jews was in response to identical behaviors toward Germans by Jews. In the midst of obvious preparations for the genocide, the French ambassador to Kigali, Georges Martre, observed, "I had dinner yesterday night with President Habyarimana; he is a nice man. I even drank champagne with him. I know him, he is a charming person."[70] Perhaps the permissive role of France was best summarized by the following statement by General Paul Kagame, commander of the RPF:

> You armed and trained the Presidential Guards; you have accepted that the Presidential Guards armed and trained, in front of you, the Hutu extremists. You have not required the President of Rwanda to abandon ethnic identity cards; vous portez donc une lourde part de responsabilité dans le génocide en cours.[71]

Or as René Lemarchand observed, "France helped to give the Habyarimana regime a degree of credibility that proved totally illusory, and thus created false expectations about its commitment to democracy ... No amount of retrospective guilt can diminish its place in history as the principal villain in the Rwandan apocalypse."[72]

As in the Armenian case and in contrast to the Holocaust, onset and magnitude are equally affected. The earlier massacres of the Tutsi in 1963–64 and 1973[73] laid the groundwork for the later magnitude of the genocide that would, given the permissive environment established by the French, begin at an extraordinarily high rate of killing. Counterfactually, had the French not helped stop the RPF offensive before Kigali in February 1993, the RPF advance might have been very swift and many more Tutsi would have been saved under RPF protection; even the genocide itself might have been averted. Diplomatic and military support of the Rwandan army and especially materiel

---

[69] Quoted in Prunier 1995, 339. Research findings refuting the claim of a double genocide are found in Verwimp 2003.
[70] Quoted in Callamard 1999, 169.   [71] *Le Figaro*, 25 June 1994; quoted ibid., 165.
[72] Lemarchand 1994, 603.   [73] Mamdani 2001, 193.

transferred to it by the French were influential not only in increasing the magnitude of the genocide, but also in establishing a climate of permission that allowed the killing to begin.

Even after much of the genocide had run its course, the French intervened forcefully in Operation Turquoise with ostensibly humanitarian goals but with very mixed consequences. Although the French were responsible for rescuing approximately 10,000–13,000 people in southwest Rwanda, they actually served to provide political cover for the many Hutu perpetrators of the genocide then fleeing to Goma in Zaire as the RPF advanced.[74] In Goma, French "humanitarian" activities actually helped the former *génocidaires* far more then the Tutsi victims who were the advertised beneficiaries.[75] Appropriately, Gérard Prunier described the "Machiavellian statesmanship" that President Mitterrand exhibited in an interview on French television in 1994 when he claimed that Operation Turquoise had saved "tens of thousands lives," that President Habyarimana had been steadily democratizing Rwanda before his death, that France had nothing to do with the genocide, and that France could not intervene during the genocide because that was the responsibility of the United Nations.[76] In point of fact, "In 1994, during the height of the extermination campaign in Rwanda, as Paris airlifted arms to Mobutu's intermediaries in eastern Zaire for direct transfer across the border to the *génocidaires*, France's President François Mitterrand said – as the newspaper *Le Figaro* later reported it – 'In such countries, genocide is not too important.' By their actions and inactions, at the time and in the years that followed, the rest of the major powers indicated that they agreed."[77]

Conclusion

Table 10.1 summarizes the preceding arguments. Two genocidal variants – cynical and brute force – are listed along with the military and genocidal targets in each case. In the first column, the cynical supporter is listed, not necessarily as a proponent of genocide, but as a formal or unspoken ally of the military goals of the perpetrator. When these military goals were transformed into genocidal ones via brute force realpolitik, then the supporters were at best transformed into bystanders, or

---

[74] Prunier 1995, 303.   [75] Gourevitch 1998, 324–25.   [76] Prunier 1995, 297.
[77] Quoted in Gourevitch 1998, 324–25.

Table 10.1 *Realpolitik and genocide*

Realpolitik variant			
Cynical		*Brute force*	
Supporter	*Perpetrator*	*Military target*[a]	*Genocidal target*
Imperial Germany	Ottoman Empire	Russia	Armenians
The Vatican	Nazi Germany	Soviet Union	Jews
France	Hutu elite	Rwandese Patriotic Front	Tutsi

Notes: [a] Only the military target relevant for the genocide is listed.

were, as in the case of the German military during World War I, actually complicit in the genocide.

This table helps suggest a method of genocide prevention.[78] Instead of targeting for diplomatic persuasion the potential perpetrator of genocide, if he or she may be fixed in the genocidal purpose and therefore intractable, the supporter or principal ally could be approached. If the Vatican or France could have been made aware of the possible consequences of their actions in supporting military goals, respectively of Nazi Germany and the Hutu elite, then it is possible that their degree of support might have diminished, with perhaps a consequent smaller probability of a later genocide. Such diplomatic entreaties would probably have been less successful in the case of imperial Germany because the ongoing world war isolated enemy coalitions from each other and made alliances such as that between Germany and the Ottoman Empire virtually unconditional.

Here we see the importance of timing and context. If widespread warfare already is underway, then there may be only very limited possibilities for prevention. On the other hand, if diplomatic approaches can be made earlier before the onset of major war, in recognition of the potential impact of influential supporters on the probability of genocide, then diplomatic venues may be more successful.

[78] See Fein 2000 and Ould-Abdallah 2000. Another approach via the mechanism of international aid is given by Uvin 1998.

In the concluding chapter, additional evidence will be presented that, in the case of Rwanda, it was not only France, the great power supporter of the Rwandan government, that played a permitting role. The behavior of the United Nations in the final moments was probably decisive in allowing the massacres in Kigali, the capital city, to spread throughout the country, yielding the genocide of 1994.

11

Cynical realpolitik and the unwanted

Thus far in this part, their use of cynical realpolitik has identified permitting agents of the Holocaust and of the genocide of the Armenians and Tutsi that undoubtedly increased the magnitude of the killing. Yet policies dictated by cynical realpolitik go beyond this relatively small company of leaders and include even the enemies of Nazism who were ultimately, at great cost, to defeat Nazi Germany in World War II. The story of this chapter is the callous disregard of the Jewish plight in virtually all potential national sites of refuge and its likely impact on the genesis and, most importantly, the magnitude of the Holocaust. Here, the cynical version of realpolitik is played out on the world stage.

The United States and Great Britain were the principal actors in this drama, for they were the main destinations sought by the Jews as the Nazi persecution worsened. Other places of potential refuge such as Canada, Australia, and New Zealand were also implicated. As might be expected, the United States was the leading actor and, "During the Holocaust, Britain's policy – much of it made in conjunction with the United States government – continued to put self-interest first, leaving minimal scope for humanitarian action."[1] Self-interest dictated by considerations of realpolitik, punctuated by occasional short-lived bursts of humanitarianism, was to characterize the policies of both countries.

The United States

According to David Wyman, "Three major factors in American life in the late 1930's tended to generate public resistance to immigration of refugees: unemployment, nativistic nationalism, and anti-Semitism."[2]

---

[1] London 2000, 1; see also Wasserstein 1999. For an overview of Western immigration policy toward Jewish refugees, see Engel 1993.

[2] Wyman 1985, 3. See also Feingold 1970 and S. Friedman 1973.

Nativism frequently shaded into outright anti-Semitism, but in itself was a force militating against admission of aliens of any origin. And the nativistic reaction to the Great Depression actually antedated the accession of the Nazis to power and the need for Jewish escape.

As early as 1930, President Hoover, when faced with the problem of increasing unemployment, sought methods to limit immigration. Seeking administrative relief from the State Department, the Hoover administration turned to a previously little-used provision of the Immigration Act of 1917 that excluded individuals who were likely to become public charges. This LPC requirement, as it came to be known, became a constant method of limiting immigration throughout the following decade and a half. Immigrants had either to possess enough money to support themselves or to have affidavits from friends or relatives in the United States that they would be supported in the event that employment could not be found. And the wording of the instructions to consular officials was elastic enough to deny entry to a large number of refugees. A White House press release of September 8, 1930, stated that, "if the consular officer believes that the applicant may probably be a public charge at any time, even during a considerable period subsequent to his arrival, he must refuse the visa."[3]

When Franklin Roosevelt assumed office, this policy was kept in place. At times this policy was eased, as in the directive of December 1936 that instructed consular officers to assess the *likelihood* of the applicant becoming a public charge, and not ... the *possibility* of it."[4] Immigration totals rose accordingly yet, on the whole, the consular officials in Germany and later Austria remained roadblocks to successful emigration. Assistant secretary of state in charge of immigration Breckenridge Long, fearful of aliens and verging on anti-Semitism, suggested to his consuls in Germany,

> We can delay and effectively stop for a temporary period of indefinite length the number of immigrants in to [sic] the United States. We could do this by simply advising our consuls to put every obstacle in the way and to require additional evidence and to resort to various administrative devices which would postpone and postpone and postpone the granting of the visas.[5]

[3] Quoted in Wyman 1985, 4.   [4] Emphasis added; quoted ibid., 5.
[5] Quoted in Zucker 2001, 41.

An unexpired passport or a police certificate attesting to good conduct was required, along with a complete financial statement, certificate from a public health official, duplicate records of all required personal information, and an affidavit by a guarantor in the United States listing the guarantor's complete assets as well as the percentage of those assets required for the new immigrant. If a single error was found in the approximately fifty pages of documentation, at best a delay was to be expected; frequently outright rejection of the application was the outcome.[6] The typical waiting time for an application to complete the screening process was nine months, even longer for those in the enemy alien category after the United States entered the war.

As early as 1933, a well-known German-Jewish historian, Dr. Mark Weschnitzer, remarked that "dozens and dozens of individuals whose credentials ... were in perfect form ... were denied visas, emphatically stating that 'the Consuls, particularly in the provinces are pretty adamant ... [and] in Berlin, too, they are so busy that they adopt the course of least resistance.'"[7] In July 1943, a visa application more than *four feet* long was introduced along with the need for *two* American sponsors who would attest to the absence of any danger to the United States from the applicant[8] – this at a time when Washington was already fully aware of the ongoing destruction of European Jewry.

One incident is revealing. A German-Jewish refugee in France had her visa approved in Washington in November 1941. But after American entry into the war one month later, now categorized as an enemy alien, she had to begin the process all over again. According to a report of the Unitarian Service Committee in October 1942, "In spite of what seemed to be a favorable reception of her case when it was presented by her niece in Washington, the visa was refused and this meant her case could not be reopened for six months. There was nothing we could do. A few days ago came word of her deportation."[9]

Of course, state security, an essential element of realpolitik, was operative here after December 7, 1941. There was an ongoing fear of spies introduced into the United States under the guise of refugee status. Given the relatively large US German-speaking population and the ability of such a spy to submerge in its midst, this was a real concern. Yet, as we saw in the preceding incident of the deported refugee, all too many genuine victims of Nazism were lost in the process, soon to be murdered.

---

[6] Ibid.   [7] Quoted ibid., 175.   [8] Wyman 1984, 127.   [9] Quoted ibid., 126.

Even those who were offended by the Nazis' treatment of the Jews nevertheless opposed any liberalization of the immigration laws. Here, nativism and anti-Semitism merge with a realpolitik that together put the interests of the state over those of increasingly desperate human beings. George Messersmith, as consul-general in Berlin, minister in Vienna, and later assistant secretary of state of immigration matters among other positions, embodied this syndrome. Despite hundreds of reports detailing the Nazis' barbaric behavior, according to his biographer, his "visceral Americanism" included "a selfish side that recommended selective immigration policies"[10] especially concerning Jewish applications, and he sought to preserve American democracy by excluding "those who might become an added burden on democracy."[11] Messersmith admitted opposing any "tampering with that existing order which ... vests final authority in the Consular Service."[12] And when, in 1933 American universities developed a plan to admit German-Jewish professors, Messersmith averred that such individuals were dangerous because they, "while designated as 'liberal,' are in reality in direct opposition to our own social order."[13] Realpolitik in the form of friendly relations between Germany and the United States also was important to him. When, in 1933, a German-Jewish physician came to the consulate to complain of Nazi atrocities against Jews in Berlin's hospitals, Messersmith burst out, "You Jews are always afraid of [sic] your own skins. The important thing for us is to preserve friendly relations between the two countries."[14]

As an indicator of the overall effectiveness of the many obstacles to immigration, the following statistics are revealing. Although the immigration quotas allowed for Germany and Austria in the 1930s would have been insufficient to meet the demand, they were never filled. According to Bat-Ami Zucker, "During this period, quota fulfillment ranged from a low of 5.3 percent in 1933 to a high of 40.6 in 1939, with an average for the entire period of 17.5 percent."[15]

When the number of refugees itself is examined, both Jewish and non-Jewish, the total admitted between 1933 and 1943 rises to no more than 280,000,[16] a small fraction of the total possible under law (2,154,306).[17]

Realpolitik has another dimension, in addition to that of state security. When the focus is on the state, of course state security is paramount. But when the focus shifts to leadership, tenure in office is the *sine*

[10] Zucker 2001, 176.   [11] Ibid.   [12] Ibid., 175.   [13] Quoted ibid., 176.
[14] Quoted ibid.   [15] Ibid., 60.   [16] Davie 1947, 27.   [17] Zucker 2001, 60.

qua non, especially in democratic polities. In their sensitivity to widespread anti-Semitism, the actions of the Roosevelt administration and its counterpart in Britain reflected this aspect of a cynical realpolitik.

As early as 1920, Henry Ford set the stage for the emergence of political anti-Semitism with his personal newspaper, the *Dearborn Independent*, with a circulation of 700,000. He chronicled the supposed misdeeds of Jews and their threat to the republic. The infamous tsarist forgery, *The Protocols of the Learned Elders of Zion*, a staple of anti-Semitism up to the present time, was published serially by the *Independent* in 1920.[18] Articles in the *Independent*'s series "The International Jews: The World's Problem" were bound in volumes and mailed to members of Congress and other prominent officials. One observer, Carey McWilliams, concluded that "it would be difficult to overestimate the damage which Ford's vicious, persistent, and heavily financed anti-Semitic campaign caused the Jews of the world."[19]

Ford was the first American to be awarded the Grand Cross of the German Right. As early as 1922, his portrait hung in Hitler's private office.[20] Articles in the *Independent* were translated and distributed widely in Germany. Hitler openly noted the importance of Ford's "contribution." With the onset of the Depression, 121 American anti-Semitic organizations emerged during the 1930–40 period.[21]

Important among them were the Silver Shirts, headed by William Dudley Pelley. Predominantly a Protestant movement, at its maximum in 1934 it had about 15,000 members. Although nominally national in scope, many of its officers came from the Ku Klux Klan, thus giving it a regional southern flavor. Most of its propaganda activities were found west of the Appalachians.[22]

More influential in the 1930s was the movement established by Father Coughlin, a Roman Catholic priest based in Royal Oak, Michigan. Initially attractive to working people of all faiths, including many Jews, because of its emphasis on social justice (the name of Coughlin's periodical), by the mid-1930s it had turned openly anti-Semitic. He gave Sunday afternoon radio talks that by one estimate in 1939 reached 3,500,000 people. He formed the National Union for Social Justice as a vehicle for espousing his political views, and later the Christian Front in New York, which consisted of anti-Semitic thugs ready to take to the streets at a moment's notice. Coughlin published the *Protocols* in 1938.

[18] Baldwin 2003, 141.   [19] Quoted in Zucker 2001, 21.   [20] Baldwin 2003, 173.
[21] D. Strong 1941.   [22] Zucker 2001, 22.

Much of the Coughlinite anti-Semitic propaganda centered on the notion of the "international" Jew who could not be successfully integrated into American life; the *Protocols*, of course, were a pillar of this worldview. But even more insidious was the implication and direct accusation that Jews were somehow alien to American life and a danger to the republic. The connection between Jews and communism was consistently emphasized both on the radio and in print. Only after US entry into the war were Coughlin's activities curtailed, and *Social Justice* was banned from the mails in 1942.

The influence of Ford, Pelley, Coughlin, and other anti-Semites was to be found in the prevalence of anti-Jewish activities in the 1930s and 1940s. A series of surveys between 1938 and 1941 showed that between one-third and one-half of the American populace believed that Jews had "too much power in the United States."[23] During the war years, the survey found that the proportion rose to 56 percent. Jewish power was earlier thought to be located principally in "business and commerce" and in "finance." Later it was extended to "politics and government."[24]

From August 1940 and later through the war, 15 to 24 percent of respondents viewed Jews as "a menace to America"; Jews were seen as more threatening than "Negroes," Catholics, Germans, or Japanese (with the exception of 1942 for the latter two groups). Between 1938 and 1945, 15 percent of respondents would have supported an anti-Jewish campaign, with 20 to 25 percent sympathizing with it. Another 30 percent would have opposed it, with the rest remaining neutral. Thus, nearly 40 percent of the population would have approved of an anti-Jewish campaign.[25]

The results of these polls must have been known to President Roosevelt and influenced him accordingly. Although he was at first outwardly sympathetic to the plight of Germany's Jews, as time passed, concerns about the United States in the war – a fundamental state security tenet of realpolitik – replaced any residual sympathies he had for them.

As early as 1938, Roosevelt was trying to publicly resolve the Jewish refugee crisis without opening any additional American doors. The Anschluss of 1938 between Austria and Germany yielded an additional flood of refugees. In addition to combining the Austrian and German US immigration quotas, and allowing this consolidated quota to be

---

[23] Quoted in Wyman 1984, 14.   [24] Ibid., 15.   [25] Ibid.

completely filled, a major result was the Evian conference, held in July 1938.

The conference, called by Roosevelt, was billed as a major intergovernmental effort to resolve the refugee crisis that threatened to reach flood-like proportions, as the Nazis hastened Jewish emigration from newly acquired Austria. The conference had a humanitarian face but somewhat darker origins. In a State Department memorandum of 1938 summarizing the year's refugee program, pressure from liberal writers such as Dorothy Thompson and "certain Congressmen with metropolitan constituencies" were claimed to have led to the conference. Demands emanating from those quarters were deemed to be "both exceedingly strong and prolonged." As a consequence, Secretary of State Cordell Hull, Undersecretary Sumner Welles, and Assistant Secretary Messersmith concluded that, instead of resisting this pressure, it would be preferable to "get out in front and attempt to guide it," primarily to forestall any efforts to liberalize immigration policy.[26] By making everyone in the world responsible for the fate of the refugees, essentially no one would be, including the United States.

And that was the basic outcome of the conference. With the exception of Italy, all thirty-two invited countries attended the conference at Evian-les-Bains, but only one, the Dominican Republic, agreed to increase its quota for Jewish immigration. Another outcome was the formation of the Intergovernmental Committee on Refugees, which was to prove to be largely ineffectual as a vehicle for Jewish immigration. As former undersecretary of state Sumner Welles averred after the war, "The committee could have been responsible for an outstanding humanitarian achievement prior to and during the war years, but ... the final results amounted to little more than zero. The Government of the United States itself permitted the committee to become a nullity."[27]

Two aspects of the conference were noteworthy. One was the open rejection by most countries of even the possibility of Jewish immigration. Countries such as Belgium, the Netherlands, and France indicated that they were already saturated with Jewish refugees. Australia would not encourage any large-scale immigration because, they said, "as we have no real racial problem, we are not desirous of importing one."[28] New Zealand pointed to its economic problems, as did Canada, in limiting immigration. Unemployment was cited as a major factor by Latin American countries, with the aforementioned exception of the

[26] Quoted in Wyman 1985, 44.   [27] Quoted ibid., 51.   [28] Quoted ibid., 50.

Dominican Republic. Cynical realpolitik, in the sense of a perceived national self-interest placed over and above the human rights of persecuted peoples, was the dominant response.

The American public responded in a similar vein. In July 1938, at the time of the conference, a *Fortune* poll revealed that two-thirds of respondents (67.4 percent) agreed with the statement regarding refugees that "with conditions as they are we should keep them out." Organs of public opinion such as the Jesuit weekly *America* and the Catholic *Tablet* published in Brooklyn essentially agreed with this view, although the liberal Catholic *Commonweal* supported the possibility of Jewish refuge in the United States.[29] In Congress, Edward T. Taylor, Democrat of Colorado, wanted to be assured that the proposed Evian conference did not amount to "an invitation to use the United States as a dumping ground for all of these people."[30] This sentiment was typical of many in Congress who opposed opening doors to the burgeoning number of refugees.

Even non-German sources threatened to worsen the refugee problem. Both Poland and Romania sought to attend the Evian conference in an effort to lessen their own "Jewish problems." In common with Nazi Germany, which allowed observers to attend from both the German and Austrian Jewish communities, the conference was seen by Poles and Romanians as a vehicle for the reduction of their own Jewish populations. Both countries were refused attendance.

The German government, of course, was well aware of these events. At the time of the conference, Hitler declared in Königsberg, "I can only hope and expect that the other world, which has such deep sympathy for these criminals, will at least be generous enough to convert this sympathy into practical aid. We, on our part, are ready to put all these criminals at the disposal of these countries, for all I care, even on luxury ships."[31] Awareness of the unwillingness of the West to respond openly to the Jewish refugees was indicated by Vienna's *Völkischer Beobachter*, which stated: "We cannot take seriously President Roosevelt's appeal to the nations of the world as long as the United States maintains racial quotas for immigrants."[32] And at the close of the conference, a spokesman for the Wilhelmstrasse (where the German foreign policy making agency was based) "exultingly announced that Western countries wanted the Jews no more than did the Germans themselves."[33]

[29] Wyman 1984, 64.   [30] Quoted in Wyman 1985, 46.   [31] Quoted in Morse 1968, 204.
[32] Quoted ibid., 205–06.   [33] Quoted in Marrus 1985, 172.

This rejection of the Jewish refugees would be even more dramatically revealed by events surrounding two vessels, the *St. Louis* and the *Struma*. In May 1939, the former ship set sail for Havana from Hamburg with Jewish refugees aboard. Although the Cuban government had abruptly canceled all landing permits already issued, the ship landed at Havana and 907 of the refugees were refused entry. Nor would the US government intervene on behalf of the more than 700 of the passengers who had registered for American visas and had their support documents in order. The *New Republic*, for one, was outraged that these passengers were not permitted to land, taken in on temporary visas, and later counted toward the new quota. After sailing back to Europe and desperate entreaties from refugee organizations, Britain, France, Belgium, and the Netherlands agreed to take them in.

The *Struma*, with 769 passengers, would meet a far worse fate. Embarking for Palestine, initially from a Romanian port, the *Struma* reached Istanbul in February 1942, but was forbidden to land without prior British approval for entry to Palestine. This the British refused to grant (see pp. 246–47 for more details on British Palestine policy). Forced to sail from Istanbul in an unseaworthy ship, the *Struma* was towed from port and exploded shortly thereafter. There was a total of two survivors.[34]

Great Britain and Commonwealth countries

British immigration policy toward Jewish refugees differed little from that of the United States. Louise London[35] estimates that a final total of approximately 80,000 Jews from Germany, Austria, and Czechoslovakia were permitted to escape through the United Kingdom. Given that the population of the UK was roughly one-third that of the United States at that time, this number on a per capita basis is comparable to the maximum cited earlier of 280,000, including both Jews and non-Jews, allowed to enter the United States.[36] There were, however, two major exceptions. The first is the admission of 20,000 Jewish children from Austria and Germany after the Anschluss, something the United States refused to agree to, and the problem of Palestine, then governed by Britain under a League mandate.

Historically, the ungenerous British immigration policy had roots similar to the American. Both emerged from the nativist and strong

[34] Wyman 1985, 38–39. [35] London 2000, 12. [36] Zucker 2001, 60.

anti-communist feelings permeating Anglo-American society after World War I. As in the "Red Scare" immediately after the war in the United States, immigrants from Russia in London, most of them Jews, were viewed with deep suspicion. In 1920, elements of the government even agreed that Russian immigrants were to be interned en masse in time of war.[37] During the 1930s, immigrants from Germany, also principally Jewish, were to be interned in the event of war.

Anti-Semitism in official circles also paralleled the American variant. While expressing sympathy for the persecuted Jews (e.g., George Messersmith in the United States), officials often held anti-Semitic views that inevitably found their way into immigration policy. The British ambassador to Germany in 1933, Sir Horace Rumbold, is a case in point. He was strongly anti-Nazi, wrote a critique of *Mein Kampf* that was required reading within the Foreign Office, and even lectured Hitler on the wrong-headedness of his anti-Jewish policies. Yet he also sought explanations for German anti-Semitism in the behaviors of the Jews themselves. In particular, he contrasted the undesirable behavior of "bad Jews," especially immigrants to Germany, with the upright actions of the native "good Jews"; Rumbold aided refugee Jews in Britain after his retirement in August 1933, even while continuing to express anti-Semitic views.[38]

Cynical realpolitik was at the heart of British policy, as in the United States. According to London, this policy was driven by "self-interest, opportunism and an overriding concern with control"[39] and was "ruled by priorities formulated in terms of the national interest."[40] As a result, these policies were hostile both to immigration substantial enough to alleviate the ever-growing problem and to international agencies such as the Intergovernmental Committee on Refugees (IGC) of the League of Nations engaged in humanitarian work.

Palestine presented a major problem for British policy making. Ultimately, cynical realpolitik considerations won the day. Although eventually 140,000 Jewish refugees reached Palestine, both legally and illegally,[41] Arab opposition to Jewish immigration, culminating in the 1936 riots, led to the closing of that venue. The UK governmental White Paper of May 1939 limited Jewish immigration into Palestine to a total of 75,000 during the next five years, after which no further immigration would be allowed without Arab consent. Clearly, a general war appeared

---

[37] London 2000, 21.   [38] Ibid., 32.   [39] Ibid., 14.   [40] Ibid., 94.
[41] Ibid., 12.

to be on the horizon, and Arabs throughout the Middle East were to be propitiated if not appeased by this policy. Hence, the national interest trumped the humanitarian needs of Jewish refugees.

Nor would the Dominions of the British Empire be of any help to the Jews. When approached about the possibility of admitting German-Jewish scientists, Lord Bledisloe, governor-general of New Zealand, stated that, even if there were immigration possibilities, he would be unlikely "to take any step ... from humanitarian motives which might leave the impression that German Jews of any description were being welcomed to this Dominion during a period of acute economic depression to the possible detriment of New Zealanders."[42] Further, he feared that "immigrants from Germany might be at heart, if not openly, Communists, and spread revolutionary propaganda to the social unsettlement of the local community."[43]

Canada was especially hostile to Jewish immigration. It is worthwhile quoting at some length the response of Frederick Charles Blair, director of the Immigration Board at this time. Writing to a strong opponent of Jewish immigration, he stated:

> I suggested recently to three Jewish gentlemen with whom I am well acquainted, that it might be a very good thing if they would call a conference and have a day of humiliation and prayer which might profitably be extended for a week or more where they would honestly try to answer the question of why they are so unpopular almost everywhere ... I often think that instead of persecution it would be far better if we more often told them frankly why many of them are unpopular. If they would divest themselves of certain of their habits I am sure they could be just as popular in Canada as our Scandinavians ... Just because Jewish people would not understand the frank kind of statements I have made in this letter to you, I have marked it confidential.[44]

The prime minister of Canada, Mackenzie King, believed that if Jewish refugees "of even the best type" were allowed to land on Canadian soil, they would destroy the country. In his diary he wrote, "We must seek to keep Canada free from unrest and too great an intermixture of foreign strains of blood."[45] He feared the "pollution" of the Canadian bloodstream and that Canadian unity would be undermined by any increase in the Jewish population.[46] Canada did take a substantial number of

---

[42] Quoted ibid., 43.   [43] Quoted ibid.   [44] Quoted in Abella and Bialystok 1996, 755.
[45] Quoted ibid., 756.   [46] Ibid.

non-Jewish refugees from Czechoslovakia in 1938–39, but fewer than 5,000 Jews between 1933 and 1945.[47]

With doors increasingly closed to Jewish refugees, and the ongoing Holocaust now well known to the Allies, an Anglo-American conference on refugees was called for April 1943 in Bermuda. According to David Wyman, "The conference's minutes reveal once more the deep fear the two powers shared that a large exodus of Jews might take place."[48] And Richard Law, the head of the British delegation, confided that "It was thought in London that the most favourable thing that could be done in opening negotiations with Hitler was the receipt of a blank negative to any proposals made by the United Nations – that this clearly was the hope in England."[49] Even in the face of mass murder on a literally unimaginable scale, cynical perception of the national interest, here understood in terms of limited or nonexistent immigration, dominated the political landscape.

Impact on the Holocaust

We know that from the outset the Nazi government was keenly aware of emigration possibilities. Indeed, they did all they could to encourage if not mandate that emigration. Hitler himself had taken such an interest. As early as 1933, British ambassador Horace Rumbold reported that, according to an informant, at a meeting of the German cabinet, Hitler requested "information about the number of Jews who had left Germany recently and remarked that he hoped, in time, to get rid of every Jew in the country."[50]

This report, of course, is consistent with Hitler's and other German reactions to the Evian conference indicated above. The Germans, in their efforts to encourage emigration, even went so far as to omit the "J" for Jewish from passports of Jews they knew were attempting to enter Palestine illegally.[51]

There are two possible conclusions. First, the limiting of emigration possibilities implied that Germany and Austria would not easily dispose of their Jews in this fashion. When during the war literally millions of additional Jews were added to territory under German control, then clearly thoughts of mass annihilation came to mind. Second, the near-universal rejection of mass immigration by Jews implied their

[47] London 2000, 45.   [48] Wyman 1984, 114.   [49] Quoted in London 2000, 213.
[50] Ibid., 28.   [51] Ibid., 175.

dehumanization, which reaction to the *St. Louis* and *Struma* incidents by the international community must have powerfully reinforced.

Added to this was the refusal of the Allies to interfere in any way with the mass extermination process. As late as 1944, when events surrounding the Holocaust were well known in Allied capitals, the refusal of President Roosevelt to bomb Auschwitz was symptomatic of the influence of cynical realpolitik on Allied decision making. Although John McCloy, the assistant secretary of war, had been excoriated for his refusal to authorize the bombing, most recently an interview with him revealed that he had been acting at the president's behest. When McCloy brought the suggestion to Roosevelt, he was "irate." Roosevelt exclaimed "Why, the idea! They'll say we bombed these people, and they'll only move it down the road a little way and [we'll] bomb them all the more. If it's successful, it'll be more provocative, and I won't have anything to do [with it] ... *We'll be accused of participating in this horrible business.*"[52] It is the last sentence that is most revealing. Instead of the symbolic and real support of Jews faced with annihilation, the reputation of the United States and of Roosevelt, in particular, assumed priority. The Nobel laureate Elie Wiesel, a survivor of Auschwitz, indicated that he would have welcomed the bombing. "We were no longer afraid of death – at any rate, not of that death."[53] Thus did the personal and perceived national interests of leaders trump all humanitarian concerns.

But this form of dehumanization would have additional implications. Beyond suggesting the primacy of a cynical realpolitik on a worldwide basis, at least regarding the fate of the Jews, this universal rejection suggested that others besides the Nazis perceived the risks (often unrealistic) associated with the Jewish presence. (Note especially the reactions of the Canadian and New Zealand prime ministers.) Thus, when faced with large concentrations of Jews after the invasion of the Soviet Union and increasing difficulty in prosecuting the war, the Nazis would call upon their own now-buttressed dehumanization of the Jews to eliminate this risk. The mass killings by the *Einsatzgruppen* would receive additional justification[54] well beyond the early anti-Semitism of the Nazi Party and continuity with mass murder in the East, as well as its validation, during the Russian Civil War.

---

[52] Emphasis added; quoted in Beschloss 2002, 66.   [53] Quoted ibid., 65.
[54] As Saul Bellow 2000, 178, commented, "The war made it clear that almost everybody agreed that the Jews had no right to live."

12

High victimization: the role of realpolitik

Consistent with the purpose of explaining the magnitude of the killing, the remaining chapters in this part focus initially on reasons for the high victimization rate in certain occupied countries during the Holocaust. Realpolitik is emphasized, followed by inequality and failures of mutual identification among the victims. This part of the book concludes with a comparison among Jewish ghettos in Eastern Europe and the reasons for revolt in one such ghetto, but a higher survival rate in another that did not revolt. Paradoxically, revolt and ultimate survival will prove to be independent of each other in these ghettos. Also, somewhat counter-intuitively, individual and community survival will appear to be inconsistent with each other.

Two cases of high victimization now occupy our attention. Why should Hungary and the Netherlands stand out for the mass murder of high percentages of their Jewish populations, especially when Hungary was occupied by the Germans only very late in the war (March 1944), and the Netherlands had a uniquely tolerant social landscape that virtually eliminated the possibility of widespread anti-Semitism? What are the salient causes?

Hungary

The Holocaust in Hungary also conforms to the model of the contraction of socioeconomic space as a progenitor of anti-Semitic practice, but it was German brute force realpolitik that sealed the fate of 70 percent of Hungarian Jewry.

Prior to World War I, the Hungarians joined with the Austrians in administering the Austro-Hungarian Empire, a dual monarchy in which they jointly ruled the largest empire in East-Central Europe comprising today's Austria, Hungary, Czech Republic, Slovakia, Slovenia, Croatia, Bosnia-Herzegovina, and large swaths of southeastern Poland and western Ukraine, most notably Galicia. Hungarian Jews were increasingly

"Magyarized" in their support of the Hungarian aristocracy. After the emancipation of the Jewish community in 1867, the same year as the dual monarchy was formed to permit Hungarian accession to power, Magyars and Jews entered a "golden age" of cooperation. Jews advanced economically and socially while providing almost all of the middle-class economic development that Hungary badly needed.

A mutually advantageous relationship developed between the still largely feudal Hungarian aristocracy and the rising Jewish bourgeoisie. Jews also provided a buffer against the increasingly vocal Slavic minorities who were agitating for a share of political power, something the Jews were perfectly willing to leave to the Hungarian aristocracy, as the Jews themselves became increasingly acculturated and assimilated. The Magyar aristocracy established an umbrella of political protection under which the Jews prospered economically and socially as they developed a modern economic infrastructure within Hungary.[1] By 1910, the Jews constituted 23 percent of Budapest's population. Overall, they comprised "over 40 percent of all journalists, 52 percent of all industrial employers, 59 percent of medical personnel, 61 percent of all lawyers, and 64 percent of those engaged in trade and finance."[2] In Budapest, Jewish prominence was even greater, where the better-known newspapers were owned by Jews and approximately 70 percent of journalists were Jewish. Prominent scientists, writers, poets, and artists were predominantly Jewish.[3]

Although this newly achieved Jewish visibility led to tensions with elements of the Hungarian population, it was World War I and its aftermath that began the process of institutionalized Hungarian anti-Semitism. Two factors were to be salient in this transformation. After World War I, instead of sharing almost equally in the governance of a geographically large and populous European great power, "Hungary had lost two-thirds of its historic territory, one-third of its Magyar people, and three-fifths of its total population."[4]

The Trianon Treaty of June 4, 1920, was signed between the victorious Allied Powers and a newly independent Hungary created from the dismemberment of the Austro-Hungarian Empire. Large amounts of territory were ceded to Romania, Czechoslovakia, and the Kingdom of Serbs, Croats, and Slovenes (soon to be called Yugoslavia). Approximately 3 million Magyars now found themselves under

---

[1] Braham 2000, 19–20.   [2] Cesarani 1997a, 10.   [3] Deák 1965, 368.
[4] Braham 2000, 22.

Romanian or Czech administration. "Retaining less than a third of the territories [Hungary] had once ruled: of 282,870 square kilometers she kept 91,174, and of a population of 18 million only 8 million were left."[5]

A truncated Hungary had become one additional small landlocked European country to be the object of great power manipulations. With the exception of the Jews, Hungary was now essentially a homogeneous state. No longer were the Jews required as a loyal, increasingly Magyarized minority to offset the Slavic influence. Jews came to be viewed as foreigners, an unhealthy interposition within the body of the Hungarian people. The large number of poor, rural, Yiddish-speaking Jews who were widely seen to be unacculturated and unassimilable added to this perception. A not-insignificant number of these Jews had recently fled the violence attendant upon the Bolshevik Revolution in nearby Ukraine, an uprising that had inspired many pogroms by right-wing counterrevolutionaries.

This contraction of physical and demographic space with its associated consequences was to be caused, in part, by an event similar to that which transpired in Bavaria, a left-wing revolution in which Jews were to play a prominent role. Perceptions of Jews as alien were to be enormously facilitated by this revolution.

Following the collapse of the Habsburg Empire and dismemberment of the Hungarian Kingdom in 1919, a Communist dictatorship led by Béla Kun, along with other Jews such as Georg Lukács, seized power. Although soon overthrown by an intervening Romanian army,[6] the harsh period of Kun's governance left a bitter legacy. While Jews also found that government distasteful, perhaps doubly so because of their own middle-class status and classification as followers of an organized religion, nevertheless, anti-Semitism substantially increased after the overthrow of Kun's government. A counterrevolutionary terror followed that in fact dwarfed the preceding Red terror in magnitude and ferocity.[7] István Deák considers the brief Bolshevik reign and the presumption of Jewish responsibility for its excesses to be "one of the determining factors in [later] Hungarian policy."[8]

Counterrevolutionary leaders gathered in Szeged consisted of many of those who had been dispossessed one way or another by the massive contraction: military officers who had lost their positions because of the lost war or Kun's purges, civilians affected by the inflationary spiral, and

---

[5] Weber 1964, 88.   [6] Cesarani 1997a, 12.   [7] Braham 2000, 21–22.
[8] Deák 1965, 370.

especially the "homeless, propertyless, and embittered [who] first placed their hope in the Károlyi and Kun regimes. Disappointed over the violation of their traditional class interests, subsequently they whole-heartedly embraced the counterrevolution. They were easily swayed by the ideologues of the Szeged movement who placed the blame for their suffering on the 'alien' Jews and Bolsheviks."[9] Former public servants constituted the majority of the 300,000 Magyar refugees who fled into Hungary after 1918.[10]

Significantly, this counterrevolutionary group gave rise to a philosophy or ideology known as the "Szeged Idea." Its central themes included fomenting anti-Semitism, struggle against Bolshevism, extreme national-ism, and revanchism. In many respects, the founders of this group were, as they claimed, the forerunners of fascism and Nazism. Indeed, the first military units to flaunt death as their symbol were not those of the German SS, but the Hungarian counterrevolutionary "Black Legion of Death" that initiated numerous pogroms leading to the deaths of thou-sands of Jews. Only the fear of stern Allied reaction to these atrocities led to their forced cessation by the new conservative Hungarian leadership.[11] Gyula Gömbös, a Szeged leader and later to be Hungarian prime minister, actually was the first to openly suggest a German–Italian alliance, as early as the 1920s.[12] He spoke of himself as a Hungarian National Socialist as early as 1919.[13]

Yet the Kun revolution and its counterterroristic aftermath culminat-ing in the truncated territory of Trianon Hungary had societal conse-quences that went beyond a radicalization of the Hungarian right. Everyday decisions were being made on the basis of this truncation. For example, in 1922, a chief judge in a town near Budapest refused to grant permission to a Jewish entrepreneur to start a new industry. His reasoning was: "The request will be refused because on the territory of truncated Hungary the primary task of officials is to guarantee the living conditions of Hungarians. If he granted the request of a member of a different race, a chief judge would act against his obligations."[14] Indeed, this statement may be seen as paradigmatic for all defeated and/or truncated entities of the interwar period and World War II. First the majority must be tended to, and then, and only then, might some consideration be given to "alien" minorities.

---

[9] Braham 1981, 18.   [10] Nagy-Talavera 2001, 78.   [11] Braham 1981, 18–19.
[12] Nagy-Talavera 2001, 79.   [13] Weber 1964, 90; Payne 1995, 132.
[14] Quoted in Pók 1997, 151.

Conservative governments, for the most part, were the order of the day during the interwar period. Surely, as in Bavaria, the threat to a traditional, often Roman Catholic way of life was palpable to many Hungarians. A status reversal, with the Jews as politically dominant, was probably the most threatening aspect of Kun's revolution.

Given these spatial and demographic contractions, as well as the threatened status reversal, it is not surprising that Hungary was the first European state to institute anti-Jewish measures. In 1920, a Numerus Clausus act was adopted, which restricted Jewish admissions to higher education institutions to at most 6 percent of the student body,[15] in a first effort to uproot "social disproportionality."[16] By 1938, the then prime minister Kálmán Darányi announced the essential abolition of the 1867 act that had granted the Jews the same civil and political rights enjoyed by the Christian majority.[17] Following that speech, four pieces of legislation were introduced limiting Jewish participation in economic life.

The first of these bills, passed in 1938, was to reduce Jewish participation in the economy by limiting the proportion of Jewish labor in businesses with more than ten employees to no more than 20 percent of the total. The remaining laws were to strengthen the barriers to Jewish participation in the economic life of the country even to the point of requiring male Jewish participation in public labor projects, a kind of corvée that laid the foundation for the later notorious labor brigades within the Hungarian army. A large proportion of productive Jewish males lost their lives in these brigades on the Soviet front after the German invasion of June 1941.[18]

These "firsts" for anti-Jewish legislation in the interwar period were complemented by another of far more sinister dimension. Although the anti-Jewish legislation was only laxly enforced, and the number of Jews affected was far fewer than these laws required, far worse was to come. The purpose of the legislation promulgated by traditional Hungarian conservatives was in part to appease the radical anti-Semitic right. Now these anti-Semites were to be appeased in bloody fashion.

As foreign Jews migrated into Hungary to escape the hardships of German rule after 1939, especially in Poland, all were required to register with the National Central Alien Control Office (KEOKH). Ultimately, the category of "alien Jews" consisted of refugees who found a haven in Hungary from the Nazi persecutions in Poland and Slovakia, Jews who

---

[15] Braham 2000, 22.   [16] Don 1997, 48.   [17] Ibid.   [18] Ibid., 66.

had fled to Hungary during World War I to escape the privations of that period, and, finally, Jews who came under Hungarian rule in newly acquired territories during 1938–41.[19]

Upon Hungary's entry into the war against the Soviet Union on June 27, 1941, officers of the KEOKH hatched a scheme to deport "alien" Jews to areas of Poland and Ukraine now under German rule. Beginning in July, all foreign Jews registered with the KEOKH were rounded up by the Hungarian authorities and, indeed, were not limited only to "aliens." In the haste and extent of the roundup, Hungarian-Jewish citizens, even entire communities in Carpatho-Ruthenia, were crammed into freight cars. By August 19, 15,567 Jews had been handed over to the SS. First taken in trucks, they were then marched in columns of 300–400 to temporary homes in Kamenets-Podolsk.

Unprepared for the mass arrival of the Jews, the Germans actually tried to halt the deportations, but to no avail because of Hungarian opposition. Complaints by Wehrmacht officers that their lines of communication were being affected by this large number of Jews led to the SS-Obergruppenführer Franz Jäckeln to order their execution. On August 27–28, the mass murder was carried out. In the Operational Report on the killing, Jäckeln put the total number at 23,600 (16,000 from Hungary), the first massacre of this size in the history of the Final Solution.[20] Although the deportations ceased when news of the mass murder was received in Budapest, Hungarian authorities nevertheless had undertaken delivery of these victims to the SS. This fact alone substantially distinguishes the Hungarian from other European governments who were not accomplices to mass murder, Belgium and the Netherlands among them. The latter two will be treated shortly.

Yet the vast majority of Hungary's Jews were still alive in mid-1942. Even Hungarians inclined to genocidal thinking did not yet think in terms of complete annihilation. György Ottlik, a member of the Foreign Affairs Committee of the Upper House of the Hungarian parliament, after his meeting with Döme Sztójay, the Hungarian minister in Berlin, recounted Sztójay's views that

> It would be appropriate if Hungary did not wait until [the Germans] raised the issue sharply, but would expedite the tempo of the changing of the guards [sic] and resettle a sizable portion of our Jewish population in occupied Russia. Our minister first spoke of about 300,000 but then

[19] Braham 1981, 274.   [20] Braham 2000, 33–34.

bargained himself down to 100,000. On my interjected remark he did not keep it a secret that "resettlement" meant execution.[21]

Thus a realistic maximum for the massacre of Hungarian Jewry, even after the Final Solution was already being enacted throughout occupied Europe, was set at approximately 14 percent. By early 1944, when the vast majority of Jews in these occupied lands had been murdered, the condition of Hungarian Jews had not changed appreciably. This condition of relative stasis was about to change radically. And the cause of this abrupt departure was not principally Hitler's wish to extend the Final Solution throughout Hungary, desirable as that outcome might be to him. "The German decision to occupy Hungary resulted from a series of political-military factors; the 'unsolved' Jewish question, though important, was not the determining consideration."[22]

The key consideration was Hungary's decision to withdraw from the war in the face of unrelenting Soviet pressure in the East. Italy had already withdrawn from the war and Hungary had recognized the Badoglio government that replaced Mussolini's. As early as January 1943, the dismal performance of the Hungarian military in support of the Germans at Voronezh during the previous year had soured the Nazi leadership on Hungarian commitment to their cause.[23] Now, at the start of 1944, the Hungarian government was preparing to repatriate Hungarian troops from the Eastern front for the defense of the Carpathian mountains. Most important was the strategic position of Hungary directly in the path of several approaching Soviet armies.[24] With a Hungarian withdrawal from the war and large numbers of Jews in the Carpatho-Ruthenian regions presumably highly receptive to a Bolshevik entry, the Soviet advance could be rapid indeed. To forestall this possibility, the Nazis decided to occupy Hungary. The catastrophic consequences for Hungarian Jews, especially for the less urbanized section in the east, followed directly from that decision. After a conference in March 1944 between the top Hungarian and German leadership in Schloss Klessheim, including Hitler and the Hungarian regent, Admiral Horthy, the Hungarians agreed to the occupation. When the issue of deportation was raised, especially of "shtetl" Jews of Galician descent, Horthy acquiesced. According to László Endre, a key figure in the ghettoization process, Horthy stated:

[21] Quoted ibid., 58.   [22] Ibid., 53.   [23] Murray and Millett 2000, 292.   [24] Ibid., 410.

> The Germans ... want to deport the Jews. I don't mind. I hate the
> Galician Jews and the Communists. Out with them, out of the country!
> But you must see ... that there are some Jews who are as good
> Hungarians as you and I. For example, here are little Chorin and Vida –
> aren't they good Hungarians? I can't allow these to be taken away. But
> they can take the rest.[25]

To be sure, Horthy wanted to save as many of the Magyarized Jews as
possible. According to another account, the regent raised no objection
to the deportations, saying that the sooner the operation was concluded,
the sooner the Germans would leave the country.[26] Horthy's preferences
essentially would dictate the contours of the bloodletting that would
follow in the next several months and would account for most of the
569,507 Hungarian Jews murdered, out of the 725,000 in Hungary just
prior to the German occupation.

Given the hypothesized dependence of the killing on war-related
matters, one would expect the most rapid and extensive deportations
to occur first in the areas most vulnerable to the Soviet westward
advances. And this is precisely what happened. The whirlwind ghettoization and deportation of Jews in Carpatho-Ruthenia and northeastern
Hungary took place immediately after the German occupation, to be
followed by those in northern Transylvania, northern Hungary, southern Hungary, southwestern parts of the country, and finally Budapest
and its immediate vicinity.[27] Proximity to the advancing Soviet armies
and implications for security of the Third Reich were the principal
criteria.

Note the similarity between this pattern of deportation of Hungarian
Jews and that demonstrated in the deportation of Armenians (see
chapter 2). In each case, the sequence began with removal of the victims
from the zone of greatest threat posed by an onrushing enemy (Soviets
in the former instance and tsarist Russians in the latter) and ended at the
locus of least threat, more distant from the enemy.

On April 28, 1944, the decree authorizing the establishment of the
ghettos was scheduled to go into effect. However, the roundup and
concentration of Jews actually began in Carpatho-Ruthenia and northern Hungary twelve days earlier, suggesting not only the extreme importance of this region in relation to the Soviet advance, but also the
necessity for haste in light of proximity to that advance. Although in

---

[25] Quoted in Braham 2000, 61.   [26] Ibid.   [27] Ibid., 113–14.

response to various international and domestic pressures Horthy ceased
the deportations on July 7, in the period between April and early June,
several hundred thousand Jews already had been deported during the
most rapid rate of annihilation of the entire Holocaust. A later government led by the Nyilas – the pro-Nazi Arrow Cross Party – resulted in
the deaths of many more Jews. In all, of the 825,000 individuals targeted
as Jews (including converts and Christians of part-Jewish origin),
569,507 were murdered, or nearly 70 percent of the total.[28]

Comparison with Romania

A contrast between the outcomes in Hungary and Romania is puzzling.
Despite the barbarity of the Romanian authorities, approximately half of
Romania's Jews survived, a larger percentage than in Hungary. Out of
756,000 Jews in Romania in 1930, 375,000 survived the war, the vast
majority in Regat Romania. Why? There are essentially two reasons for
this outcome, both consistent with the theoretical framework put forward here emphasizing losses at the outset. First, as Radu Ioanid put it,

> In regard to the experience of the Jewish community of Regat, one thing
> was clear during the Holocaust: not having come into contact with the
> Soviets in 1940, the Jews were not held accountable for the loss of
> Bessarabia and Northern Bukovina and therefore not singled out for
> prompt punishment at the beginning of the war.[29]

Thus, Jews in the Regat were not murdered to the same extent as those
in Bessarabia and northern Bukovina, because they were not held
responsible for the Romanian territorial losses and consequent refugee
migrations.

Second, despite Romanian refusals to initiate these deportations, the
Germans might still have intervened directly in Romania to effect
deportations under different geopolitical circumstances. And here we
find one of the crucial distinctions between Romanian and Hungarian
behavior. Whereas the Romanians could refuse the German requests for
deportation for their own reasons, having to do principally with the fear
of Allied reprisals after the increasingly likely German defeat, the
Hungarians could not. In contrast to Romania, Hungary lay directly in
the path of the Soviet westbound march. In the Nazi view, as we saw
earlier, the large concentration of Jews in Hungary constituted a

---

[28] Ibid., 252.   [29] Ioanid 2000, 238.

potentially collaborating fifth column that could ease the Soviet advance to the Reich heartland. Hence, direct German intervention was required.

Although geopolitically important principally due to the Ploesti oil fields, Romania did not lie directly in the path of the main Soviet advance and was not required for a strategic defense of the eastern reaches of the Reich. At this stage of the war, after Allied bombing of the oil fields and the absence of a perceived direct strategic threat to Germany of Romania's remaining Jews, an intervention was not required for strategic defense. It is ironic that a country with a far more virulent and barbaric anti-Semitic tradition could save a larger percentage of its Jews than one with an earlier history of strong Hungarian–Jewish collaboration. Yet here we see the importance of geopolitical imperatives, an important component of realpolitik (as identified in the three models of realpolitik in chapter 5), in effecting these unexpected outcomes. Additional reasons stemming from the socioeconomic structures of both the Hungarian- and Romanian-Jewish communities will emerge in chapter 13.

Finally, the pattern of Hungarian-Jewish deportations suggests a transition even within imprudent–brute force realpolitik. Whereas the choice of genocidal behavior clearly was imprudent at the start of Operation Barbarossa in mid-1941, three years later, even to German opponents of Nazism, it could now appear to be prudent. By this time, the Germans could reason, many Hungarian Jews would have heard of the genocide elsewhere in Europe and would have become determined opponents of the Nazi regime. Aid to the oncoming Soviets would have been forthcoming. Having created this body of potential fifth columnists by their own unbridled brutality, the Germans were forced to live with the consequences. Deportation and death of this Jewish population then could easily have been seen by the Germans to be absolutely required in order to protect the German state and its population from Soviet revenge.

The Netherlands

And what of comparisons with a country that witnessed an even larger proportion of its Jews murdered during the Holocaust, yet whose government did not play a significant role in that process? How can we reconcile the finding that two perpetrating states, Romania and Hungary, had larger percentages of their Jews saved than did an essentially nonperpetrating state, the Netherlands, with an approximate

85 percent victimization[30] rate to be compared with 50 percent and 70 percent for Romania and Hungary, respectively? Perhaps even more revealing of the importance of the geopolitical component of realpolitik is the comparison between the Netherlands and a neighboring nonperpetrating state, Belgium, in which the victimization rate was 40 percent, less than half that of the Netherlands. And even France, another perpetrating state (in the Vichy-controlled region), had only a 25 percent victimization rate. We have seen how the geopolitics of the wartime period affected France, Hungary, and Romania. The relevance of geopolitical considerations is no less true of the Netherlands in comparison with Belgium.

As in our other cases, the initial conditions defined the ultimate contours of the Holocaust and its outcomes. A major difference between the Holocaust in the Netherlands and Belgium was the prime military importance of the latter. Belgian territory is far closer to Britain than is Dutch soil. An invasion of Europe from Britain would be far more likely to traverse the English Channel to land in Belgium than to land in the Netherlands. For these and other reasons having to do with traditional Dutch neutrality prior to the war (or leaning toward the German side as in the extensive German use of Dutch Fokker aircraft in World War I), in contrast to Franco-Belgian cooperation, the German administration in the Netherlands was civilian.

In Belgium, as in unoccupied France, the German administration was military. Tensions therefore were introduced between the Wehrmacht (the German army) and other German authorities such as the SS.[31] Often, points of friction surrounded the economic impact of Jewish deportations. The diversion of badly needed transport from military uses to Jewish deportations or, in some cases, the potential alienation of sympathetic local non-Jewish populations, especially later in the war when it appeared as if Germany would lose, upset Wehrmacht leaders. The ideologically motivated SS would often ignore these increasingly salient factors. SS–Wehrmacht frictions occurred with far greater frequency in the West, in contrast to the East, with its large concentrated Jewish populations presumably infected with the Bolshevik virus generating substantial agreement between the two agencies.

A consequence of this civilian administration in the Netherlands was the exaggerated prominence of the SS. The Reichskommissar, Arthur Seyss-Inquart, was a loyal Nazi who was directly responsible to Hitler

---

[30] Moore 1997, 259–60.   [31] Blom 1989, 338.

and took his honorary SS rank seriously.[32] He was aided by four Generalkommissare: Hans Rauter of the SS; Fritz Schmidt representing the Nazi Party; and two acquaintances, Frederick Wimmer and Hans Fischbock. All except Schmidt were from Austria, thus facilitating communication and fulfillment of common purpose with higher-level SS functionaries, such as Adolf Eichmann and Ernst Kaltenbrunner, also from Austria. The depth of Austrian anti-Semitism and active participation in the Holocaust has been well documented. A measure of the SS presence in the Netherlands is the number of men found there – 5,000 – in comparison with only 3,000 in France with a much larger territory and Jewish population.[33]

These factors begin to explain how the Netherlands, with the virtual absence of any tradition of political anti-Semitism, experienced such a high victimization rate for its Jewish population. Yet there is more to be said, for even with the disproportionately large SS presence, according to Willi Lages, head of the German Security Police and SD (intelligence arm of the SS), "The main support of the German forces in the police sector and beyond was the Dutch police. Without it, not 10 percent of the German occupation tasks would have been fulfilled ... Also it would have been practically impossible to seize even 10 percent of Dutch Jewry without them!"[34] This testimony was corroborated by an Amsterdam police detective who testified after the war that "The cells were full of Jews day after day, so there was no room for ordinary criminals. I was sometimes unable to find a single police van for serious criminals, but when a hunt for Jews was called there were no problems, then the vans were ready to take off."[35]

In explaining the apparent anomaly, there are at least two levels of explanation. The first pertains to the general political culture of Dutch society of which the police, of course, were an integral part; the second refers directly to police structure and behavior.

As in Germany, cooperation with the prevailing political authority was a leading Dutch societal value. The utterly one-sided German victories on land over all opponents early in the war, of course, reinforced this tendency. Thus, after Jewish ritual slaughter was banned, forms A (for "Aryans") and B (for "non-Aryans") were distributed to the Dutch civil service and routinely signed, and then Jews were dismissed from the civil service; there was little formal opposition by the

---

[32] Marrus and Paxton 1982, 704.   [33] Blom 1989, 339.
[34] Quoted in Hirschfeld 1988, 173.   [35] Quoted ibid., 177.

secretaries-general who constituted the Dutch leadership under
the Germans after escape to London of the government itself.[36] To be
sure, there were courageous figures such as the theologian
Dr. J. Koopmans, who from the beginning openly protested the
German requirements and who tirelessly worked to help persecuted
Jews.[37] And a strike on February 25, 1941, initiated by the Dutch
Communist Party in support of Jewish workers deported to the
Mauthausen concentration camp, was one of the few public actions in
Nazi-occupied Europe taken by non-Jews in support of their Jewish
countrymen.[38] Yet, deference to authority prevailed not only among the
Dutch bureaucrats, especially the police, but also among Jews themselves. J. Presser, a Dutch-Jewish survivor and author of *The Destruction
of the Dutch Jews*,[39] could not find a single case of Jews who deliberately
avoided registering as required by the Germans.[40] Compliance was rife
throughout Dutch society. Perhaps the comfort they felt as Dutch
citizens with little experience of anti-Semitism lulled the native Jews
into thinking that they were safe.

For this reason alone, one would not have expected the police to
behave differently when confronted with orders emanating initially
from the German occupiers and transmitted through the Dutch police
leadership. Additionally there were severe sanctions for noncompliance.
Not only could the individual officer lose his livelihood but, beginning
in July 1942 at the start of the massive roundup of Jews, officers who
refused to undertake a task assigned to them had to face trial before a
special German SS and police court.[41] At the same time, bonuses were
given to police who exceeded expectations in rounding up Jews or other
"distasteful" tasks such as the capture of downed British airmen.

Yet there were instances of police help to Jews in warning of forthcoming roundups, and earlier in the lax enforcement of regulations
forbidding Jewish entry to parks and swimming pools. In October
1942, for example, between 13,000 and 15,000 Jews were apprehended.
Yet despite the presence in this action of more men than all other
agencies combined (German police and Nazi Party functionaries,
Dutch National Socialists and SS), the Dutch police arrested only 700
of the total number of Jews.[42]

Perhaps one indication of the lack of enthusiasm of police for the
roundups is given by the "reeducation" efforts of the Germans in

---

[36] Presser 1969, 6–31.   [37] Ibid., 24.   [38] Moore 1997, 72.   [39] Presser 1969.
[40] Moore 1997, 64.   [41] Hirschfeld 1988, 173.   [42] Moore 1997, 98.

attempting to bring the police around to the German viewpoint. When this failed, they set up a special police training program at Schalkhaar. Most of the Schalkhaarders, as they were called, now ideologically programmed by the Germans, were deployed in Amsterdam and may account for the police cooperation in Jewish detentions noted earlier. In May 1942, Rauter also set up a Voluntary Auxiliary Police composed of Dutch SS and Dutch National Socialist Party members. They were committed Jew-hunters and served the Germans admirably in their deportation efforts.[43] Thus, special efforts to effectively craft Dutch police units in the German (actually SS) image may have gone far to account for the extent of police cooperation with the Germans. Beginning in 1943, when forced labor requirements and food restrictions began to be imposed on the Dutch themselves, and the war appeared to be turning against the Germans, many police began to openly defy the Germans. However, by this time, the majority of Dutch Jews had gone to their deaths.

Finally, the structure of the Jewish community itself and failure of Jews to identify with each other, in class, religious outlook, or other life circumstances, undoubtedly contributed to the ease with which German exterminatory goals were satisfied. This topic will be dealt with extensively in the following chapter.

---

[43] Ibid., 199–200.

13

Inequality and absence of identification

Genocide, as we have seen, is a massive event that lends itself to analysis at various levels. As before, most of this chapter and its successor concentrate on the victims, a necessary addition to the analysis.[1] Here we continue our exploration at the societal level as a means of understanding two things: (1) how so many perpetrators could be induced (of their own will or otherwise) to commit mass murder and (2) how so many victims, especially in the Holocaust, could be persuaded to collaborate in their own annihilation.

One perspective enables us to shed light on both questions; it emerges from our initial identification of the centrality of loss in the form of the diminution of socioeconomic space experienced by both perpetrator and victim, although at different times. Earlier, we saw the emotional and cognitive reaction of perpetrators to the consequence of contraction. The pitiful or at least unsettling condition of refugees and economic chaos were principal consequences of territorial loss. Now we focus on an additional consequence of loss – the nexus between inequality and identification, and how the interplay between the two variables affects victimization. Specifically, economic scarcity leads to economic inequality between individuals and groups, which in turn limits the ability to establish mutual identifications among the goals and life circumstances of the affected parties.

Inequality and absence of identification between perpetrators and victims

By way of introduction, as we saw in chapter 3, the first mass murder of Jews in the twentieth century occurred in Ukraine after the Bolshevik Revolution of 1917 and the truncation of tsarist Russia. This process had

---

[1] D. Michman 2003.

an inequality component, one that emerged even in the midst of some economic expansion. According to Elias Heifetz:

> The well-being of the population both Christian and Jewish had increased considerably. It was the time of unlimited speculation in goods and money, of smuggling in and out of Soviet Russia and the neutral zone. The peasants, however, could not increase their earnings in the same measure as the others. The products of the land were taken from them by force, at low prices, and carried to Germany. On the basis of exaggerated reports of "the wealth of the Jews," there developed among the peasants a feeling of envy and a desire for city products (manufactured goods, shoes), of which there was nothing in the Ukrainian village, rumor having it that the Jews in the larger centers enjoyed a superfluity of such things.[2]

Because Jews were concentrated in the towns and peasants in the countryside, with only limited contact between them, reports of Jewish wealth could be magnified beyond all proportion. The prominence of some Jews within the Soviet government further magnified the envy of the peasantry so that they asked "What, you want to rule over us?,"[3] in stark contrast to the earlier tsarist prohibition against Jews holding any state or public office. Heifetz further comments that "The Ukrainian peasant had a tendency to impute to the Jewish commissars and generally to the whole Jewish population in the neighboring towns and districts all the sins committed against him by the new regime (requisitioning, mobilization, barrage troops, executions by order of the extraordinary commissions)."[4] Hence, *perceptions* of inequality outpaced the inequality that actually existed. Peasant hostility toward the Jews would be channeled into the pogroms of the Civil War, and the deaths of up to 150,000 people, as we saw in chapter 3.

It has been known for some time now that scarcity and inequality are strongly linked. The greater the scarcity of desiderata (generally commodities, but also societal status), the greater the inequality among potential recipients.[5] Thus the greater the contraction of socioeconomic space, the greater the inequality between haves and have-nots, and the diminished extent of identification between societal sectors. Urban Jews in Kiev or Odessa with access to an expanding economy could be contrasted with poorer and discomfited Ukrainian peasants without such access and vulnerability to German and later Soviet expropriation of farm products. German nationalists could contrast comfortable

---

[2] Heifetz 1921, 7–8.   [3] Ibid., 8.   [4] Ibid., 9.   [5] M. Midlarsky 1982, 1988b, 1999.

German Jews, living in Berlin after World War I, with recently arrived
dispossessed Baltic or East Prussian Christian ethnic Germans.
Identifying with the dispossessed German, the nationalist (e.g., Hitler;
see p. 89) would deeply resent the better-off status of the Jew. A sense of
commonality and community would be fostered between the two
German-speaking coreligionists, to the exclusion of the Jews whose
economic comfort would be increasingly resented.

One can, of course, make the same argument for Hungarian nationalists witnessing the arrival of hundreds of thousands of Christian
Hungarian public servants rendered jobless by the massive truncation
of Hungary after dismemberment of the Austro-Hungarian Empire.
Here resentment of the Jew would even be greater because of the virtual
control of the nonagricultural sector of the Hungarian economy by the
Jewish bourgeoisie, as we saw in the preceding chapter, in comparison
with the much smaller extent of relative Jewish economic empowerment
in Germany. And, indeed, Hungarian political anti-Semitism was widespread after World War I, leading to the first overtly anti-Semitic
legislation in all of Europe during the interwar period. In contrast,
German anti-Semitism was not as widespread, and, even after the Nazi
electoral victories of 1932 and 1933, the Nazi-sponsored economic
boycott of Jewish businesses in April 1933 was a grand failure.[6] The
Nazis garnered votes mostly for other reasons,[7] a fact that led them to
rely on the fomenting of anti-Semitism during the later 1930s and the
war years.[8] Thus, the *extent* of socioeconomic contraction and contrast
with the better-off Jew is predictive of the degree of popular political
anti-Semitism in these two cases.

Inequality and absence of identification among the victims

Similar arguments apply to Jews herded into ghettos far too small to
adequately accommodate the large number of newcomers. The Jews
were divorced from the national economy by the German occupiers,
so the unavailability of productive work immediately distinguished the
affluent from the poor. Those who were able to bring with them large
amounts of cash or diamonds, a frequently used form of currency, were
able to purchase temporary exemptions from deportation or simply to
use their influence with ghetto leaders to prolong their lives in the
expectation that in the end they would survive, an unattainable goal

[6] Kershaw 1998.   [7] Abel [1938] 1986; Merkl 1975.   [8] Obenaus 2000.

for the vast majority. After early 1942, Nazi policy was to ultimately murder every last Jew in occupied Europe. But the vast majority of Jews had no way of knowing this hideous fact, and, even when apprised of Nazi intentions, many simply chose to disbelieve this apparent flouting of all moral restraints.

East European ghettos

In the East European ghettos, it was not only socioeconomic class that distinguished among inmates, but point of geographic origin that tended to be crucial in establishing failures of mutual identification. Refugees and expellees from other regions tended to be treated differently from the native Jews, even in the ghettos. In the Warsaw ghetto, for example, "in refugee homes between 20 and 25 people would be forced to live in a room measuring 4 by 6 meters. In the homes of natives, up to seven persons lived in one room."[9] The average density across natives and "foreigners" was less than 4 m^2 per person in the Łódź ghetto, and in Kaunas (Lithuania), 2.25 m^2 per person.[10]

Because of the massive resettlement efforts by the Germans, the space problem was enormous:

> The dimensions of the mass migration are best illustrated by the fact that, according to the official German population census of April 18, 1941, 1,365, or 26 percent, of the 5,239 Jews in Kutno were refugees from 75 different localities. In the small town of Zagorów (Konin district), with a Jewish population of 2,170 in 1940, 1,582, or 73 percent were refugees ... According to the report of the Warsaw Ghetto refugee committee of December 31, 1940, there were in the Warsaw Ghetto 78,625 refugees from 73 towns (14,823 from Łódź, 6,230 from Kalisz, 2,097 from Włocławek, among others). Refugees numbered 20 percent of all the Jews registered in the ghetto at that time. During the period from January to April 1941, over 70,000 Jews from the western part of the district were driven into the Warsaw Ghetto, and by mid-1941 the refugee population rose to almost 150,000 souls, one-third of all the ghetto inmates.[11]

Living in squalid, overcrowded conditions that beggar the imagination, the death rate of refugees even before they were deported exceeded that of the natives. Because they were forced to leave their homes almost immediately, they had few garments, no furniture, very little money, and

---

[9] Trunk 1972, 109.   [10] Ibid.   [11] Ibid., 129–30.

virtually no space in which to live. Often what little they could take with them was stolen by either the German or Polish authorities. Indigence was a problem in Polish cities such as Lublin and Kielce even before the war. Now it became a problem literally without solution, except for the rapid deaths of the many indigent refugees.[12]

In addition to the different life circumstances of refugees and natives as well as class distinctions, there were frequent additional intrusions to minimize identification among the ghetto inhabitants. For example, in the fall and winter of 1941–42, approximately 20,000 Jews from Austria, Germany, and Prague were "resettled" in the Łódź ghetto. Because of their much better life circumstances before the war and less rapid dislocation by the German authorities, many were able to bring with them quantities of cash, diamonds, or other personal belongings that simply were unknown in the poverty-stricken Jewish communities of Eastern Europe. As a result of this sudden infusion of cash and valuables, inflation rapidly increased and the ghetto currency plummeted in value. In short, the newcomers could buy food and additional necessities of life, while others in the ghetto could not.[13] As Zygmunt Bauman put it, "In the ghetto, distance between classes was the distance between life and death."[14] Disparities of this kind were significant in turning Jew against Jew and diminishing substantially the prospects for cooperation against the Nazis. Equality, as we know from the work of Morton Deutsch and others, is a strong vehicle for cooperation.[15]

The Netherlands

Yet one did not require a ghetto with its horribly constricted spaces to yield critical differences among Jews. Although an Amsterdam ghetto was contemplated, it never came into existence, despite the presence of a fairly well-defined "Jewish quarter." Perhaps the fact that this neighborhood did not contain a majority of Amsterdam's Jews influenced the outcome.[16] Differences among Dutch Jews predated the Holocaust by several centuries. As early as the middle of the seventeenth century, two major groups of Jews resided in the Netherlands: Ashkenazic Jews (those

---

[12] Ibid., 131.
[13] Ibid., 97. Recently released photographs of the Łódź ghetto vividly illustrate the gap between a small privileged elite celebrating birthdays and other occassions and the destitute majority barely managing a day-to-day subsistence (Alvarez 2005).
[14] Bauman 1989, 146.   [15] Deutsch 1985; M. Midlarsky 1999.   [16] Moore 1997, 67–68.

of Central and East European origin) and Sephardic Jews (mainly Portuguese in origin). According to Bob Moore, "The Sephardim chose to avoid any contact with their Eastern European co-religionists, which necessitated the continuance of separate religious and secular organizations by each community."[17] Indeed, this was a characteristic of Dutch society in general in which four vertical *zuilen* (pillars) – Protestant, Roman Catholic, social democratic, and so called liberal or neutral – divided the society, with the Jews tending to associate with the two nonreligious pillars.[18] Although class inequality was not a factor in this societal segmentation, nevertheless, cooperation among the four categories was not substantial.

According to Moore, among the many divisive elements in the Jewish population, degree of religious observance within both Ashkenazic and Sephardic groups was not the least important. "Nevertheless, the crucial factor seems to have been the chasm between the Jewish elite and proletariat."[19] Class differences were significant. Jews were markedly overrepresented in lower middle-class or proletarian occupations such as diamond cutting, which did not enjoy high earnings.[20]

Added to this mix of divisive elements is national origin. By 1940, as the result of immigration, nearly 16 percent of the Jews in the Netherlands originated from Central and Eastern Europe.[21] The Dutch Jews had little in common with these German- or Yiddish-speaking Jews, culturally, socially, or linguistically. Even economically, there were disparities. Some of the refugees, especially those from Germany, were better off than the native Dutch Jews. Many of the German Jews settled in the more affluent sections of Amsterdam and its suburbs. "Indeed, the refugee enclaves became so well-known that in some quarters the number 24 tram was re-christened the 'Berlin express,' and the number 8 reputedly had a sign that the conductor also spoke Dutch."[22] There were further resentments of the apparent arrogant attitude of the German-Jewish refugees toward their Dutch-Jewish hosts. Despite fleeing Germany, the refugees tended to tout German culture as decidedly superior to the native Dutch variety.

At the other end of the economic spectrum, the East European Yiddish speakers tended to inflate the ranks of the proletariat. Poorly educated or trained for the workplace (although well-versed in their religion), these Jews could find no better places on the economic ladder

[17] Ibid., 21.   [18] Ibid., 10.   [19] Ibid., 24.   [20] Ibid., 26.   [21] Ibid., 259.
[22] Ibid., 31.

than its lowest rungs. Thus, economic inequality that was relatively severe prior to the immigration of the 1930s was worsened considerably at the end of this period. Although the immigrants numbered no more than 16 percent of the Jewish population, they tended to concentrate in Amsterdam, thereby increasing the large-scale urban visibility of this inequality.

Much has been written about the Amsterdam Jewish Council, especially the extent of its cooperation with the German authorities. My purpose here is not to pass judgment on any of the actions of this council or on its East European Judenrat counterparts. As Moore in his comments on the Amsterdam Jewish Council[23] and Isaiah Trunk in his judgments of the Judenrate make clear,[24] the extraordinary moral complexity of their highly constrained situations make any condemnations morally uncertain, if not outright derelict. Yet one can examine the quality and extent of collaboration as a measure of the unwillingness of many Jews to cooperate with their besieged coreligionists in thwarting the Nazi goals. Effectively, the Dutch Jewish council was exceptional in the efforts of its leadership to protect the middle- and upper-class Dutch-Jewish population, especially the families and friends of those within the leadership circle. To this end, the leadership of the council demanded absolute cooperation by Jews with the German authorities. All German demands of the Jewish community were funneled through the council; they were instantly obeyed. As Moore put it, "Each time it was asked for a concession in the form of co-operation or the compilation of lists or choices of who should be eligible for labour service or deportation, the Council complied."[25]

The council probably gave the Jewish population the illusion of some security when in fact there was none. Many Jews hoped that the cooperation demanded by the councils, acting as intermediaries with the Germans, was a means to an end – survival. This, as we know, was a false hope, which leaders of the council may in fact have realized as early as 1942 when reports of massacres in the East began to be received in the Netherlands. Professor David Cohen, one of the two Amsterdam council leaders, explicitly dismissed these reports as irrelevant in the current circumstances, for how could the Westernized Jews of the Netherlands be treated by the Germans the same as the poor "shtetl" Jews of Poland?

After the war, Cohen, who survived, argued that to save the community a certain portion had to be retained (the "elite," to use his own

---

[23] Ibid.   [24] Trunk 1972.   [25] Moore 1997, 109.

word) while the remainder (presumably the "nonelite") had to be sacrificed.[26] In response to this assertion,

> Cohen's argument that he had to protect and preserve a nucleus of the elite for the eventual rehabilitation of the community, and if necessary leave the others to their fate, is unacceptable – an excuse for saving members of a protected class to which the heads of the Council themselves belonged. Indeed, the results show that to the extent to which matters depended on the Council, it was the rich and the intellectuals who were saved.[27]

That a form of class warfare was being practiced is borne out by available statistics. For example, in Amsterdam, 62.9 percent of deportation exemptions were distributed by the council to middle- and upper-class neighborhoods, but only 38.8 percent of the Jewish population was found in these neighborhoods. In the Hague, also with a collaborating council, 75 percent of the lower classes had been deported by April 1943 and 59 percent of the middle classes, but only 43 percent of the upper class.[28] This was despite the tendency of the Nazis to destroy the Jewish leadership early in the extermination process to avoid the possibility of rebellion. Apparently the Dutch Jewish councils were judged to be sufficiently cooperative to avoid any early Nazi attacks on their leaders.

To the great misfortune of the Dutch Jews, the German judgment proved to be correct. After the war, the following dialogue with Willi Lages, head of the German central office for Jewish affairs in the Netherlands (the Zentralstelle), was recorded:

> "How was the Jewish Council used?"
> "In every possible way."
> "Did you find them easy to work with?"
> "Very easy, indeed."[29]

Elsewhere, Lages commented that "without the Jewish Council we would not have achieved anything."[30]

Dutch Jews, in their inequality of class as well as diversity of national origin and extent of religious observance, failed to identify with each other in opposition to the German oppressor. Indeed, if anything, the leadership of the council, especially Abraham Asscher and David Cohen, may have to a certain extent identified with the aggressor, while

---

[26] Presser 1969, 205.   [27] J. Michman 1989, 834.   [28] Moore 1997, 112–13.
[29] Quoted in Presser 1969, 271.   [30] Quoted in Moore 1997, 246.

demanding absolute obedience from the Jewish masses. Privileges were
conferred on both men that simply were not available to other Jews.
Asscher, for example, was able to use his bicycle and telephone, could
ride in automobiles and trams, and even asked Lages for permission to
travel first-class to visit the transit camps of Westerbork and Vught
where Jews were held prior to deportation to Auschwitz.[31] Cohen did
not avail himself of all of these privileges but nevertheless had greater
freedoms than other Jews. Both Asscher and Cohen along with their
families eventually were deported, the former to Bergen-Belsen and the
latter to Theresienstadt, where they were afforded substantially better
treatment than the vast majority of Dutch Jews, thereby enabling them
to survive the war. Other Jews were deported ultimately to Auschwitz
where they were generally murdered immediately upon arrival, especially the children and elderly.

A wry joke circulating among the remaining Jews in 1943–44 concerned an interchange between Asscher and Cohen. They are the only
Jews left, "and the Germans demand the deportation of one of them.
Says Cohen to Asscher: It had better be you, Abraham – lest worse befall
the rest of us."[32] Despite strong differences in geopolitics, history, and
war-related events, the experience of Hungarian Jews was strikingly
similar. Again, the failure among disparate Jewish communities to
mutually identify likely contributed to the high victimization rate.
Inequality was a major component of this failure.

Hungary

Prior to the German occupation in 1944, two so-called Jewish laws were
passed in Hungary. The first, passed in May 1938, as we saw in the
preceding chapter, if implemented seriously, would have had significant
effects on Jewish economic life. More than half of the Jewish lawyers,
almost half of the Jewish physicians, and a substantial number of
journalists, engineers, and other professionals would have been dismissed from their positions. In all, approximately 15,000 Jewish professionals would have been rendered jobless, along with an additional
35,000 tradesmen.[33]

But in order to minimize damage to the Hungarian economy, the law
was only laxly enforced. Its purpose was to appease Germany and its
ideological allies on the extreme Hungarian right. The second Jewish

[31] Presser 1969, 275.   [32] Quoted ibid., 276.   [33] Don 1997, 51–52.

law, enacted in early 1939, however, "extended discrimination deep into all aspects of political and civil life."[34] Jewish tradesmen were to be excluded from many, even most, of their traditional occupations. Quota restrictions of 12 percent in white-collar jobs and 6 percent in the liberal professions (lawyers, physicians, pharmacists) were imposed, thus limiting Jewish employment to numbers far below their earlier levels. In contrast to pre-quota employment of close to 100 percent, imposition of quotas resulted in employment rates varying between 20 percent and 60 percent, depending on occupation. By 1942, anywhere between 140,000 and 222,000 people had lost their sources of livelihood.[35] However, because of the strong connections that remained between the Jewish entrepreneurial upper class and the Hungarian aristocracy, few of the Jewish entrepreneurs were affected. "The Jewish laws seemed to make little visible impact on the fortunes of the very large Jewish industrial enterprises."[36] Nevertheless,

> The overall economic effects of the Jewish Laws on the Jewish public were highly regressive. They dramatically widened the income and wealth gap within the community, between the well-to-do classes and the lower middle classes. While the income of the upper echelon was hardly impaired and probably improved as a result of wartime prosperity and inflation, the peddler, the artisan, the white-collar employee and the average liberal professional became impoverished, first, by losing their jobs and, second, by losing through inflation the value of their savings. The wealth factor further widened economic inequality. Until the German occupation Jewish wealth, except farmland, was not directly affected. Neither was income from property affected. This applied, naturally, only to those who owned property and did not have to sell it to survive. The wealth factor thus reinforced the regressive tendencies caused by the selective implementation of the Jewish laws.[37]

The second major source of disparity and divisiveness stemmed from the social, cultural, and religious orientation of Hungarian Jews. In contrast to the upper class of Jewish (or formerly Jewish) magnates who had deep ties to the Hungarian aristocracy, most Jews led social and religious lives that principally involved other Jews. This was especially true of the provinces, which yielded by far the highest number of victims.

---

[34] Ibid., 56.   [35] Ibid., 59.   [36] Ibid., 68.   [37] Ibid., 71.

There were three sources of Hungarian-Jewish immigration. Two of them, the Austro-German and Bohemian-Moravian, were to eventually coalesce into a fairly homogenous group who called themselves "Magyars of the Israelite faith." Religiously, they were Neolog (roughly equivalent to contemporary Reform Judaism) in religious affiliation and were highly assimilated culturally. By the early 1940s very few, if any, spoke Yiddish. Many could not even remember a family ancestor who did. These were the Jews who were most prominently found in Trianon Hungary (territory that remained to Hungary after the Trianon Peace Treaty of 1920), especially in Budapest.

By way of contrast, the Jews of Carpatho-Ruthenia to the northeast were Yiddish-speaking, religiously Orthodox, frequently Hasidic, and had little in common with the remainder of Hungarian Jewry. Whereas, the former were mostly middle-class, the Jews of Carpatho-Ruthenia were engaged either in rural business or most frequently in manual labor.[38] Additionally, in contrast to the assimilated Jews of Trianon Hungary, those of Carpatho-Ruthenia were extraordinarily resistant to assimilation:

> The resistance to assimilation in Carpatho-Ruthenia may be gauged from the statistics on mixed marriages in the various regions of pre-World War II Czechoslovakia. While the proportion of Jewish men taking non-Jewish wives was 30 percent in Bohemia, 19 percent in Moravia, and 5 percent in Slovakia, it was only 0.4 percent in Carpatho-Ruthenia. Jewish women who married non-Jewish husbands constituted 26 percent in Bohemia, 16.6 percent in Moravia, 4.8 percent in Slovakia, and 0.9 percent in Carpatho-Ruthenia.[39]

Moreover, while only 5.9 percent of Carpatho-Ruthenia Jews declared themselves to be Hungarian in nationality in the 1930 census, 92.6 percent considered themselves to be Jewish.[40] Transylvania to the east, the third major region to be found in wartime Hungary, reflected a mix of Orthodoxy, Hasidism and a Hungarian cultural orientation even among the religiously observant.

In addition to the typical granting of "special status" to Jewish leaders in order to gain their cooperation,[41] thereby limiting identification between elite and mass, the diverse nature of Hungarian Jews made for extreme difficulties in identification among them. Even within the Orthodox community, say in Transylvania, there were many who did

---

[38] Braham 1981, 81–82.   [39] Ibid., 83.   [40] Ibid., 1, 83.   [41] Braham 2000, 77.

not speak Yiddish, suggesting a strong contrast with Orthodox, even non-Hasidic, Jews who spoke only Yiddish in Carpatho-Ruthenia. (I am personally acquainted with one Hungarian Orthodox Jewish woman who learned to speak Yiddish only in the displaced persons camps of postwar Germany, as her only means of communicating with many non-Hungarian Jews.) Also contributing to this dizzying mix of identities was the fact that most Jews from Carpatho-Ruthenia were relatively recent immigrants from Polish Galicia, and that Carpatho-Ruthenia along with portions of Transylvania was alternately ruled by Czechoslovak or Romanian political authorities prior to 1940. In contrast, no such political transfers occurred in Trianon Hungary.

For Hungarian Jews, especially in the provinces, the result of inequalities and failures to identify was catastrophic. While David Cohen in the Netherlands could assume with perhaps some justification in prior history that murderous events in the East simply could not be repeated in the more civilized West, no such assumption could be made in Hungary, especially regarding Galician-descended Jews in Carpatho-Ruthenia. Their brethren in Poland already had gone to their deaths, and this fact was now well known in Hungarian-Jewish circles. As early as the late summer of 1941, the news of the mass murder of 16,000–18,000 "alien" Jews deported to Kamenets-Podolsk had reached Hungary. The more general exterminatory activities of the *Einsatzgruppen* were also by now well known.[42]

Other sources of news existed as well. Thousands of Jewish refugees had escaped into Hungary from Poland and Slovakia, bringing with them word of the extermination camps. More specific information was provided from the relative safety of Slovakia. The working group of the Bratislava Jewish Council was active in forwarding information to Hungarian-Jewish counterparts. On March 24, 1943, a full year before the beginning of the Hungarian deportation, Gisi Fleischmann of the Slovakian group identified annihilation centers in Poland where the only Jews left alive were those deemed fit to work. Most remaining Polish Jews had been murdered. Additionally, "though bitterly complaining about the callousness and insensitivity of the Hungarian Jewish leaders, Fleischmann continued to forward further details about the annihilation of the European Jews in Poland. Her report of September 5, 1943, was quite specific: 'We know today that Sobibor, Malkyne-Treblinki, Belzec, and Auschwitz are annihilation camps. In the camps

[42] Ibid., 88.

themselves small work parties are being maintained to create the impression that they are ordinary camps.'"[43]

Finally, two escapees from Auschwitz, Rudolf Vrba and Alfred Wetzler, collected detailed information about the annihilations while inmates in that camp. Reaching Slovakia, that information, including the number and origin of Jews gassed at Birkenau (the location next to Auschwitz where the mass murders actually took place), apparently was then relayed to Hungarian-Jewish leaders. Vrba states that he was assured by Slovak-Jewish leaders that the report was sent to Hungary before April 26, 1944. Further, the report was corroborated by two additional escapees from Auschwitz, Arnost Rosin and Czezlaw Mordowicz.

Hungarian-Jewish leaders such as Samu Stern, head of the Budapest Jewish Council, were aware of these events:

> I – nor others I suppose – was not taken in by the faked good will, hypocrisy, and treachery of the Gestapo's debut. *I knew what they had done in all German-occupied states of Europe.* I knew their activities to be a long, long sequence of murders and robberies . . . I knew the Nazis' habits, deeds, and terrifying reputation, and yet I accepted the chairmanship of the Council. *And the others knew as much as I did when they joined the Council as members.*[44]

And Rudolph Kasztner, president of the Zionist organization of Hungary, stated "We had, as early as 1942, a complete picture of what had happened in the East to the Jews deported to Auschwitz and the other extermination camps."[45]

In early May 1944, *Hauptsturmführer* Dieter Wisliceny was visited by Kasztner at his home in Budapest: "He told me [Kasztner] that it had finally been decided – total deportation."[46] Kasztner already was in possession of the Vrba–Wetzler report. Despite those admissions of virtually complete knowledge of the impending deportations and the near-certain fate of the Jews when deported, neither the provincial Jewish leaders, nor the Jewish masses, nor even the Hungarian authorities (themselves probably already well aware of the consequences of deportation) were informed by the Hungarian-Jewish leadership. The Jewish leaders held the Vrba–Wetzler report to be "confidential" and kept their knowledge secret so as "not to create panic."[47] Thus were the

---

[43] Quoted ibid., 90. [44] Emphasis in original; quoted ibid., 92.
[45] Quoted ibid., 93. [46] Quoted ibid., 94. [47] Ibid., 95.

vast majority of Hungarian Jews in the provinces kept in the dark as to the ultimate goal of the ghettoization, deportation, and ultimately Jewish annihilation in a totally *Judenrein* Hungary.

Romania

By way of contrast, we do not find an abandonment of vast numbers of Jews by the Jewish leadership in Romania, despite the widespread anti-Semitism and malevolent intent of the government. Indeed, quite the opposite appears to have been the case. From the start, Wilhelm Filderman, president of the Union of Jewish Communities of Romania, was adamant in his support of all Jews under Romanian authority, even including recent refugees from Poland. Shortly after the invasion of the Soviet Union during the summer and fall of 1941, various local and national edicts were passed requiring Jews to wear the infamous yellow star. Filderman was active in opposing them all. He met with the deputy minister of the interior, Popescu, twice, sent memoranda to Mihai Antonescu, vice president of the Council of Ministers, and to Ion Antonescu, the head of state, requesting, even demanding, that these orders be rescinded. Although he was not entirely successful, the star was not imposed in most of the Regat.[48] Filderman also effectively used his contacts with non-Jews such as Dr. Nicolae Lupa, a National Peasant Party leader who was sympathetic to the Jews. Indeed, Filderman was so active on behalf of his Jewish brethren that this, among other factors, influenced the Romanian government to dissolve the Union of Jewish Communities of Romania and replace it with a Central Jewish Office controlled by the government, effectively a Romanian Judenrat.[49]

During the summer of 1942, negotiations were proceeding between Romanian and German officials for deportation of Romania's remaining Jews, mainly from Moldavia, Wallachia, and southern Transylvania. According to a census in the spring of 1942, approximately 300,000 Jews remained in Romania. Raul Hilberg summarizes the result:

> On July 26, 1942, the Eichmann Referat of the [Reich Security Main Office] reported that its representative in Bucharest, Hauptsturmführer Richter, had scored a complete breakthrough. "Political and technical preparations for a solution of the Jewish question in Romania," reported

[48] Ioanid 2000, 33.   [49] Ibid., 34.

Eichmann, "have been completed by the representative of the Reich Security Main Office to such an extent that the evacuation transports will be able to roll in a short time. It is planned to remove the Jews of Romania in a series of transports beginning approximately September 10, 1942, to the district of Lublin, where the employable segment will be allocated for labor utilization, while the remainder will be subjected to special treatment."[50]

Yet the deportations did not take place. Why? Apparently the intercession of Jewish leaders such as Filderman made the difference. Chief Rabbi Alexandru Şafran intervened with Metropolitan Bălan (himself an anti-Semite) pleading with him to approach Ion Antonescu on behalf of the Jews. Apparently he did. Andrea Cassulo, the apostolic nuncio, also interceded with Antonescu. Wealthy Jews like Max Auschnitt, or converts to christianity such as Baron Neumann, donated large amounts (or arranged for their donation) to Ion Antonescu's favorite charities. One of these was Maria Antonescu's Patronage Society; another was the Palace of the Handicapped directed by Antonescu's personal physician, Dr. Stroescu, who then intervened directly with Antonescu. This particular charity was the recipient of funds directly from the Jews of Transylvania and Banat.[51]

At the same time, the indefatigable Filderman along with another Jewish leader, Dr. Stefan Antal, repeatedly intervened with General Vasiliu, inspector general of the gendarmerie, which would have carried out the deportations. Vasiliu recommended canceling the deportations because of the weather, recommending their initiation the following spring. Antonescu followed this recommendation and, probably on October 11, cancelled the deportation order. The deportations were never to be carried out.[52] Later, in November, when the danger certainly was not over, Filderman even intervened on behalf of Polish-Jewish refugees on Romanian soil[53] and repeatedly sought clemency for the Jews of Bessarabia and Bukovina.[54] Why, then, do we find the ability of Filderman, Antal, Şafran, Auschnitt, and even Baron Neumann to identify with the Jewish masses of Romania, to the extent of an ultimately successful rescue of approximately 300,000 persons?

The Jews of Romania, although of course differentiated in many ways, nevertheless constituted a more homogenous body than those of Hungary and, even with respect to class, those of the Netherlands.

---

[50] Hilberg 1985, 784.   [51] Ioanid 2000, 242–43.   [52] Ibid., 246.   [53] Ibid., 261.
[54] Ibid., 275.

Most Romanian Jews were at least nominally Orthodox and spoke or at least understood Yiddish. Whereas the Magyarized Jews of Hungary could identify with Hungarian and to some extent French or German culture, Romanian Jews, many of them very recent arrivals from Poland or Russia, had assimilated to a far lesser extent. For the most part, they maintained their own communities and were not encouraged to assimilate as were Hungary's Jews. In contrast to Hungary, the Romanian political elite did not see any particular advantage to an economic alliance with the recent arrivals, not only Yiddish-speaking, but many Hasidic as well.[55] Only in Wallachia was Yiddish relatively unknown, but those of Wallachia constituted only a small percentage of Romania's Jews as of the census of 1930.[56] Bucharest, in Wallachia, had a small Sephardic community, but as in Holland, the division between Ashkenazim and Sephardim was not a critical determinant of exterminatory outcomes. Although the Jews of Transylvania and Bessarabia were oriented to Hungarian and Russian culture respectively, the prevalence of a Yiddish-based culture was a common cement.

Despite the existence of a traditional Jewish entrepreneurial elite that was distinguished from the mass of Romanian Jews, much of it had been bankrupted during the depression of the 1930s. As Ioanid put it, "Although the standard of living among Romanian Jews was higher than that of Polish Jews, many were virtual paupers."[57] Class differences were present, but not to the same extent as in the Netherlands and Hungary. The ability of a Jewish leadership to identify with the interests of a majority of the Jewish population was far more pronounced in Romania than in the Netherlands or in Hungary.

On the possibilities of survival

Identification presupposes certain basic socioeconomic equalities. The Nazis understood this full well when they decided to stigmatize Jews with the required yellow Jewish star. Once equal to their Christian neighbors, Jews were now identified by something new that suggested their manifest inequality with others. The Nazi leadership also likely understood the consequences of appointing Jewish council leaders such as Asscher and Cohen, even giving them virtually unlimited power over their coreligionists. With the prewar socioeconomic and cultural inequalities between council leaders and Jewish masses augmented

[55] Lindemann 1997, 311–12.   [56] Ioanid 2000, xx.   [57] Ibid.

immeasurably by the new power over life and death, especially concerning deportations and exemptions which were now in the hands of
council leaders, the gap between elite and mass was transformed into a
chasm. The principal advisor to Professor Cohen summarized these
powers in a memorandum to members of the finance committee of
the Amsterdam Jewish Council:

> The reality is … that the joint presidents, and only they, are the men with
> whom, in the final analysis, the governing authorities negotiate, to whom
> they relay their instructions, and whom they hold fully responsible for
> everything that happens or does not happen. Since it is they who are held
> responsible to the outside authorities, they must also be given full
> responsibility in the inner circles, both formally and substantively. All
> members are subordinate to the presidents, and they alone make the final
> decisions. This means that all the other members, all the way down the
> line, are in effect *advisors only*.[58]

SS officers charged with administering the Jewish councils frequently
were careful to treat the Jewish leaders with respect, as if to consecrate
their elite status and presumed immunity from deportation. Promises of
such immunity were frequently conferred, only to be broken when the
last Jews, including the leadership, were themselves deported.

Effectively, the inequality was two-tiered. At the societal level, prior to
the war, there were differences of class, culture, language, and religious
observance. During the occupation, the apparently unlimited power
(at least over life and death) vested in the Jewish leadership and the utter
powerlessness experienced by the Jewish masses were superimposed
upon these earlier fissures.

These vastly differing circumstances can have profound consequences. In a now-classic experiment by Philip Zimbardo and his
colleagues,[59] dividing college-age students into prison guards and
inmates, with appropriate uniforms, the guards treated the prisoners
in an utterly inhuman manner. They forced the prisoners to defecate in
buckets, to clean toilets with their bare hands, and to be utterly submissive to their every whim. Stripped of human dignity, the prisoners
became objects of derision and near-sadism by the guards. The social
arrangement, not any inherent personality flaws, led to the cruelty. Or as
Zygmunt Bauman avers, "What mattered was the existence of a polarity,

---

[58] Emphasis in original; quoted in J. Michman 1989, 826.
[59] Haney et al., 1973.

and not who was allocated to its respective sides. *What did matter was that some people were given a total, exclusive and untempered power over some other people.*"[60]

The absolute power of the SS was transmitted, albeit temporarily, to the Jewish council heads who then acted accordingly. But if that same leadership could have found some points of commonality with its charges, then perhaps some of the extreme consequences could have been mitigated.

We now arrive at a critical counterfactual issue. Could a greater number of Jews have survived had the Jewish leadership in the Netherlands, Hungary, and other locations acted differently? Certainly, Jacob Robinson's conclusion is in agreement with the facts set out by historians such as Isaiah Trunk. "It would appear, then, that when all factors are considered, Jewish participation or nonparticipation in the deportations had no substantial influence – one way or the other – on the final outcome of the Holocaust in Eastern Europe."[61]

One may even take Robinson's conclusion beyond Eastern Europe and apply it to the Netherlands as well. For example, Joseph Michman concludes that, relative to other leaderships of Jewish councils in Nazi-occupied Europe, "such a comparative investigation would reveal that the leaders of the Jewish Council of Holland fell below par in comparison with many of their colleagues in other lands in questions of political sagacity, preservation of Jewish honor, and even in placing the good of the community above personal interests."[62] Michman also counsels us to "remember those who forced them into their actions or inactions."[63] Even the most sagacious and honorable of Jewish council leaders did not have the luxury of freedom of choice relative to ultimate Nazi exterminatory goals.

But what of Central Europe, principally Hungary, in which approximately 750,000 Jews remained alive in early 1944? The Jewish councils in the Netherlands (principally Amsterdam and The Hague) and Judenrate in East European ghettos shared a salient common feature. In these cases, the deportations began almost immediately after the provisions of the Wannsee conference had been implemented, that is, in mid-1942. German prospects for victory, at least to the casual observer, still appeared to be bright. Resistance to the Nazis appeared to be futile,

---

[60] Emphasis in original; Bauman 1989, 167–68.
[61] J. Robinson 1972, xxxv.   [62] J. Michman 1989, 843.   [63] Ibid.

and, in places of high population density such as the Netherlands, there were few places to which one could flee.

The Holocaust in Hungary, however, began two years later, when Soviet troops were fast approaching Hungary's borders; a German defeat seemed inevitable. In this instance, warnings to provincial Jewish leaders and even directly to the Jewish masses could have saved tens of thousands, perhaps even hundreds of thousands of lives. Flight to the forests in a much less densely populated country was a possibility denied to others far to the west. Survival until the soon-to-be-consummated Soviet victory was possible, at least for the younger and hardier elements of the population. Simply the imposition of difficulties in the roundup and deportation of Jews could have saved lives. Eichmann had only 150–200 SS men[64] with whom to do the job of deporting approximately half a million Jews. He relied on the local Hungarian gendarmerie and the cooperating Jewish authorities. If open opposition to the roundups began, with the inevitable cruel German responses, even some of the Hungarian gendarmerie might have balked. Open declaration by the Jews that their opposition was predicated on awareness of the Final Solution might have given pause to the Hungarian leadership, especially in light of the proximity of the Soviet army and possible Allied retribution after the war. Indeed, Horthy's ultimate halting of the deportations was based precisely on this logic.

Additional German troops might have been required to put down the disturbances, exacerbating the already-tense relations between the SS and Wehrmacht in certain quarters. All available German troops were desperately needed to counter the Soviet advance. And the Germans had already indicated their unwillingness to have the deportations and "resettlement" openly advertised as mass murder. Earlier in the winter of 1943, 1,700 Jewish men married to non-Jewish women were rounded up in Berlin and were being held by the Gestapo pending their deportation to the "East." The wives of these Jewish men began demonstrating publicly, demanding the return of their husbands. Unwilling to arrest the women and thereby risk advertising the genocide, especially after defeats in the East had unsettled the Nazi regime, Goebbels ordered the release of these Jews. They were also reclassified as "protected" Jews and allowed to remove the identifying yellow star. Hitler agreed with Goebbels's decision.[65]

---

[64] Braham 2000, 24.   [65] Heidenrich 2001, 106–07.

Now, the Hungarian countryside was not the same as Berlin, the political heart of Germany. Yet the international press could still have gotten wind of the mass attempts to flee by the threatened Jews, and of the massive protests against deportation taking place throughout Hungary. Why would such a widespread, desperate reaction occur unless it was based on the fear of annihilation? Even nearby Wehrmacht troops needed for the battle against the Soviets but diverted to quell the disturbances might have been an unwelcome conduit for the news to reach Germany. The claim that these were communist sympathizers, thereby justifying the earlier *Einsatzgruppe* mass murders upon the invasion of the Soviet Union, would have been more difficult to justify in a Central European region, formerly part of the Austro-Hungarian Empire.

Had the Hungarian-Jewish leaders, already branded as "callous and insensitive" by Gisi Fleischmann in late 1943, felt an identification with the threatened Jewish provincial population, they might have acted differently. Certainly many lives would have been saved.

Equality and identification between Jews and non-Jews

One may gain further insight into the importance of equality and identification by examining the rescue of Jews by non-Jews during the Holocaust. Identification, as we have seen, may or may not occur *within* the variegated social structure of a particular group. Of course, the same holds true for identification, or its absence, *between* groups.

Consider first the political identification between Christian and Jewish Danes that facilitated the rescue of Danish Jewry. Although at first considered a "model protectorate" by the Nazis largely because of a perceived "Aryan similarity" and absence of overt opposition to their rule, things begin to change in 1943. After a dock strike in August 1943 along with other strikes, riots and sabotage, the Danish government was forced to resign. Danish parliamentary government was replaced with direct military rule.

Shortly after the assumption of direct command by the Nazis, a raid was planned against the Jews. As the result of warnings received from a German shipping official in Copenhagen and relayed to the Jews by the leadership of the Danish Social Democratic Party, the chief rabbi publicly warned the community just before the start of the Jewish New Year. Warnings were spread by Social Democrats, priests, politicians, and others. As a result, when the first raid was carried out on October 1–2,

1943, very few Jews were found at home. The vast majority were in hiding, ready to be ferried to Sweden in fishing boats. Even many of the 475 who were seized were saved from death in Theresienstadt by the constant intercession of Danish officials, shipments of food parcels from Denmark, and other expressions of concern.

As Leni Yahil describes it,

> For two or three weeks, the Danes, identifying the Jews' fate with their own, became totally involved in the rescue operations. They viewed the rescue of the Jews as a manifestation of their national revolt against the Germans, and thus the rare situation was created in which it was not the Jews who were asked or sought to prove their identification with the host country, but rather it was the Danes who proved by their response and actions how great the identification was between their national interests and the fate of the Jews.[66]

Similar arguments apply to the later help given to Jews by the Christian Dutch, but only after most Jews already had been deported. Earlier, as we saw, the Dutch authorities were complicit with Nazi rule. As B. A. Sijes remarks, "The Dutch authorities, and in particular the Secretaries-General, who had been invested with governmental authority by the departing Dutch Government, were the first who must bear part of the responsibility for separating Jews and non-Jews by implementing laws which were completely contrary to existing Dutch law. This was the starting point for the development of a barrier between the two groups."[67] Only later, in 1944, when the Dutch themselves were experiencing difficulties with the German occupation, especially labor conscription, did resistance movements develop that were of some help to the Jews. As Helen Fein suggests, "Why did a movement to aid people in hiding emerge almost a year after it would have been of most benefit to the Jews hunted for extermination? One answer, advanced by de Jong, cites the belated development of identification with Jews and the ambivalence or antipathy among the founders of this movement, who came from different social classes and regions than did most Jews."[68]

Consider, finally, relations between Jews and non-Jews in Nazi Germany. Given the middle-class nature of German Jewry in the period from the formation of the German Empire in 1871 to the rise of the Nazis, one would expect a predominance of helping Jews, or at least active opposition to the Nazis, among the German middle class. Equality

---

[66] Yahil 1977, 620–21.   [67] Sijes 1977, 552.   [68] Fein 1979, 287.

of circumstance here is predicted to promote cooperation or helping.[69] And this is what Sarah Gordon's data generally demonstrate.

In an exhaustive analysis of archives from the Nazi period, Gordon extracted data on opponents to Nazism found in the Gestapo files of the Governmental District of Düsseldorf (GDD). There were "203 Gestapo files on individuals who aided Jews, 42 files on critics of racial persecution, and 30 files on individuals suspected of aiding Jews. The archive also holds 137 files on Germans who had sexual relations with Jews, 40 files on persons who were suspected of having sexual relations with Jews."[70]

The Nazis labeled those who gave direct help as *Judenfreunde* (friends of Jews), while those who had sexual relations with Jews were termed *Rassenschänder* (disgracers of the race). Sexual relations with Jews were forbidden to Germans by the Nüremberg Laws and therefore involved at least an element of risk, if not outright opposition to the regime. In Gordon's statistics, she does not differentiate between the two categories in overt class-based opposition. However, in a comparison between *Judenfreunde* and *Rassenschänder* during the different phases of persecution (1933–34, 1935–37, 1938–39, 1940–44), there were no substantial differences in percentages between the two categories.[71]

Table 13.1 presents the statistics of greatest interest in Gordon's study. Percentages of Jews in Germany in 1933 in the various occupational categories are compared with percentages of Jews in the Rhine province to establish that there are no visible differences of serious magnitude between the two data sets. This lack of difference suggests that the percentages of opponents in the Governmental District of Düsseldorf are likely (but not certain) to be representative of the pattern of opposition throughout Germany. It is clear that middle-class (independents and white-collar workers) opponents of the Nazis are vastly overrepresented relative to the working class. This is all the more surprising because for a substantial portion of this period, 1939–44, the Jews remaining in Germany were mainly blue-collar (58.3 percent). Thus, the opportunity for a blue-collar Christian to help the blue-collar Jewish colleague would have been greater than for a middle-class Christian, especially given the 51.1 percent of the GDD labor force that was blue-collar.[72]

---

[69] Deutsch 1985; Leventhal et al. 1980.   [70] Gordon 1984, 211.   [71] Ibid., 216.
[72] Ibid., 323

Table 13.1 *Occupational distribution of Jews and opponents of anti-Semitism in Germany, the Rhine Province, and the Governmental District of Düsseldorf (in percentages)*

	Jews in Germany, 1933	Jews in Rhine Province, 1933	Jews in Germany, 1939	Opponents of anti-Semitism in the Governmental District of Düsseldorf (GDD), 1933–44
Independents (professional and self-employed)	51.7	53.4	16.2	33.6
Civil servants	1.1	1.0	0.0	6.6
White-collar	37.5	35.6	25.5	44.4
Blue-collar	9.8	9.9	58.3	15.3

Source: After Gordon 1984, 227, who cites the following: for the occupational distribution of Jews in 1933, see *Statistik des Deutschen Reichs*, 470 (1937), 1: 8; for 1939, see 552 (1944), 4: 74; for the occupational distribution of Jews in the Rhine Province in 1933, see *Statistik des Deutschen Reichs*, 455 (1936), 16: 60. For the occupational distribution of opponents of anti-Semitism, see Gordon 1984, appendix B, 324–25.

This finding concerning the predominance of middle-class opponents of the Nazi racial policies is even more surprising given the conventional wisdom of middle-class electoral support for the Nazis. One would expect, therefore, a diminution of middle-class helping of Jews and perhaps a predominance of blue-collar support of Jews, especially in light of communist opposition to the Nazi regime. Yet such is not the case. The theory of equality and identification, on the other hand, predicts this finding of greater helping by middle-class Germans, based on perceptions of similarity between middle-class Germans and their Jewish counterparts and, perhaps at some level, common fate. This outcome is supported in the data of table 13.1.

14

On the possibility of revolt and altruistic punishment

The preceding chapter detailed the impact on victim survival of inequality and identification among the victims. That chapter also examined identification between the victims and potential non-Jewish helpers – how that identification affected the differential likelihood of early death at the hands of the Nazis, or salvation from it. Now I examine the impact of identification not on the likelihood of death and its timing, but on the manner of dying. Why did the Warsaw ghetto end in a massive rebellion in which the remnants of the Jewish population chose to go to their deaths fighting, while a neighboring large Jewish ghetto, that of Łódź, exhibited virtually no sign of revolt, not even at the very end? And an intermediate case, that of Vilna, demonstrated an intent to revolt by a group of organized youth, but was persuaded to abandon that alternative when faced with the unique political circumstances of the moment. As we shall see, altruistic punishment was a major unifying factor in the successful organization of the Warsaw ghetto revolt.

Łódź

Ordered to be established on February 8, 1940, by the Łódź chief of police, SS Brigadenführer Johannes Schäfer, the Łódź ghetto was the oldest of the large Jewish ghettos in Poland.[1] It was located in the Warthegau, a portion of prewar Poland annexed to the Reich after the Polish defeat of 1939. This most westerly of the large Jewish ghettos, therefore, was to be a major recipient of Western Jews deported from the old Reich, Czechoslovakia (principally Prague), and Austria (mostly Vienna). And, as we saw in the preceding chapter, this entry of approximately 20,000 Western Jews at least temporarily resulted in an enormous increase in the level of inequality. The recorders of the chronicles of the ghetto are explicit on this point. Most of the newcomers in

---

[1] Dobroszycki 1984, xxxvii.

the spring of 1942 brought extra food with them. The chroniclers record
that on May 7, "Prices shot up from one hour to the next, and in a short
time the price of a loaf of bread had risen to 25 marks, whereas in
previous conditions a price of 10 marks would have seemed sky
high."[2] And by May 30 it was no longer 25 marks but "the price of
a loaf of bread rose to 600 marks, one kilogram of margarine to 1,000
marks, one kilogram of potatoes to 90 marks, one cigarette, without
mouthpiece, to 4 marks, and so on."[3] Clearly only those who could
afford these prices could buy bread or a little horsemeat, a minimal
protein staple of the ghetto. The vast majority, mostly native Polish
Jews, could not. Mutual identification across the geographic divide
of national origin was unlikely under these circumstances.

Another distinguishing feature of the Łódź ghetto was its condition of
isolation. Whereas the Warsaw ghetto abutted "Aryan" Warsaw and was
occasionally open to contact with the outside world, the Łódź ghetto was
virtually hermetically sealed. Very little interchange between the Jewish
and "Aryan" side took place, in contrast also to Vilna where at least the
possibility existed of escape to the forests to join the Partisans, as did
many young fighters in the end. All of the workshops, factories, and
other places of employment were found within the barbed wire of the
Łódź ghetto. Residents were simply not exposed to news emanating
from other parts of the world, other ghettos. Even the fate of Jews subject
to "resettlement" was known with less certainty in Łódź than in either
Vilna or Warsaw.

Without these sources of news, the ghetto population could
be manipulated more readily by its "Eldest of the Jews" Mordechai
Chaim Rumkowski. Appointed by the Germans in October 1939, he
very quickly took the reins of power (all that was allowed by the
Germans), eventually becoming a virtual dictator. Indeed, he used
that word in response to questions concerning strikes at a meeting
of administrative officials and workshop managers on December 2,
1940. He stormed: "Strikers are criminals! I'll act like a dictator! I'll
stamp them out, them and their families! I'll arrest them and send them
to labor camps!"[4] In a more specific response to a nurses' strike, he
threatened, "And now, only force will be used. No one is going to deal
with the nurses but me. I will break them. If they had come to me instead
of leaving their jobs, I'd have extended my hand."[5]

[2] Ibid., 165–66.   [3] Ibid., 191.   [4] Quoted in Tushnet 1972, 26.
[5] Quoted in Adelson and Lapides 1989, 98.

These are the hallmarks of a totalitarian mentality, one that would brook no opposition or dissidence. He eliminated all sources of such opposition, including separate organizational soup kitchens, private meetings of Zionist or Bundist parties, smuggling groups that could indicate to the Germans that he, Rumkowski, was not in full control, and any other indication of independent activity in the ghetto.[6] His was a collectivist sensibility; the individual frequently had to be sacrificed for the common good. Perhaps this was expressed most tragically in his speech of September 4, 1942, when the Germans demanded deportation of children under the age of ten, the sick, and the elderly, he proclaimed "In my old age I must stretch out my hands and beg: brothers and sisters, hand them over to me! Fathers and mothers, give me your children! . . . Give me the sick. In their place, we can save the healthy."[7]

Even more directly, on October 17, 1943, he stated: "Please understand this. I appeal to you as human beings and Jews! Please accept that you must show consideration for the ghetto as a whole and subordinate your personal interests to the collective interest. Do not force me to use methods I would rather not."[8] Others such as Adam Czerniakow, chairman of the Warsaw Judenrat, upon meeting Rumkowski in Warsaw on May 17, 1941, declared "In the Community Rumkowski was recounting his activities in Łódź. The individual does not exist for him. He uses a *Sonderkommando* for the purpose of requisitioning. He has been collecting diamonds and furs."[9]

The designation *Sonderkommando* was copied from SS usage, thoroughly consistent with Rumkowski's frequent appearance in public wearing Gestapo boots.[10] His sense of the collective goal, however, was thoroughly distorted. In contrast to Maimonides's (perhaps the greatest Jewish philosopher of the past two millennia) injunction – if idolaters were to demand the life of a single Jew under the threat of collective annihilation if refused, then all should allow themselves to be killed – Rumkowski supervised the deportation of tens of thousands including, as we saw, the children. Perhaps this distortion resulted from his rumored pedophilia, for which we also have first-hand testimony,[11] or his desperate desire to be recognized in some fashion by the Jewish community, a goal that eluded him before the war. Whatever the source,

---

[6] Tushnet 1972, 31–33.   [7] Quoted in Adelson and Lapides 1989, 328–29.
[8] Quoted ibid., 390.   [9] Quoted in Czerniakow 1979, 237.
[10] See photographs, Adelson and Lapides 1989, 52, 54.   [11] Eichengreen 2000.

he is quoted as saying, "If I can save a hundred Jews in the ghetto, everything will have been worthwhile."[12]

A survivor of the Łódź ghetto, Lucille Eichengreen, comments, "The enormity and monstrosity of Rumkowski's words appalled me. One hundred Jews, and no more! This is what he considered an achievement! Not a thought had been spared for those already deported, and not a thought or concern had been expressed for the tens of thousands of small children he had demanded we hand over to the Germans. They were gone, and would never be seen again."[13]

This obsession with seeing at least a remnant survive led Rumkowski to take actions that precluded any possibility of revolt. By February 1944, the Łódź ghetto was the only place in Poland where Jews existed in fairly large numbers. Approximately 80,000[14] were found in the ghetto, mostly working in the factories and workshops that produced much-needed materiel for the German armed forces. In Rumkowski's mind, this was to be the solution for "his Jews," as he liked to think of them. If they could prove themselves indispensable to the Wehrmacht and hold out long enough for the Soviet armies to reach Łódź in their drive westward, then perhaps these Jews might be saved. Accordingly, no break in production was to be allowed. The Nazi war machine was to be served with almost-fanatical devotion to forestall the increasingly likely mass deportation, as the German losses mounted.

Accordingly, on February 15, Rumkowski issued orders severely restricting freedom of movement. In his speech, he ordered, among other things:

(1) To begin with, distribution points will remain closed during working hours, that is from 7 AM to 5 PM. The same will hold for the outpatient clinics and other institutions and offices dealing with the public.
(2) The factories will remain hermetically sealed from 7 AM to 5 PM. No one will be permitted to leave his plant. All persons on a plant's official roster must in fact be there ...
(3) I order those working at home to remain there and work continuously under all circumstances. Loitering in the street, on whatever pretext, must stop.
(4) I order a regular inspection of apartments ...

---

[12] Quoted ibid., 83.   [13] Ibid.   [14] Dobroszycki 1984, 301.

(5) From now on, no one will be able to leave his job site, factory, or office during working hours without a pass. Every manager will appoint someone to take responsibility for this, along with the gatekeeper, who is to let no one out. Passes will be administered in such a way that it will be easy to know to whom and how often a pass has been issued. Anyone found in the street will have to show his papers. Furthermore, the work card will indicate the worker's shift. If he works at night, there is no reason why he cannot be outdoors during the day.[15]

This was the end product of Rumkowski's draconian centralization of authority in his own person and a consequent atomization of ghetto society. There was little opportunity for residents of prime working age, hence most fit for battle, to organize effectively and confront the Germans in one last battle, that would salvage at least a modicum of honor and revenge. The Warsaw ghetto, with half the number found in Łódź, roughly 40,000, would provide a stark contrast.

Warsaw

Once again, it is useful to approach the problem of ghetto revolt through the medium of the leader, in this case the chairman of the Judenrat, Adam Czerniakow. Leadership plays a crucial role here because to the extent they thought possible, and to maximize efficiency, the Nazis vested virtually all of their authority in a single individual. And in the Warsaw ghetto, events were to take a very different course from that in Łódź, in large measure because of Czerniakow's far more humane and tolerant attitude toward organized Jewish life and the individuals that comprised it. In contrast to Rumkowski, "Czerniakow was a caretaker, not so much of a community, as of its countless afflictions, and his entire official life was much less a singular daily effort to save a people than a whole series of efforts to save people every day."[16]

Czerniakow was appointed chairman of a spontaneously formed Jewish council in September 1939,[17] a position that he sought. With the assumption of the civil administration of Warsaw by the Gestapo, in the following month, Czerniakow found himself chairman of the Warsaw Judenrat.

---

[15] Quoted in Adelson and Lapides 1989, 409.   [16] Hilberg and Staron 1979, 65.
[17] Ibid., 68.

In further contrast to Rumkowski, Czerniakow encouraged the development of civil life in the ghetto without his immediate supervision. Vocational schools were opened and specific training courses begun. Teacher-training courses were encouraged; elementary schools were opened. Even a professional conference on the consequences of hunger (appropriate for the ghetto) took place.[18]

Under Czerniakow's aegis, a rather astonishing event took place. Consistent with their overall policy of discouraging if not destroying the infrastructure of Jewish communal life, on January 20, 1940, the Germans ordered that all synagogues, *yeshivas* (Jewish parochial schools), and *mikvahs* (ritual baths) be closed. Even small *minyanim* (prayer services with ten or more men) were forbidden. Yet at the end of April 1941, Czerniakow persuaded the Germans to allow the opening of three synagogues. He even suggested to a delegation of rabbis that they choose a chief rabbi and begin to rebuild the synagogues. On June 1, 1941, Czerniakow prayed in the Great Synagogue.[19] Only after the December 1941 decision to murder all available European Jews and the subsequent Wannsee conference in January were the synagogues ordered closed. On March 3, 1942, Czerniakow received a letter from the German Kommissar, Heinz Auerswald, ordering that the Great Synagogue and neighboring buildings be emptied by March 20.[20]

Czerniakow's desire to be an effective "caretaker" led him to avoid cracking down on smuggling operations or other efforts to supplement the wholly inadequate food rations legally allowed by the Germans. He records that, in November 1941, legal imports to the ghetto were 2 million złotys in value, unlike illegal imports amounting to 80 million złotys.[21]

In a similar vein, he worked to ameliorate the inequalities of ghetto life. According to Josef Kermisz, "The *Judenrat* represented mainly the well-to-do, was closer to the upper classes, and more frequently backed these classes during the selection for the camps where the Jews were sent for forced labor and extermination."[22] The wealthy, for example, were almost entirely exempt from direct taxation. Indirect taxation also fell disproportionally on the poor, especially taxes on food coupons and medicaments.

In this, the Warsaw ghetto and its Judenrat did not differ substantially from others. Yet Czerniakow did try to ameliorate the consequences of

[18] Kermisz 1979, 8–9.   [19] Ibid., 10.   [20] Czerniakow 1979, 331.
[21] Kermisz 1979, 12.   [22] Ibid., 5.

this inegalitarian tendency, sometimes to no avail, but at other times successfully. On January 6, 1942, he managed to increase by 10,000 the number of vouchers that would be free of the bread tax. The total number of exemptions now reached 150,000, a substantial portion of the ghetto population.[23] On April 20, 1942, and again on May 21, Czerniakow instructed the ghetto police to raid the stores that displayed luxury food items. Those included sardines, chocolate, fats, and cakes. Cakes were distributed to the orphanages.[24]

From the earliest stages of the ghetto, the political parties (the Yiddishist and Socialist Bund, Communist, Zionist) ignored the ban on their activities. Czerniakow tried to incorporate their activities into those of the Judenrat but, when they balked, he did not in any way suppress them. In this, as in virtually all other matters of consequence, Czerniakow acted as a "transmission belt" for German orders and not as a satrap having discretionary powers.[25] Even raids by left-wing groups on clubs and restaurants of the wealthy brought only warnings from Czerniakow and no action against the perpetrators. Political parties conducted meetings in "secret" and published underground newsletters. Thus, when the massive deportations began in July 1942 resulting in the deaths of approximately three-quarters of the residents by September, the parties and their youth auxiliaries were in place to plan resistance activities.

Shortly after the start of the German *Aktion* against the Jews (some say on the day after it began, i.e., July 23, 1942), a meeting took place between the representatives of the organized parties, with the exception of Mizrachi (a middle-class-oriented Zionist party) and the Revisionists (a semi-militarized right-wing Zionist party). The absence of the Revisionists at the first meeting in Warsaw will have echoes later in the failure of the Vilna underground to stage a revolt against the Germans. In Warsaw, it was even to affect the timing and composition of the Jewish fighters, for a degree of mutual identification was necessary for a revolutionary organization to form.

At this meeting in Warsaw, the issue of resistance was raised immediately, but several participants argued strongly against it. Zisha Frydman representing the Agudah, an ultra-Orthodox organization, deemed it necessary to place the future of Warsaw Jewry in the hands of God, as virtually all intensely observant Jews had done for millennia. Salvation could be found only in God's hands. Representing a more

---

[23] Czerniakow 1979, 312.   [24] Ibid., 345, 356.   [25] Tushnet 1972, 120.

commonly held view at the time was a veteran Zionist, Dr. Ignacy Schipper, who held that Jews episodically had to accept a period of bloodletting in order to insure the survival of at least a portion of the community and, therefore, Jewish continuity. Resistance would only provoke the Germans to intensify their blood lust. Only certain representatives of young Zionist groups (Dror Hehalutz and Hashomer Hatzair), generally leftist in orientation, argued for armed resistance.

With views this divergent in scope, the parties were unable to reach agreement. Each of them attempted to respond to the emergency individually through various self-help measures that of course would prove to be futile in light of the recently adopted Nazi exterminatory policy.

At the end of the first week of the *Aktion*, representatives of three Zionist youth movements met to form the organization that would carry out the revolt the following April. These were Hashomer Hatzair, Dror Hehalutz, and Akiva (Orthodox labor Zionist). The Jewish fighting organization was given a Polish name, Żydowska Organizacja Bojowa, commonly called by its acronym ŻOB. The purpose of the organization initially was to make contact with Polish sources of arms, obtain as many as possible in the shortest amount of time, and send emissaries to other Polish ghettos announcing the organization's existence. According to Yisrael Gutman, "the flurry of organizational activity and uprising in a number of places – Cracow, Będzin, Sosnowiec, Częstochowa, and to some degree Bialystok – should be viewed as expressions of a dynamic that was set in motion in Warsaw in July 1942."[26] However, none of these events was to have the scope, intensity, and ultimately the significance of the Warsaw uprising.

Although the deportations were continuing on a daily basis, after much debate, the founders of ŻOB decided not to immediately attack the Germans. Younger members were eager to do so, but cooler heads prevailed after pointing out the necessity to obtain arms, detail a plan of action, and choose an appropriate time. Until then, any spontaneous outburst would be easily put down, and therefore short and without any lasting significance. Whether such a decision would have been made had the ŻOB known that the *Aktionen* would end in September only after nearly three-quarters of the population had been murdered[27] is an open question. Tactics of the organization during this period included the posting of handbills in public places and other clandestine activity urging Jews to avoid reporting to the Umschlagplatz (from which they

---

[26] Gutman 1982, 237.   [27] Ibid., 211.

were deported) when ordered to, and in any way possible avoid both the Jewish police and the German authorities. In addition, an assassination attempt was made on the life of the commander of the Jewish police, Jósef Szeryński, himself a convert to Christianity and an open anti-Semite before the war. Apartments of deported Jews also were burned to prevent their possessions from falling into the hands of the Germans.[28]

By January 1943, there were some 40,000 Jews living in the ghetto.[29] Despite progress in obtaining some quantities of small arms and developing an infrastructure in preparation for the planned uprising, the rebels were not yet ready. Yet an *Aktion* by the Germans was upon them, and the surprised but partially ready fighters responded with force. For the first time, the Germans had to be wary of a Jew carrying a revolver and willing to shoot. An observer, Shmuel Winter, recorded in his diary, "thanks to the resistance, during today's *Aktion* there wasn't a single instance of the murderers seeking people out in cellars; they were simply afraid to go down [into them]."[30]

Only some of the groups forming the ŻOB fought in this encounter, and they were primarily those which had met in July 1942 to form the initial framework. They also were among the Jews that had weapons, always in very short supply. At the forefront stood the commander of the organization, Mordechai Anielewicz, who would lead the major uprising in April, and a band from his Zionist movement, the left-wing Hashomer Hatzair. The fighting was sporadic, but had several important consequences. First, the idea of resistance gained credibility in the ghetto. The Jews concluded that the relatively small number of Jews removed from the ghetto, approximately 5,000,[31] was a consequence of the resistance. In point of fact, this is only partially true. The Germans had planned a limited *Aktion* to begin with, expecting to cull about 8,000 from the ranks of the ghetto.[32] The Jews, exposed to the massive deportations of the preceding summer, assumed that this relatively small number was entirely a consequence of the resistance. Nevertheless, Winter commented in his diary: "Combat groups went out to war again, at Mila 34. Today they took a thousand plus a few hundred more Jews. Blessed be those youngsters."[33]

Second, the combat groups gained valuable experience in street fighting and even combat within buildings or on rooftops. This experience

---

[28] Ibid., 238–40.   [29] Ibid., 307.   [30] Quoted ibid., 310.   [31] Ibid., 311.
[32] Ibid., 307.   [33] Quoted ibid., 317.

would prove to be invaluable in prolonging the much larger uprising in April.

Third, among many Poles, the ŻOB won respect. Although the estimated number of German dead tended to be inflated by the Poles, probably inevitable in such observation from a distance, nevertheless the conclusions of one important underground publication resonated widely. Writing in the *Biuletyn Informacyjny*, the official organ of the AK (the Home Army, largest of the militarized Polish underground groups), the commentator observed, after a detailed recounting of the armed clashes, that "the valor of those who have not lost their sense of honor during the saddest moments of Jewish history inspires admiration, and it is a glorious chapter in the history of Polish Jewry."[34] More important to the ŻOB was the delivery at the end of January of the largest shipment of arms from the AK command. Fifty large revolvers and fifty grenades were smuggled into the ghetto. Without the events of January, it is most unlikely that the Poles would have been willing to part with these weapons.

Finally, the self-sacrifice of the Jewish fighters, ultimately outnumbered, outgunned and killed by reinforced German units amounted to an altruistic punishment by the Jewish youth. According to Marek Edelman, a Bundist and one of the few leaders of the April revolt to survive: "The ŻOB had its baptism by fire in the first substantial street battle on the corner of Mila and Zamenhofa. We lost the cream of our organization there. The commander of the ŻOB, Mordechai Anielewicz, was saved by a miracle and only thanks to the fortitude of [their] courage."[35] Their "valor," as we saw, impressed not only the Poles, but more immediately the Jews of the ghetto. In addition to the possibility of staving off future deportations, Jewish groups that had remained aloof from the ŻOB decided to cooperate, as did the Poles in their arms shipment. The Poles also established ties with ŻOB representatives on the "Aryan" side of Warsaw.

Although we have little information on when an alternate group the ŻZW (Jewish Military Union) was founded, its formation and eventual relationship with the ŻOB undoubtedly were influenced by the January events. The Revisionists, as we saw, did not attend the July 1942 meeting that laid the foundation for the ŻOB. They eventually founded the ŻZW which was able to obtain arms through contacts with Polish former military officers. Although they probably had to pay dearly for it,

[34] Quoted ibid., 320.   [35] Quoted ibid., 313–14.

nevertheless, this group was able to obtain a machine gun somehow smuggled into the ghetto, demonstrating relatively close relations with elements of the Polish military underground. There is no record of any military activities of the ŻZW in the January clashes. During the April uprising it became essentially subordinated to the ŻOB.[36] Ideological differences and disagreements over organizational structure (the Revisionists demanded, among other things, that the ŻOB have a commander drawn from their group) prevented an early union between the two fighting groups.[37] By April, both groups, now under the command of the ŻOB, were able to field about 500 fighters from the ŻOB and 250 from the ŻZW.[38]

But it was not only some key Poles and a major dissident Jewish organization that were drawn into cooperative relations with the primary Jewish fighting organization. After January, many Jews sought to join the ŻOB and some the ŻZW, but the shortage of weapons, fear of informers among individuals who were not well known, and the intent to maintain an elite fighting unit kept the numbers down. When the widespread fighting erupted, the ŻOB leadership under Anielewicz wanted to be certain that the fighters would be fully prepared to confront the German army in highly unequal combat. The Jews who were turned away or who did not know whom to approach spent much time digging bunkers that might not only help save some Jews from the Germans, but also could serve as places from which resistance could be maintained even after the street battles had been lost.

Known informers, at least those not already assassinated by the ŻOB, were shunned and isolated by the vast majority. Whereas before January informers had played a significant role in suppressing dissent and atomizing the ghetto, this had now ceased. Thus, the events of January were to have a considerable impact on the April uprising. It lasted from April 19 until at least May 16 when General Jürgen Stroop, commander of the German forces quelling the uprising, declared that the "Grand Aktion" was over.[39] Yet even afterward, until May 26, Jews survived in bunkers, sewers, and cellars, some to reemerge occasionally to shoot at the Germans, or to make their way to the "Aryan" side. Many of those who survived in this fashion were to fight and die in the general Warsaw uprising the following April. Some groups actually survived in the ghetto into October.[40]

[36] Ibid., 349.   [37] Ibid., 295.   [38] Ibid., 365.   [39] Ibid., 399.   [40] Ibid.

Perhaps most telling was the strategy that Stroop was forced to adopt. Confronted with the tenacity of the Jewish fighters, mounting German losses, and the warren of bunkers that the residents had constructed, on April 26, seven days after the revolt's outbreak, he resorted to setting successive housing blocks afire until the entire ghetto was razed to the ground.[41] Only in this fashion could he put down the revolt in anything resembling a reasonable amount of time and with a minimal casualty rate. Elsewhere, and for a different purpose, I commented,

> The modern Warsaw Ghetto revolt of 1943 had clear antecedents in the earlier, almost equally destructive rebellion of the Jews against Rome in 66–70. The ability to act collectively even in defeat against overwhelming odds and to make the rebellion endure – four years in the instance of Rome and one month in the instance of hopelessly outgunned men, women, and children in Warsaw – created a historical linkage of Jewish national life that would feed powerfully into the formation of modern Israel in 1948.[42]

Vilna

Vilna is the third great East European Jewish community that can be examined through the prism of leadership policies that influenced the likelihood of revolt. On September 6, 1941, the Vilna ghetto was established by the Germans, after approximately half of the Vilna Jewish population was massacred at Ponar, a location outside the city. Shortly afterward, a smaller "second ghetto" was liquidated when its residents were killed at Ponar.[43] Although initially only the chief of the ghetto police, Jacob Gens was quickly established as the effective leader of the ghetto. Gens's military background and connections with Lithuanian Christians facilitated his effectiveness. A Judenrat was established, but because of his good relations with Franz Murer, the Nazi deputy for Jewish affairs, Gens frequently bypassed it until July 11, 1942, when Murer dissolved it. At that time, Gens was officially appointed by Murer head of the ghetto, with two assistants, one for administrative matters and the other for police matters.[44]

In matters pertaining to civic life in the ghetto (with the exception of cultural events and historical chronicles that all three encouraged),

[41] Ibid., 386.   [42] M. Midlarsky 1999, 136.   [43] Harshav 2002, xliii.
[44] Kruk 2002, 326.

Gens's policies were situated somewhere between those of Rumkowski and Czerniakow. Whereas Rumkowski quashed almost all of the organizational activity of the Łódź ghetto and Czerniakow encouraged such activity in Warsaw, Gens was guarded in his support. Food smuggling was a common activity, in stark contrast to its complete absence in Łódź and difficulty in Warsaw despite Czerniakow's encouragement. In part this was a result of Gens's status as a former officer in the Lithuanian army, who commanded the respect of Lithuanian guards at the ghetto entrance. They actually saluted him as he entered and exited the ghetto. They were bribable. Even the Germans called him "the Proud Jew."[45] Because of the smuggled food, in contrast to Warsaw, there were no outright deaths from starvation in the Vilna ghetto, and no deaths from tuberculosis as in Łódź.[46]

Most important, for our purposes here, of course, was Gens's relationship with the nascent underground movement. Whereas Rumkowski worked hard to suppress underground activity, and Czerniakow tried to coopt it into the Judenrat, eventually winking at its existence, Gens studiously ignored it until the question of weapons became important to him, by which time the underground was already established. "Unlike Rumkowski, who used any excuse to get rid of 'troublemakers,' when the Germans asked [Gens] for a list of Bundists and Communists in the ghetto, he told them he knew of none. He also told them that only foolish children talked about resistance, that no partisans had connections with the ghetto, that all the ghetto Jews were solid workers."[47] Gens was even aware that his deputy, Joseph Glazman, was a commander of the United Partisan Organization, the FPO.[48]

As in Łódź and Warsaw, the question of mutual identification among Jews was crucial. Such identification tends to be linked to cooperation that, all other things being equal, may enhance the probability of survival. Because of the relatively widespread availability of food and absence of Jews from outside the region, in contrast to Łódź, the issue of socioeconomic inequality was not critical. However, in the diary of Herman Kruk, deep political fissures were revealed between the non-Zionist Bund and other groups of Jews, all of whom, with the exception of the Communists, had Zionist leanings. Kruk, the Bundist (Yiddishist and socialist), commented on a New Year's Eve party on January 1, 1942, hosted by Gens, a supporter of the right-wing Zionist Revisionist Party

[45] Tushnet 1972, 161.   [46] Ibid., 165.   [47] Ibid., 169.
[48] Farynikte Partizaner-organizatsye; ibid., 171.

that actually had prewar contacts with the Italian fascists: "Il Duce of the ghetto, the Revisionist police chief Gens, held a New Year's Eve party, attended by 25 persons, in his apartment. At 12 o'clock at night Il Duce took the floor and said that despite the hard year this was and despite his hard work, he recalls how he stood at the gate and saw Jews taken away; some we may never see again, others we may perhaps meet sometime – nevertheless, he thinks he has done important work."[49]

Elsewhere in the diary Kruk also comments on the virtual monopoly of power that the Revisionists had accumulated (e.g., "police Revisionists"),[50] despite Gens's efforts to instill unity among all groups not directly affiliated with the partisans.

After the formation of the FPO, the primary resistance organization, in late January 1942 (21st, 23rd, or 24th),[51] the question of participation arose for inhabitants of the ghetto. Kruk tells us that, "if not for the specific tragic situation in which the ghetto finds itself, none of our group would have agreed to cooperate with the Revisionists, Shomrim [Hashomer Hatzair, left-wing Zionists], and Comm(unists). Not wanting to remain isolated, we, too, were forced to join the FPO. Naturally, the Reds took over the institution. They harnessed the partners in the supposed organized self-defense while turning it into a fortress of their own. Having no alternative, our group swallowed all that."[52] Ultimately, the Bund members agreed among themselves not to participate in any armed rebellion: "We must try to influence the ghetto police. But by no means to allow a social and historical crime of exploding the ghetto."[53] The commanders of the FPO were Itzik Wittenberg, a Communist, Abba Kovner, a member of Hashomer Hatzair, and Glazman, the Revisionist.

The question remains whether politicization of the ghetto administration in the form of known Revisionists occupying key roles (head of the ghetto and the Jewish police) led to important strategic decisions based on political criteria. Without such apparently overt politicization (like that in Vilna) in the Warsaw ghetto administration, the Warsaw fighters of the ŻOB included Bundists such as Marek Edelman, a leader of the Warsaw ghetto April uprising, and one of its few survivors after the war.

Gens's policies allowed the formation of a reasonably broadly based partisan organization, albeit mostly Zionist (the Yiddishist Bund members were opposed to a Jewish national home). The organization quickly

[49] Kruk 2002, 148.   [50] Ibid., 135.   [51] Ibid., 453.   [52] Ibid., 561.
[53] Quoted ibid., 562.

began to assemble a cache of smuggled weapons that not only swelled but exceeded that held by the ŻOB and ŻZW in Warsaw. They had "thirty revolvers, five machine guns, fifty grenades, several rifles and thousand [sic] of rounds of ammunition. To these were added the weapons secretly made in the ghetto machine shops, enough to arm every fighter and to have a reserve."[54] Why then did not the ghetto residents rebel, as did those of Warsaw when intimations of impending ghetto liquidations were all around them? On July 1, 1943, the long-time ghetto Kommissar Franz Murer was replaced by a so-called Jewish expert, a Gestapo man by the name of Kittel with a reputation as a liquidator of Jewish ghettos.[55] This, among other events, heightened the sense of foreboding.

Earlier, on June 26, in a confrontation between members of the Jewish police and the FPO, the former were shown to be representative of an essentially politically bankrupt organization. The ghetto police were ordered to arrest the vice commander of the FPO, Joseph Glazman, and escort him to neighboring Resza. For a while, the ghetto authorities may have been concerned about the organized resistance, the presence of arms in the ghetto, and increasing numbers of ghetto residents "going to the forest." The "exile" of Glazman may have been an effort to disrupt these processes, especially after the Warsaw ghetto uprising in April–May. Glazman refused to go peacefully and was forced by the Jewish police to exit the ghetto. Suddenly, a group of about fourteen to seventeen FPO commanders attacked the small group of police and rescued Glazman, to the cheers of the onlooking ghetto residents. For a short time, it was the partisan organization, not the Jewish police in the service of the German authorities, that had control of the streets. After an intercession by Gens to avoid a threatened assumption of direct control by the Germans, Glazman agreed to go to Resza under the protection of Gens and the Jewish police chief Salek Dessler.[56] As Kruk remarked: "Today has an absolutely historical meaning for the ghetto. It was the first contest between the not-yet-dead ghetto society and the empty hollowness of the ghetto rulers. The street said that the police are undermined. The danger that the disagreements inside the ghetto will explode the ghetto hovers over everyone."[57]

Yet, in contrast to Warsaw, the ghetto did not explode. Why should this have been the case? Subsequent events were to provide the answer. On July 9, in preparation for the liquidation of the ghetto and the

[54] Tushnet 1972, 179.   [55] Kruk 2002, 580.   [56] Ibid., 573–74.   [57] Ibid., 575.

transport of residents to work camps in Estonia, shooting at Ponar, or mass murder at Majdanek, the FPO commander, Wittenberg, was arrested as ordered by the Germans. Upon being apprehended while attending a meeting with Gens at his invitation, Wittenberg was freed from Jewish police custody by members of the FPO. Kittel issued an ultimatum that, if Wittenberg was not given up to the ghetto authorities, the ghetto itself would be liquidated. Instead of rising in revolt, the panicked residents descended on the FPO demanding that Wittenberg be surrendered.[58] Gens himself incited the residents with his slogan "1 or 20,000," meaning that, if Wittenberg were to escape, then all 20,000 residents would be murdered in reprisal. As Benjamin Harshav describes the scene: "Underworld characters and Jewish police, masses of ghetto Jews besieged partisan headquarters with screams: 'We want to live!' The Germans were staying out of it. For the partisans, it made no sense to start the uprising then and there because that would mean fighting the Jews rather than the Germans. In a terrible bind, the partisan leadership decided to let Wittenberg go alone to the Gestapo. He apparently got hold of a cyanide capsule and committed suicide the same day."[59]

Afterwards, the FPO decided to send its membership in small groups to the forests where together they fought the Germans until the end of the war. The ghetto itself was liquidated in four waves, between August and September.[60] The remaining FPO members engaged the Germans in combat on September 1 and then fled the ghetto. By September 24, the ghetto was no more.[61] Gens himself was shot on September 14 by the Gestapo chief, Neugebauer.[62]

Comparisons among the three ghettos

Clearly the Vilna ghetto response to the Wittenberg affair was crucial, for the FPO leadership decided against the revolt upon perceiving the mood of the majority. But why was this mood different from that in Warsaw the previous April? The Glazman episode as a precursor may be telling, just as the January combat between the ŻOB and the Germans was decisive for the April uprising in Warsaw. Whereas the Germans were directly engaged in combat with the ŻOB, only the Jewish police were attacked by the FPO. Germans died in the Warsaw encounter, and it appeared as if Jews were saved from deportation by the Jewish fighters. No one was

[58] Ibid., 585, 592.   [59] Harshav 2002, xlvi.   [60] Ibid.   [61] Kruk 2002, 592.
[62] Tushnet 1972, 196.

killed in the Vilna incident, and it even appeared as if the confrontation was futile because of Gens's interession and the "exile" of Glazman. Moreover, by this time, after the Warsaw uprising, the Germans were sensitized to the possibility of revolt by a well-armed group, hence the desperate search for weapons during this later period by the Jewish police at German instigation, and the attacks on the FPO leadership, especially on Glazman and Wittenberg.

Perhaps most important, if we seek to understand the absence of cooperation against a hated enemy, the absence of altruistic punishment may be decisive. In the January Warsaw combat, not only were Germans killed, but so were Jews willing to save their people from deportation. Entire groups of Jewish fighters were annihilated, as we saw. This example of valor in death, wherein one's own life is sacrificed for the sake of punishing the enemy and promoting the ultimate survival of one's own group, was abundantly evident in Warsaw.

Although the Warsaw ghetto was liquidated and the preponderance of Jewish lives was lost, the altruism of the fighters in the Warsaw ghetto uprising served as an example of heroism and solidarity to the struggling Jewish community in Palestine. Most of the leadership of the uprising was Zionist, as were many of the participants. As the East European Jewish communities were rapidly disappearing in the Nazi death camps, the future of the Palestinian-Jewish community must have been salient in the thinking of these Zionists. Such heroic altruistic actions were absent in Vilna.

Leonard Tushnet comments that all three ghetto leaders were not only personally ambitious in their efforts to save their ghetto populations, but were "in a way bound up with an altruism amazing under the circumstances."[63] Certainly Rumkowski and Gens could have saved themselves, if they so wished. Gens was married to a non-Jew, had excellent relations with the earlier Gestapo administration, and was even warned a day earlier about his impending execution by a Nazi officer, Martin Weiss, who took a liking to him.[64] Gens could easily have escaped to his wife's dwelling or to the forests, where his military training and native strategic talents would have been invaluable. Rumkowski was offered the option of remaining in the ghetto with his wife and adopted son after the vast majority of Jews were deported to Auschwitz.[65] Both chose death, as did Czerniakow (a suicide) earlier in the process when he perceived the Germans' exterminatory intentions.

---

[63] Ibid., 204.   [64] Ibid., 195.   [65] Ibid., 61.

Yet none of the three engaged in the altruistic punishment that can yield societal cooperation in the most grievous circumstances. Perhaps, by his suicide, Czerniakow attempted to signal his desire to resist the Germans,[66] but no Germans died in the process, and so active cooperation against them had to wait until the following April.

Yitzhak Zuckerman, one of the few surviving leaders of the April revolt, concludes that "the January revolt made the April revolt possible."[67] And Yisrael Gutman, perhaps the foremost chronicler of the Jews of Warsaw during the war period, argues that "an analysis of the course of events leads to the conclusion that the January uprising was an indispensable step that allowed the ghetto to unite and prepare for the April revolt."[68] In this fashion, the inequalities and failures of mutual identification were overcome, cooperation was fostered by the altruistic punishment of January, and the April revolt was far more stunning in its eventual impact then even its planners foresaw.

Certainly this revolt, along with other historical instances of Jews defying the odds and battling far stronger adversaries, enhanced the resolve of the Palestinian-Jewish community in the immediate aftermath of the war. Not even the combined military might of the surrounding Arab states could deter them from establishing the State of Israel. And many Jewish communities from Europe, the Caucasus, North Africa, and the Middle East were saved from eventual extinction (by assimilation or pogrom) through the existence of Israel as a destination of choice.

Yet the Jews of the Łódź ghetto survived in far greater numbers than those of any other ghetto. In addition to the 877 people who were left to clean up the ghetto and avoided death because of the hasty departure of the Germans as the Russians approached,[69] it is estimated that approximately 10,000 survived the ghetto's liquidation.[70] The enormous number of Jews at Auschwitz in the summer of 1944 (mainly from Hungary) led to the deportation of some Łódź Jews to non-exterminatory labor camps, thereby increasing the probability of their survival. In reality, only the herculean efforts of Rumkowski, the parvenu, alleged pedophile, and dictator, kept the ghetto so productive for the Germans that it became the last place in Poland with a significant number of Jews, even more than a year after the liquidation of the Warsaw and Vilna ghettos.

---

[66] Ibid., 130.   [67] Quoted in Gutman 1982, 320.   [68] Ibid.
[69] Dobroszycki 1984, lxvi.   [70] Adelson and Lapides 1989, 493.

It is a great irony that Rumkowski's efforts to save a community led to the salvation of a not insignificant number of individual Jews, whereas the deaths of the Warsaw ghetto fighters increased the likelihood of Jewish communal continuity in Israel. Perhaps their recognition of the possibility that Jews in Palestine or elsewhere might not be willing to fight for Jewish continuity without the precedent of intense resistance during the Holocaust led the Zionists to be among the earliest and most prominent leaders of the ghetto fighting organizations. If Jews themselves would not fight for Jewish honor, then who would was a question that those young men and women likely posed to themselves. Their answer was found in battles on the streets of Warsaw and in the forests near Vilna. Rumkowski, despite his Zionist sympathies, never really asked that question. Because of his efforts, though, there are Jews from the Łódź ghetto who, to this day, credit their survival to his dictatorial policies.[71]

Conclusion: the role of altruistic punishment

In the final analysis, did inequality within the ghettos have a major impact on the differential outcomes in the three cases? Certainly the Łódź ghetto with its large influx of German and Central European Jews experienced the largest gaps between socioeconomic categories, and the Vilna ghetto experienced the smallest such disparities. Yet the non-economic failures of mutual identification probably were more salient. Wealth differentials can affect the tendencies of people to identify with each other but, as in the Vilna ghetto, political identification was at least as important, if not more so. The failure of the Yiddishist Bund to identify with the Zionist and Communist factions comprising the FPO was crucial in the consequent failure of the FPO to encompass the entirety of the potential opposition to the Germans. Vilna was home to YIVO (Yiddisher Visenshaftlekher Institut), one important indicator of the importance of Yiddish language and culture in Vilna. Another was the acronym, FPO, that stood for the *Yiddish* name for the partisan organization, in contrast to the Polish ŻOB and ŻZW in Warsaw. Had the Bund joined the FPO as the organizational representative of Yiddishism, it is possible that a significantly larger number of people would have been sympathetic to the FPO and supported a revolt within the ghetto at the critical moment.

[71] Ibid.

What is clear, though, is that the massive inequalities in Łódź combined with (or enabling via atomization) Rumkowski's dictatorial policies virtually precluded any possibility of revolt. It is also clear that the altruistic punishment of the January battles in Warsaw facilitated the unity that made possible the later general uprising in April. No such facilitating event occurred in Vilna. Whether the emergence of widespread political identification thereby incorporating the Vilna Bund in the FPO could have made a significant difference is, of course, an open question.

Our focus on the victims is now complete. To end the overall analysis, it is necessary to consider exceptions to the patterns identified thus far. If, for example, it is found that German allies with *expanded* socioeconomic space did *not* collaborate with the Germans in the killing of their Jewish citizenry, as did allies with *contracted* socioeconomic space (see chapter 9), then the salience of loss as a progenitor of genocide will have been reinforced.

PART V

Exceptions

15

A dog of a different nature: the Cambodian politicide

Exceptions to the patterns identified thus far are now considered. First, the Cambodian politicide is contrasted with the genocides of Jews, Armenians, and Tutsi. This is a matter of some importance because of the frequent claim that the Cambodian mass murders between 1975 and 1979 amounted to genocide. The overall pattern in this instance, however, does not conform to that identified in the genocides analyzed in previous chapters.

The succeeding two chapters present cases where genocide was not committed even where it might have been expected to occur. In the first of the two chapters, I examine Bulgaria and Finland as exceptions to the pattern established in collaborating and perpetrating states in the Nazi orbit (Italy, Vichy France, and Romania). Territorial expansion prior to the Holocaust characterized the former two countries, whereas the three perpetrating states experienced territorial contraction. And in the last chapter of this part, a major deterrent to genocide, the ethnoreligious or ideological affinity to the victims on the part of powerful populations or governments, is suggested. Again, genocide did not take place where it might have been expected to occur.

Turning to Cambodia, the mass killings in that country during Pol Pot's murderous regime are often categorized with other seemingly identical instances. Cambodia and Rwanda, for example, are typically treated as genocides that differ little from each other in essential characteristics. However, the victimization rates for the two countries are similar only when treated as proportions of the *total* country population systematically murdered. Although the mass murders in Cambodia are frequently categorized as genocide, I argue that in fact genocidal activity was only a small proportion of the killing and that the vast majority of Cambodians died in a politicide, substantially different in origin from the genocides we have been examining. The matter of etiology lies at the root of my distinction here, not definitional semantics. If we lump the Cambodian case with other instances of systematized mass murder, then the sources of all of them become hopelessly muddled.

Between April 1975, the date of the victory of the Khmer Rouge over the Lon Nol government, and January 1979, when the Cambodian Communist government was toppled by the invading Vietnamese, enormous numbers of people were slaughtered. Ben Kiernan estimates that 1,671,000 residents of Cambodia were killed, or approximately one in five Cambodians.[1] Yet, as we shall see, a fundamental difference exists between Rwanda and Cambodia in regard to the selective exclusivity of the murders. In Rwanda, the vast preponderance of the murdered was Tutsi, with a much smaller number of Hutu moderates opposed to the genocide also having been slaughtered. In Cambodia, the killing ranged over virtually all sectors of the population. The 70 percent victimization rate of the Tutsi contrasts sharply with the 20 percent killing rate in Cambodia. We will see the detailed ideological basis of the Cambodian killings in contrast to the virtual absence of any articulated ideology (other than Hamitic origin) in the Rwandan case, or in our other instances of genocide: the Holocaust and the Armenian case.

Essentially, I argue that genocides stem from a primitive identification of the "collective enemy" in Carl Schmitt's sense, whereas politicides, at least of the Cambodian variety, are attributable to more detailed ideological considerations. Further, the Cambodian case falls under the rubric of state killings, having a particular affinity with earlier practices in the Soviet Union and China. Indeed, an arc of Communist politicide can be traced from the western portions of the Soviet Union to China and on to Cambodia. Not all Communist states participated in extensive politicide, but the particular circumstances of Cambodia in 1975 lent themselves to the commission of systematic mass murder. Because an element of Cambodian state insecurity existed in this period, especially vis-à-vis Vietnam, a genocidal element is found in the killing of identifiably non-Khmer peoples such as the Vietnamese, who comprised a small proportion of the total.

To begin with, it is useful to set out the agenda of Pol Pot, the leader of Democratic Kampuchea (DK) as it was then called, immediately after taking power. Because of the civil war that raged between 1970 and 1975, Pol Pot had a great deal of time to consider his options and to formulate a detailed agenda. According to eyewitness testimony, Pol Pot made eight points in a special meeting of military and civilian officers of the new regime called for May 20, 1975. They are:

[1] Kiernan 1996, 458.

(1) Evacuate people from all towns.
(2) Abolish all markets.
(3) Abolish Lon Nol regime currency and withhold the revolutionary currency that had been printed.
(4) Defrock all Buddhist monks and put them to work growing rice.
(5) Execute all leaders of the Lon Nol regime beginning with the top leaders.
(6) Establish high-level cooperatives throughout the country with communal meals.
(7) Expel the entire Vietnamese minority population.
(8) Dispatch troops to the borders, particularly the Vietnamese border.[2]

Most of the subsequent major political events, although occurring at different times during the next three and a half years, were dictated by this agenda. When the killing began, one observer identified three principal categories and their approximate numbers of deaths:

(1) Between 100,000 and 200,000 deaths were attributed to the execution of Lon Nol regime personnel including family members.
(2) Another murdered cohort, estimated to be as many as 200,000, consisted of party members caught in the never-ending purges of the Communist Party of Kampuchea (CPK). A measure of the extent of these purges is given by the fact that nearly one-third of Pol Pot's cabinet of 1976 did not survive until early 1979, the end of Democratic Kampuchea.[3]
(3) Finally, the greatest proportion of deaths is attributed to the so-called assertive killings resulting from the formal evacuations from towns and other resettlements, as well as ethnoreligious murders. Included in this category are those who died of overwork or outright starvation.[4]

The so-called new people, or those resettled from elsewhere, had the highest total victimization among the general Khmer population.

Variation in victimization

A breakdown of the number dead in several categories will prove to be helpful in assessing the etiology of the killings. First, although small in total numbers, the proportion of ethnic Vietnamese affected stands out

[2] Quoted ibid., 55.   [3] Chandler 1999, 108.   [4] Thion 1993, 166–67.

at 100 percent. Of the 20,000 ethnic Vietnamese remaining in Cambodia in 1975, all had been expelled, fled the country, or were murdered by early 1979. Indeed, as early as the end of September 1975, 150,000 ethnic Vietnamese residents of Cambodia had been expelled to Vietnam.[5] Crucially, and in contrast to other societal categories, no difference in victimization rate is found between urban and rural Vietnamese. Despite the fact that ethnic Chinese were virtually all urban in origin, anathema for the Khmer Rouge, 50 percent died during this period. Next in order are the Lao (40 percent), Thai (40 percent), and Cham (36 percent), all rural,[6] with the distinguishing feature of the Cham being their Muslim faith. The vast majority of Cham spoke Khmer, and the two peoples were linked by "language, lifestyle, a long shared exis-tence and a good mutual understanding."[7] The Cham also shared with the Khmer a history of conflict with the Vietnamese, which nevertheless did not compensate for their "alien" belief system. Among the "New" or resettled people, often urban in origin, the victimization rate for Khmer was 25 percent, whereas among the "Base" or *in situ* population it was 15 percent.

Victimization rates for Vietnamese, Thai, and Lao on the one hand, and Chinese on the other, are revealing, for they point to two principal characteristics of the mass murder. A clear genocidal component existed in the killing of ethnic minorities and indeed conforms generally to the three principal cases considered earlier. The Vietnamese clearly consti-tuted a threat to Cambodian state security both historically and in the perception of the CPK. Historic Vietnamese domination was to be avoided at all costs. Potential allies of the Vietnamese such as the Lao and Thai also suffered. Most ethnic Vietnamese were expelled by 1975; those that remained, often intermarried with Khmer, were murdered. The ethnic Chinese, almost all urban, were killed not so much for their ethnicity but for their presumed beliefs and socioeconomic character-istics, assumed to be incompatible with the new Kampuchea.

Genocide of the Vietnamese

Difficulties with Vietnam began almost immediately after the Khmer Rouge victory in April 1975, when several Vietnamese-held islands in the Gulf of Siam were attacked by the Cambodian forces.[8] Tensions with

[5] Kiernan 1996, 107.   [6] Ibid., 458.   [7] Ner, quoted ibid., 256.
[8] Chandler 1999, 219–20.

the Vietnamese were highlighted in September 1976 in a dispute within the CPK over whether the party's origins were to be traced back to 1951 when the "Indochinese Communist Party" was founded essentially under Vietnamese tutelage, or 1960 when a special congress was called in Phnom Penh, which named Pol Pot and Ieng Sary, among others, to the party's Central Committee.[9] Those who favored the latter date were supporting the independence of Cambodia from the perceived threatening hegemony of Vietnam in the former French Indochina. That threat was accentuated by the treaty of cooperation between Vietnam and Laos signed in July 1977.[10] Cambodia appeared to be surrounded by potentially hostile forces. Soon after, in September 1977, the Vietnamese congratulated Pol Pot on his speech announcing the existence of the CPK and its relation to Cambodian history. Vietnamese radio reported that the Vietnamese "always considered their *special relationship* with ... Kampuchea as their sacred cause."[11] As David Chandler notes, "with friends like that, Pol Pot may have mused, what would Cambodia do for enemies?"[12]

The situation deteriorated very quickly thereafter. In response to repeated incursions of DK forces into Vietnamese territory and the refusal of DK to negotiate with Vietnam, a major invasion by Vietnamese troops was mounted in late 1977. Most returned to Vietnam within several months, taking with them Cambodians who could be groomed for future governance in a Vietnamese-dominated Cambodia. Conflict continued throughout 1978. Chinese diplomatic support of Cambodia was coupled with a Soviet like-minded effort on behalf of Vietnam. At around this time, Deng Xiaoping referred to the Vietnamese as "the Hooligans of the East."[13] In December 1978, the Vietnamese mounted a major offensive that led to the end of Democratic Kampuchea in January 1979.

Why the unabated, ultimately suicidal, hostility of the Khmer Rouge toward Vietnam? Had not the Vietnamese fully supported the Cambodian Communists' successful campaign to overthrow Lon Nol? Here, of course, lay the not-so-hidden threat of Vietnamese dominance in league with the Soviets. And the Chinese were prepared to give full diplomatic support (but not the requested troops) to the Cambodians.[14] Yet such incessant hostility, including the thorough extinction of all

[9] Carney 1989b, 18.   [10] Chandler 1999, 220.
[11] Emphasis added by Chandler; quoted ibid., 136.   [12] Ibid.
[13] Quoted in Chandler 2000, 223.   [14] Morris 1999.

remaining Vietnamese in the country after the earlier expulsion, requires further explanation. We find it in the person of Ieng Sary, the deputy prime minister for foreign affairs.[15] He was born in Kampuchea Krom, essentially the Mekong River region of Vietnam, was a Khmer Krom – ethnic Khmer originating in Vietnam – and actually had to learn the Khmer language. According to Marie Martin:

> The fact that Ieng Sary was a native of Kampuchea Krom certainly influenced his conduct of foreign policy, above all toward Vietnam. If the Khmers organized their first guerrilla units in accordance with the advice and aid of the Vietnamese, Ieng Sary remained distrustful and waited for the hour of vengeance to come: the Vietnamese of the north and south had to pay for the suffering they had imposed on the Khmer *krom* [sic] over the last twenty years. The ease with which the Americans abandoned the game politically, the failure of the Khmer republicans, and the submission of the inhabitants at the entrance of the *yothea* [Khmer Rouge soldiers] into Phnom Penh caused the leaders to lose what little sense of proportion they had. Ieng Sary was able to give free rein to his desire for vengeance and to convince the victorious Pol Pot without difficulty that the reconquest of Kampuchea Krom was within striking distance.[16]

Not only was Ieng Sary able to implement his vision of an annexed Kampuchea Krom through his own ministerial position, but he had also named his nephew, Hong, as the secretary general of foreign affairs.[17] By 1978 Ieng Sary himself was now fully in charge of international relations as he was the only deputy prime minister for foreign affairs, having relegated his colleague, Son Sen, formerly also a deputy prime minister, to a ministerial position.[18]

Here, we find, as in chapter 7, the domain of losses – Vietnamese domination of Kampuchea Krom – operating to increase risk acceptance, even in what would appear to be a fruitless venture. Vietnam was attacked; ethnic Vietnamese along the border were murdered as part of a process of risk minimization. After the late 1977 decisive Vietnamese defeat of the Khmer Rouge forces,[19] even non-Vietnamese residents of the east closest to Vietnam would be subject to Khmer Rouge butchery. But, after the defeat, even more important from our perspective is the extension of the killing of remaining Vietnamese, part-Vietnamese, and Khmer Krom throughout Cambodia.[20] In other words, a close parallel

---

[15] Carney 1989a, 101.   [16] Emphasis in original; M. Martin 1994, 212.   [17] Ibid., 162.
[18] Carney 1989a, 102.   [19] Morris 1999, 102.   [20] Kiernan 1996, 123–24.

to our cases of genocide is found here in the imprudent eliminationist DK behavior vis-à-vis the Vietnamese. Risk acceptance in the aggressive military behavior at the border was to be coupled with the risk minimization of the killings of ethnic Vietnamese at the border, and eventually loss compensation associated with the mass killings of a thoroughgoing genocide of the ethnic Vietnamese.

And if this was the sum total of the mass killing in Cambodia, then we could easily place Cambodia (especially the annihilation of the Vietnamese) alongside the Holocaust, the Armenians, and the Tutsi as an exemplar of genocide. But, as we know, this is not the case. The murdered 10,000 Vietnamese, even including the additional residents of the east murdered with them, amount to only a small fraction of the total. Other sources to be found in Communist ideology and behavior are far more relevant. One immediate source is to be found in the Chinese Great Leap Forward of 1958–61 and the later Cultural Revolution of the mid-1960s.

The Communist models

China in the late 1950s and Cambodia in 1975 faced similar problems. Both were largely peasant societies with enormous aspirations to industrialize along the lines of Communist ideology and rhetoric. To accomplish this goal quickly and at the same time maintain control over a highly reluctant and potentially seditious peasantry, collectivization was introduced. One observer commented on a speech by Pol Pot to students in an "educational" seminar. "He was the only one to speak during two days. He wanted the country to be first in all domains and to become the model for all nonaligned countries; he wanted agricultural yields to be higher than Japan's. He told us that Cambodia was an underdeveloped country, that it had to wake up quickly, make progress, a great leap."[21]

As in Cambodia later in the 1970s, new Chinese communes were established by pouring millions of city people into them. The traditional village as the hallmark of rural China was to be abandoned in favor of the communes. Work was to be organized collectively; no longer would the peasant have his or her own plot of land. Living was on a communal basis with common dining rooms. Also to be found later in Cambodia was a reliance on "barefoot doctors," often children with no knowledge

---

[21] Quoted in M. Martin 1994, 202.

of medicine but who nevertheless possessed the folk wisdom of the
people. Estimated deaths from starvation in these ill-advised transformations during 1959–62 in China run as high as 20 million people.[22]

An even earlier Communist antecedent is to be found in the minimum of 6 million dead in Stalin's collectivization efforts of 1929–33.[23]
Here, too, famine was an essential reason for the deaths. When famine
did not eliminate the recalcitrant Ukrainian farmer and kulak "land-
owner," opponents of the collectivization effort were shot immediately
or deported to regions from which few returned. Exposure to the
Stalinist French Communist Party during the early 1950s likely influenced Pol Pot's later policy choices.[24]

The Cultural Revolution provided the next model for Pol Pot's
revolution. Indeed, he visited China in 1966 just as the Cultural
Revolution was in full swing.[25] Kenneth Quinn identifies several characteristics of the Cultural Revolution that were found in Cambodia a
decade later.[26] A first similarity can be found in the emphasis on youth
purity, and its critical role in the revolution. The Chinese Red Guards,
the guarantors of Mao's virtually perpetual revolution, were almost all
very young and poorly educated. They were to be preferred to the
tainted and especially Westernized older people, frequently urban,
who simply could not be trusted.

In Cambodia, the Khmer Rouge were young, poorly educated, and
frequently illiterate, yet precisely because of these characteristics were far
less infected by the "microbes" that haunted the Democratic
Kampuchean imagination. According to a CPK report issued in 1976:

> The heat of the peoples' revolution and the democratic revolution were
> not enough ... The level of people's struggle and class struggle meant
> that [when] we searched for evil microbes inside the party, we couldn't
> find them. They were able to hide. Now that we are advancing on an all-
> embracing socialist revolution ... in the party, in the army, among the
> people, we can find the evil microbes. They emerge, pushed out by the
> true nature of the socialist revolution.[27]

The purity that was so valued by the Khmer Rouge was to be found only
in the young, or alternatively in the hill peoples found in the northeast of
the country. These poor minority peoples, many of whom could not

---

[22] Quinn 1989a, 225.   [23] Conquest 1986, 303.   [24] Jackson 1989b, 249.
[25] Chandler 1999, 71–73.   [26] Quinn 1989a, 226–31.
[27] Quoted in Chandler 1990, 169.

write Cambodian, were highly valued by the Khmer Rouge, especially during their sojourn in that region while fighting the Lon Nol forces. The Khmer Rouge considered "the hill tribes to be pure elements and, fascinated by their social organization, decided to apply the tribal social model to all Cambodia."[28] As one might expect, their victimization rate was the lowest of all groups, sharing this fortunate circumstance (15 percent) only with the rural Khmer "Base People," those not relocated from other cities or regions.[29]

A second shared characteristic is found in the attack on vested interests. Four groups in China were targeted by the Cultural Revolution:

(1) The majority of rural cadre[s] who had reached accommodations with the peasants or were afraid of losing their positions;
(2) Low-ranking officials whose loyalty was to their bosses;
(3) Ordinary peasants with kinship ties or other ties to village leaders, which gave them a favored position;
(4) Peasants with an economic stake in the status quo, such as the "rich peasants" who by 1962 were reemerging in the villages as the government's emphasis turned to increased production.[30]

Bureaucratization, kinship, and other forms of "nonrevolutionary" association were, in Mao's view, strangling the Communist revolution. To overcome them, young cadres from far regions were relocated into communes, factories, or universities. These strangers would not in any way be subservient to the current structure of deference. Accordingly, they could freely attack the institutional infrastructure.

In Cambodia, too, similar processes were initiated by the CPK. As early as 1971, well before the final victory over the Lon Nol forces, unknown young cadres (political leaders) were appearing in conquered southwest Cambodia to purge local cadres and then implement the new Khmer Rouge policies. In June 1973, these cadres destroyed existing hamlets and villages and upon their ashes built the new communes. Already in this early process we see the systematic relocation of Cambodians. These communes appeared to be fairly close imitations of those established in the Chinese Great Leap Forward.

Third, politics were primary in both revolutions. And here, as we shall see, lies the core of the politicide. Apparently the slogan of the Chinese revolution was "better red than well read."[31] Expertise,

---

[28] M. Martin 1994, 209.   [29] Kiernan 1996, 458.
[30] T. Robinson 1971, 16–17, quoted in Quinn 1989a, 227.   [31] Quinn 1989a, 227.

the *sine qua non* of modern Westernized society, was to be eschewed in favor of political views thoroughly consonant with those of the revolution. In 1957, Mao delivered a speech titled "On Contradictions," in which he cited the supposed contradiction between the intellectuals and the peasants as the chief obstacle standing in the way of the revolution. Those with the expertise, or the intellectuals, were too prone to command attention, thereby emerging as a leadership class with its own interests, frequently at odds with those of the revolution. In China, this elite emerged prior to the revolutionary transformations desired by Mao. As a consequence, during both the Great Leap Forward and the later Cultural Revolution, administrators, managers, and technicians were sent to the countryside to be replaced by untrained youths who would presumably succeed at their jobs through political zeal and revolutionary steadfastness.

To avoid this problem, Pol Pot decided to short-circuit this process and, immediately after seizing power, preemptively send urban populations directly to the rural areas where they could do no damage to the revolution. Eventually, many died from malnutrition, disease, starvation, or outright execution. Haste was required in order to prevent any entrenchment of urban and Westernized elites in the new bureaucracy. Haste also was required to place the revolution on a firm footing prior to the eventual confrontation with Vietnam. Despite Vietnamese reluctance to go to war, especially after their quarter-century of war against Japan and the Western powers, the Khmer Rouge fully expected such a war of domination to take place shortly after their victory over the Lon Nol forces. Thus, avoidance of limitations of the Chinese experience and the Khmer Rouge perceptions of a threatening environment conspired to yield the hasty emptying of the cities and rapid communalization of the countryside. Both the Great Leap Forward and the Cultural Revolution failed in their objectives. With a much smaller and therefore manipulable political stage and avoidance of the problems encountered by Mao, the Khmer Rouge thought they could achieve success in both revolutionary transformation and maintenance of their sovereignty.

A simultaneous anti-urban and anti-Western orientation permeated the Great Leap Forward and Cultural Revolution. This is the fourth element of commonality between the Chinese and Cambodian revolutions. The Chinese revolution exhibited a strong preference for communalization of the countryside and a consequent deemphasis on the importance of cities. At the same time, Chinese independence from the West and ultimately even from the "revisionist" Soviet Union was to be vigorously maintained. The Chinese revolution was to be untainted by foreign influences.

In Cambodia too, the anti-urban and anti-Western sentiments were to be strongly manifested. And where these policies were to be present in Chinese formulation, they were to be exaggerated, perhaps even carica-tured in the Cambodian revolution. Cities were to be emptied almost immediately after victory, and the degree of isolation of DK was extra-ordinary. Diplomatic relations were maintained only with China and North Korea, themselves international isolates (though, in the Chinese case, not to the same degree as the others).[32] The world of Cambodian communism was small and was restricted only to the Asian models that were worthy of emulation. No other societies were worthy of even minimal contact.

Finally, individual incentives were eschewed in favor of collectivism in both the Chinese and Cambodian revolutions. Rewards were to be collective in both the Great Leap Forward and the Cultural Revolution, as well as in Cambodia.

A particular form of collectivism was favored during the Cultural Revolution. This was the so-called *Tai Chai* system, which favored rewards for communal effort instead of any to be bestowed on indivi-duals.[33] Mao himself wrote of this successful experience in inaugurating a "Learn from Dazhai" (*Tai Chai*) campaign.[34] This was to be the model for the Cambodian communes in their collective efforts to improve their agricultural output. A "red flag honor program" was instituted to reward communes which had performed in the honored *Tai Chai* fash-ion. Indeed, in late 1977, a Chinese Politburo member, Chen Yonggui, visited Cambodia with the purpose of educating the Cambodians about the accomplishments of *Tai Chai*.[35] "Tachai was symbolic of the possi-bilities which the 700 million people of China could realize if they would but bend their backs and their collective will to the task."[36] He toured agricultural sites, always accompanied by Pol Pot, lecturing the Khmer about the achievements of the agricultural work brigades in northern China under his supervision in the 1960s.[37]

Yet despite these profound similarities and the evidence of close contact between Chinese and Cambodian leaders, there were differ-ences. In the final analysis, the Chinese revolution simply was less draconian than the Cambodian. The expulsion of urbanites from cities

---

[32] Ibid., 229.   [33] Ibid.   [34] Kiernan 1996, 354.   [35] Milton and Milton 1976, 74.
[36] Chandler 1999, 140–41.   [37] Ibid., 233, n. 7.

was far less complete in China than in Cambodia. And most important, at least for our purposes here, the victimization rate was far lower. Pol Pot undoubtedly observed this *relatively* benign behavior and finally came to the conclusion that this Chinese restraint, along with other factors, had led to the failure of the Cultural Revolution. The sheer size of the country made a sweeping revolution envisioned by Mao more difficult to accomplish successfully. Additionally, Chinese leaders such as Zhou Enlai or Deng Xiaoping exercised moderating influences on Mao.

Cambodia, on the other hand, was a much smaller country. Resistance to authority that could be made effective by distance from the capital or living in remote mountainous regions simply was far less likely to flourish within the confines of the small Cambodian state. Chinese social and economic institutions also had a greater durability historically than did those of the Khmer; in contrast, few such moderating influences existed to affect the DK central leadership. To minimize the possibility of failure, the total emptying of cities and the unprecedented use of violence were tactics chosen by a united Khmer leadership. And here the Stalinist model was available; the similarities between Pol Pot's policies and those of Stalin are many and important.

In contrast to the Chinese experience, both the Cambodian and Soviet authorities were more narrow in their classification of people amenable to reeducation and consequent inclusion in the new society. According to Alexander Dallin and George Brandover, "whereas the Maoist strategy defines the 'out-group' – those who, in Bolshevik jargon, are destined for the garbage heap of history – so narrowly as to leave open the possibility of reeducating most class-alien elements, the Stalinist variant is marked ... by a far narrower definition of the 'in-group' – those who can be trusted as and those who can be made over into 'good Communists.'"[38]

As a consequence, in the Soviet Union entire categories of people were marked for elimination. The kulaks or those deemed to be "landowners" by virtue of owning small plots of land and perhaps employing a worker or two, were deported or eliminated *in situ*, as the collectivization process advanced in the late 1920s and early 1930s. A reasonable estimate of the number of dead in the dekulakization process is the 6.5 million given by Robert Conquest.[39] Added to this should be the 7 million dead in the famine

---

[38] Dallin and Breslauer 1970, 7.   [39] Conquest 1986, 306.

associated with the collectivization process.[40] This process is comparable to that imposed on the vast number of "New" people and others victimized in the Cambodian revolution.

Yet another similarity is to be found in the antecedents of both Stalin and Pol Pot's campaigns of terror. The period of the Russian Revolution and Civil War (1917–23) was extraordinarily murderous. One estimate, including deficit in births as the result of the mass murders and starvation, rises to 23 million. Another estimate actually yields 26 million losses. The brutality of the revolutionary and Civil War period was exceptional. Here, too, we see famine (approximately 5 million dead) that would be repeated in somewhat different form less than a decade later.[41] Although the killings were not as coordinated as they would be later under Stalin's reign, nonetheless the precedent of vast numbers killed, whether by design or happenstance, would certainly predispose the later regime to indulge in a similar level of brutality and neglect.

The Cambodian experience prior to Pol Pot's victory in April 1975 was also exceptionally morbid. Between 1970 and 1975, large numbers of Cambodians died either as the direct result of combat in the civil war, famine, or disease, or as a consequence of the beginning of hamlet destruction and replacement by communes even prior to the Khmer Rouge victory. Even at the height of the US bombing campaign of 1973, itself a contributor to the mass destruction and CPK recruitment,[42] the communization process was proceeding rapidly in those areas already conquered by the Cambodian Communists.[43] In a sense, both Stalin and Pol Pot directly coordinated processes of mass destruction that in significant ways aped their own chaotic but no less destructive precedents. In Stalin's case, in comparison with Pol Pot's, the preceding period was the more deadly of the two. Nevertheless, Pol Pot had not only his own previctory period to draw upon, but also Stalin's own policies in the 1930s as a Communist model. Both Stalin and Pol Pot moved to collectivize with great speed and determination once they had the reins of power. In this too, they showed a basic similarity.

Purges

Because the Chinese were more optimistic in their expectations as to the consequences of reeducation, they paid a price. According to Dallin and Breslauer:

[40] Ibid.   [41] Pipes 1993, 508–09.   [42] Kiernan 1996, 22.   [43] Chandler 1999, 100.

> The Chinese leadership failed to eliminate potentially rival elites before embarking on its major mobilization tasks ... Many who were written off as members of "out-groups" in Russia and Eastern Europe were in China allowed to survive ... And, once the Maoist wholesale effort at restructuring human attitudes had visibly failed, in key spots within the society there remained not only the unreformed (more precisely, the un-thought-reformed) members of "in-groups" but also the alienated survivors whose counterparts elsewhere in the Communist world would have been purged.[44]

Accordingly, to avoid this problem, Pol Pot, as we saw, decided to purge the party to get at the "microbes" still persisting within its ranks. The model was already Stalinist. According to one estimate, by 1938, 80 percent of the Central Committee members of 1934 in the Soviet Union had been arrested. Almost all of those arrested were murdered in captivity.[45] This wholesale elimination of potential opposition, both real and imaginary, led to the following: "By 1939, some 80 percent of its [the party's] members had joined after the midpoint of the decade, and hence were products of the new socialism, wedded both psychologically and ideologically to its achievements and personally beholden to its master builder."[46]

Apparently, in the new Cambodia of the late 1970s, as in the case of the Soviet Union of the late 1930s, there was significant opposition to regime policies emerging even from the depths of the ruling party. And in Cambodia the opposition was virulent enough to lead to an attempted coup in September 1976. Alarmed by the extent of violence in revolutionary DK, military leaders and senior party officials, among them Hou Yuon, a former minister of the interior and cooperation, planned to overthrow the existing regime. Pol Pot was to be assassinated by poison and a new leadership installed. The plot was foiled; its aftermath included the first of the great purges that followed in 1977. All party leaders, governmental officials, and military leaders associated with the plot were hunted down. Hou Yuon was executed, as were other senior officials, including their wives, children, and other close family members. More than 16,000 dossiers on victims were found, including 1,200 pictures of children.[47] The purge was then extended beyond the confines of officialdom. In one district, of the 70,000

[44] Dallin and Breslauer 1970, 79–80.   [45] Mann 1997, 153.   [46] Malia 1999, 307.
[47] Quinn 1989b, 198.

residents, 40,000 were claimed to be traitors and were dealt with accordingly.[48]

A second coup attempt was initiated by Cambodian elements sympathetic to the Vietnamese leadership in Hanoi, apparently at its instigation. Beginning in late 1977 or early 1978, a second purge was initiated in which all officials and others suspected of Vietnamese sympathies were eliminated, among them Von Vet, the vice premier responsible for economic policy. As before, the party organization, military structure, and governmental ranks were heavily depleted by the violent purges. In one district in Battambang Province, a district chief was removed, followed by his replacement within the period of one year. Reportedly they were both killed as enemies of the state. Political commissars also were among those murdered. The extent of the purges even led true Pol Pot supporters to side with the Vietnamese in the forthcoming invasion because of fears for their safety.[49]

Summary comparisons

Summarizing the etiology of events in Cambodia between 1975 and 1978, Kenneth Quinn probably put it best when he stated that: "In short, Pol Pot was implementing Mao's plan with Stalin's methods."[50] Serge Thion categorized the motives of the killings in more detail:

> Generally speaking, people were persecuted under DK because of what they believed, or were supposed by security organs to believe, and because of family links with those suspected of harboring wrong beliefs or thoughts detrimental to the state. Killings based on racist hatred involved only the small number of Vietnamese residents left after the May 1975 evacuation and the wanton murdering of Vietnamese farmers in the raids across the border in 1977–1978 ... Chinese and Sino-Khmers were not murdered as such, but as traders and capitalists in the greatest need of "reformation," killed mostly by hard labor.[51]

The core of the motivation, then, was belief or presumed belief, and the low probability of successfully reeducating certain categories of people. This stands in stark contrast to the unyielding decision to massacre *all* Jews, Armenians, and Tutsi based on "racial" or ethnoreligious characteristics. Religious conversion could not help the hunted Jews, or the Armenians except in the infrequent instances of young and mostly

---

[48] Ibid., 200.   [49] Ibid., 206–07.   [50] Quinn 1989a, 236.   [51] Thion 1993, 172.

attractive girls who could be taken into Muslim households as servants, concubines, or in other capacities that required, of course, conversion to Islam. The only Tutsi who managed to survive the killing in Rwanda were those who hid themselves effectively (or were hidden), or who masked their ethnicity and even in some cases participated in the murder of their own relatives. Victimization rates in all three instances of genocide ranged between 66 and 70 percent. The 20 percent victimization rate in Cambodia is much more in keeping with the scripted mass murders initiated by Stalin and Mao.

16

Dogs that didn't bark I: realpolitik and the absence of loss

In order to establish valid causal inference, instances must be found where genocide might be expected to occur, but did not. Theoretically, the national experience of loss and the demands of imprudent realpolitik, especially unnecessary risk minimization, are suggested to lead to genocide. If even one of these explanatory components is absent, then genocide also should be absent. The following two chapters explore these themes.

In this chapter, I argue that the absence of loss may be sufficient to avert genocide. Thus, the Bulgarian and Finnish experiences of territorial expansion at the start of World War II are contrasted with the territorial loss and contraction experienced by the genocidal and perpetrating states examined in the preceding chapters. Specifically, the pre-genocide histories of Germany, Austria, the Ottoman Empire, the Hutu-led Rwandan state, Italy, Vichy France, and Romania entail the experience of loss, while those of Bulgaria and Finland are associated with gain. At the same time, the genocidal and perpetrating states were complicit in the mass murder of their own citizenry, while Bulgaria and Finland refused to enter that abyss. Germany, Austria, Italy, Vichy France, and Romania also demonstrated very different behaviors before and after their loss experiences.

In chapter 17, the second chapter treating instances in which potential genocide did not occur, I examine the importance of the affinity condition in preventing genocide. That is, even when other facilitating conditions exist, the presence of affine populations or governments (ethnoreligiously similar or ideologically sympathetic) serves to diminish the probability of genocide. Chapter 17 examines the consequences of a necessary minimization of risk in order to maximize security of the state. If, for example, identification of "defectors" (such as the Jews) requires their removal in order to maximize state security, at the same time, the risk of removal itself to the perpetrating state should not be too great. The affine population or government serves a protective function via the implicit or explicit threat of retaliation against the genocidal state. It is this affinity condition that will be explored in the succeeding chapter. In this later chapter, Nazi Germany is examined before and after the invasion of the Soviet Union, and the Ottoman Empire in its differing behaviors toward Armenians and Greeks. These analyses are followed by explorations of the behaviors of nonperpetrating states that might otherwise have been inclined to genocidal behavior: late eighteenth-century Poland, the British in Ireland in 1916–21, and, briefly, the Israelis in Intifada II (2000–present).

Bulgaria

Bulgaria illustrates the influence of prudent realpolitik at the highest levels of decision making and the absence of the impact of loss. Additionally, the Bulgarian Orthodox Church protested even the earliest introduction of anti-Jewish legislation. The demands of any sort of realpolitik at this time could be flouted by the Bulgarian church hierarchy because, in contrast to the Vatican (see chapter 10), an independent state-like existence simply did not exist for the Bulgarian Orthodox Church. Neither, of course, did it exist in France at the time of the French Roman Catholic protests against the deportations.

Prudent realpolitik nevertheless was evident in the Bulgarian governmental decision to propitiate Nazi Germany in the hopes of immediate gain. And these hopes were realized. On February 15, 1940, the German-educated and strongly Germanophile Bogdan Filov was appointed premier by King Boris III,[1] replacing the earlier moderately pro-Western Georgi Kyoseivanov. Also appointed was the new interior minister, Petâr Gabrovski, a former member of a leading Bulgarian fascist organization, the Ratniks (Guardians). Between August and December, the Law for the Defense of the Nation was prepared in the National Assembly and officially promulgated on January 23, 1941.[2] The law defined precisely who was a Jew and proceeded to limit Jewish participation in the professions, property ownership, and even places of residence.[3] During this period, the Germans interceded on behalf of the Bulgarians in Vienna on September 7, 1940, at which time the Bulgarians received southern Dobrudja from Romania.[4] In March 1941, Bulgaria formerly adhered to the Axis Powers and, with German permission, assumed control of

---

[1] Oren 1968, 92.   [2] Ibid., 93.   [3] Todorov 2001, 4.   [4] Chary 1972, 19.

Thrace and Macedonia.[5] As Nissan Oren comments: "In the main, the Law for the Protection of the Nation was to pave the way for the fast developing *rapprochement* with Germany and solidify Bulgaria's position within the Axis."[6]

King Boris III, virtually the absolute authority since 1934, actually suggested the Law of the Defense of the Nation, remarking that such legislation had been imposed in Romania, Hungary, "and even France."[7] As Frederick Chary indicates: "If alliance with the Reich meant an anti-Semitic law, Boris knew that Bulgaria must have such a law, although he tried to make it as mild as possible."[8] Thus, with Nazi Germany in the political and military ascendancy throughout Europe, Bulgaria, a small, militarily insignificant country, demanded a prudent realpolitik in its foreign policy, lest it be overwhelmed by the much stronger European great power. In that event, the plight of the Jews would be far worse than the mild application of the Law of the Defense of the Nation. The territorial rewards were ample and the safeguards were significant, especially as Hitler trusted and admired the king, at least in the early stages of the war.[9] Later in the war, in March 1943 after the massive German defeat at Stalingrad, Boris responded positively to the plight of the Jews, effectively preventing their deportation.

How did this state of affairs come about? More precisely, in addition to the diminishing threat of Nazi Germany and a required corresponding change in prudent realpolitik, what were the domestic circumstances that allowed Boris to essentially thwart Hitler's intention to eradicate Bulgarian Jewry?

The Bulgarian National Assembly is said to have been influential in mustering a protest against the deportations that led to their postponement and ultimate cancellation. Here, a minority of parliamentarians, although a sizeable group from the government's own party, protested this operation, never achieving abrogation of the decree, but postponing it just enough for other political forces to emerge that would render the temporary permanent.[10] Boris was obviously influenced by this protest from a substantial portion of his own party's deputies. But even more important, and consistent with demands of a prudent realpolitik, the king "needed as much support as possible. He had to convince the Germans that his decision to stop or delay deportation was the result

---

[5] Todorov 2001, 5. [6] Oren 1968, 93. [7] Quoted in Todorov 2001, 4.
[8] Chary 1972, 186. [9] Oren 1968, 91. [10] Chary 1972, 190.

of a series of strong protests that coming, as they did, from very influential circles, could not be ignored."[11]

At the same time, recent scholarship has shifted to an emphasis on one member of the National Assembly in particular, its vice chairman, Dimitâr Peshev. It was he who organized the petition signed by one-third of the government's own party members. When he heard of a roundup of Jews in his own electoral district, the town of Kyustendil, he acted. Attempting to speak to Bogdan Filov, the prime minister, he was allowed to see the minister of internal affairs, Petâr Gabrovski, in charge of the deportations. Peshev pointed out to Gabrovski that these unpublicized deportations violated Bulgarian constitutional law; Gabrovski initially denied any knowledge of this operation. Peshev, his colleagues Mikhalev and Ikonomov, and other deputies refused to leave Gabrovski's office until all telephone or telegraph contacts had been made that were necessary to free the Jews who had been arrested.[12]

In order to ensure that the arrests would not shortly resume, Peshev organized the parliamentary petition that ultimately led to his removal as vice chairman of the National Assembly, but postponed further any deportation plans to the more distant future.[13] By then, the war would be nearly over, as Peshev and his colleagues suspected, and even the thought of such mass killing would be abhorrent.

Nevertheless, not denying the goodness that Tzvetan Todorov attributes to Peshev, this is not the whole story. It is instructive to examine the manner in which Peshev was informed. When Bulgarians in Kyustendil heard of the arrests, they quickly made plans to send forty of their number to the National Assembly in Sofia. After deliberation, they chose only four, all non-Jews, to plead the case of their Jewish townspeople.[14] Although Peshev had already heard of the arrests through other avenues, he was heartened by the concern of his non-Jewish constituents. Thus, in addition to the basic decency of the man and his supporters in the National Assembly, we must consider the milieu that made it possible. Why, in contrast to France and Romania, not to mention Germany, was Bulgaria so free of anti-Semitism that it could yield Peshev's success?

One answer, of course, is the absence of territorial loss and its accompanying refugee influx. Without the large number of refugees of like ethnoreligious identity, sympathy can actually be extended to others

[11] Boyadjieff 1989, 140.   [12] Todorov 2001, 37.   [13] Ibid., 39.   [14] Ibid., 9–10.

of a different identity, who, through no fault of their own, are subject to deportation and a probable death. Thus according to Peshev:

> As I was trying to understand what was happening and why, I received a visit from Dimitâr Ikonomov, the deputy of the National Assembly from the town of Dupnitsa ... He told me that he had just returned from a visit there and was extremely depressed by what he had witnessed taking place in the street. He described a distressing scene – Thracian Jews, old people, men, women, and children, carrying their belongings, defeated, desperate, powerless people, begging for help as they crossed the town on foot, dragging themselves towards some unknown destination. He was saddened and utterly outraged to see helpless people being sent to some destination that could only be surmised, to a fate that conjured up everyone's darkest fears. He spoke of the effect of this horrible scene on the residents of Dupnitsa, their anger and outrage, their inability to remain indifferent to the tragedy that was unfolding before their eyes: This multitude of women and children and old people who were being taken who knows where. To hear Ikonomov tell it, the townspeople's despair was so great that many had been moved to tears.[15]

Here, Peshev refers to a failure of Bulgaria to protect the Jews of Macedonia, Thrace, and a small portion of Serbia, now under Bulgarian authority. The Germans demanded these deportations and, in order to placate them, the Bulgarian government complied, at the same time asserting that these were residents of newly occupied territory, not Bulgarian citizens subject to Bulgarian constitutional law. In all, 11,393 Jews from these regions were deported to Poland, almost all perishing in the extermination camps.[16] Later in the concluding section of this chapter, Bulgaria's behavior will be compared to that of Vichy France.

Coincidentally, February 2, 1943, the day that SS-Obersturmführer Theodor Dannecker and Gabrovski agreed that the Bulgarian government would deliver to the Germans all Jews in Thrace and Macedonia,[17] was the same day that the last message was transmitted from the German pocket still holding out at Stalingrad.[18] Thus, the period subsequent to this agreement was one in which news of the massive German defeat was being widely disseminated. Boris clearly was aware of these military developments.[19] By the following month, a reevaluation of Bulgarian policy toward the Jews was undertaken.

---

[15] Quoted ibid., 158.   [16] Chary 1972, 127.   [17] Oren 1968, 95.
[18] Murray and Millett 2000, 291.   [19] Boyadjieff 1989, 147–48.

Despite evacuation from the capital Sofia to about twenty other cities (probably to mollify the Germans), as were non-Jews eight months later for their own safety during the Allied bombing, the 45,000 Jews of Bulgaria[20] were not deported from the country and survived the war.

Finally, in all of our cases of genocidal or perpetrating states, victim prominence has been cited. But in Bulgaria this element is decidedly absent. Jews were conspicuously absent from the political and economic leadership of the country. In an open letter to the National Assembly deputies, journalist and politician Christo Punev remarks:

> The vast majority of Jews in Bulgaria are working-class people: small grain merchants, pushcart vendors, retail tradesmen, labourers and maids, all of them working for a living and all of them going hungry. Have you not walked by the children of Yuchbunar on the streets of the capital? Little children and students, have you not seen them, famished, jaundiced, wasted and ragged, marching alongside Bulgarian children on Cyril and Methodius' Day? ... We are seven million people, yet we so fear the treachery of 45,000 Jews who hold no positions of responsibility at the national level that we need to pass exceptional laws to protect ourselves from them ... And then what?[21]

The combustible mix of territorial loss, threatening ethnoreligious identity, and class conflict is absent, as is outright collaboration in the genocide of a state's own citizenry. Thus, the absence of territorial loss and consequent refugee migration allowed sympathy for the Jews to develop, especially after the deportations from Thrace and Macedonia were witnessed by elements of the Bulgarian population. Perhaps it was this sympathy which led Assa Ben Solomonov to proclaim: "If one looks for a single denominator to ascribe the success to a single name, I would say that this is the Bulgarian people themselves, who saw the light and produced also sons who were up to the task of successfully carrying through this great humanitarian deed."[22]

At the same time, a prudent realpolitik that earlier suggested a limited cooperation with the Germans, after the decisive German defeat at Stalingrad indicated less cooperation, and ultimately frustration of the Nazi goal of deporting Bulgaria's Jewish citizens. In this fashion, Bulgaria would be better prepared politically to greet the Allied victors.

---

[20] 48,000 according to Boyadjieff 1989, 1.   [21] Quoted in Todorov 2001, 51.
[22] Quoted in Boyadjieff 1989, 143.

Finland

The Jewish community of Finland numbered approximately 2,000 in the early 1930s, before the addition of several hundred foreign Jews who had been granted asylum. Nearly all escaped deportation.

After an extended analysis, Hannu Rautkallio concludes that the visits of Hitler and Himmler to Finland, respectively in June and July of 1942, "proved how much the Führer valued the contribution of Finland as a co-belligerent fighting a common enemy in the East ... The Jewish Question was therefore left in the background of Finnish–German relations; in fact, this issue was never brought forcefully to the attention of the Finns."[23] Here, the Germans were exercising a prudent realpolitik. Finnish participation on the Eastern front was required, and so other matters such as the Jewish Question were not unduly emphasized. German pressure was minimal; hence the Finns could act with considerable latitude in regard to their Jewish residents, including support for their civil liberties. Why the absence of anti-Jewish animus? One answer is found in territorial expansion.

As in the case of Bulgaria, Finland *gained* territory prior to its brush with genocide. By the start of the later Continuation War with the Soviet Union, in December 1941, the Finns had regained all of the territory lost to the Soviets in the Peace of Moscow of March 1940 ending the earlier Winter War.[24] Now, instead of losing one-ninth of their territory as in 1940, the Finns regained it all plus a substantial amount. They were to retain this territory until June 1944, well after the period during which even minor German pressure for deportation had ended.[25]

Equally important, if not more so, was the status of refugees. In 1940, 11 percent of the total population was relocated westward on newly created holdings, a process that proved to be a colossal undertaking.[26] After the territorial advances of 1941, these refugees returned to their old homes. Instead of refugees streaming into the country invoking feelings of anger and identification with their unfortunate ethnic kin, the nation could feel satisfied that this earlier wrong had been corrected. We would expect, as in the case of Bulgaria, a sympathetic response to other refugees in Finland, many of them Jewish.

And this is indeed what we find. Despite the absence of "forceful" German pressure, in October 1942 the Finnish government did plan to

---

[23] Rautkallio 1987, 170.   [24] Polvinen 1986, 282.   [25] Kirby 1979, 141.
[26] Jutikkala and Pirinen 1974, 279.

deport foreign Jews. When the plan became known, 200 citizens of the
town of Pietarsaari signed a petition asking that the government not
deport these Jews.[27] This effort parallels that which occurred in the
Bulgarian town of Kyustendil, as we saw in the preceding section.
After a public dispute leading to a reduction in the number of deportees,
on November 6, eight Jews including two children were deported to
Tallinn in Estonia and then to Auschwitz after which only one adult
survived the war.[28]

Although seemingly incomparable in one respect – the sacrifice of
foreign Jews in Bulgaria and their attempted rescue in Finland – this
difference is more apparent than real. Foreign Jews in Finland resided on
Finnish territory and had been granted asylum. Thracian and
Macedonian Jews deported by Bulgaria did not reside on Bulgarian
territory, and had not been acknowledged in any way by the Bulgarian
government. Similar dynamics were at work in a population outraged by
the prospect of violating Finnish hospitality, and in one horrified by the
treatment of the Thracian and Macedonian Jews. Without the popular
anger that might have erupted over treatment of their own indigenous
refugees, had they existed at the time, the routine sympathies of ordinary
people could be activated.

The cases of Bulgaria and Finland both share the impact of realpolitik
in their relations with Nazi Germany. In the former, the worsening
German fortunes on the battlefield suggested a distancing of Bulgaria
from Germany. In the latter, German dependence on Finnish participation to maintain the integrity of the Eastern front tended to minimize
the intensity and extent of pressure for Jewish deportation from Finland.
At the same time, the absence of territorial loss and refugee influx in
both cases freed both populations from feelings of anger that could
easily have been directed against the Jews. Realpolitik at the state level
and absence of loss at the popular level tended to reinforce each other in
yielding these relatively benign outcomes.

Comparisons

We have now laid the foundation for comparisons across genocidal
states, perpetrators, and exceptions. In the context of the Holocaust as
well as genocides of the Armenians and Tutsi, territorial contraction and
its corollary of refugee influx are important progenitors of mass killing.

[27] Cohen and Svensson 2001, 205.   [28] Ibid.

In our genocidal states, Germany and Austria, and two of the perpetrating states, Vichy France and Romania, the mix of territorial loss, refugees, and issues of social class was prominent; in Italy, the state itself was threatened by the ongoing territorial loss (see chapter 9). Only in Bulgaria and Finland, where the vast majority of Jews was saved, were these elements absent.

One may argue that a large proportion of France's Jewish citizens, although not as large as Bulgaria's, also survived the war, and France did indeed suffer severe truncation and territorial loss. Yet until World War II, France was the home of continental European liberalism, never having promulgated an anti-Semitic law after the time of Napoleon I. Pogroms in France were unknown. Bulgaria, on the other hand, had experienced episodic pogroms including the most famous one in Pazardzhik (1895), as well as Sofia (1884), Vratsa (1890), Lom (1903), and Kyustendil (1904). Most were sparked by rumors of ritual Passover murders by Jews, the infamous Blood Libel.[29] Thus, for France, the leap to state-supported anti-Semitism and complicity in Jewish deportation, including many French citizens, was far greater than that for Bulgaria and certainly for Romania. Although Romania did take that plunge into the abyss, as did Vichy France, Bulgaria ultimately declined.

As it does not differentiate effectively between Vichy France and Bulgaria, emphasis on a history of anti-Semitism as a potential explanation for genocidal behavior also does not distinguish between Italy and Finland. In both instances, before the 1930s, widespread anti-Semitism was virtually unknown in the modern period, yet the outcomes differed in the two cases.

Romania, in its twentieth-century history, like Vichy France, demonstrated radically different behaviors upon expansion and later after contraction. Only after substantial shrinkage of the Romanian state in 1940 did it embark on its genocidal path. These considerations suggest that one must examine a perpetrating state's behavior not only in comparison with others, as in the comparisons among Italy, Vichy France, Romania, Bulgaria, and Finland, but also in light of its own history. The behaviors of these states, as well as those of Germany and Austria, suggest enormous changes in state policy regarding Jews only after the experience of territorial loss and, in four of these states, Germany, Austria, Vichy France, and Romania, refugee migration. Political elites concerned with state security may be more directly

---

[29] Chary 1972, 32.

sensitive to territorial loss in itself, as was Mussolini, while refugee migration, often associated with territorial loss, can lead to mass disaffection and popular violence directed against targeted minorities.

Finally, there is the issue of symbolic representation. For many French people and, as a percentage, many more Romanians, as for many Germans, there was the indelible but vastly exaggerated connection between Jews and communism. Any gains for the Soviet Union (as in the instance of the territories forcibly ceded to the Soviet Union by Romania in 1940) were frequently laid at the Jewish doorstep. Thus, in addition to the psychosocial implications of loss suggested by prospect theory, identification with the downtrodden of one's own ethnicity, anger at the presumptive "other," and economic competition within a shrunken spatial environment, there are issues of political responsibility that emanate from territorial transfers. Jews, Armenians, and Tutsi were to pay a heavy price for an unwarranted culpability emerging from the national experience of loss, made palpable in the everyday lives of people by the often-ubiquitous presence of refugees.

17

Dogs that didn't bark II: affinity and vulnerability reduction

Now we examine potential victimizers, apart from the Axis collaborating countries of World War II. There are seemingly innumerable available instances, but several strong possibilities present themselves based on variables already introduced in chapter 5. These are countries: (1) situated within the domain of losses, (2) experiencing threats to state security, (3) undergoing substantial risks, and (4) potentially targeting victims that have large affine populations or governments (ethnoreligiously similar or ideologically sympathetic, frequently in neighboring countries) with substantial political and/or military influence – the affinity condition.

This last variable is suggested to distinguish between potential genocides that eventuated in that outcome and those that did not, largely because of the prudent recognition by the potential victimizer of the importance of affinity. The targeted victim should not be in a position to react effectively or be able to call upon effective help from like-minded or ethnoreligiously similar populations. The existence of such potential allies, if deemed to be sufficiently powerful or at least influential in the international arena, could deter genocidal activity by a potential victimizer. Essentially, victim vulnerability, a necessary condition for genocide, can been reduced by the affinity condition.

However strong the genocidal impulse in a potential victimizer, a prudent realpolitik demands avoidance of the extreme risk of offending a large affine population or powerful government that can come to the aid of the victim. Of course, the fog of war increases the likelihood of an imprudent realpolitik that can be genocidal. War can strongly increase the perceived threat of potential victims and their kin in neighboring countries and, as we shall see in the concluding section of this chapter, can nullify the affinity condition.

As before, the Holocaust is complex enough that we will find the disappearance of the affinity condition associated with the rapidly worsening treatment of the European Jewish population. Interestingly, the Ottoman Empire demonstrates the presence *and* absence of affinity, with respect to two separate populations, the Ottoman Greeks (ultimately expelled in 1922–23 in an exchange of populations after the failed invasion of Turkey by Greece) and the Armenians. As a final requirement for the cases to be examined here, potential perpetrators must have been keenly aware of the genocidal choice as a policy option, preferably in their own past experience.

These considerations led to the examination of the Ottoman Empire in its very different treatment of Armenians and Greeks, and Nazi Germany before and after the invasion of the Soviet Union. Here the behavior of perpetrators differs over space (Ottoman Empire) and over time (Nazi Germany). To complete the comparison, three nongenocidal potential victimizers are chosen: late eighteenth-century Poland, the British in Ireland in 1916–21, and, briefly, the Israelis in the second Intifada. Poland experienced extreme losses in the late eighteenth century, and clearly fulfills the remaining conditions for inclusion, as do the other two cases. As we shall see, the Poles recognized the availability of genocide or at least widespread massacre as an option. The British and Israelis understood full well the possibility of genocide as a policy option. The Israelis, of course, have the recent memory of the Holocaust in which many family members of the Jewish population were slaughtered during World War II. The British had the long, tortured history of Anglo-Irish relations, the charge of genocidal behavior in Ireland having been leveled against them during at least three historical moments.

Affinity and genocide

The absence of affinity is understood as the absence of any affine population or government (ethnoreligiously similar or ideologically sympathetic) with the power and influence to actively intervene or provoke intervention on behalf of the victims. Larger neighboring populations, especially if they appear to have political influence, can serve as protective umbrellas for threatened populations. The affinity does not have to be ethnoreligious, although in practice that is most frequently the case.

The actual presence of affinity can be signified in two ways. First, the *direct* protection of the potentially victimized population is available through the political influence of a neighboring affine population. For example, the influence of highly placed Soviet Jews may have given pause to whatever German genocidal intent toward Jews may have existed prior to June 1941, as an expanded and more powerful Greece protected ethnic Greeks in the Ottoman Empire. Second, an *indirect* two-tiered process may protect the potential victims. Here a smaller protecting state itself is protected by one or more great powers that then, by extension, protect the potential victims as well. Ethnic Greeks living in the Ottoman Empire were subject to both the direct and indirect varieties – the existence of an independent Greece and European great powers intent on its welfare – thereby distinguishing them from the far more threatened Armenians without either protection.

Greeks in the Ottoman Empire

We begin with differential outcomes for Armenians and Greeks in the Ottoman Empire. Ethnic Greek communities had existed in Anatolia since ancient times. After the independence of Greece from the Ottomans in 1832,[1] these communities remained under Ottoman rule, numbering 1,792,206 Greeks out of a total of 18,520,016 Ottoman citizens in 1914, or nearly 10 percent of the total population.[2] Economically, of all ethnic groups including Turks, Arabs, Armenians, and Jews, the Greeks were predominant in 1912, controlling 43 percent of internal trade, 49 percent of industry and crafts, and 44 percent of the professions.[3] Given this degree of prominence outweighing even the Armenians (roughly 1.3 million in number and averaging 25 percent economic dominance), and the obvious Ottoman preference for a religiously if not ethnically homogeneous society, why were the Greeks not targeted for extinction along with the Armenians, or even before them?

Beyond their size and economic importance, both communities were threatening to the Ottomans. While the Armenians established nationalistic groups and made separatist claims, the Greeks "vastly expanded the activities of their *syllogues*, the political organizations they dubbed 'literary and scientific' associations. With financial support from the Greek government and rich Greeks … the *syllogues* sprang up in all the major Ottoman localities inhabited by Greeks and added political momentum to the cultural awareness disseminated by the existing Greek educational institutions. In the Istanbul area alone the Greeks

---

[1] Kourvetaris and Dobratz 1987.   [2] S. Shaw and Shaw 1977, 241.   [3] Issawi 1980, 14.

had over one hundred schools as early as 1878, and the number had nearly doubled by the end of the century."[4]

While the Armenians were perceived as threatening in eastern Anatolia and to some extent in Constantinople, the Greeks were even more numerous in that city.[5] Perhaps most important, the Greek population was situated principally along the shores of the Black, Aegean, and Mediterranean Seas, making them a prime target for subversion of the Ottomans by British and Russian naval emissaries. And the loyalties of Ottoman Greeks were highly suspect, even those of Greek deputies of the Ottoman Assembly who espoused widely held pan-Hellenic sympathies. In the widely quoted words of one of them, Boşo (Boussios) Efendi, "I am as Ottoman as the [foreign-dominated] Ottoman Bank."[6] Armenians, Jews, and Maronites were far more welcome in the Ottoman administration than were Greeks.[7]

One may counter that the Germans, for example, seeking to rid the East of Poles and Jews, after murdering the Polish leadership and intelligentsia chose to commit genocide only against the Jews. But the Poles were far more numerous than the Jews (10 percent of Poland's prewar population was Jewish) and the Germans simply did not have the facilities to murder so many people simultaneously. In contrast, Greeks in the Ottoman Empire were little more populous than Armenians, numbering approximately 500,000 more.

Perhaps the greatest threat came from Greek adherence to the "Great Idea." This was the overriding goal of Greek foreign policy from the inception of the state until the early 1920s. With Greek boundaries guaranteed by Great Britain, France, and Russia in the three-power treaty of 1827, foreign policy concerns extended principally to the unincorporated Greek communities. Or as Theodore Couloumbis et al. put it, "That goal, most commonly designated the 'Great Idea,' was the liberation of Greeks still subject to the Ottoman Empire or, in the case of the Ionian Islands until 1864 and Cyprus after 1878, those living under British colonial rule. It involved their incorporation into a greater Greece and therefore presupposed territorial aggrandizement."[8]

Precisely because the Greek state initially incorporated only about one-third of ethnic Greeks in the Mediterranean region, the Great Idea became the most pressing concern of Greek foreign policy. With a small

[4] Karpat 2001, 324–25.   [5] S. Shaw and Shaw 1977, 242.
[6] Quoted, for example, in Ahmad 1982, 409.   [7] Ortaylı 1999, 165.
[8] Couloumbis et al. 1976, 22.

nearby state agitating for incorporation of large numbers of Ottoman citizens, the Ottoman state must have perceived threats to its security that genocide could have averted.

There were two forms of threat to the integrity of the Ottoman state. The first threatened direct incorporation of territories inhabited principally by Greek communities. The classic expression of this form of threat (essentially the Great Idea) was put forward in a speech by Ioannis Kolettis before the Constituent Assembly in Athens in 1844:

> The Kingdom of Greece is not Greece. [Greece] constitutes only one part, the smallest and poorest part. A Greek is not only a man who lives within this kingdom but also one who lives in Jannina, in Salonika, in Serres, in Adrianople, in Constantinople, in Smyrna, in Trebizond, in Crete, in Samos and in any land associated with Greek history or the Greek race ... There are two main centres of Hellenism: Athens, the capital of the Greek kingdom, [and] 'The City' [Constantinople], the dream and hope of all Greeks.[9]

The second possible strategy was less bellicose in its implications, but no less threatening to the social and religious coherence of the Ottoman state. Through the good offices of the Ottoman state, educational and cultural life of the Greek communities could expand at will, as we just saw in the near doubling of Greek schools between 1878 and the end of the nineteenth century in the Constantinople area alone. Paraphrasing the written views of Pavlos Karolidis, a Greek deputy in the Ottoman parliament of 1908 and a leading intellectual, Richard Clogg tells us that:

> From an economic point of view the Ottoman Empire already constituted a Greek state, since all economic life and many public works were carried out either by Greeks or by Greek capital. Greek and unbiased foreign observers seeing these things, the newspaper continued, deplored the hostile policy of Greece towards the Ottoman Empire, believing the Hellenization of the Ottoman state to be a simple matter of time. Although expressed with characteristic hyperbole such attitudes were by no means uncommon among both Greeks of the empire and Greeks of the kingdom.[10]

In this view, the Ottoman state itself would eventually fall into Greek hands if they simply waited for these socioeconomic processes to continue on this course.

---

[9] Quoted in Clogg 1982, 193.   [10] Ibid., 197.

Yet the Greek state prior to World War I possessed another property that brings us to the first direct affinity condition protecting the Ottoman ethnic Greeks. The Greek state of 1914 was no longer the tiny truncated state of 1832, the year of its formation. As a result of the Balkan Wars, by 1913 Greece had acquired most of Macedonia, southern Epirus, many Aegean islands, and Crete, a major foreign policy goal for decades. Greece had increased its territory by 68 percent and its population from approximately 2.7 to 4.4 million. And, "for the first time since independence, Greece had expanded territorially as a result of its own efforts rather than through the good graces of the powers."[11]

Thus, Greece had emerged as a significant Mediterranean power in its own right. If that power were to be activated, then the Ottomans would face another opponent in the context of World War I and its grave uncertainties.

Events within Greece would further counsel extreme Ottoman caution. With the outbreak of World War I, two opposing foreign policy camps arose within Greece, one led by the prime minister, Eleftherios Venizelos, arguing for entry into World War I on the side of the Entente and the other, headed by King Constantine I, seeking to support the Central Powers, or at least to reinforce neutrality. Aggravating the dispute was Venizelos's strong emotional attachment to Britain and France, while Constantine was married to the sister of Kaiser Wilhelm II of Germany and was himself an honorary field marshal in the German army.[12] War-related events were to force each side to take opposing views of the Greek future. Venizelos's adherence to the Entente had the purpose of implementing the Great Idea of incorporating Ottoman territories containing ethnic Greeks, while Constantine and his supporters advocated "a small but honorable Greece." Venizelos invited British and French forces to occupy Salonika in support of the Serbs; they landed in October 1915. Constantine for the second time in six months called for Venizelos to resign. Further conflict ensued, first, when the government in Athens, now headed essentially by Constantine, refused to allow Serbs to cross Greek territory to reform their front and, second, when British and French forces landed in Piraeus and Athens to enforce Greek neutrality but were forced back in an ignominious retreat.

Two governments now existed, one in Athens headed by Constantine controlling all of southern Greece (principally the area of Greece prior to

---

[11] Couloumbis et al. 1976, 35.   [12] Clogg 1992, 86–87.

1913) while Venizelos governed the 1913 conquests (including Crete), plus Thessaly conquered by Venizelists and the Allies between September 1916 and June 1917.[13] Clearly, any Ottoman attack on ethnic Greeks during the period of genocidal activity against the Armenians (1915–16) would unify the Greek state around Venizelos's support of the Great Idea. A new opponent added to the array of allies opposed to the Central Powers and especially the Ottomans would be particularly undesirable. On the other hand, as long as the newly empowered (as of 1913) Greek state was divided, Greece would likely continue to remain neutral. Without Ottoman provocation, neutrality was indeed observed until June 1917, when the Allies forced Constantine's abdication. By the time Greece was actively engaged in the September 1918 offensive on the Macedonian front, the war's trajectory was clearly in favor of the Allies. Genocide of the ethnic Greeks by the Ottomans would have been an extraordinarily foolhardy action.

The second, the indirect form of the affinity condition, is that provided by great power(s) protection of the affine country. Even before the beginning of Greek statehood, the great powers had been active in support of Greek independence. By the Treaty of London in 1827, Great Britain, France, and Russia agreed to mediate the conflict between insurgent Greece and the Ottoman Empire. This policy led to the Battle of Navarino in October 1827 – the last major naval battle with opposing ships of sail – in which an allied fleet led by the British admiral, Sir Edward Codrington, utterly destroyed a combined Turco-Egyptian fleet.[14] The later treaty of May 1832 among the three powers placed the new Greek state "under their protection," with Otto of Bavaria accepting the Greek throne.[15]

The interests of Greece were protected and even advanced during the nineteenth century. In 1864, the British ceded the Ionian islands to Greece, increasing the population by roughly a quarter of a million.[16] In the aftermath of the Russo-Turkish War of 1877–78 and the ensuing Congress of Berlin, Greece was allowed to annex Thessaly and the Arta district of Epirus in 1881, adding a territory roughly 25 percent of pre-war Greece and a sizable population.[17]

Although Britain was in the forefront of these activities, by 1913 France and Germany also sought to woo the expanding Greek state. For example, although the Greek government under pressure was prepared to yield one of the furthest of its conquests in the Second Balkan

---

[13] Ibid., 92.   [14] Ibid., 42.   [15] Ibid., 47.   [16] Ibid., 61.   [17] Ibid., 73.

War, Kavala, both France and Germany supported its retention by Greece.[18] Even Austria-Hungary, represented by Count Johann von Pallavicini in Constantinople, lectured the Turks on their "foolish" persecution of the Greeks in Thrace.[19]

Culturally, all of the European powers felt indebted to the Greek heritage. Great Britain and France emphasized ancient Greek democracy, Germany the archeological and literary treasures of Greece, and Russia its religious heritage of Orthodoxy. Given these political and cultural ties, wholesale attacks on the Ottoman Greeks would have profoundly angered not only the Entente Powers, but Germany and Austria-Hungary as well, the allies upon whom the Ottomans were deeply dependent. Under these conditions, genocide of the Ottoman Greeks simply was not a viable option.

Many, however, were massacred by the Turks, especially at Smyrna (today's Izmir) as the Greek army withdrew at the end of their headlong retreat from central Anatolia at the end of the Greco-Turkish War. Especially poorly treated were the Pontic Greeks in eastern Anatolia on the Black Sea. In 1920 and particularly in 1921, as the Greek army advanced, many were deported to the Mesopotamian desert as had been the Armenians before them.[20] Nevertheless, approximately 1,200,000 Ottoman Greek refugees arrived in Greece at the end of the war. When one adds to the total the Greeks of Constantinople who, by agreement, were not forced to flee, then the total number comes close to the 1,500,000 Greeks in Anatolia and Thrace enumerated in 1914.[21]

Here, a strong disjunction between intention and action is found. According to the Austrian consul at Amisos, Kwiatkowski, in his November 30, 1916, report to the foreign minister Baron Burian: "on 26 November Rafet Bey told me: 'we must finish off the Greeks as we did with the Armenians . . .' on 28 November Rafet Bey told me: 'today I sent squads to the interior to kill every Greek on sight.' I fear for the elimination of the entire Greek population and a repeat of what occurred last year."[22] Or according to a January 31, 1917, report by Chancellor Hollweg of Austria:

> The indications are that the Turks plan to eliminate the Greek element as
> enemies of the state, as they did earlier with the Armenians. The strategy
> implemented by the Turks is of displacing people to the interior without

---

[18] Couloumbis et al. 1976, 38.   [19] Bridge 1984, 45.   [20] M. Smith 1998, 211.

[21] For the estimated number of Greek refugees, see Hirschon 2003, 14, while the 1914 estimate of Greeks in Anatolia and Thrace is found in Karpat 1985, 188.

[22] Quoted in Halo 2000, 123.

taking measures for their survival by exposing them to death, hunger, and illness. The abandoned homes are then looted and burnt or destroyed. Whatever was done to the Armenians is being repeated with the Greeks.[23]

Massacres most likely did take place at Amisos and other villages in the Pontus. Yet given the large numbers of surviving Greeks, especially relative to the small number of Armenian survivors, the massacres apparently were restricted to the Pontus, Smyrna, and selected other "sensitive" regions.

Jews in Eastern Europe

Having juxtaposed the radically different outcomes for two ethnic communities in the Ottoman Empire, we can now turn to a diachronic analysis of Jews in Eastern Europe before the worsening of relations between Germany and the Soviet Union in the autumn of 1940, and after the German invasion of the Soviet Union in June 1941. According to Christopher Browning, "the invasion of the Soviet Union would ultimately have an immensely radicalizing effect on Nazi Jewish policy, from which no Jews in the German empire – and those in Poland in particular – would be spared."[24]

As we saw in chapter 7, prior to mid-August 1941, the Nazis had not yet experienced the losses that would invoke their memory of World War I and its domain of losses, which inspired their movement from the outset. Thus, one would not expect a wholesale extermination policy to be implemented before that August. Nevertheless, despite the great importance of these losses in initiating the Holocaust, one can still see the impact of affinity in the relatively restrained (for the Nazis) early treatment of Jews in comparison with the brutality meted out to Poles immediately after the invasion of September 1939.

We now consider both the reality and the reputation of Jews in the Communist Party. The equation of Jews with Soviet communism was, of course, a longstanding axiom of Nazi ideology. But how did this come about? In answering this question we will also be able to understand the initial avoidance of systematized mass murder of Jews in Poland and the later onset of genocide across all of occupied Europe.

From the beginning, the European socialist parties had a dispropor-tionate number of Jews. As Albert Lindemann put it, "Considering that

[23] Quoted ibid., 124.   [24] Browning 2004, 137.

the Jewish population of Europe was approximately 2 percent of the total, the Jewish participation in socialism, revolutionary and democratic, was remarkably large."[25] Even more important, the proportion of visible socialist leaders of Jewish origin was extraordinarily high. One has only to mention the names of Moses Hess, Karl Marx, Ferdinand Lassalle, Eduard Bernstein, Otto Bauer, Rosa Luxemburg, Julius Martov, Leon Trotsky, and Léon Blum to see this striking contribution. Of course, many other leaders such as Friedrich Engels, Vladimir Ilyich Lenin, August Bebel, and Georgy Plekhanov were not Jewish, but even many of the non-Jews were so-called Jewifiers (in the parlance of anti-Semites) who valued the Jews even more than they valued their own nationalities. Lenin, for example, commented to Maxim Gorky that "an intelligent Russian is almost always a Jew or someone with Jewish blood in his veins."[26]

But even Lenin, the non-Jew, had a Jewish grandfather who had converted to Christianity in marrying his grandmother, who was herself of Christian German origin. Although culturally Great Russian, he was widely believed by anti-Semites to be Jewish. Mikhail Kalinin, the president of the Soviet Union, was considered by Jewish Bolsheviks to be "more Jewish than the Jews" possibly because of his open expression of emotion. For example, in a speech describing the pogroms of the Civil War (see chapter 3), he broke down and cried, and was unable to complete the speech.[27] Felix Dzerzhinsky, head of the Cheka, the Soviet secret police, was originally a member of the Polish gentry and learned to speak Yiddish in his youth in Vilna. He was friendly with many Jews and was married to one.

Even Winston Churchill, along with other English intellectuals such as Hilaire Belloc and G. K. Chesterton, bought into the idea of Jewish dominance of the Bolsheviks. According to Churchill, "this amazing race has created another system of morality and philosophy, this one saturated with as much hatred as Christianity was with love."[28]

Much of this British reaction, like that of other nations, was based on the reality and exaggeration of Bolshevik atrocities during the Civil War, which were equaled if not surpassed by the opposing White and Ukrainian nationalist armies (see chapter 3). According to David Vital,

[25] Lindemann 1997, 425.   [26] Quoted ibid., 426.   [27] Ibid., 433.
[28] Quoted ibid., 434.

The counter-revolutionaries believed that at the root of the Russian Revolution lay a Jewish–Bolshevik conspiracy, that "the Jews" were ultimately responsible for Russia's disasters – for how else were those disasters to be explained? – and that, more generally, the Jews had engineered themselves into a position of great political power. It was a view that they held with great tenacity, and which they proceeded, with some success, to spread round the world.[29]

Among those deeply influenced by these events, as we saw, were Hitler and Himmler. With their firm belief in the veracity of the tsarist forgery *The Protocols of the Learned Elders of Zion*, and the news from the East brought back by returning German soldiers after World War I, the Jewish–Bolshevik connection became firmly rooted in the Nazi mind. Indeed, the infamous and influential "stab in the back" accusation that Kaiser Wilhelm II made on his way out of Germany had its origin partly in the East. Walther von Kaiserlingk, the German Admiralty's chief of operations visited Petrograd (St. Petersburg) in the winter of 1917–18. He saw the government as "run by Jews in the interests of Jews; it was 'insanity in power,' and it presented a mortal threat not only to Germany but to the civilized world. Wilhelm agreed that the Russian people had been 'turned over to the vengeance of the Jews, who are connected with all the Jews of the world.'"[30]

Who were these Jews? First among them and initially second only to Lenin in power and authority was the leader of the Red Army, Leon Trotsky (né Bronstein). Grigori Zinoviev (Radomyslsky), a celebrated orator, was president of the Communist International and chairman of the Petrograd Soviet. Lev Kamenev (Rosenfeld) was a member of the party Central Committee, edited *Pravda*, the party newspaper, and chaired the Second Congress of Soviets. He also briefly was nominal head of state and chaired the Moscow Soviet. Adolf Yoffe was chair of the Revolutionary Military Committee of the Petrograd Soviet, headed the Soviet delegation negotiating the Treaty of Brest-Litovsk with Germany, and then became Soviet ambassador to Germany. Yakov Sverdlov was secretary and principal organizer of the Bolshevik Party in 1917, and in 1918 was head of state after Kamenev. Moisei Uritsky was head of the Cheka (Soviet secret police) in Petrograd where the Communist terror was especially brutal. Other Jewish leaders were Grigori Sokolnikov, once editor of *Pravda* and head of the delegation

---

[29] Vital 1999, 726.   [30] Quoted in Lindemann 1997, 424.

that signed the Treaty of Brest-Litovsk after Yoffe's voluntary departure from that position, and Karl Radek, a leading political figure.[31]

Most important, the Cheka employed a significant number of Jews right up to the start of World War II. For example, in 1937 at least 10 percent of the 407 Cheka officials who had been decorated had obviously Jewish names.[32] High-level Jews at that time were a close associate of Stalin, Lazar Kaganovich, the head of the secret police, Genrich Yagoda, and the diplomat Maxim Litvinov who, although dismissed as foreign minister prior to the Nazi–Soviet Pact of 1939, nevertheless continued in power until 1943, occupying the extremely important position of ambassador to the United States with its large Jewish community.

Deeply offending powerful Jews in the Soviet Union by killing Polish or other Jews based on "racial" classification would not have been in the Nazi self-interest for at least three reasons. First, the Soviets were allied with the Nazis after June 1939, an alliance that brought considerable benefit in the successful invasion of Poland, an outcome that would not have been possible without Soviet neutrality, if not support. Second, a frequently overlooked element of the alliance was the population resettlement policy of the Nazi regime that required Soviet cooperation. For example, immediately after the transformation of the Baltic states into Soviet republics, on July 21, 1940, Himmler ordered preparations for the resettlement to Prussia of ethnic Germans from Lithuania and later Estonia and Latvia.[33] On September 5, a German–Soviet pact was signed authorizing the transfer of German minorities from Bessarabia and northern Bukovina.[34] If a genocidal policy had been adopted by the Nazis at that time, then resettlement agreements of this kind, essential to Hitler's goal of establishing a homogenous Reich, would have been difficult if not impossible to consummate.

Finally, the timing of the war with the Soviet Union might have been affected. Perhaps more than any other contemporaneous leader, Hitler understood the value of surprise in both war and politics. He also understood the value of careful preparations in anticipation of a major military action, especially one that entailed the extraordinary risks associated with an invasion of the Soviet Union. If leading Jews in the Soviet Union had been alarmed unduly by the onset of genocide, then early Soviet preparations for war might have forced Hitler's hand and the onset of a war for which Germany would not have been adequately prepared. By not engaging in excessively brutal behaviors toward Jews,

[31] Ibid., 431–32.   [32] Ibid., 454.   [33] Aly 1999, 93.   [34] Ibid., 98.

at least not highly visible ones, Hitler could retain the initiative to be utilized at a time and place of his own choosing. Stalin's utter surprise and consequent misconduct of the war immediately after the Nazi invasion is a vindication of this early restraint by Hitler.

Another of the Nazis' fears, of course, was Jewish influence in the United States that could lead it into war against Germany.[35] Genocide in Europe might have galvanized action in the United States, leading to the two-front war so dreaded by the Nazis. Ever mindful of the international situation, especially in wartime, Hitler would exercise caution in attempting to avoid the major pitfall of simultaneous war with the Soviet Union and the United States.

Poland at the time of the Partitions

Now, instead of a diachronic comparison, let us consider cases where genocide might have been expected to occur, but did not. The affinity condition will prove to be important, even decisive.

As before, the Polish experience, because of its large concentration of Jews, becomes emblematic. The Jews of Poland found themselves at a critical juncture in late eighteenth-century Poland. The Partition of Poland of 1772 had shorn the country of nearly 30 percent of its territory and 35 percent of its population. Austria received not only 83,000 km² and 2,650,000 inhabitants but some of the most fertile and densely populated lands with valuable salt mines. Russia received the lion's share of territory – 92,000 km² – but fewer inhabitants, 1,300,000 in all, and fewer fertile lands with no appreciable mineral assets. The Prussian share was the smallest at 36,000 km² of territory and 580,000 inhabitants.[36] This apparent inequity was strongly compensated for by its presence at the mouth of the Vistula River. As a consequence of this geopolitical coup as well as Prussia's control of areas in Silesia and later Pomerania, the overwhelming proportion of Polish trade had to pass through Prussian territory. Trade treaties, ratified in 1775, imposed heavy customs duties on goods leaving Poland, low duties on those entering Poland, and exorbitant charges on Polish transit trade. There

---

[35] As Richard Breitman summarizes George Messersmith's view of Nazi policies during the 1930s: "It was only the realization that antisemitic actions could injure Germany's interests that exerted a check on the regime's actions against Jews" (Breitman 2000, 505).

[36] Gieysztor et al. 1979, 281–82.

was a real danger that the new truncated Polish state could become a Prussian economic vassal.

These new economic debilities in many ways precipitated an economic crisis. "Frederick [II of Prussia]'s economic war crippled Poland," although it did not destroy it.[37] Poland had been in economic decline for more than a century; indicative of this decline was the increased dependence of royal revenues on the sale of alcohol. In 1564, in the heyday of Polish grain production, the manufacture of alcohol accounted for 0.3 percent of revenues from royal properties. By 1764 it accounted for an astonishing 37.6 percent and by 1789 over 40 percent. A reasonable interpretation of these statistics is that more than one-third of the royal income depended on an inebriated, mostly peasant population. And Jewish proprietors were at the heart of the so-called *propinacja*, a specialized form of the *arenda* (system of leases) in which Jews were leaseholders of crown estates; in the instance of the *propinacja*, the lease entailed the manufacture and sale of alcoholic beverages. Jewish-operated taverns dotted the Polish countryside. In the midst of economic crisis, the nonproductive nature of this form of economic enterprise came to the attention of many reform-minded Poles.

In other areas of the Polish economy, Jewish traders and business people of various types found themselves in competition with the Polish burghers who were approximately equal in number.[38] Here one sees the insecurities of an incipient Polish middle class in a growing state of conflict with its only domestic competition. The size of this burgher class, disproportionately small relative to the overall Polish population size, must have exacerbated its insecurities in comparison with an equally large counterpart among the Jews, despite the fact that Jews consisted of only 10 percent of the population of Poland.

The four-year Sejm (Polish national legislature), lasting between 1788 and 1792, became a focus for burgher efforts to permanently exclude the Jews from the towns. In this last-ditch effort at Polish national renewal, all sectors of Polish society attempted to exert their respective influences on the Sejm. Hostility toward Jews by the burghers reached its height in 1790, as they were agitating for Jewish exclusion. On May 15, a riot erupted in which Jews were attacked and their wares stolen; the violence did not end until the army intervened. The immediate cause of the disturbances was a contract awarded to Jewish suppliers.[39] The outcome of this violence, along with other burgher efforts, was to lead to the

---

[37] Lukowski 1999, 110.   [38] Stone 1976, 82.   [39] Levine 1991, 213.

virtual exclusion of the Jews from the towns, except when expressly permitted by the town authorities. Even more important was the exclusion of Jews as a group from the public law. Although freedom of religious practice was guaranteed by the new constitution, the Jewish community, in contrast to others, was excluded from public law. Not only was this outcome ominous for the future continued existence of this least-assimilable Polish community, but it also stood in stark contrast to its traditional legal standing.

For two centuries, between the union of 1569 and the middle to late eighteenth century, Jewish autonomy had been granted by royal charter. The *kehilla* (pl. *kehillot*), or community in Hebrew, was constituted as the legal representation of the local Jewish community. It was responsible for administering the religious and social affairs of this community and, perhaps most important, for collecting taxes, a substantial portion of which would be rendered to the Polish authorities.[40] Jewish communities, therefore, came under royal protection or, where less applicable because of distance from the capital, under the protection of local magnates. The legal standing of the *kehillot* was undisputed; beginning in the 1580s, they began to function under a larger organization called the Council of Four Lands. Such a council probably compensated for the increasing fragmentation of Polish political life and a consequent diminution of Jewish security. During the sixteenth and early seventeenth centuries, "Polish Jews had created the greatest networks of communal and educational institutions of any Jewry since the decline of the Jewish community of Babylon. This council, through its federated structures, sought to direct, regulate, and protect far-flung Jewish communities, otherwise subjected to different domains of authority and the conflicting interests of diverse segments of Polish society."[41]

By the middle of the eighteenth century, however, the political and financial difficulties of the Polish commonwealth were evident. The Szlachta (Council of the Nobility) of 1764 resolved to abolish the Council of Four Lands that had been functioning successfully for nearly two centuries.[42] Taxes would now be collected directly by the Polish representatives, a move to economize by eliminating the prior tax-collecting agent, namely the Council of Four Lands. To be sure, a certain proportion of the funds was used for administrative purposes by the council. But at the same time, Jewish communal administration, charities, religious organizations, burial societies, learned institutions and

---

[40] Davies 1982, 325.   [41] Levine 1991, 35.   [42] Dubnov 1973, 359.

the like could no longer be administered by a central Jewish organization. The individual *kehillot* were on their own.

The gradual fragmentation of the Polish state had another consequence, namely the first major communal violence targeting Jewish communities since 1648 and the Chmielnicki pogrom, which was carried out by Ukrainians, not Poles. Empress Catherine II of Russia, by this time serving as "protector" of the Polish state, now also sought to protect the rights of Eastern Orthodox Polish citizens. This action raised the question of the rights of others such as Protestants and even Jews, thereby precipitating a vigorous Roman Catholic reaction among the nobility. The Confederation of the Bar was formed under conservative Catholic leadership, which had the additional consequence of precipitating a peasant reaction to the Confederates mainly in the predominantly Orthodox areas of Ukraine. Cossack forces rampaged throughout Ukraine with the purpose of hanging from the same tree "Pole, Jew and dog – all of the same faith."[43] Estimates of the number of Jewish dead vary from conservative estimates of thousands,[44] to the 10,000–20,000 range,[45] up to tens of thousands.[46] Clearly the visibility of the Jewish *arendar* (whether or not involved in the *propinacja*) as an agent of the Polish nobleman made him a handy target for the venting of violent rage, despite the immediate origins of the violence in issues of Catholic supremacy.

Thus, the period of the First Partition in 1772, especially the four-year Sejm, was immediately preceded by two extraordinary blows experienced by the Jewish community. Its overarching communal organization had been legislated out of existence, and once again, as in the preceding century, the threat of massive violence hung over its head. In this climate of threat and vulnerability, the Jews could expect little from the four-year Sejm despite their best efforts at influence and the high praise of observers such as Jean-Jacques Rousseau among others.[47] Although the constitution resulting from this Sejm conformed to many liberal principles of the Enlightenment, it did little to respond to the Jewish predicament. If anything it worsened that plight considerably by not referring to the Jewish community. Exclusion from the public law of the time was the consequence. Ten percent of the population therefore was effectively excluded from this constitutive process. Interestingly, the book index for the most comprehensive recent treatment of this

---

[43] Quoted ibid., 364.   [44] Gieysztor et al. 1979, 278.   [45] Dubnov 1973, 366.
[46] Levine 1991, 162.   [47] Fiszman 1997.

constitution,[48] a book 562 pages in length, has not a single entry for the words "Jew," "Jewish," "Judaism," or any other variant. This exclusion stands in contrast to other European countries where Jewish corporate existence continued to be recognized both in privilege and disability.[49]

In further contrast, the Law of the Towns explicitly recognized the rights of Christian burghers, including foreigners, as well as the freedom of townspeople from feudal obligation. Burghers could now purchase estates and were granted rights to lower-level judicial and administrative appointments; several hundreds were even elevated to the level of gentry.[50] Last-minute efforts to introduce a draft resolution concerning Jewish corporate rights failed, consistent with the continued Jewish exclusion from the towns. According to Hillel Levine,

> This left Poland's Jews, even more than before the May Constitution, subject to the whims of petty local tyrants. Vis-à-vis the larger collectivity, the Polish nation, Jews were now defined administratively as nonpersons. For Jews on the brink of the modern period, a period that would witness the mightiest effort to define the Jew as a nonperson and thereby to eliminate Jews from European society, the legacy of Poland's "bloodless revolution" was insidious.[51]

Jewish reactions to this new (non)status varied, but most perceived the dangers. Perhaps most perceptive are the comments of the Briton Lord George Gordon, who was later to convert to Judaism. He wrote,

> There has been something not sincere in the Polish Revolution, a sort of false pretence in favour of Liberty, which is now too apparent, and [the Poles] themselves are suffering the fatal consequences of the deception ... The Assembly of France, you know, has prudently admitted the Nation to the equal rights of Citizens. The Jews in France were soon penetrated with admiration and respect, on beholding the multiplied acts of Justice, which proceeded from that Assembly; and they deposited in the midst of them the solemn testimony of their patriotism and devotedness: their solemn oath to sacrifice, in every instance, *their lives and fortunes* (sic) for the public good; for the glory of the nation and the king. One sole object rules and animates all their thoughts, the good of their country, and a desire of dedicating to it all their strength. In that respect they will not yield to any inhabitants of France; they will dispute the palm with all the citizens for zeal, courage and patriotism ... But what encouragement does the present Diet [another

---

[48] Ibid.   [49] Levine 1991, 229.   [50] Ibid., 218.   [51] Ibid., 221.

term for the Sejm] hold out to the Polish Jews which they did not enjoy
under the old Republican Government? None at all.[52]

In a much darker and perhaps prophetic tone, a poem was written in
1789 and published in 1790 was homicidal in content:

> How to correct this, here is a cure. Trees are in abundance, but gallows
> are sparse. So each year we must hang one hundred Jews. Crime will
> diminish ... in this way turn bad into good.[53]

Yet even here we do not see a recommendation for wholesale massacre
or genocide. However, I do identify this as a pregenocidal condition
because of commonalities with antecedents of genocide in the several
cases examined here. Moreover, Poles must have been keenly aware of
the massacre of Jews in 1768 and even more so as the result of the much
more widespread massacres (approximately 100,000 dead) of the earlier
Chmielnicki pogroms during the preceding century.

First, we have the corporate exclusion from public law. Although not
nearly so severe as the racial laws of Nazi Germany, this exclusion
nevertheless represents an abrupt departure from the explicit recognition of Jewish corporate rights in the preceding centuries. The earlier
abolition in 1764 of the Council of Four Lands likely paved the way for
this later exclusion.

Second, extensive violence against Jews leading to the probable deaths
of at least 10,000–20,000 in eastern Poland in 1768, largely unpunished,
suggests a commonality with the later massacres of 1918–20. As we have
seen, earlier massacres also occurred in our cases of genocide, fulfilling
the continuity and validation conditions.

Third, Jewish and Christian refugees must have been a major concern
during this period. The massacres of 1768 must have had the effect of
dislocating many Jews, as did the later Partition of 1772. Indeed, after
the Partition, the Prussian government simply forced the more poverty-
stricken Jews from their homes and dumped them back onto Polish
territory.[54] Within Poland itself, Jews were expelled from villages and
towns where burghers were no longer forced by the gentry or the crown
to coexist with them. A new class of 72,000 unemployed Jews and 9,000
paupers was thus generated, nearly 10 percent of the Jewish population
and a much larger proportion of its adult males.[55] In addition,

---

[52] Quoted in Solomons 1913, 257.   [53] Quoted in Levine 1991, 212.   [54] Ibid., 167.
[55] Mahler 1971, 300–01.

approximately 200,000 Germans and 300,000 Russians migrated to
Poland at this time, creating additional population pressures, although
it is unclear how many of these people were Jews.

Fourth, the First Partition in 1772 must have generated an extreme
state insecurity. After nearly a century as virtually a Russian satellite, a
status not terribly dissimilar to that of Poland during the post-World
War II era, nearly 30 percent of its territory and 35 percent of its
population were lost to three much stronger powers. Obviously, fears
of another partition were rife and led to various efforts at national
rejuvenation, including, of course, the May 3, 1791 constitution.
Clearly these efforts were not sufficient, because in 1793 and 1795 the
Second and Third Partitions ended the sovereign existence of the Polish
state. Under these conditions of extreme state insecurity, one would
expect a sharpening of antagonism toward those perceived as less cen-
trally important members of the polity.

Fifth, ideational justifications for these antagonisms were increasing.
The dissemination of the Blood Libel, a medieval calumny that claimed
Jewish use of Christian blood in the celebration of Passover (directly
contradicting a fundamental Jewish law forbidding the ingestion of even
animal blood), was on the rise. Although various high church officials, even
several popes, condemned the Blood Libel as an absurdity, nevertheless it
persisted at the local parish or regional level as a rallying cry and justification for attacks on Jews, whether verbal or physical. And as Levine indicates, from the middle of the eighteenth century, especially after one
especially heinous case in Zhitomir in 1753, the appearance of the Blood
Libel was increasing in frequency and intensity.[56] The Roman Catholic
Church rapidly emerged as a defender of Poland against all "schismatics"
(Eastern Orthodox believers) and others, such as the Jews.[57]

Given these conditions constituting a pregenocidal syndrome, why in
point of fact did a genocide of the Jews not occur? Here, again, several
reasons emerging from this analysis can be presented. First, the period
immediately after the First Partition saw the Central-East European region
at peace. The Russo-Turkish War ending in the Treaty of Kuchuk Kainardji
in 1774 was winding down and in any event did not at this time directly
involve the Poles. Indeed, a major purpose of this and the later partitions
was the avoidance of great power war.[58] An ongoing war that directly
threatens state security may in fact be a necessary condition for genocide
that no pregenocidal antecedents can overcome.

---

[56] Levine 1991, 183–90.   [57] Dubnov 1973, 363.   [58] Lewitter 1965.

Second, while ideational influences of the Roman Catholic Church fostered anti-Jewish feeling, there were clear limits to this antagonism. The Jews had experienced a protection of the church if only to continue as "witnesses" to the travails of a people that had refused to accept Christ as the Messiah. Roman Catholic theology explicitly rejected the outright murder of people, whatever their past "misdeeds."

Third, another ideational influence, this time from a very different direction, also militated against genocide. Thus, the Enlightenment in various countries including Germany immediately to the west and especially France further west was incorporating Jews into the polity and society. Clearly, the Enlightenment was influential in Poland, as the constitutional efforts of the late eighteenth century attest. Even if incomplete, especially in the exclusion of Jews as a corporate entity, the influence of the Enlightenment simply would not permit wholesale efforts at mass murder.

The fact of Jewish acceptance in revolutionary France established an affinity for Jews that likely would not permit great power and especially French approval of such a genocide. Ideas of the French *philosophes* and those emanating from the French Revolution were sufficiently wide-spread and influential in Poland to militate against any direct attack on a people that was currently being favored by revolutionary France, the soon-to-be continental hegemon.

Here is the crux of the matter. Revolutionary France, exponent of the Enlightenment and liberator of the Jews from their ghettos and restrictive legislation, was in many respects the catalyst of the new Polish constitution. To offend this once-again-rising great power by a gross victimization of the Jews was simply out of the question. Effectively France, as the guardian of both the Jewish community and Polish liberalism, played the role of affine protector.

Britain and Ireland

Before tackling the question of Great Britain and Roman Catholic Ireland after World War I – our second case of a genocide that might have been expected to occur but did not – a prior question must be addressed. Is it legitimate to suggest democracies as candidates for the commission of genocide? Clearly the histories of democracies have been vastly superior in this regard to those of autocracies.[59] Yet democracies

---

[59] Rummel 1997.

have been known to commit genocide. The Melian genocide of the Peloponnesian War is one case in point, as is the debated but nevertheless possible genocidal policy of successive US governments toward Native Americans in the nineteenth century. It remains an open question whether the use of smallpox-infected blankets given to vulnerable Indian tribes, or individual massacres such as Sand Creek in Colorado, were evidence of state-sponsored systematic mass murder as in our three instances here. Nevertheless, the Melian genocide and the suspect US policy concerning Native Americans certainly suggest the potential for democracies to commit genocide, especially against groups with ethnoreligious characteristics distinctly at variance with those of the majority.

One more issue needs to be addressed, namely the extent to which Britain was actually within the domain of losses at the time of the uprising. Although not even close to defeat (as Germany was not in 1942–43), the British by April 1916 had not won any major land victories, but did experience one humiliating loss. This was the Gallipoli invasion of March 1915 through January 1916. With the naval bombardment of March 1915 and the April landings of British and mainly Commonwealth troops, Churchill's proposed shortcut to ending the war appeared soon to be realized. The tottering Ottoman Empire, defeated by Balkan states only three years earlier, appeared to be by far the weakest major Central Power. Yet the determined stand of German-led Turkish forces forced the British to complete their withdrawal by January 1916.[60] To many observers, this would appear to signify a further weakening of the British Empire, evidenced in British difficulties in the Boer War against Afrikaner colonists some seventeen years earlier.

Much as the defeat at Mantinea saw the collapse of Athens's Peloponnesian policy followed by the Melian genocide, so did Gallipoli signify the end to any illusions of a rapid Allied march to victory. Indeed, without significant land victories (only the French had clearly won a victory on the Marne), and with only a remote likelihood at that time of American entry into the war (Wilson was already campaigning for reelection on a platform of strict neutrality), defeat was a distinct possibility. Note the timing of the unwise and excessively harsh British response to the April 1916 uprising in Dublin, to be examined more fully below.

[60] M. Gilbert 2000.

A genocidal solution of the Irish Question is found deep in Anglo-Irish history; it is most often associated with a period of English losses. As early as the late sixteenth century, there were calls for genocide against the native Irish by English colonists who were driven out in the late 1590s. They wrote to Elizabeth I, "Lett the feete of yore forces treade and trample downe these bryars that will not suffer yore plantes to prosper ... Lett them weare with theire heeles the very rootes out of the earth that they springe no more: soe shall you make Ireland a flourishing nursery for England."[61]

Edmund Spenser, one of the irate English colonists, suggested just such a genocidal program of deliberate starvation. Sensing this imprudent realpolitik, W. B. Yeats, the great Irish Protestant poet, who in his poetry distanced himself from the famine, nevertheless wrote:

> Like an hysterical patient he [Spenser] drew a complicated web of inhuman logic out of the bowels of an insufficient premise – there was no right, no law, but that of Elizabeth, and all that opposed her opposed themselves to God, to civilisation, and to all inherited wisdom and courtesy, and should be put to death.[62]

After the Anglo-Norman invasion of Ireland by Henry II in 1122, large numbers of English settlers arrived in its wake. They took root in the Dublin area, in the southeast and southwest, and more sparsely throughout virtually the entire island. But by the sixteenth century English culture was in a state of decay. Counties Kerry and Tipperary were once "studded with English settlements,"[63] but wars with the native Irish and the absorption of many Old English into the majority Gaelic culture had sapped these communities of their number. The English imagined a "golden age" of the late twelfth and thirteenth centuries in which English culture reigned supreme at least in the areas of settlement, but by the end of the sixteenth were writing of "the Irish problem."[64] "The English inhabitants of Ireland during the reigns of Henry VIII, Edward VI, Mary and Elizabeth I were convinced, correctly, that their world was shrinking day by day."[65] Even in areas close to Dublin, the heart of the English settlement, English as a language had ceased to be used on a regular basis. It was in this context of shrinkage and loss that these genocidal sentiments were uttered by uprooted English settlers.

---

[61] Quoted in Tanner 2001, 30.   [62] Yeats 1961, 361.   [63] Tanner 2001, 28.
[64] Ibid., 29.   [65] Ibid., 33.

The Irish rebellion of the late 1590s and the general decline of English culture was, in the subsequent century, to be followed by a genuine effort at the "root and branch annihilation of Irish customs" desired in the 1590s.[66] Oliver Cromwell's invasion of Ireland in 1649 was to lead to this catastrophe. A three-prong strategy was adopted by Cromwell. First was the elimination of all military resistance to the Cromwellian Protestant reforms, effectively ending the chaos that had reigned in Ireland since 1641, and the rebellion that had its origin in Ulster. This was accomplished fairly quickly and with considerable loss of life, including the infamous massacres at Drogheda and Wexford. Second, all priests and landowners implicated in the insurrection were to be removed. This process eventually entailed the wholesale dispossession of all Catholic landowners out of the three provinces of Leinster, Munster, and Ulster, effectively all of eastern Ireland, the most fertile region. Only small estates were to be allowed Catholic landowners to the west of the Shannon river. The infrastructure of the Catholic church was destroyed both organizationally and physically, entailing the murder of large numbers of clergy. Finally, Catholicism was to be supplanted with Protestantism throughout the island. To this end, large number of Protestants were to replace Catholics, either murdered or forced to move to the west of the Shannon.[67]

This process yielded a loss of approximately 750,000 persons between 1600 and 1650, reckoned as follows. At the close of the sixteenth century, Ireland had roughly 750,000 people,[68] while in 1650 it had about 800,000. Given a peacetime fertility rate (suggested by the doubling of the Irish population between 1650 and 1700 to 1.5 million people), the number of persons should have been 1.5 million in 1650, not half that number.[69]

In addition to these human losses, the losses in land were equally catastrophic. Of the 7.5 million most arable acres, 5.2 million were transferred to Irish Protestants. Although some of that land did find its way back into Catholic hands, the net effect was a massive transference of landed wealth to the Protestants.[70] From that time, the vast majority of Irish would be poor peasants, many without land, struggling to eke out a meager existence. The Protestant "Ascendancy" dates from this time.

---

[66] Ibid., 31.   [67] Canny 1991, 145–48.   [68] Ibid., 110.   [69] Tanner 2001, 145.
[70] Ibid.

The third period that some have associated with genocide is that of the famine beginning in the late 1840s. As we saw in chapter 6, if the famine was not a genocidal act overtly planned by the British, it never-theless took over 1 million Irish lives, mainly Catholics, and utterly transformed the sociopolitical face of Ireland. Just before the famine, in 1841, the population of Ireland numbered some 8,175,124. Of these, approximately 2.5 million were landless laborers, and only 10 percent of farms had more than 30 acres.[71] In this setting of rural overpopulation, the failure of the principal crop was devastating in its consequences. In the west of Ireland, the almost uniformly Catholic areas beyond the Shannon river, vast expanses of depopulation became apparent. In the words of one observer these empty villages were the "tombs of a departed race."[72]

Most importantly, the British government, which after Peel sought to allow laissez-faire (i.e., Darwinian) economics to resolve the famine crises, actually opened itself to accusations of genocide. The so-called Gregory clause of the Poor Law Amendment Act of 1847 forbade the distribution of any relief to poor who held more than one-quarter of an acre of land[73] even in the midst of widespread starvation. It is no wonder that writers such as John Mitchel directly accused the British of for-mulating a consciously genocidal policy[74] in which the famine was artificially sustained. And Mitchel was one of the first of the prominent Young Irelanders, forerunners of the Fenians who were to play a major role in the development of Irish nationalism.

Originally known as the Irish Republican Brotherhood (itself an amal-gam of Young Irelanders and Chartists, called Irish Confederates), the Fenians were actually founded in New York in 1858.[75] Many of the Fenians were to come from the pool of 150,000 or so Irish-American veterans of the American Civil War, a large reservoir of young men whose Irish consciousness was raised first by the famine they had fled, and then by rampant anti-Irish and anti-Catholic prejudices in the United States. The Fenian movement was to spread to Great Britain and, most crucially, Ireland.

And here we find one of the key elements in the development of an affine condition protecting the Irish Catholic community from system-atic mass murder. The second major consequence of the Irish famine was the emigration of large numbers of mainly young people. The scale of

---

[71] Ibid., 241.   [72] Foster 1991a, 203.   [73] MacRaild 1999, 31.
[74] Mitchel 1868; Foster 1991, 209.   [75] MacRaild 1999, 139.

the emigration can be gauged by the drop in Irish population from 8.5 million in 1845 to approximately 6.5 million six years later.[76] These numbers suggest that, in addition to the number of deaths in excess of a million, another million or so had emigrated. Additionally, this was no singular historical occurrence. A pattern had been set whereby families, especially in the Catholic west, designated certain family members to emigrate and, where possible, send money back to their impoverished relations in Ireland. This pattern had become so socially ingrained that "By 1870 more than half as many natives of Ireland were living overseas as at home. Three-fifths of the three million emigrants were in the USA, a quarter in Britain, and about one-thirteenth in Australia as in Canada. The unique decline of Ireland's population for nearly a century after the famine was mainly caused by structural emigration, which removed up to half of each generation from the country."[77]

The nearly 2 million emigrants in the USA were to be crucial, as we saw, in the establishment of the Fenians, the prototypical militant Irish nationalist movement, but also in subsequent key events. Between 1870 and 1914, at least £1 million were to be sent home annually to Ireland, typically in the Christmas "American letter," which became essential to the stability of the western rural economy.[78] And the maintenance of this relatively primitive economy was to ensure the perpetuation of this vast emigration throughout the period ending early in World War I.

Irish-Americans were crucial not only to the Irish economy but also to the furtherance of Irish nationalism. As early as the 1860s, "republicanism was seeping into the country from Famine emigrants' new home in America, gnawing away at the fibres of loyalism."[79]

The Land League, established principally by Fenians, was a response to the bad harvest, hunger, and violence of 1879. The league's purpose was to achieve peasant proprietorship and rent reduction.[80] Although peaceful in its tactics, the league would serve as a vehicle for the expression of Irish nationalism more generally. By 1881, the Land League of America had more than half a million members organized into 1,500 branches. According to Donald MacRaild, this movement represented a "'coming of age' in Irish American politics."[81] But as a consequence of the renewed and sometimes extreme Irish nationalist sentiment, violence erupted. In 1883, for example, the American Clan na Gael attempted to destroy the Liverpool Town Hall with bombs and was

[76] Ibid., 32.   [77] Fitzpatrick 1991, 213.   [78] Ibid., 216.   [79] Tanner 2001, 250.
[80] Ibid., 254.   [81] MacRaild 1999, 145.

also responsible for three explosions in Glasgow.[82] The United States was increasingly becoming an incubator for the coming Irish nationalist explosion.

In April 1916, the Fenians, now known as the Irish Republican Brotherhood, staged its revolt. Although fought by Irishmen principally in Dublin, the funding was provided by the American Clan na Gael.[83] Given Fenianism's American roots, this source of financial support was to be expected. A participant in the uprising, Eamon de Valera, later to be prime minister of Ireland, was spared execution probably because of his American birth. He later urged an "American" strategy in which Irish-Americans would be mobilized to seek American support for Irish representation at the eventual peace conference.[84] During the postwar uprising, Irish public opinion in the United States was courted and heavily mobilized in favor of Irish independence, or at least a high level of autonomy. Given this profound connection between Ireland and the United States not to mention the large Irish communities in Britain's greatest cities including London, Liverpool, and Glasgow, a genocidal solution to the Irish Question should have been excluded as an option.[85]

Yet there were strong influences in favor of a genocidal solution. Most important, perhaps, was the domain of losses noted earlier, which set the precedent for British brutality in Ireland during this period, but also to be considered is the failure of extensive British efforts to stem the tide of Irish nationalism.

Two of the most contentious issues that gave rise to groups such as the Fenians were land and religion. Inequality in Irish landholdings was enormous. To understand the scale of the inequality, a comparison with Prussia and its history of a malevolent influence of land inequality on politics is revealing. With a rough equivalency in area, "in 1870 Ireland had 400 estates of 10,000 acres or more, and 2,000 estates of 2,000 acres or more. In that year only 100 Prussian estates were 2,000 acres or more, and those of 10,000 acres were rare."[86]

Equally important politically and having even greater impact on the daily lives of Irish peasants were tenant rights. As of 1903, the vast majority of Irish farmers were tenants.[87] Tenancies were often held at the discretion of the landlord, most often a Protestant, and rents were at times increased, even though such tenures and rents were customarily

[82] Ibid., 144.   [83] Fitzpatrick 1991, 237.   [84] Ibid., 241.   [85] MacRaild 1999.
[86] Guinnane 1997, 48.   [87] Ibid., 50.

fixed; these combined to make the future appear to be very insecure to the typical Irish Catholic tenant. Poor harvests – for example, those that led to political conflict and violence associated with the Land Wars of 1879–82 – and the threat of famine easily could magnify such fears.

The Land Acts of 1870 and 1881 were designed to redress some of these grievances. The 1870 act essentially gave the force of law to that which had been customary in land tenancy, while the 1881 legislation aimed at extending the scope of tenant rights throughout Ireland and fixing rents by special land courts.[88] Elements of both acts endeavored to encourage land purchases by farmers. The Local Government Act of 1898 allowed the election of local councils in Ireland, as did the legislation of 1889 and 1894 in Britain. Additional legislation between 1885 and 1903 further encouraged land purchase.[89]

A major grievance of Irish Catholics was the existence of the Church of Ireland – a Protestant institution in a predominantly Roman Catholic land – as the established church, similar to the Protestant Church of England's established status but in a mostly Protestant country. But despite widespread evangelical Protestant efforts and relatively low levels of Protestant emigration, the number of Church of Ireland adherents actually declined from 852,000 (census of 1834) to 693,000.[90] This fact along with Fenian activity imported from the United States led to the disestablishment of the Church of Ireland in 1869, in an effort – like that of the Land Acts – to stabilize the Irish situation. According to Boyce,[91] "In 1783 the whole of Ireland was in the grip of a privileged Protestant minority; by 1901, except in Ulster, that minority had experienced the gradual transfer of power to the Roman Catholic majority. The Church of Ireland had been disestablished; local government placed in the hands of elective (and therefore mainly Roman Catholic) councils; and peasant proprietorship all but achieved."

Despite these sweeping changes, in the midst of a most difficult war, open rebellion occurred in 1916, suggesting that nothing short of a near-genocidal solution, as in Cromwell's day, could alter Irish Catholic nationalist sentiments. And the overreaction of the British authorities in 1916 is likely attributable to these considerations. Sixteen of the rebels were executed and 3,500 people were arrested, court-martialed, or interned in Britain. Given the initial, extraordinarily negative reaction of most Dubliners, who had little sympathy for the rebellion that led to the destruction of much of Dublin's center (rebels were pelted with

---

[88] Ibid.   [89] Boyce 1985, 264.   [90] Tanner 2001, 222–23.   [91] Boyce 1985, 264.

tomatoes by the public after surrendering), the British overreaction was a gift. Instead of dealing with the rebels as dissident citizens, they were viewed by the British as traitors who had "stabbed the Empire in the back"[92] and were treated accordingly. All Irish Catholics were now viewed with great suspicion. The brutality of the British forces was indiscriminate in its application. As a consequence,

> Communities previously indifferent to republican slogans were outraged at victimization of hitherto innocuous idealists, who nevertheless bene-fited from detention by meeting enthusiasts from other localities, learn-ing Irish, mastering Gaelic games, and so receiving elementary training in revolution. While the new revolutionary elite crystallized in detention, a sentimental cult of veneration for the martyrs developed outside as after previous failed risings. The conspirators thus achieved their aim of reversing the movement towards Anglo-Irish reconciliation.[93]

Yet, as we know, despite movement in this direction in 1916, and another indiscriminate brutal response by British paramilitary forces (the infamous "Black and Tans") supporting the police in suppressing the postwar rebellion of 1920–21, genocide did not occur. The affine American connection simply was too strong for the British to seriously consider this option.

Even the possibility of massacre raised red flags to incisive British observers. For example, Sir Henry Wilson, Unionist (favoring continued union between Great Britain and Ireland), member of Parliament, and former chief of the Imperial General Staff, noted in his diary in the summer of 1920: "Winston Churchill suggested arming 20,000 Orangemen [hardline Unionists] to relieve the troops from the north. I told him this would mean taking sides ... civil war and savage repri-sals, and, at the very least, great tension with America and open rupture with the Pope. Winston does not realise these things and is a perfect idiot as a statesman."[94] Noteworthy in this regard is "a resolution of sympathy for the aspirations to self-determination of the Irish people"[95] found among the reservations to the Treaty of Versailles put forward in the US Senate in 1919.

It may be objected that Jews in Europe had an American affine population as well, yet this did not serve to deter Hitler. But there are several crucial differences. First the American-Jewish community was of more recent vintage than the Irish Catholic, smaller in size, and less

---

[92] Fitzpatrick 1991, 240.   [93] Ibid.   [94] Quoted in Bew 2004, 11.   [95] Brody 1999, 23.

embedded within the overall polity and society. Irish Catholics began arriving in large numbers in the late 1840s; large-scale Jewish immigration dated from the 1890s. Whereas the Jewish community numbered approximately 4,000,000 in 1940, Americans of Irish Catholic descent numbered at least 20,000,000. More important, the hierarchy of the American Catholic Church was almost uniformly Irish Catholic in descent. As Marcus Tanner commented, "the Catholic Church in America had become a vast extension of the Irish Catholic Church."[96] To have outraged the second-largest Christian denomination in the United States would have been extreme folly on the part of the British.

Still, as implied above, the earlier relatively decent treatment meted out to Jews by the Nazis may have been pretty much due to the perceived exaggerated influence of the American-Jewish community, in tandem with similar perceptions of influential Soviet-Jewish officials. But, in the final analysis, the Soviet Union could be conquered by the Nazis, or so ran their expectation, and the United States would eventually enter the war, thus dispelling any fears of this double influence. The Holocaust would then proceed in all its ferocity. The notion of the British conquest of the United States, thereby nullifying Irish Catholic influence, was absurd. That absurdity lies at the heart of the affine protection afforded the Catholic community in Ireland.

Israel and Intifada II

As a final example, although as of this writing it has not yet come to a formal conclusion, the Israeli response to the second intifada also indicates the importance of the affine protection of potentially threatened populations. Despite the deaths of over 1,000 Israelis (and still counting) in the most recent intifada, they have been exceedingly careful to avoid any implications of genocidal activity against the Palestinians. And the haste of the Palestinians in accusing Israel of such activity even when an official UN investigation absolved the Israelis of the so-called Jenin massacre in 2002, supports the importance of the affinity condition.

In addition to the Israeli need to avoid offending the United States in its efforts to maintain cordial relations with elements of the Arab world, the overriding consideration for the Israelis is the direct threat posed by the vastly more numerous Arab populations residing on three sides of

---

[96] Tanner 2001, 298.

Israel. With roughly 5 million Jewish Israelis potentially confronting over 150 million Arabs, an affine protection is amply afforded to Arabs under Israeli governance. The common Arab identity is reinforced by a burgeoning Muslim identification in the Middle East. Faced with the possibility of a two-front or even a three-front war, if surrounding Arab states were to come to the aid of a beleaguered Palestinian population threatened with genocide, the Israelis on the whole have been cautious in responding to the suicide bombings and other Palestinian attacks. The magnitude of this caution is emphasized by the enormous disparity between the military capabilities of the Israelis and the Palestinians, that is, the gap between the damage the Israelis *could* inflict and that which they already have.

Strategically, faced with this disparity, the Palestinians have sought to goad the Israelis into genocidal activities that would force surrounding Arab states to commit themselves militarily to the intifada. Effectively, the affine population would be activated on behalf of the Palestinians. That this strategy has thus far been ineffective suggests the Israeli recognition of the importance of the affinity condition.

The impact of war

Warfare, though, may invert the affinity condition. While, earlier, East European Jews were protected by the existence of politically powerful Jews in the Soviet Union, when war broke out the Jewish "threat" had to be neutralized. Armenians protected by the February 1914 agreement between the Ottoman Empire and Russia were suddenly transformed by the war into highly threatening Russian handmaidens that needed to be dealt with harshly. And when the United Nations as a local protector decided to withdraw its troops from Rwanda, this was the signal for the genocide to be enacted throughout the country. Ottoman Greeks were saved from extinction not only by the affinity condition of extreme Allied, especially British protectiveness toward them and the existence of the Greek state itself, but by the emergence of Turkey as victorious in the later Greco-Turkish War that removed it from the domain of losses. Genocide of the Vietnamese in Cambodia accelerated rapidly as the Khmer Rouge were being decisively defeated in the quickening border war with Vietnam.

Precisely because the affinity condition restricts the decision latitude of the potential victimizer and in that sense magnifies the threat of both the potential victims and their affine protector, when war breaks out, these strictures no longer hold. Genocide then becomes a distinct possibility. This, perhaps, is the paradox of affinity – protection in peacetime, but much greater vulnerability in time of war. Yet the power of the affinity condition in preventing or at least postponing genocide is still evident, if only in the differential treatment accorded Armenians and Ottoman Greeks, even in the midst of a full-scale war in 1915–16.

PART VI

Conclusion

18

Findings, consequences, and prevention

The twentieth century witnessed the horrors of genocide and its sequelae, horrors that unfortunately have not yet ceased. A major purpose of this volume has been to identify antecedent factors that make genocide more or less likely to occur, as well as factors that increase victim vulnerability, thereby augmenting the magnitude of the killing. In this chapter, therefore, I begin by summarizing similarities and differences in the findings. Following this presentation, I include summaries of the analyses that help clarify the consequences of genocide and modes of genocide prevention including the role of democracy. If nothing else, an investigation of genocide should lead not only to an understanding of its origins and consequences, but also to ways of preventing genocide in the future. Which variables are most likely to signal the onset of genocide and how should interested parties (in the best-case scenario, the entire international community) react?

Similarities and differences

Genocide and other crimes against humanity such as ethnic cleansing share certain features in common. Most important, they are more likely to occur during wartime than during peacetime. War is associated with uncertainty, as its outcome tends to be uncertain. Given the tendency of uncertainty to increase reliance on prior knowledge or memory, as the Bayesian findings inform us, a recent history of loss looms large in its decision-making influence. Loss builds on and coalesces the tendencies toward extremism already inherent in the search for unity and continuity of mass murder. The emphasis on loss also specifies a behavioral consequence of political upheaval, a variable that has been identified as critical in yielding genocide by analysts such as Robert Melson and Barbara Harff.[1] Political upheaval, whether domestic or international,

---

[1] See Melson 1992 and Harff 2003.

369

yields winners and losers. As we have seen, losers in earlier or ongoing conflicts are the most likely perpetrators of genocide. Loss is a blatant and eminently measurable property of the human condition.

The etiology of ethnic cleansing, as in the Irish famine, is distinguished from that of genocide mainly by the presence of recent loss in the case of genocide. Realpolitik alone was prominent in explaining that famine, as well as other cases of ethnic cleansing such as that which occurred in Bosnia. In the one clearly genocidal element of the Bosnian ethnic cleansing, Srebrenica, recent or impending loss is implicated.

In the case of genocide, loss is allowed to generate its pernicious consequences. The three genocidal states – Germany, the Ottoman Empire, and Rwanda – had histories of loss that increased the probability of an imprudent–brute force realpolitik with its associated risk minimization (mostly unnecessary) and genocidal outcome, especially after loss compensation had been effected.

An implication, of course, is that, if earlier German losses in World War I had been reversed in the later conflict, then the genocide likely would not have occurred, certainly not in its eliminationist form. As we saw in chapter 7, after the defeat of France and prior to the Battle of Britain in 1940, Hitler considered the Jews to be "stupid" and not nearly as powerful as he had first thought. Following this logic, continued victory for Hitler would have led to additional contempt for world Jewry, but much less brutality. With the defeat of Britain, the British navy would no longer have been an obstacle to the mass transfer of Jews to Madagascar, the initial preferred option by the Nazis during the war.

The same argument holds for the Ottoman and Hutu extremists. Defeat of the Russian army by the Turkish, instead of the latter's rout in 1915, and reversal of the Rwandese Patriotic Front territorial gains, especially those of February 1993, would likely have thwarted the genocidal process.

At the same time, vulnerability of the targeted group with real or purported connection with an enemy state (e.g., ethnic kin within that state) is a necessary condition for the genocide to occur. Thus, not all experiences of loss by states will lead to genocide.[2] Continuity of the killing with earlier massacres, which demonstrates vulnerability, and validation – killing without punishment – facilitate occurrence of the later genocide. Whether

---

[2] For example, although Mexico was a substantially truncated state after the Mexican–American war of 1846–48, genocide did not occur. There was no vulnerable ethnic group within truncated Mexico that could be accused of facilitating the Mexican defeat and territorial loss.

continuity and validation rise to the level of necessary conditions is still an open question, although in fact they may be just that.

Essentially, the explanations offered here apply to three genocides of the most destructive variety and involving the deaths of far more people than many mass murders combined. To err on the conservative side, I should make no claim that this explanatory framework extends to other instances, although, in fact, it might. Most recently, I discovered that the Vendée, a series of late eighteenth-century mass murders (estimated 117,000 dead within a relatively small area in northwestern France) by French revolutionary troops following a major counterrevolutionary revolt, occurred immediately after a military defeat of the French revolutionary army at Neerwinden in Belgium.[3] This loss emphasized the precarious condition of the French revolutionary state in the face of both internal and external enemies. Applicability of the present framework to the current ethnic cleansing with possible genocidal behavior in the Darfur region of western Sudan will be examined later in the section on genocide prevention.

Defeat of the Khmer Rouge by the Vietnamese army signaled the military weakness of Democratic Kampuchea followed by the thoroughgoing genocide of ethnic Vietnamese in Cambodia. This finding was an unexpected byproduct of analyzing the Cambodian politicide.

There are differences among our cases. Most notably, the Cambodian politicide emerged within the historical and geographic arc of communist governance stretching from Central Europe through Siberia and China, and extending down to the French Indochinese successor states. In contrast to the genocidal states that had little ideological uniformity, a single ideology of Marxism-Leninism (albeit with regional variations) established the parameters of governance, despite genocide of the ethnic Vietnamese largely within the domain of losses and risk minimization. It is not surprising, therefore, that the Cambodian politicide exhibited the goals of Mao's Cultural Revolution implemented by Stalin's methods. Pol Pot's frequent contact with the Chinese Communists, along with his

---

[3] For descriptions and analyses of the Vendée, see Tilly 1964 and Secher 2003. Although comprising a series of mass murders like those of the Armenians in 1894–96, certainly not a genocide, these cases suggest the possibility that large-scale mass murders also may be associated with prior or ongoing loss. In the Armenian case, it was the attempt by Armenians to enforce the liberal reform provisions of the Treaty of Berlin of 1878 imposed on the Turks after their disastrous losses in the Russo-Turkish War of 1877–78, followed by the unification (and expansion) of Bulgaria in 1885 at Ottoman expense, that led to the mass murders (Dadrian 1997, 113–84).

earlier sojourn in Paris and the influence of the Stalinist French Communist Party, established the contours of his later decision making.

Another major difference is found in matters of scale. Although the Holocaust victimized approximately six times as many people as the next most extensive genocide, that fact, horrifying as it is, turned out not to be critical to the analysis. What was crucial analytically was the presence of the Holocaust in twenty European countries, which allowed comparisons among perpetrating states.

Among the findings of analyses of these countries, several are prominent. The experience of territorial loss distinguished between perpetrating states such as, on the one hand, Italy, Vichy France, and Romania, which victimized their own citizenry, and on the other Bulgaria and Finland, which saved most of their Jews after having their borders expanded at the start of World War II. At this time, both Vichy France and Romania were severely truncated, and Italy was in the process of experiencing territorial loss. Implications of that loss, as in the genocidal states (Germany, Austria, the Ottoman Empire, and Rwanda), were extensively developed theoretically.

Inequality and especially mutual identification among victims turned out to be important in understanding two things: first, how so many people could be murdered by the Germans using collaborators among the Jewish leaders, and, second, why at least one East European ghetto rebelled on a large scale, but others did not.

Victim vulnerability, a seldom-examined subject, is salient here. Whether the number of Jewish victims in the Netherlands could have been reduced if there had existed greater equality and mutual identification among them is unknown. Yet, if the extensive collaboration between the Amsterdam Jewish Council leaders and the SS had been reduced, then perhaps delaying tactics might have led to the survival of a larger number of Jews at the war's end. This speculation is somewhat problematic because of the early (1942) destruction of so much of the Dutch-Jewish community.

Much less problematic is the contrast between behaviors of the Hungarian-Jewish leaders and those of Romania. Despite intense Romanian anti-Semitism and the participation of Romania in the killing of more Jews than any other state besides Germany,[4] 300,000 were saved by the intense efforts of Jewish leaders identifying with their coreligionists. Before the war, among five European countries examined, Romania had by far the highest number of anti-Semitic acts per million population between 1899 and 1939, more than three times the rate of Germany.[5] In Hungary,

---

[4] Hilberg 1985, 759.   [5] Brustein and King 2004, 43.

on the other hand, with much less identification among different sectors of the Jewish community, more than 500,000 went to their deaths in the absence of warnings from the Jewish leadership that annihilation was imminent. In mid-1944 when these killings took place, the probabilities of escape and survival until the Soviets arrived were much higher than earlier in the war.

Absence of mutual identification also helps explain the failure of revolts to develop among Jews in ghettos such as Łódź and Vilna. In the former, the presence of wealthier foreign Jews militated against such identification, while in the latter the resistance organization was not all-inclusive, omitting important groups such as the Yiddishist Bund because of deep political antipathies. In Warsaw, on the other hand, the April ghetto revolt exploded with all resistance groups cooperating.

Even more important, as we saw, is the likely impact of altruistic punishment occurring in the earlier January revolt on the unity characteristic of the later, much more widespread, April revolt. Not only was that unity achieved among the victims, at least in this one instance, but the concept of altruistic punishment also helps answer Michael Marrus's question of why so many victimizers were willing to follow Hitler down his murderous path. Altruistic punishment as a generator of unity within a fractious population was found to be important in answering this question. It also was critical in helping understand how a violence-averse person such as Himmler could still engage in mass murder on a horrendous scale.

At the same time, altruistic punishment may have been less important in the genocides of Armenians and Tutsi. We have some evidence of inclinations in the direction of altruistic punishment by Ottoman leaders such as Enver Paşa and Talât, both of whom died shortly after World War I in circumstances that can be interpreted as sacrificial for unity of the state.[6] Sacrifice of the *génocidaires* was found in the refugee camps of Zaire and the deaths of many at the hands of the RPF.

If altruistic punishment was less important and perhaps even irrelevant to the Rwandan genocide, which process could augment or replace it in encouraging unity of leaders and followers? The evidence thus far suggests the role of fear of both the oncoming RPF and the genocidal Hutu leaders who might kill Hutu peasants if they did not obey orders to murder Tutsi. Interviews with *génocidaires* have revealed both

---

[6] As minister of the interior, Talât was responsible for deportation of the Armenians; he was assassinated by an Armenian in Germany in 1921. Enver Paşa continued to battle the Soviets after World War I and was killed by them in 1922.

motivations as sources of the widespread killing.[7] Fear of the oncoming Russian army as well as of disobeying Ottoman officers charged with the genocide was probably a major factor in the Armenian instance, as were elements of altruistic punishment.

Yet altruistic punishment as a voluntary form of sacrifice is more effective. Without the sacrifice of Captain Wesreidau and others of like mind on the battlefield (see chapter 8), the German front might have collapsed much earlier in the war, as it did in World War I, thereby saving many Jewish lives and rendering the genocide less complete. The more than half a million Hungarian Jews along with Romanian, Slovak, French, Polish, and other Jews killed later in the war could have been saved.

We are now at the point of identifying the relative impact of several key variables. Analyses here have indicated that both loss and imprudent–brute force realpolitik are clearly implicated in all three cases of genocide, both in generating the onset of genocide and in magnifying the extent of victimization. Using the language of necessary conditions,[8] one can argue that these variables rise to the level of necessity because of their appearance in all cases of genocide and absence in the instances where genocide might have been expected to occur, but did not. I prefer to use the language of probabilities, wherein these variables can be said to greatly increase the probability of genocide's occurrence and extent of victimization. Alone, the search for unity probably was not influential in regard to either the onset or magnitude of genocide, but *was* consequential in affecting magnitude in concert with altruistic punishment (in the case of the Holocaust), or with fear (in the case of the Tutsi).

On the other hand, there are variables that principally affect the magnitude of the genocide. Altruistic punishment is one such variable, as we just saw, and cynical realpolitik is certainly another both in the denial of refuge that undoubtedly increased the number of victims, and in the effective permission granted to genocidal governments by cynical bystanders. Inequality and especially absence of mutual identification were significant in allowing Hungarian Jews to go to their deaths without warning that might have saved many, given the proximity of Soviet forces.

The consequences of loss, imprudent and cynical realpolitik, altruistic punishment, and failures of mutual identification individually or in some combination exist beyond the confines of genocide. Mass murder may be occasioned by loss and an imprudent realpolitik, as in the

[7] Berkeley 2002.   [8] Goertz and Starr 2003.

Vendée, and realpolitik alone is influential in the genesis of ethnic cleansing. The rise of suicide bombing, in particular, may stem from a sense of loss and altruistic punishment intended to maximize cooperation among the aggrieved population.[9] Bayesian findings that emphasize the role of uncertainty in diminishing the bases of rational calculation and lead to reliance on memory are especially applicable to almost any situation clouded by the fog of uncertainty.

The fog of war is what it implies – a blanket of uncertainty that obscures features of the physical and social landscape; most important, it renders uncertain the war's outcome. All three of the genocidal states and the genocidal component of the single politicide occurred within the context of war.[10] Without war, it is exceedingly unlikely that genocide would have occurred. Precisely because of the importance of war, the international dimension of genocide has received the lion's share of attention.

Consequences of genocide

If the study of genocide can lead to the understanding of crimes against humanity beyond the strict confines of the phenomenon in question, the consequences of genocide too can be multifaceted and far-reaching both geographically and in longevity of outcomes. All three genocides had such wide-ranging consequences.

The Holocaust

In addition to the removal of the majority of Jews from Europe by death or migration, a principal outcome of the Holocaust was the formation of the State of Israel. If, at the outbreak of World War II, the majority of world Jewry was not Zionist, within a few years after its end it would be. As we saw, significant proportions of the Jewish population were Yiddishist (often Bundist, supporting Yiddish as the main language of the Jews and opposing Zionism), and so were opposed to the idea of a Jewish state and the use of Hebrew as a daily language as it was evolving in the Jewish community of

---

[9] M. Midlarsky 2004.
[10] For general associations between genocide and war, see Markusen 1987 and M. Shaw 2003. The context of war profoundly influenced the Cambodian genocide of the ethnic Vietnamese, for it occurred very shortly after the defeat of Lon Nol's forces, conquest of South Vietnam by the North, ongoing military engagement of the Khmer Rouge with the Vietnamese, and the earlier highly destructive US bombing of Cambodia.

Palestine. Another segment was Orthodox, frequently Hasidic, organized typically into separate communities. Support for a Jewish state was absolutely forbidden among many of these communities because of their belief that only arrival of the long-awaited Messiah could justify the ingathering of Jews into the Promised Land.

Sometimes, entire nationalities such as the Hungarian Jews, whatever their level of observance, were only weakly Zionist, if at all, because of assimilation (see chapter 12), the presence of Hasidism, or simply the absence of a history of persecution comparable to that of the Jewish communities of Poland and Russia under the anti-Semitic tsars. Franz Josef II of the Austro-Hungarian Empire presided over a tolerant government that in the view of most Hungarian Jews obviated the necessity of seeking a Jewish national home. Finally, the level of assimilation, not only in Hungary, but in Austria, Germany, and even Poland–Russia, excluded the possibility of Zionism as an option for many Jews.

The Holocaust changed all that. The vast majority of Hasidim were murdered. Assimilated as well as observant Jews were killed along with their families with apparent equanimity; no distinctions were made in this thoroughly egalitarian enterprise of mass murder. In this milieu, practicing Christians with Jewish parental or even grandparental ancestry were pushed into the gas chambers along with bearded and earlocked Hasidim. Theodor Herzl, author of *The Jewish State* and the father of modern Zionism, appeared to be correct. There was no hope for the Jew in Europe, even if thoroughly Christianized.

Support for an independent Israel, then, grew to transcend the bounds of the Jewish community, not only in Europe, but importantly also in the United States. Staunch Arab opposition to this development, both within Palestine and outside it, led to the invasion of Palestine by surrounding Arab governments and the defeat of these forces by the now-organized Jewish defenders. And, as argued in chapter 14, the Warsaw ghetto revolt of 1943 against vastly superior German forces, as in the much earlier revolt against Rome in 66–70, suggested the precedent for limited and perhaps even, under different conditions, substantial Jewish success against seemingly overwhelming odds.[11]

---

[11] Israel Gutman notes that "The Warsaw Ghetto Uprising ... has become a symbol of Jewish resistance and determination, a moment in history that has transformed the self-perception of the Jewish people from passivity to active armed struggle. The Uprising has shaped Israel's national self-understanding" (1994, xi).

A consequence, of course, was the displacement of most Palestinian Arabs from the boundaries of Israel, the beginnings of the Palestinian refugee problem, and desire for revenge by the defeated Arabs whether Palestinian, Egyptian, Syrian, or Iraqi. The various Arab–Israeli wars, Intifadas I and II, and the current (as of this writing) impasse in Israeli–Palestinian negotiations then followed. If the populations of the European Union believe that Israel is a greater threat to world peace than North Korea or Iran,[12] it is precisely because of the legitimation of Zionism by the Holocaust, occurring of course, on European soil.

The Armenian genocide

Strangely, as we shall now see, an important consequence of the Armenian genocide and its corollary, the ethnic cleansing of the Anatolian Greeks, will intersect with that of the Holocaust. This is the secularization of modern Turkey under Kemal Atatürk after dissolution of the Ottoman Empire at the end of World War I. Stanford Shaw and Ezel Shaw describe the condition of modern Turkey at its inception in 1923:

> The disruption was massive. Most non-Muslims were gone, with the Greek community reduced from 1.8 million to 120,000[,] the Armenians from 1.3 million to 100,000. No less than 2.5 million Turks had died during the war, leaving a population of 13,269,606 in Anatolia and eastern Thrace. Foreign trade had fallen drastically, exports from 2.5 to 0.8 billion kuruş, imports from 4.5 to 1.4 billion kuruş between 1911 and 1923. State revenues declined from 2.87 to 1.8 billion kuruş.[13]

And, as we saw in chapter 7, prior to World War I, ethnic Turkish participation had been limited to 15 percent in internal trade, 12 percent in industry and crafts, and 14 percent in the professions. Armenians and Greeks controlled the lion's share (between 66 and 79 percent) of the non-agricultural Ottoman economy. Turks themselves therefore, had to fill these enormous gaps after the genocide and ethnic cleansing.

Atatürk himself was keenly aware of these deficiencies. In a speech to a conference held in Izmir (formerly Smyrna) in February 1923, Atatürk began, "I shall not describe the state the country is in. You know it."[14] Knowledge of the country's backwardness should be an impetus to unity

[12] As of the fall of 2003, according to the Monitoring Institute on Racism and Xenophobia of the European Commission.
[13] S. Shaw and Shaw 1977, 373.   [14] Quoted in Mango 2000, 375.

in its redevelopment, was Atatürk's principal message: "Those who conquer by the sword are destined to be defeated by those who conquer by the plough; the economy is everything: it is the totality of what we need to live, to be happy."[15]

Atatürk was acutely aware of the absolute dependence of Turks on Armenian and Greek craftsmen. According to Andrew Mango, "Muslim Turks lacked the most basic technical skills. Famous as cavalrymen, they had to rely on Armenian farriers to shoe their horses."[16] And his only address to a popular audience during the War of Independence was one given to graduates of a newly created school for military farriers. The Turkish nation, according to Atatürk, was dependent on non-Turks for everything "from needles to thread, from nails to pegs." Continuing, he stated that "the simplest trade is the most honourable. Shoemakers, tailors, carpenters, tanners, blacksmiths, farriers – these are trades most worthy of respect in our social and military life."[17] All of these trades traditionally had been occupied by non-Muslims.

An interesting sidelight on this conference is its location. Smyrna was formerly occupied almost entirely by Greeks, Armenians, Turks, and Jews, but after its destruction by Atatürk only the Turkish and Jewish sectors were left standing. Because of the widespread destruction, many of the conferees were hosted in Jewish homes, signifying the longstanding security felt by Jews even in the emergent modern nationalist Turkey. Noteworthy here is the position of Jews as a distant third, after Greeks and Armenians, among non-Muslims in control of the economy, in contrast to Hungary, Romania, Poland, Austria, and Germany. The threat of Jewish economic dominance as a component of potential loss in Turkey, therefore, was minuscule, in comparison with these European states prior to World War II.

Traditional Islamic teaching simply would not do. The *medreses*, or religious schools, frequently were headed by *müftüs*, who were woefully ignorant even of their own traditions. Encountering one such *müftü* attempting to teach Arabic, Atatürk proclaimed "I do not know Arabic, but as I had served in Arab lands, I knew more of the language than the *müftü* ... Let us send people to Syria or Arabia to learn Arabic, but let us not waste time in all our *medreses*, where people who neither know nor can teach are uselessly occupied."[18] Only the study of modern business and technology could restore Turkey to a semblance of its economic

---

[15] Quoted ibid.   [16] Ibid., 368.   [17] Quoted ibid.   [18] Quoted ibid., 374.

performance prior to the war. And this was one of the first orders of business facing the republic.

A modern system of education was instituted that was divorced from religion. The study of religion was delegated to the family or to small private schools in smaller villages. Although Islam was never abolished and mosques were allowed to remain open for prayers, clergy who had once been extraordinarily influential were relegated to the sidelines. State reforms would proceed without interference from the Muslim clergy so that enormous losses engendered by the disappearance of the Armenians and Greeks (at least a century of growth according to the US consul Leslie Davies; see chapter 4) could be recouped.

When in late 1923 the caliph, as the supreme Muslim leader, became a political focus for opponents of the new regime and asked for increasing privileges, Atatürk reacted. Writing to the last caliph, Abdulmecit: "Let the caliph and the whole world know that the caliph and the caliphate which have been preserved have no real meaning and no real existence. We cannot expose the Turkish Republic to any sort of danger to its independence by its continued existence. The position of Caliphate [sic] in the end has for us no more importance than a historic memory."[19] On March 3, 1924, the caliphate was abolished, ending the Muslim seat of ecclesiastical governance for the entire Middle East and beyond.

And here we find one of the genuinely incalculable consequences of the Armenian genocide and Greek expulsion. In his haste to secularize and thereby make up much lost economic ground, all threats to that process had to be blunted. Vestiges of the religious hegemony of Islam embodied in the caliphate were eliminated. And this is precisely the historical event that exercised the staunch Islamism of the Egyptian Sayyid Qutb, arguably the single most influential philosopher of Muslim extremism, and his most accomplished follower, Osama bin Laden.

With the dissolution of the Ottoman Empire in 1921, elimination of the caliphate in 1924, and the emergence of secular Turkey under Kemal Atatürk as a successor state, the empire unifying the Muslim peoples of the Middle East had been replaced by a horrendous model to be avoided at all costs. Qutb's solution, enthusiastically adopted later by Egyptian Islamist groups and still later by Al Qaeda, was resurrection of the Muslim caliphate whose institutional vestiges had been destroyed by Atatürk's regime.

---

[19] Quoted in S. Shaw and Shaw 1977, 368–69.

Osama bin Laden explicitly harks back to this time of Muslim "humiliation" after World War I. Remarking that the United States was "filled with horror" after the attacks of September 11, bin Laden goes on to say, "Our Islamic nation has been tasting the same for more [than] 80 years, of humiliation and disgrace, its sons killed and their blood spilled, its sanctities desecrated."[20]

Had the Armenians and Greeks remained in Turkey as economic prime movers, it is likely that the secularization drive would have been much slower and perhaps would never have come into existence. The old *millet* with its autonomous religious communities would still have been needed, and sensitivity to Muslim sentiments could have continued. As in Abdulhamit's reign as the last sultan of the Ottoman Empire, Islam could have been seen as societal cement, but one limited by strictures of the *millet* system.

And here lies the convergence of consequences of the Holocaust and the Armenian genocide. Both Israel as an immediate outgrowth of the Holocaust and secularism in the modern Islamic world inspired by the Turkish model have invoked the wrath of Islamists ranging from the Palestinian Hamas to the Egyptian Islamic Jihad, including, of course, Al Qaeda. Perhaps it is a measure of the enormity of genocide that events occurring in different parts of the world, with seemingly little overt connection, can generate trajectories that join many years later in widespread but connected oppositional movements with similar themes.

The Tutsi genocide

Finally, we have the immediate consequences of the Tutsi genocide. As of 2004, it had resulted in the deaths of at least 3.8 million people in the Democratic Republic of the Congo (formerly Zaire),[21] and the active involvement of neighboring African countries such as Rwanda, Uganda, Tanzania, Angola, and Zambia. Hutu *génocidaires* escaping the victorious RPF spilled over the borders into Zaire, followed by troops of the RPF and other Tutsi seeking vengeance. Attempts to depose the Laurent Kabila government led to civil war involving local political and tribal groups, with substantial external involvement, principally Rwandan. French-led troops came as peacekeepers, to be replaced more recently by a force of Bangladeshi, Pakistani, Nepalese, and Uruguayan

---

[20] Quoted in Berman 2003, 117.
[21] According to the International Rescue Committee (Lacey 2004).

composition.[22] Given the magnitude of the killing and the involvement of so many African countries signifying Congo's size and geographic centrality, it is doubtful that we have seen the last of the consequences of the Rwandan genocide.

As in our other two cases, unforeseen events and currently inconceivable political trajectories may have been set in motion by the mass killings first in Rwanda and then in Zaire. The future political unity of the Democratic Republic of the Congo may have been seriously jeopardized, with implications for the unity of the other African states with borders stemming from the colonial period. This is but one of the potential consequences of the Rwandan genocide, in addition to the millions already murdered in Congo.

Genocide prevention and the role of democracy

Has the analysis here suggested ways of preventing genocide? Well, both yes and no. To the extent that genocide originates in war, a military force exclusively devoted to intervention in potential genocides[23] would be helpful. But if the potential victimizer is a great power, as occurred in two of the three cases of genocide analyzed here, then such an international force would be of little utility. Judicial arenas such as the International Court of Justice, created in 1946 but without enforcement powers, had little effect even on the course of the Rwandan genocide, or genocidal elements of the Bosnian ethnic cleansing. The newly created International Criminal Court, in its ability to try and sentence individuals for criminal behavior defined by the Rome Statute,[24] may be more successful, but still may not deter the tendencies toward impunity of the most powerful states.

Among those who have examined the issue of prevention, John Heidenrich[25] explores the potential for prevention of various forms of rescue, and the role of organized religion, among other agencies, in limiting either the onset or extent of genocidal killing once begun.[26] Helen Fein reviews the findings of studies that have revealed the sources of genocide.[27] Among them are regime type (democracy, nondemocracy), presence or

---

[22] BBC News, UK Edition, June 11, 2004, http://news.bbc.co.uk/1/hi/world/africa.
[23] Bauer 2002.
[24] For the contents of the Rome Statute of the International Criminal Court, see http://www.un.org/law/icc/statute/contents.htm.
[25] Heidenrich 2001.   [26] See Kolodziej 2000.   [27] Fein 2000, 48–49.

absence of civil liberties, political exclusion as the result of ethnic hierarchy, conflict over land use, growth of hate movements, and immunity from external restraint.

Here, I propose to examine variables identified in previous chapters that have the potential to limit or prevent genocidal activity. On the whole, following emphases of this book, these variables are international. If, as we saw, variables that increase threat to state security also increase the probability of genocide, then decreasing that threat would be of paramount importance. Most important analytically is the situation of the state within the domain of losses. Identifying countries or populations that have experienced recent losses internationally (or interethnically), especially if the losses are territorial, might be an important first step in pinpointing a potential genocide. Recency is important because of the still palpable emotional reaction and (as yet) little recompense for the loss. If memories of loss are kept alive within schools, say in refugee populations, then this activity can be functionally equivalent to recency.

Loss compensation and affinity

The experience of loss and the importance of loss compensation in effecting genocide suggest a potential preventive measure. Instead of loss compensation taking the form of genocide, as it has in our three cases (and in the instances of Srebrenica and the ethnic Vietnamese in Cambodia), it can be introduced much earlier in relations between states or communities. For example, Allied recognition of the potential impact of German territorial concessions at Versailles, especially in light of the massive relinquishing of non-German territories occupied by German troops (including territories governed by Prussia since the late eighteenth century), might have led at that time to Allied compensations. Reparations might have been imposed, as they were, but then immediately forgiven, as they were not. Only after the French occupation of the Ruhr in 1923 to guarantee payment had embittered many Germans and massively energized the Nazi Party were the reparations ultimately forgiven. Clear readmission into the network of European great power politics also could have yielded compensation in the form of increased international status.

Compensation also can take the form of credible territorial guarantees to compensate countries for major territorial losses. If the Ottoman Turks had been convinced that, despite the war, the whole of Anatolia would remain Ottoman and not be divided into Turkish, Greek, and

Armenian enclaves, then the Armenian genocide and ethnic cleansing of the Greeks would have been less likely to occur. Great power guarantees of continued Hutu political influence in Rwanda in proportion to their number, not envisioned in the Arusha Accords, could have compensated for Hutu concessions in those accords. For countries experiencing serious losses, even the substantial effort by significant international actors to achieve loss compensation could go far in allaying fears about an extremely uncertain future. This is a form of prudent real-politik for great powers that replaces the far more prevalent (historically) cynical variety, and can avoid the imprudent–brute force realpolitik of mass political violence.

And here we find the first suggestion (another will be examined later) that democracy may not be a universal palliative in protecting human rights.[28] After the four years of intense propaganda efforts by the Allies in painting the "Huns" as evil autocrats, thereby stimulating the war effort at home, could the leaders of Britain and France have agreed to a compensatory peace at Versailles and still retained office? Woodrow Wilson, on the other hand, leading a country at war for less than half that time, with many fewer casualties per capita, and proportionately less inhibited by these government-generated domestic hostilities toward the Central Powers, was able to craft the fair-minded set of Fourteen Points, effectively constituting a compensatory peace that, alas, could not carry the day against British and especially French obstructionism. Without the need to satisfy energized and in the French case security-minded electorates, it is possible that a more compensatory peace could have evolved, thereby avoiding the intense feelings of loss and their ultimate consequences for war and genocide.

Even the limited compromises Georges Clemenceau agreed to at Versailles – for example, accepting the promise of security guarantees by the United States and Britain in place of French occupation of the left bank of the Rhine – were distasteful to the French public. When, after Versailles, these guarantees failed to materialize within the United States, mainly for political reasons, the Clemenceau government fell in January 1920.[29]

---

[28] For evidence of the pacific effects of democratic governments on genocide within their own countries, see Rummel 1997 and Harff 2003, despite differences in the domains of inquiry between these studies and my own. For the pacific impact of democracy on civil wars, see Hegre et al. 2001.

[29] Brody 1999, 25.

Russia and the Ottoman Empire

Based on this analysis, is it possible to predict the current likely perpetrators of genocide? Certainly the country with the largest domain of
losses is Russia, having lost not only its satellites in Central and Eastern
Europe with the collapse of the Soviet Union, but even long-time
ethnically cognate major components of the old tsarist empire such as
Ukraine and Belarus. Correspondingly, we have seen the brutal Russian
attempts to stamp out efforts at Chechen autonomy. To the extent that
these activities have killed a significant number of Chechens, Russia
could already be accused of genocide based on the United Nations
definition. However, insofar as Russia has not sought to eradicate all
Chechens, including women and children, it cannot be classified as a
genocidal state according to the definition adopted here.

Why has the Russian government not sought to entirely eradicate the
Chechen people? Answers are to be found in the gradual incorporation
of Russia into Europe and the dangers of rupturing these relations.
European powers and even the United States might not only eschew a
policy of cynical realpolitik that could allow a genocidal venture against
the Chechens, but might even become affine governmental protectors of
the Chechens, especially if nearby large Muslim-majority states such as
Kazakhstan, Uzbekistan, and notably Turkey become alarmed. There
existed a near-universal recognition that Russia after 1991 bore strong
similarities to Weimar Germany after 1919, including the rise of nationalist extremists such as Vladimir Zhirinovsky who could profit politically from the Russian experience of loss.[30] Western policy toward
Russia during this period, on the whole, sought to avoid the isolation
and near-pariah status accorded Weimar Germany after World War I,
which reinforced the sense of loss. Instead of committing genocide in
order to ensure that Chechen territory remains within the Russian
Federation, compensatory policies in the economic and political realm
have been reincorporating Russia into the global system with its own
substantial rewards.

Here we see a fundamental difference in analytical consequence
between use of the definition adopted in this book – attempted total

---

[30] As early as October 1990, even before the actual disintegration of the USSR, at a
conference held at the Institute of USA and Canada Studies of the Soviet (now
Russian) Academy of Sciences, statements to this effect by Soviet speakers were
heard. Some written hints of it are to be found in chapters stemming from the
conference published in M. Midlarsky et al. 1994.

eradication – and partial loss of group members noted by the United Nations definition as sufficient for the accusation of genocide. Although compensation for losses and affinity could not save all of the Chechens, nevertheless these processes very likely were instrumental in mitigating the ferocity of the Russian governmental response, thereby allowing most Chechens to survive. These mitigating variables emerged from the present analysis that focuses only on the few contemporary attempts at ethnoreligious eradication. It is less likely that these variables would have emerged from a large-N analysis that necessarily is not limited to the most egregious cases. Less policy-specific variables such as political upheaval have emerged from such analyses.[31]

Interestingly, a comparison between Russia in 1991 and the Ottoman Empire in 1914 is equally appropriate for purposes of distinguishing between the emergence of brutality, even mass killing on the one hand, and outright genocide on the other. Both Russia and the Ottoman Empire had suffered grievous territorial losses and were deeply concerned about the territorial integrity of their truncated states. Genocide of the Armenians was partly a product of that Ottoman concern in 1915. Extreme brutality toward the Chechens is the contemporary analogue, with the previously mentioned constraints – affinity and compensation – preventing genocide. Effectively, both prudential (recognition of affinity) and imprudent–brute force realpolitik are found in the effort to maximize state security in both the Ottoman and Russian cases but, in the absence of uncompensated loss, the violence has stopped short of genocide in the Russian instance. Additionally, the absence of widespread warfare dampened the genocidal impulse.

Widespread warfare, of course, is decisive in vastly increasing the probability of genocide. Losses during war, such as those experienced by the Ottoman Empire, Nazi Germany, and Rwanda, are extremely difficult to compensate. First, while the war is ongoing, battlefield position is almost always non-negotiable. Second, especially during the opening stages of battle, losses generate uncertainty – the fog of war – that, as we have seen, leads to magnification of the losses in decision-makers' perceptions and that may yield genocidal outcomes. Precisely because of these considerations, Clausewitz is almost certainly wrong in his well-known assertion that war is politics carried out by other means.[32] Absence of loss compensation at the outset and loss magnification during the war yield very different conceptions and behaviors from

---

[31] See, for example, Harff 2003.   [32] Clausewitz 1968.

those stemming from the give-and-take of ordinary political discourse. Losses in war build on earlier losses experienced in older wars (Nazi Germany) or nationalist uprisings (Ottoman Empire). Loss of freedom as the result of political subjugation becomes a possibility once again as a consequence of more recent losses in war (Rwanda).

Darfur

Although territorial loss in war with its seemingly irreversible quality tends to be decisive, the *expectation* of such loss, if uncompensated, can also have horrific consequences. In the Darfur region of western Sudan we may have an illustration of just such a consequence as a form of loss compensation by means of self-help, in contrast to compensation that could be offered by the international community.

As a result of protocols signed on May 26, 2004,[33] between southern Sudanese leaders of the black, predominantly Christian Sudanese People's Liberation Army (SPLA) and the Arabized Muslim leaders of the north, a six-year interim period would be specified, after which a referendum would take place allowing for the possibility of independence for the oil-rich south. This outcome would lead to the loss of approximately one-third of Sudanese territory including its oil. The possible presence of oil in the Darfur region as well makes this territory potentially as valuable economically as the oil-rich south. If Darfur were to be Arabized through the massacre and ethnic cleansing of its black population, then it could serve as compensation for losses in the south, especially in the face of an incipient rebellion by the black Africans in Darfur.

Encouraged by the success of the black southern rebels both on the battlefield and at the conference table, two groups of black Muslims from Darfur rebelled, apparently representing black populations persecuted through raids and other violence by nomadic Arabized tribes. Confronted by another separatist rebellion like that of the SPLA, ethnic cleansing of another black population was unleashed, with a possible genocidal component of tens of thousands dead.[34] One purpose of this effort has been to compensate for the potential losses in the south by ensuring that another potentially valuable territory, Darfur, remains within an Arab-dominated Sudan.

---

[33] BBC News, World Edition, May 27, 2004, http://news.bbc.co.uk/2/hi/africa.
[34] Marquis and Lacey 2004.

As in the Rwandan case, the international community was intensely concerned that a settlement between the Khartoum government and the SPLA be reached. Colin Powell, then the US secretary of state, visited the negotiations between the SPLA and Khartoum leaders in October 2003 and Darfur itself in June 2004.[35] The United Nations has also taken an active role. And like Arusha in the Rwandan case, an international agreement implying heavy losses in the future, whether in political power (Rwanda, territory already having been lost to the RPF) or valuable territory (Sudan), may have spurred this effort at loss compensation. Also like the Interahamwe in Rwanda, much of the killing and ethnic cleansing has been carried out by a government-supported militia, the Janjaweed, an Arabized military group.

These considerations suggest that even more active intervention is required to stem these massacres and ethnic cleansing. A pairing of the two regions of Sudan, Darfur and the south, should be a focus of international diplomacy, without forsaking one region for the other. Unfortunately, just the opposite appears to have occurred. According to John Prendergast, a former African affairs director at the National Security Council under President Clinton, "When the secretary [Colin Powell] was in Naivasha [location of the negotiations between the Khartoum government and the SPLA], and a major problem was getting worse in Darfur, everyone agreed to deal with the southern problem first and with Darfur later. That was a monumental diplomatic error."[36]

Integration of Sudan into elements of the international economy, including appropriate financial incentives (e.g., firmly guaranteed access to oil in the south in the event of southern independence), might serve at least as a partial loss compensation to offset the loss of one or both regions.

All of this indicates that, as in any medical or social pathology, early intervention is required to avoid a fatal outcome. Hitler in Germany and Zhirinovsky in Russia experienced very different historical trajectories in part because of the contrasting reactions of international diplomacy in the two cases.

At the same time, potentially victimized populations without affine protection are the most vulnerable to future genocide. In contrast to

---

[35] Ibid.

[36] Quoted in Weisman 2004. Actually, I encountered this negative assessment of current US policy *after* having written this section suggesting a simultaneous diplomatic approach to both the south and Darfur based on the present theory.

other cases such as the Greeks in Anatolia or the Roman Catholic Irish in the twentieth-century United Kingdom, at the time of their respective genocides, the Armenians, Jews, and Tutsi did not enjoy the protection of affine populations and/or governments powerful enough to shield the threatened populations in time of war.

Realpolitik

Far more difficult to pinpoint with some precision are the various forms of realpolitik, especially the matter of prudence and its antecedent, reasoned scrutiny. Amartya Sen himself admits that the concept is not easily translatable into practical application[37] or, what is the same thing, ease of operationalization. Yet, perhaps as in the case of pornography, following Supreme Court Justice Potter Stewart's dictum, imprudent realpolitik can be recognized when it is seen. Difficulties in defining pornography and distinguishing it from art are similar to those encountered in recognizing an imprudent realpolitik distinct from the prudential variety. Yet there may be one criterion that clearly sets the imprudent apart from the prudential version: the end justifying the means. When any and all methods, including the most brutal, are justified for state preservation or expansion, then imprudent realpolitik is evident. Genocide, of course, is one such illustration, as are unnecessary resorts to force when diplomacy or other peaceful methods might achieve the same or an equivalent goal.

Admittedly, short of unwarranted, frequently brutal means in relation to a particular end, the divide between prudent and imprudent realpolitik is not a clear line, but a zone in which one shades into the other. Proportionality in response to provocation is critical in evaluating the matter of prudence. Within that grey zone between prudence and imprudence, proportionality may be the criterion of choice for evaluating state responses. Disproportional responses, of course, fall into the imprudent category.

Imprudence can have a dynamic all its own; as we saw in the deportation of Hungarian Jewry (chapter 12), imprudence can actually be self-generating. What appeared to be imprudent to many Germans on the battlefield – the start of the mass murder of Jews in mid-1941 – might actually have had the appearance of prudence in mid-1944 and the threatened entry into Germany of Soviet forces with Hungarian-Jewish

---

[37] Sen 2002, 48–52.

help. Having created a Hungarian-Jewish population of determined opponents as the result of the earlier genocide, protection of the German heartland and its population appeared to require the elimination of this fifth column. Greater support for imprudent–brute force realpolitik had been generated, even among Germans who had initially opposed the genocidal policy.

Yet, in the final analysis, we cannot allow the subjective perceptions of perpetrators to condition our analytic judgment. As suggested in chapter 4, in evaluating the presence or absence of rationality and prudential or imprudent realpolitik, it is the outcome that is decisive. Genocide is genocide, whatever processes may have led to its commission; it is a particularly noxious form of brute force–imprudent realpolitik.

Interestingly, cynical realpolitik is somewhat less difficult to identify. When the lives of human beings are jeopardized for state purposes without direct activity of that state, then cynical realpolitik is evident. Bystanders who could alleviate the condition of victims but do not for reasons of state, or permitting agents who could be influential in preventing genocide but do not for the same reason, can be said to engage in a cynical realpolitik – one that ignores the essential humanity of the victim.

At the same time, among the different types of realpolitik, cynical realpolitik may be most easily altered, at least in the long run. A case in point is the Vatican, which has gone far in acknowledging its past indiscretions that possibly made the Holocaust more likely to occur and almost certainly increased its magnitude. Anti-Semitic references in the Roman Catholic liturgy have been reduced if not eliminated entirely. Earlier, admittedly limited efforts by several popes to reach out to Jewish communities have culminated in John Paul II's unprecedented activities in this domain. The image of this pope praying at the Western Wall in Jerusalem, Judaism's holiest site, is indelible. A cynical realpolitik as practiced by Pius XII is most unlikely to occur again, at least in the foreseeable, even distant future.

This change of behavior suggests a possible preventive strategy, namely targeting the most relevant and powerful bystanders who could intervene on behalf of potential victims. Governments with affine populations are likely to be most influential because of the increased probability of their intervention in a potential genocide, and at the same time they are susceptible to diplomatic appeals. Affinities do not have to be ethnic, but also can be religious, suggesting the potential influence of religious institutions. They can even be political, as in the strong influence of revolutionary France on Poland and the likely consequence of that influence on the prevention of any government-inspired mass violence against Jews at the time of the Polish Partitions. Other geographically or ethnoreligiously proximal bystanders also could be persuaded to exert some diplomatic influence on behalf of intended victims. However, war, during which genocides typically occur, makes such efforts difficult. Hence, any effort to dehumanize and isolate a distinct ethnoreligious population, or the prevalence of cynical realpolitik in its treatment, is a signal to the international community that, if war were to break out, this population is in danger.

Preventing politicides, as in the communist template, is more difficult because of the reclusive nature of such regimes. The only significant influences on their domestic behavior emanate from other strong states of the same kind. If these states (e.g., communist) are rare, then the possibilities of external restraint are circumscribed, and are not likely to be easily found.

The sources of cynical realpolitik are important and instructive for future preventive efforts. Consider, for example, the refusal of the United States to intervene actively on behalf of the Tutsi in Rwanda, or even to countenance a UN presence in Rwanda that somehow could involve US military forces. As early as April 7, 1994, after the first massacres in Kigali, the United States opposed expanding the United Nations Assistance Mission for Rwanda.[38]

To this end, the term *genocide*, with its implications for requiring UN intervention, was desperately avoided both by US policy-makers directly and in their behind-the-scenes influence on UN Security Council resolutions. At the start of the genocide, Christine Shelly, speaking to reporters on behalf of the US State Department concerning use of that term, noted that:

> The intentions, the precise intentions, and whether or not these are just directed episodically or with the intention of actually eliminating groups in whole or in part, this is a more complicated issue to address ... I'm not able to look at all of those criteria at this moment and say yes, no. It's something that requires very careful study before we can make a final determination.[39]

---

[38] Des Forges 1999, 603.
[39] Quoted in Power 2002a, 360.

She further maintained that the UN genocide convention did not contain an "absolute requirement ... to intervene directly,"[40] so that even if the "g" word were used, this fact would not commit the United States to action. The term *genocide* did not appear in any official US or UN statement. And when the Security Council did seek to make a statement, US and British diplomats insisted on the word's exclusion. At the same time, Secretary of State Warren Christopher instructed the American UN delegation to push for UN withdrawal, lest American troops be involved.[41] By April 25, 1994, most of Roméo Dallaire's UN troops were evacuated. Even as late as mid-May when nearly 500,000 Rwandans were already dead, the United States was still putting disabling conditions on the Security Council's authorization of humanitarian rescue.[42]

Why this extreme aversion to US military involvement? The one prior event that would be most salient to US policy-makers was the Somalia fiasco in which American troops were attacked and killed by Somali forces (possibly supported by Al Qaeda), and the American public was horrified to witness on television the body of a dead American Marine dragged through the streets of the capital, Mogadishu. Thus,

> The fear, articulated mainly at the Pentagon, was that what would start as a small engagement by foreign troops would end as a large and costly one by Americans. This was the lesson of Somalia, where US troops had gotten into trouble after returning to bail out the beleaguered Pakistanis. The logical outgrowth of this fear was an effort to steer clear of Rwanda entirely and be sure others did the same. Only by yanking Dallaire's entire peacekeeping force could the United States protect itself from involvement down the road.[43]

Even the pending 1993 US intervention in Haiti was influenced by the Somalia debacle. A small gang of Haitian toughs threatened to create "another Somalia" for the United States if American troops landed in Port-au-Prince. The transport ship *Harlan County* carrying American troops then left Haitian waters. The subtitle of the *New York Times* article reads "As Peacekeeping Falters in Somalia, Foes of the US Effort in Haiti Are Emboldened."[44] And the *New York Times* went on to comment on the first page, "A clearer demonstration of the global village

---

[40] Quoted ibid.   [41] Ibid., 367.   [42] Dallaire 2003, 372.
[43] Power 2002a, 366; See also Barnett 2002.   [44] Apple 1993, A1.

that modern communications have created ... would be difficult to imagine."[45]

In Rwanda, a cynical realpolitik was invoked based on the fear that future US military embarrassment, as in Somalia, could jeopardize the Clinton administration at the polls. This was especially important as the election of 1996 was already on the political horizon. Certainly Bill Clinton, the consummate politician, was preparing for it, if only in the avoidance of any future pitfalls that could thwart his reelection.

The lesson for future genocide prevention is clear. When salient embarrassing events such as the Somalian intervention occur, the probability of immobilizing even potential great power interveners increases, thereby also increasing the probability of imprudent–brute force actions such as genocide. Efforts to thwart this immobility must be redoubled. As Michael Walzer suggests, establishing norms or rules of external intercession on behalf of threatened populations may be the best way to encourage humanitarian intervention.[46]

Included among these norms should be a more vigorous response by peacekeepers when opposed by indigenous forces intent on mass murder. In this way, the "Somalia effect" – in which not only was the United States immobilized, but Hutu *génocidaires* along with the Haitian thugs became aware of this potential immobilizing response – could be avoided. Indeed, some of the aggressive actions of the *génocidaires* toward Belgian and other UN peacekeepers were based precisely on this logic of immobility.[47] When faced with casualties to their forces, the international peacekeepers would withdraw, allowing the extremists free rein to scuttle the Arusha Accords, or to do far worse, as we have seen, in the face of the resumed RPF military advances.

Democracy

And now we arrive at a paradox of genocide prevention. Although one of the best preventives of the genocide of a state's minority population is the existence of a liberal democratic regime *within* that state, quite the opposite is true of democracy in *bystander* states. Here, the desire to be reelected, as in the case of the Allied governments at Versailles, or simply to avoid negative public reaction, may preclude any governmental

---

[45] Ibid.
[46] Walzer 2002. For additional perspectives, see Ignatieff 2002 and Power 2002b.
[47] Dallaire 2003, 240.

action on behalf of endangered citizens of another state. Recall in chapter 11 President Roosevelt's refusal to authorize the bombing of Auschwitz because of the fear of embarrassment, not to mention his earlier narrowing of immigration possibilities for Jews seeking refuge in the United States. Opinion polls had revealed the high level of anti-Semitism in the United States that might make his governing more difficult and, of course, his reelection as well. The British followed a similar path, as did President Clinton more recently in the Rwandan genocide.

At the Evian immigration conference in 1938 (chapter 11), the only state to open its borders to Jewish immigration was the Dominican Republic under Rafael Trujillo, a dictator who was among the least responsive to public opinion. The Western democracies were extremely uncooperative in opening their borders. To be sure, public outcry on behalf of a threatened population potentially may reach a larger audience in a democracy than in an autocracy, if allowed, but on the whole the presumption in democracies, almost universally accepted, is that the electorate will be far more responsive to issues directly concerning its own perceived well-being than to the concerns of "alien" people.

Even more recently, the reaction by the Spanish people after the bombings of March 11, 2004, may serve to illustrate the limitations associated with democracy. Despite efforts of the coalition forces to secure a democratic regime in Iraq that would no longer countenance the mass killings of the Saddam era, after the bombings, the Spanish electorate ousted the Conservative government (the election favorite before the bombings), which had authorized Spanish participation in the occupying coalition in Iraq. Note that the election did not raise the issue of the invasion of Iraq. That event had already occurred. The only issue remaining was continued participation of Spanish forces that had incurred Al Qaeda's fury and Spanish civilian casualties. The Spanish electorate effectively ignored any domestic needs of the Iraqi people for the stability that an effective and temporary occupation could offer.

Democracy, therefore, is a double-edged sword. On the one hand, its spread will make the lives of minorities more secure within states that democratize successfully. This conclusion is suggested by the findings of Rudolph Rummel[48] and Barbara Harff.[49] On the other hand, populations threatened with genocide may find fewer islands of refuge within democratic states. Recent restrictions on the granting of political asylum

[48] Rummel 1997.   [49] Harff 2003.

in European countries, not to mention greater difficulties generally in immigrating to Europe, and all of this even after the European Holocaust experience, suggest the importance of this distinction.

Validation

Finally, the role of validation must be considered. We saw that failures to adequately punish the perpetrators of earlier massacres either of Armenians in 1894–96, Jews in Ukraine in 1918–20, or Tutsi in Rwanda beginning in 1959 likely contributed to the perceived vulnerability of these groups.

With the rise of contemporary mass communications, perhaps even resulting in a global village in the half-century since the Holocaust, validation does not have to be confined to the *earlier* unpunished murder of the potential victims *themselves*. If the *ongoing* process of massacre is not addressed, then victimizers anywhere in the world may conclude that mass killing will not be interrupted or punished, even if in a different location and with different victims. A process of this type likely occurred prior to the Rwandan genocide, and specifically in the early stages of the Bosnian conflict two years earlier. At this time, it had all the appearances of genocide, at least to many observers. The fact that the apparent mass murder of tens if not hundreds of thousands in Bosnia[50] went unopposed, at least militarily in the opening, most influential stages of the conflict, made it appear that genocidal activities could be accomplished without serious external constraint in the post-Cold War climate of the 1990s. In other words, "if they can get away with it, so can we."

Regarding another African conflict, "I call it the copycat syndrome," said Dame Margaret Anstee, who was the UN secretary general's special envoy in Angola in the early 1990s. She said that, in 1992, when the rebel leader Jonas Savimbi "chose bullets over ballots," he had been watching the Bosnian Serb leader Radovan Karadzic "getting away with murder."[51] This interpretation accords with the finding of Stuart Hill and Donald Rothchild that receptivity to outside political violence is conditional upon a recent history of domestic strife, amply found in both Angola and Rwanda.[52] The fighting between Hutu and Tutsi in 1959–64, the sporadic persecutions after independence (especially in 1973), and

[50] Daalder 1996.   [51] Quoted in Crossette 1999, 16.   [52] Hill and Rothchild 1986.

the ongoing strife after the RPF invasion of 1990 amply satisfy this condition.

Widespread massacres anywhere in the world, particularly in regions with powerful states such as Europe, have the potential to be extremely influential, especially if these states do nothing to stop the massacres. If power disparities between potential interveners and victimizers are substantial, again as in Europe in the early 1990s, and no intervention occurs, then validation of massacre, if not genocide itself, can be even more pronounced. Thus, prevention of genocide in one location is dependent on prior occurrences not only in that location, but in almost any place in the world in which successful intervention to prevent mass murder could have occurred, but did not. As in understanding the etiology of genocide, prevention is a complex matter requiring vigilance and awareness of the appropriate antecedent variables.

Coda

A Jewish mother walking in the Ukrainian woods with her children in September 1941,[53] an Armenian working on the Berlin–Baghdad railway in late 1915, a Tutsi sitting in a crowded Rwandan church in the spring of 1994, or a Cambodian teaching her class of twelve-year-olds in 1976 most likely never would be seen again. It is my hope that this book has accurately charted pathways from the mundane to the bizarre and unthinkable. That chart, of course, does not consist of a simple linear trajectory, but requires several analytic nodes to encompass it. Given the enormity of genocide and politicide, one should expect nothing less.

---

[53] After writing this passage, I read Jonathan Safran Foer's *Everything Is Illuminated* (2002). Although fictional, it is the single most compelling evocation of the end of a Ukrainian shtetl that I have read.

REFERENCES

Abel, Theodore. [1938] 1986. *Why Hitler Came into Power*. Cambridge: Harvard University Press.

Abella, Irving and Franklin Bialystok. 1996. "Canada," in David S. Wyman and Charles H. Rosenzveig, eds., *The World Reacts to the Holocaust*. Baltimore: Johns Hopkins University Press, 749–81.

Abramowicz, Hirsz. 1999. *Profiles of a Lost World: Memoirs of East European Jewish Life Before World War II*, trans. Eva Zeitlin Dobkin, ed. Dina Abramowicz and Jeffrey Shandler. Detroit: Wayne State University Press.

Adelman, Howard and Astri Suhrke, eds. 1999. *The Path of a Genocide: The Rwanda Crisis from Uganda to Zaire*. New Brunswick, NJ: Transaction Publishers.

Adelson, Alan and Robert Lapides, eds. 1989. *Lodz Ghetto: Inside a Community Under Siege*. New York: Viking.

Ahmad, Feroz. 1982. "Unionist Relations with the Greek, Armenian, and Jewish Communities of the Ottoman Empire, 1908–1914," in Benjamin Braude and Bernard Lewis, eds., *Christians and Jews in the Ottoman Empire: The Functioning of a Plural Society*, vol. I. New York: Holmes and Meier, 401–34.

Albrecht-Carrié, René. 1958. *A Diplomatic History of Europe Since the Congress of Vienna*. New York: Harper.

Alvarez, Lizette. 2005. "Hesitantly, Holocaust Survivors Revisit Past." *New York Times*, January 18, E1, E7.

Aly, Götz. 1999. *"Final Solution": Nazi Population Policy and the Murder of the European Jews*, trans. Belinda Cooper and Allison Brown. London: Edward Arnold.

Anderson, Benedict R. 1991. *Imagined Communities: Reflections on the Origin and Spread of Nationalism*, rev. ed. London: Verso.

Anderson, Matthew S. 1966. *The Eastern Question, 1774–1923: A Study in International Relations*. London: Macmillan.

Angier, Natalie. 2002. "The Urge to Punish Cheats: It Isn't Merely Vengeance." *New York Times*, January 22, F1, F6.

Apple, R. W. Jr. 1993. "Policing a Global Village: As Peacekeeping Falters in Somalia, Foes of the US Effort in Haiti Are Emboldened." *New York Times*, 13 October, A1, A13.

Arendt, Hannah. 1951. *The Origins of Totalitarianism*. New York: Harcourt Brace.
    1964. *Eichmann in Jerusalem: A Report on the Banality of Evil*, rev. and enl. ed. New York: Viking.

Aschheim, Steven E. 1982. *Brothers and Strangers: The East European Jew in German and German Jewish Consciousness, 1800–1923*. Madison: University of Wisconsin Press.

Auron, Yaïr. 1998. *Les juifs d'extrême gauche en Mai 68: une génération révolutionnaire marquée par la Shoah*, trans. from the Hebrew by Katherine Werchowski. Paris: Albin Michel.

Axelrod, Robert. 1984. *The Evolution of Cooperation*. New York: Basic Books.

Axelrod, Robert and William D. Hamilton. 1981. "The Evolution of Cooperation." *Science* 211 (March 27): 1390–96.

Babel, Isaac. 1998. *Collected Stories*, ed. Efraim Sicher, trans. David McDuff. London: Penguin Books.
    2002. *The Complete Works of Isaac Babel*, ed. Nathalie Babel, trans. Peter Constantine, intro. Cynthia Ozick. New York: W. W. Norton.

Balakian, Peter. 2003. *The Burning Tigris: The Armenian Genocide and America's Response*. New York: HarperCollins.

Balakrishnan, Gopal. 2000. *The Enemy: An Intellectual Portrait of Carl Schmitt*. New York: Verso.

Baldwin, Neil. 2003. *Henry Ford and the Jews: The Mass Production of Hate*. New York: Public Affairs.

Bankier, David, ed. 2000. *Probing the Depths of German Antisemitism: German Society and the Persecution of the Jews, 1933–1941*. Jerusalem: Yad Vashem.

Barnett, Michael. 2002. *Eyewitness to a Genocide*. New York: Cornell University Press.

Baron, Salo W. 1976. *The Russian Jew Under Tsars and Soviets*. New York: Macmillan.

Bartov, Omer. 1992. *Hitler's Army: Soldiers, Nazis, and War in the Third Reich*. New York: Oxford University Press.
    1994. "The Conduct of War: Soldiers and the Barbarization of Warfare," in Michael Geyer and John W. Boyer, eds., *Resistance Against the Third Reich 1933–1990*. Chicago: University of Chicago Press, 39–52.
    2003. *Germany's War and the Holocaust: Disputed Histories*. Ithaca, NY: Cornell University Press.

Bauer, Yehuda. 1994. *Jews for Sale?: Nazi–Jewish Negotiations, 1933–1945*. New Haven, CT: Yale University Press.
    2001. *Rethinking the Holocaust*. New Haven, CT: Yale University Press.
    2002. "Holocaust and Genocide in the Wake of the Twin Towers," paper presented at the Aegis Conference, Nottinghamshire, England, January.

Bauman, Zygmunt. 1989. *Modernity and the Holocuast*. Ithaca, NY: Cornell University Press.

Bellow, Saul. 1982. *The Dean's December*. New York: Pocket Books.
     2000. *Ravelstein*. New York: Penguin Books.
Bendersky, Joseph W. 1983. *Carl Schmitt: Theorist for the Reich*. Princeton, NJ: Princeton University Press.
Benford, Robert D. and David A. Snow. 2000. "Framing Processes and Social Movements: An Overview and Assessment." *Annual Review of Sociology* 26: 611–39.
Berkeley, Bill. 2002. "Road to a Genocide," in Mills and Brunner 2002, 103–16.
Berman, Paul. 2003. *Terror and Liberalism*. New York: Norton.
Beschloss, Michael. 2002. *The Conquerors: Roosevelt, Truman and the Destruction of Hitler's Germany, 1941–1945*. New York: Simon and Schuster.
Bew, Paul. 2004. "Versions of Murder." *Times Literary Supplement* 5281 (June 18): 10–11.
Black, Eugene C. 1993. "Lucien Wolf and the Making of Poland: Paris, 1919," in Polonsky 1993, 264–95.
Blakeslee, Sandra. 2001. "Watching How the Brain Works as It Weighs a Moral Dilemma." *New York Times*, September 25, F3.
Blom, J. C. H. 1989. "The Persecution of the Jews in the Netherlands: A Comparative Western European Perspective." *European History Quarterly* 19 (3): 333–51.
Bodenhausen, Galen V., Lori A. Sheppard, and Geoffrey P. Kramer. 1994. "Negative Affect and Social Judgment: The Differential Impact of Anger and Sadness." *European Journal of Social Psychology* 24 (1): 45–62.
Bodger, Alan. 1984. "Russia and the End of the Ottoman Empire," in Kent 1984, 76–110.
Boehm, Christopher. 1999. *Hierachy in the Forest: The Evolution of Egalitarian Behavior*. Cambridge: Harvard University Press.
Boettcher, William A. III. 1995. "Context, Methods, Numbers, and Words: Prospect Theory in International Relations." *Journal of Conflict Resolution* 39 (September): 561–83.
Boia, Lucian. 2001. *History and Myth in Romanian Consciousness*. Budapest: Central European Press.
Bourget, Pierre and Charles Lacretelle. 1980. *Sur les murs de Paris et de France: 1939–1945*. Paris: Hachette Réalités.
Bowles, Samuel and Herbert Gintis. 2002. "Behavioural Science: *Homo Reciprocans*." *Nature* 415 (January 10): 125–28.
Boyadjieff, Christo. 1989. *Saving the Bulgarian Jews in World War II*. Ottawa: Free Bulgarian Center.
Boyajian, Dickran H. 1972. *Armenia: The Case for a Forgotten Genocide*. Westwood, NJ: Educational Book Crafters.
Boyce, D. G. 1985. "Ireland: From Ascendancy to Democracy," in Christopher Haigh, ed., *The Cambridge Historical Encyclopedia of Great Britain and Ireland*. Cambridge, UK: Cambridge University Press, 261–64.

Boyd, Robert and Peter J. Richerson. 1992. "Punishment Allows the Evolution of Cooperation (or Anything Else) in Sizable Groups." *Ethology and Sociobiology* 13 (2): 171–95.

Braham, Randolph L. 1981. *The Politics of Genocide: The Holocaust in Hungary,* vol. I. New York: Columbia University Press.

2000. *The Politics of Genocide: The Holocaust in Hungary,* condensed ed. Detroit: Wayne State University Press.

Breitman, Richard. 1991. *The Architect of Genocide: Himmler and the Final Solution.* Hanover, NH: Brandeis University Press and University Press of New England.

2000. "American Diplomatic Records Regarding German Public Opinion During the Nazi Regime," in Bankier 2000, 501–10.

Bridge, F. R. 1984. "The Habsburg Monarchy and the Ottoman Empire, 1900–1918," in Kent 1984, 31–51.

Bridgman, Jon M. 1981. *The Revolt of the Hereros.* Berkeley: University of California Press.

Brody, J. Kenneth. 1999. *The Avoidable War,* vol. I, *Lord Cecil and the Policy of Principle, 1933–1935.* New Brunswick, NJ: Transaction Publishers.

Broszat, Martin. 1981. *The Hitler State.* London: Longman.

Browning, Christopher R. 1992. *Ordinary Men: Reserve Police Battalion 101 and the Final Solution in Poland.* New York: HarperCollins.

2004. *The Origins of the Final Solution: The Evolution of Nazi Jewish Policy, September 1939–March 1942.* Jerusalem: Yad Vashem, and Lincoln: University of Nebraska Press.

Brustein, William I. and Ryan D. King. 2004. "Anti-Semitism in Europe Before the Holocaust." *International Political Science Review* 25 (1): 35–53.

Bueno de Mesquita, Bruce, Alastair Smith, Randolph M. Siverson, and James D. Morrow. 2003. *The Logic of Political Survival.* Cambridge: MIT Press.

Bullen, Roger. 1974. *Palmerston, Guizot and the Collapse of the Entente Cordiale.* London: Athlone Press.

Burg, Steven L. and Paul S. Shoup. 1999. *The War in Bosnia-Herzegovina: Ethnic Conflict and International Intervention.* New York: M. E. Sharpe.

Burleigh, Michael. 2000. *The Third Reich: A New History.* New York: Hill and Wang.

Burrin, Philippe. 1994. *Hitler and the Jews: The Genesis of the Holocaust,* trans. Patsy Southgate. London: Edward Arnold.

1996. *France Under the Germans: Collaboration and Compromise,* trans. Janet Lloyd. New York: New Press.

Buruma, Ian. 1995. *The Wages of Guilt: Memories of War in Germany and Japan.* London: Vintage.

Callamard, Agnes. 1999. "French Policy in Rwanda," in Adelman and Suhrke 1999, 157–83.

Canny, Nicholas. 1991. "Early Modern Ireland, c. 1500–1700," in Foster 1991b, 104–60.

Cargas, Harry J., ed. 1998. *Holocaust Scholars Write to the Vatican*. Westport, CT: Greenwood.

Carney, Timothy. 1989a. "The Organization of Power," in Jackson 1989a, 79–107.
   1989b. "The Unexpected Victory," in Jackson 1989a, 13–35.

Carpi, Daniel. 1977. "The Rescue of Jews in the Italian Zone of Occupied Croatia," in Gutman and Zuroff 1977, 465–525.

Cesarani, David. 1977a. "Introduction," in Cesarani 1997b, 1–28.
   ed. 1997b. *Genocide and Rescue: The Holocaust in Hungary 1944*. Oxford: Berg.

Chadwick, Owen. 1986. *Britain and the Vatican During the Second World War* Cambridge, UK: Cambridge University Press.
   1989. "Weizsäcker, the Vatican, and the Jews of Rome," in Michael R. Marrus, ed., *The Nazi Holocaust*, vol. VIII, part 3. Westport, CT: Meckler, 1263–83.

Chalk, Frank. 1999. "Hate Radio in Rwanda," in Adelman and Suhrke 1999, 93–107.

Chalk, Frank and Kurt Jonassohn. 1990. *The History and Sociology of Genocide: Analyses and Case Studies*. New Haven, CT: Yale University Press.

Chamberlain, Muriel E. 1987. *Lord Palmerston*. Washington, DC: Catholic University of America Press.

Chandler, David P. 1990. "A Revolution in Full Spate: Communist Party Policy in Democratic Kampuchea, December 1976," in David A. Ablin and Marlowe Hood, eds., *The Cambodian Agony*. New York: M. E. Sharpe, 165–79.
   1999. *Brother Number One: A Political Biography of Pol Pot*. New York: Westview Press.
   2000. *A History of Cambodia*, 3rd ed. Boulder, CO: Westview Press.

Chang, Iris. 1997. *The Rape of Nanking: The Forgotten Holocaust of World War II*. New York: Basic.

Charny, Israel W. 1994. "Toward a Generic Definition of Genocide," in George Andreopoulos, ed., *Genocide: Conceptual and Historical Dimensions*. Philadelphia: University of Pennsylvania Press, 64–94.

Chary, Frederick B. 1972. *The Bulgarian Jews and the Final Solution, 1940–1944*. Pittsburgh: University of Pittsburgh Press.

Chorbajian, Levon. 1999. "Introduction," in Levon Chorbajian and George Shirinian, eds., *Studies in Comparative Genocide*. New York: St. Martin's Press, xv–xxxv.

Cienciala, Anna M. and Titus Komarnicki. 1984. *From Versailles to Locarno: Keys to Polish Foreign Policy, 1919–1925*. Lawrence: University Press of Kansas.

Cioffi-Revilla, Claudio. 1998. *Politics and Uncertainty: Theory, Models and Applications*. Cambridge, UK: Cambridge University Press.

Clausewitz, Karl von. 1968. *On War*. London: Routledge and Kegan Paul.

Clogg, Richard. 1982. "The Greek *Millet* in the Ottoman Empire," in Benjamin Braude and Bernard Lewis, eds., *Christians and Jews in the Ottoman Empire: The Functioning of a Plural Society*, vol. I. New York: Holmes and Meier, 185–207.

    1992. *A Concise History of Greece*. Cambridge, UK: Cambridge University Press.

Cohen, William B. and Jürgen Svensson. 2001. "Finland," in Walter Laqueur, ed., *The Holocaust Encyclopedia*. New Haven, CT: Yale University Press, 204–06.

Committee of the Jewish Delegations. 1927. *The Pogroms in the Ukraine Under the Ukrainian Governments (1917–1920)*. London: John Bale, Sons and Danielsson, Ltd.

Condell, Bruce and David T. Zabecki, eds. 2001. *On the German Art of War: Truppenführung*. Boulder, CO: Lynne Rienner.

Connolly, S. J. 1995. "The Great Famine and Irish Politics," in Póirtéir 1995, 34–49.

Conquest, Robert. 1986. *The Harvest of Sorrow: Soviet Collectivization and the Terror-Famine*. New York: Oxford University Press.

Conway, John W. 1968. *The Nazi Persecution of the Churches, 1933–1945*. New York: Basic Books.

Cooper, Matthew. 1990. *The German Army, 1933–1945: Its Political and Military Failure*. Lanham, MD: Scarborough House.

Cornwell, John. 1999. *Hitler's Pope: The Secret History of Pius XII*. New York: Penguin Books.

Couloumbis, Theodore A., John A. Petropulos, and Harry J. Psomiades. 1976. *Foreign Interference in Greek Politics: An Historical Perspective*. New York: Pella Publishing.

Crossette, Barbara. 1999. "The World Expected Peace: It Found a New Brutality." *New York Times*, January 24, Section 4:1, 16.

Curtis, Michael. 2002. *Verdict on Vichy: Power and Prejudice in the Vichy France Regime*. New York: Arcade Publishing.

Czerniakow, Adam. 1979. *The Warsaw Diary of Adam Czerniakow: Prelude to Doom*, ed. Raul Hilberg, Stanislaw Staron, and Josef Kermisz, trans. Stanislaw Staron and the staff of Yad Vashem. New York: Stein and Day.

Daalder, Ivo H. 1996. "Fear and Loathing in the Former Yugoslavia," in Michael E. Brown, ed., *The International Dimensions of Internal Conflict*. Cambridge: MIT Press, 461–88.

Dadrian, Vahakn N. 1997. *The History of the Armenian Genocide: Ethnic Conflict from the Balkans to Anatolia to the Caucasus*. Providence, RI: Berghahn Books.

    1999. *Warrant for Genocide: Key Elements of Turko-Armenian Conflict*. New Brunswick, NJ: Transaction Publishers.

Dallaire, Roméo. 2003. *Shake Hands with the Devil: The Failure of Humanity in Rwanda*. Toronto: Random House Canada.

Dallin, Alexander and George W. Breslauer. 1970. *Political Terror in Communist Systems*. Stanford, CA: Stanford University Press.

Daly, Mary E. 1995. "The Operations of Famine Relief, 1845–1857," in Póirtéir 1995, 123–34.

Davie, Maurice R. 1947. *Refugees in America: Report of the Committee for the Study of Recent Immigration from Europe*. New York: Harper and Brothers Publishers.

Davies, Norman. 1982. *God's Playground: A History of Poland in Two Volumes*, vol. I, *The Origins to 1795*. New York: Columbia University Press.

Dawidowicz, Lucy. 1986. *The War Against the Jews, 1933–1945*. New York: Bantam Books.

Deák, István. 1965. "Hungary," in Hans Rogger and Eugen Weber, eds., *The European Right: A Historical Profile*. Berkeley: University of California Press, 364–407.

de Gaulle, Charles. 2002. *The Enemy's House Divided*, trans. Robert Eden. Chapel Hill: University of North Carolina Press.

de Grazia, Sebastian. 1989. *Machiavelli in Hell*. Princeton, NJ: Princeton University Press.

de Quervain, Dominique J.-F., Urs Fischbacher, Valerie Treyer, Melanie Schellhammer, Ulrich Schnyder, Alfred Buck, and Ernst Fehr. 2004. "The Neural Basis of Altruistic Punishment," *Science* 305 (August 27): 1254–58.

Des Forges, Alison. 1999. *"Leave None to Tell the Story": Genocide in Rwanda*. New York: Human Rights Watch.

DeSteno, David, N., Nilanjana Dasgupta, Monica Y. Bartlett, and Aida Cajdric. 2004. "Prejudice from Thin Air: The Effect of Emotion on Automatic Intergroup Attitudes," *Psychological Science* 15 (5): 319–24.

Deutsch, Morton. 1985. *Distributive Justice*. New Haven, CT: Yale University Press.

Dieckmann, Christoph. 2000. "The War and the Killing of the Lithuanian Jews," in Herbert 2000b, 240–75.

Dinkel, Christoph. 1991. "German Officers and the Armenian Genocide." *Armenian Review* 44 (Spring): 77–133.

Dobroszycki, Lucjan, ed. 1984. *The Chronicle of the Łódź Ghetto 1941–1944*, trans. Richard Lourie, Joachim Neugroschel, and others. New Haven, CT: Yale University Press.

Don, Yehuda. 1997. "Economic Implications of the Anti-Jewish Legislation in Hungary," in Cesarani 1997b, 47–76.

Donnelly, James S. Jr. 1995. "Mass Eviction and the Great Famine," in Póirtéir 1995, 155–73.

Drechsler, Horst. 1980. *"Let Us Die Fighting": The Struggle of the Herero and Nama Against German Imperialism (1884–1915)*, trans. Bernd Zöllner. London: Zed Press.

Dubnov, Simon. 1973. *History of the Jews: From the Congress of Vienna to the Emergence of Hitler*, vol. V, trans. Moshe Spiegel. New York: Thomas Yoseloff.

Eichengreen, Lucille. 2000. *Rumkowski and the Orphans of Lodz*. San Francisco, CA: Mercury House.

Elster, Jon. 1986. "Introduction," in Jon Elster, ed., *Rational Choice*. New York: New York University Press, 1–33.

Engel, David. 1993. "The Western Allies and the Holocaust," in Polonsky 1993, 407–22.

Erickson, Edward J. 2001. *Ordered to Die: A History of the Ottoman Army in the First World War*. Westport, CT: Greenwood Press.

Evans, Richard J. 2004. *The Coming of the Third Reich*. New York: Penguin Books.

Farnham, Barbara. 1992. "Roosevelt and the Munich Crisis: Insights from Prospect Theory." *Political Psychology* 13 (June): 205–35.

Fehr, Ernst and Simon Gächter. 2000. "Cooperation and Punishment in Public Goods Experiments." *American Economic Review* 90 (September): 980–94.

2002. "Altruistic Punishment in Humans." *Nature* 415 (10 January): 134–40.

Fein, Helen. 1979. *Accounting for Genocide: National Responses and Jewish Victimization During the Holocaust*. New York: Free Press.

1984. "Scenarios of Genocide: Models of Genocide and Critical Responses," in Israel W. Charny, ed., *Toward the Understanding and Prevention of Genocide*. Boulder, CO: Westview, 3–31.

1990. "Genocide: A Sociological Perspective." *Current Sociology* 38 (Spring): 1–126.

2000. "The Three P's of Genocide Prevention: With Application to a Genocide Foretold – Rwanda," in Neal Riemer, ed. *Protection Against Genocide: Mission Impossible?*. Westport, CT: Praeger, 41–66.

2004. "To Prevent and to Punish Genocide: Rwanda," paper presented at the Remembering Rwanda: Conference on the Rwanda Genocide 10th Anniversary, New York, May 8.

Feingold, Henry L. 1970. *The Politics of Rescue: The Roosevelt Administration and the Holocaust, 1938–1945*. New Brunswick, NJ: Rutgers University Press.

Feldman, Gerald D. 1993. *The Great Disorder: Politics, Economics, and Society in the German Inflation, 1914–1924*. New York: Oxford University Press.

Fischer, Klaus P. 1998. *The History of an Obsession: German Judeophobia and the Holocaust*. New York: Continuum.

Fiszman, Samuel, ed. 1997. *Constitution and Reform in Eighteenth-Century Poland: The Constitution of 3 May 1791*. Bloomington: Indiana University Press.

Fitzpatrick, David. 1991. "Ireland Since 1870," in Foster 1991b, 213–74.

1995. "Flight from Famine," in Póirtéir 1995, 174–84.

Fleming, Gerald. 1984. *Hitler and the Final Solution*. Berkeley: University of California Press.

Foer, Jonathan S. 2002. *Everything Is Illuminated: A Novel*. Boston: Houghton Mifflin.

Foreign Relations of the United States. Washington, DC: US Government Publications Office, Superintendent of Documents.

Foster, R. F. 1991a. "Ascendancy and Union," in Foster 1991b, 161–211.

ed. 1991b. *The Oxford Illustrated History of Ireland*. Oxford: Oxford University Press.

2001. "Remembering 1798," in Ian McBride, ed., *History and Memory in Modern Ireland*. Cambridge, UK: Cambridge University Press, 67–94.

Fraenkel, Ernst. 1941. *The Dual State*. New York: Oxford University Press.

Frei, Christoph. 2001. *Hans J. Morgenthau: An Intellectual Biography*. Baton Rouge: Louisiana State University Press.

Friedländer, Saul. 1966. *Pius XII and the Third Reich: A Documentation*, trans. Charles Fullman. London: Chatto and Windus.

1967. *Prelude to Downfall: Hitler and the United Sates, 1939–1941*. New York: Knopf.

1997. *Nazi Germany and the Jews*. New York: HarperCollins.

Friedman, Milton. 1953. *Essays in Positive Economics*. Chicago: University of Chicago.

Friedman, Saul S. 1973. *No Haven for the Oppressed: United States Policy Toward Jewish Refugees, 1938–1945*. Detroit, MI: Wayne State University Press.

1976. *Pogromchik: The Assassination of Simon Petlura*. New York: Hart.

Gaddis, John L. 2002. *The Landscape of History: How Historians Map the Past*. New York: Oxford University Press.

Gartner, I. 1991. "Ukrainian Nationalism After World War II," in Sabrin 1991, 227–31.

Garver, Eugene. 1987. *Machiavelli and the History of Prudence*. Madison: University of Wisconsin Press.

Gellately, Robert. 2001. *Backing Hitler: Consent and Coercion in Nazi Germany*. New York: Oxford University Press.

Geraghty, Tony. 1998. *The Irish War*. New York: HarperCollins.

Gergel, N. 1951. "The Pogroms in the Ukraine in 1918–1921." *YIVO Annual of Jewish Social Science* 6: 237–52.

Gerlach, Christian. 2000a. "German Economic Interests, Occupation Policy, and the Murder of the Jews in Belorussia, 1941/43," in Herbert 2000b, 210–39.

2000b. "The Wannsee Conference, the Fate of German Jews, and Hitler's Decision in Principle to Exterminate All European Jews," in Omer Bartov, ed., *The Holocaust: Origins, Implementation, Aftermath*. New York: Routledge, 108–61. Reprinted from *Journal of Modern History* 70 (December 1998): 759–812.

German Foreign Office. 1940. *Documents on the Events Preceding the Outbreak of the War*. New York: German Library of Information.

Geyer, Michael. 1986. "German Strategy in the Age of Machine Warfare, 1914–1945," in Peter Paret, ed., *Makers of Modern Strategy: From*

Machiavelli to the Nuclear Age. Princeton, NJ: Princeton University Press, 527–97.

Gieysztor, Aleksander, Stefan Kieniewicz, Emanuel Rostworowski, Janusz Tazbir, and Henryk Wereszycki. 1979. *History of Poland,* 2nd ed. Warsaw: PWN-Polish Scientific Publishers.

Gilbert, Felix. 1986. "Machiavelli: The Renaissance of the Art of War," in Peter Paret, ed., *Makers of Modern Strategy: From Machiavelli to the Nuclear Age.* Princeton, NJ: Princeton University Press, 11–31.

Gilbert, Martin. 1989. *The Second World War: A Complete History.* New York: Henry Holt.

1999. "Forward to the Second Edition," in Weinreich 1999, v–xi.

2000. *The Straits of War: Gallipoli Remembered.* Stroud, UK: Sutten.

Glaser, Charles L. 1996. "Realists as Optimists: Cooperation as Self-Help." *Security Studies* 5 (Spring): 122–66.

Glenny, Misha. 1996. *The Fall of Yugoslavia: The Third Balkan War,* 3rd ed. New York: Penguin Books.

Gnamo, Abbas H. 1999. "The Rwandan Genocide and the Collapse of Mobutu's Kleptocracy," in Adelman and Suhrke 1999, 321–49.

Göçek, Fatma M. 1996. *Rise of the Bourgeoisie, Demise of Empire: Ottoman Westernization and Social Change.* New York: Oxford University Press.

Goebbels, Joseph. 1983. *The Goebbels Diaries 1939–1941,* trans. Fred Taylor. New York: Putnam.

Goertz, Gary and Harvey Starr, eds. 2003. *Necessary Conditions: Theory, Methodology, and Applications.* Lanham, MD: Rowman and Littlefield.

Goldberger, Leo, ed. 1987. *The Rescue of the Danish Jews: Moral Courage Under Stress.* New York: New York University Press.

Goldhagen, Daniel J. 1996. *Hitler's Willing Executioners: Ordinary Germans and the Holocaust.* New York: Knopf.

Gomme, A. W., A. Andrewes, and K. J. Dover. 1970. *A Historical Commentary on Thucydides,* vol. IV. Oxford: Clarendon Press.

Gordon, Sarah. 1984. *Hitler, Germans, and the "Jewish Question."* Princeton, NJ: Princeton University Press.

Gourevitch, Philip. 1998. *We Wish to Inform You That Tomorrow We Will Be Killed with Our Families.* New York: Farrar, Straus and Giroux.

Greenberg, Eric J. 2005. "Letter Reveals Vatican Policy on Children of Holocaust." *Forward,* January 7.

Greene, Joshua D., R. Brian Sommerville, Leigh E. Nystrom, John M. Darley, and Jonathan D. Cohen. 2001. "An fMRI Investigation of Emotional Engagement in Moral Judgment." *Science* 293 (September 14): 2105–08.

Gross, Jan T. 2001. *Neighbors: The Destruction of the Jewish Community in Jedwabne, Poland.* Princeton, NJ: Princeton University Press.

Grynberg, Henryk. 1993. *The Victory*, trans. Richard Lourie. Evanston, IL: Northwestern University Press.

Guinnane, Timothy. 1997. *The Vanishing Irish: Households, Migration, and the Rural Economy in Ireland, 1850–1914*. Princeton, NJ: Princeton University Press.

Gürün, Kamuran. 1985. *The Armenian File*. New York: St. Martin's Press.

Gutman, Yisrael. 1982. *The Jews of Warsaw, 1939–1943: Ghetto, Underground, Revolt*, trans. Ina Friedman. Bloomington: Indiana University Press.

[Gutman, Israel]. 1994. *Resistance: The Warsaw Ghetto Uprising*. Boston: Houghton Mifflin.

Gutman, Yisrael and Efraim Zuroff, eds. 1977. *Rescue Attempts During the Holocaust*. Jerusalem: Yad Vashem.

Haffner, Sebastian 1979. *The Meaning of Hitler*, trans. Ewald Osers. New York: MacMillian.

2002. *Defying Hitler: A Memoir*, trans. Oliver Pretzel. New York: Farrar, Straus and Giroux.

Halder, Franz. 1988. *The Halder War Diary: 1939–1942*, ed. Charles Burdick and Hans-Adolf Jacobsen. Novato, CA: Presidio.

Hale, William, 2000. *Turkish Foreign Policy 1774–2000*. Portland, OR: Frank Cass.

Halo, Thea, 2000. *Not Even My Name*. New York: Angel Hat Ink.

Hamann, Brigitte. 1999. *Hitler's Vienna: A Dictator's Apprenticeship*, trans. Thomas Thornton. New York: Oxford University Press.

Hamburg Institute for Social Research. 1999. *The German Army and Genocide: Crimes Against War Prisoners, Jews, and Other Civilians in the East, 1939–1944*, trans. Scott Abbott. New York: New Press.

Haney, Craig, Curtis Banks, and Philip Zimbardo. 1973. "Interpersonal Dynamics in a Simulated Prison." *International Journal of Criminology and Penology* 1 (February): 69–97.

Harff, Barbara. 2003. "No Lessons Learned from the Holocaust? Assessing Risks of Genocide and Political Mass Murder Since 1955." *American Political Science Review* 97 (February): 57–73.

Harff, Barbara and Ted Robert Gurr. 1988. "Toward Empirical Theory of Genocides and Politicides: Identification and Measurement of Cases Since 1945." *International Studies Quarterly* 32 (September): 359–71.

Harshav, Benjamin. 2002. "Introduction: Herman Kruk's Holocaust Writings," in Kruk 2002, xxi–lii.

Hatzfeld, Jean. 2003. *Une saison de machettes: récits*. Paris: Seuil.

Hayton, David. 1985. "Ireland: Planters and Patriots," in Christopher Haigh, ed., *The Cambridge Historical Encyclopedia of Great Britain and Ireland*. Cambridge, UK: Cambridge University Press, 214–17.

Hegre, Håvard, Tanja Ellingsen, Scott Gates, and Nils Petter Gleditsch. 2001. "Toward a Democratic Civil Peace? Democracy, Political Change, and Civil War, 1816–1992." *American Political Science Review* 95 (March): 33–48.

Heiber, Helmut, ed. 1968. *Reichsführer! Briefe an und von Himmler.* Stuttgart: Deutsche Verlags-Anstalt.

Heidenrich, John G. 2001. *How to Prevent Genocide: A Guide for Policymakers, Scholars and the Concerned Citizen.* Westport, CT: Praeger.

Heifetz, Elias J. U. D. 1921. *The Slaughter of the Jews in the Ukraine in 1919.* New York: Thomas Seltzer.

Heim, Susanne. 2000. "The German-Jewish Relationship in the Diaries of Victor Klemperer," in Bankier 2000, 312–25.

Helmreich, Ernst C. 1979. *The German Churches Under Hitler: Background, Struggle, and Epilogue.* Detroit, MI: Wayne State University Press.

Herbert, Ulrich. 2000a. "Extermination Policy: New Answers and Questions About the History of the 'Holocaust' in German Historigraphy," in Herbert 2000b, 1–52.

2000b. *National Socialist Extermination Policies.* New York: Berghahn Books.

Hickey, Michael. 1995. *Gallipoli.* London: John Murray.

Hilberg, Raul. 1985. *The Destruction of the European Jews,* rev. ed. New York: Holmes and Meier.

Hilberg, Raul and Stanislaw Staron. 1979. "Introduction," in Czerniakow 1979, 25–70.

Hill, Stuart and Donald Rothchild. 1986. "The Contagion of Political Conflict in Africa and the World." *Journal of Conflict Resolution* 30: 716–35.

Himmler, Heinrich. 1938. *Once in 2000 Years: Secret Speech Delivered to the German Army General Staff.* New York: American Committee for Anti-Nazi Literature.

Hirschfeld, Gerhard. 1988. *Nazi Rule and Dutch Collaboration: The Netherlands Under German Occupation 1940–1945,* trans. Louise Willmot. Oxford: Berg.

Hirschon, Renée, 2003. "The Consequences of the Lausanne Convention: An Overview," in Renée Hirschon, ed., *Crossing the Aegean: An Appraisal of the 1923 Compulsory Population Exchange Between Greece and Turkey.* Oxford, UK: Berghahn Books, 13–20.

Hitler, Adolf. 1939. *Mein Kampf.* Boston: Houghton Mifflin.

[1942] 2000. *Hitler's Table Talk, 1941–1944: His Private Conversations,* trans. Norman Cameron and R. H. Stevens, intro. Hugh R. Trevor-Roper. New York: Enigma Books.

Höhne, Heinz. 1970. *The Order of the Death's Head: The Story of Hitler's SS,* trans. Richard Barry. New York: Coward-McCann.

Holmes, Oliver Wendell. 1897. "The Path of the Law." *Harvard Law Review,* 10 (March): 458–78.

Horne, John and Alan Kramer. 2001. *German Atrocities, 1914: A History of Denial.* New Haven, CT: Yale University Press.

Horowitz, Donald L. 2001. *The Deadly Ethnic Riot.* Berkeley: University of California Press.

Horowitz, Irving Louis. 2002. *Taking Lives: Genocide and State Power,* 5th edition. New Brunswick, NJ: Transaction Publishers.

Hürten, Heinz. 1992. *Deutsche Katholiken: 1918–1945*. Paderborn: Ferdinand Schöningh.

Huth, Paul K. 1996. *Standing Your Ground: Territorial Disputes and International Conflict*. Ann Arbor: University of Michigan Press.

Huttenbach, Henry R. 2002. "From the Editor: Towards a Conceptual Definition of Genocide." *Journal of Genocide Research* 4 (2): 167–76.

Ignatieff, Michael. 2002. "Intervention and State Failure," in Mills and Brunner 2002, 229–44.

Ioanid, Radu. 2000. *The Holocaust in Romania: The Destruction of Jews and Gypsies Under the Antonescu Regime, 1940–1944*, foreword Elie Wiesel. Chicago: Ivan R. Dee.

Issawi, Charles. 1980. *The Economic History of Turkey: 1800–1914*. Chicago: University of Chicago Press.

Jäckel, Eberhard. 1981. *Hitler's World View: A Blueprint for Power*, trans. Herbert Arnold. Cambridge: Harvard University Press.

Jackson, Karl D., ed. 1989a. *Cambodia 1975–1978: Rendezvous with Death*. Princeton, NJ: Princeton University Press.

1989b. "Intellectual Origins of the Khmer Rouge," in Jackson 1989a, 241–50.

Janjić, Dušan. 1995. "Resurgence of Ethnic Conflict in Yugoslavia: The Demise of Communism and the Rise of the 'New Elites' of Nationalism," in Payam Akhnavan and Robert Howse, eds., *Yugoslavia, the Former and Future*. Washington, DC: Brookings Institution Press, 29–44.

Jelavich, Barbara. 1983. *History of the Balkans*, *vol.* II. Cambridge, UK: Cambridge University Press.

Jervis, Robert. 1992. "Political Implications of Loss Aversion." *Political Psychology* 13 (June): 187–204.

1999. "Realism, Neoliberalism, and Cooperation." *International Security* 24 (Summer): 42–63.

Jonassohn, Kurt and Karin S. Björnson. 1998. *Genocide and Gross Human Rights Violations in Comparative Perspective*. New Brunswick, NJ: Transaction Publishers.

Jones, Bruce. 1999. "The Arusha Peace Process," in Adelman and Suhrke 1999, 131–56.

2001. *Peacemaking in Rwanda: The Dynamics of Failure*. Boulder, CO: Lynne Rienner.

Judah, Tim. 2000. *The Serbs: History, Myth and the Destruction of Yugoslavia*. New Haven, CT: Yale University Press.

Jünger, Ernst. 1975. *The Storm of Steel: From the Diary of a German Storm-Troop Officer on the Western Front*, trans. Michael Hoffman. New York: H. Fertig.

Jutikkala, Eino and Kauko Pirinen. 1974. *A History of Finland*, rev. ed., trans. Paul Sjöblom. New York: Praeger.

Kagan, Donald. 1981. *The Peace of Nicias and the Sicilian Expedition*. Ithaca, NY: Cornell University Press.

Kahneman, Daniel, Jack L. Knetsch, and Richard H. Thaler. 1990. "Experimental Tests of the Endowment Effect and the Coase Theorem." *Journal of Political Economy* 98 (December): 1325–48.

    1991. "The Endowment Effect, Loss Aversion and Status Quo Bias." *Journal of Economic Perspectives* 5 (Winter): 193–206.

Kahneman, Daniel and Amos Tversky. 1979. "Prospect Theory: An Analysis of Decision Under Risk." *Econometrica* 47 (2): 263–92.

    eds. 2000. *Choices, Values, and Frames.* Cambridge, UK: Cambridge University Press.

Kaiser, Hilmar. 1999. "The Baghdad Railway and the Armenian Genocide, 1915–1916: A Case Study in German Resistance and Complicity," in Richard G. Hovannisian, ed., *Remembrance and Denial: The Case of the Armenian Genocide.* Detroit: Wayne State University Press, 67–112.

Kaplan, Chaim A. 1973. *The Warsaw Diary of Chaim A. Kaplan,* ed. and trans. Abraham I. Katsh. New York: Collier.

Karpat, Kemal H. 1985. *Ottoman Population, 1830–1914: Demographic and Social Characteristics.* Madison: University of Wisconsin Press.

    2001. *The Politicization of Islam: Reconstructing Identity, State, Faith, and Community in the Late Ottoman State.* Oxford: Oxford University Press.

    2002. *Studies on Ottoman Social and Political History: Selected Articles and Essays.* Leiden: Brill.

Kasaba, Reşat. 1999. "Economic Foundations of a Civil Society: Greeks in the Trade of Western Anatolia, 1840–1876," in Dimitri Gondicas and Charles Issawi, eds., *Ottoman Greeks in the Age of Nationalism: Politics, Economy, and Society in the Nineteenth Century.* Princeton, NJ: Darwin Press, 77–87.

Katz, Steven. 1994. *The Holocaust in Historical Context,* vol. I, *The Holocaust and Mass Death Before the Modern Age.* New York: Oxford University Press.

Keates, Jonathan. 2004. "Blood then Brandy." *Times Literary Supplement* 5258 (January 9): 8.

Keesing's Contemporary Archives. London: Keesing's Limited.

Kenez, Peter. 1992. "Pogroms and White Ideology in the Russian Civil War," in John D. Klier and Shlomo Lambroza, eds., *Pogroms: Anti-Jewish Violence in Modern Russian History.* Cambridge, UK: Cambridge University Press, 293–313.

Kent, Marian, ed. 1984. *The Great Powers and the End of the Ottoman Empire.* London: George Allen and Unwin.

Kermisz, Josef. 1979. "Introduction," in Czerniakow 1979, 1–24.

Kershaw, Ian. 1998. *Hitler, 1889–1936: Hubris.* New York: Norton.

    2000a. *Hitler, 1936–1945: Nemesis.* New York: Norton.

    2000b. *The Nazi Dictatorship: Problems and Perspectives of Interpretation,* 4th ed. London: Edward Arnold.

Kiernan, Ben. 1996. *The Pol Pot Regime: Race, Power, and Genocide in Cambodia Under the Khmer Rouge, 1975–79.* New Haven, CT: Yale University Press.

Kinealy, Christine. 1994. *This Great Calamity: The Irish Famine 1845–1852.* Dublin: Gill and MacMillan.

Kinross, Patrick B. 1977. *The Ottoman Centuries: The Rise and Fall of the Turkish Empire.* New York: Morrow.

Kirby, D. G. 1979. *Finland in the Twentieth Century.* Minneapolis: University of Minnesota Press.

Klier, John D. 1995. *Imperial Russia's Jewish Question, 1855–1881.* Cambridge, UK: Cambridge University Press.

Klier, John D. and Shlomo Lambroza, eds. 1992. *Pogroms: Anti-Jewish Violence in Modern Russian History.* Cambridge, UK: Cambridge University Press.

Knutson, Brian. 2004. "Sweet Revenge?." *Science* 305 (August 27): 1246–47.

Kolodziej, Edward A. 2000. "The Great Powers and Genocide: Lessons from Rwanda." *Pacifica Review* 12 (June): 121–41.

Körding, Konrad P. and Daniel M. Wolpert. 2004. "Bayesian Integration in Sensorimotor Learning." *Nature* 427 (January): 244–47.

Korzec, Pawel and Jean-Charles Szurek. 1993. "Jews and Poles Under Soviet Occupation (1939–1941): Conflicting Interests," in Polonsky 1993, 385–406.

Kourvetaris, Yorgos A. and Betty A. Dobratz. 1987. *A Profile of Modern Greece in Search of Identity.* Oxford: Clarendon Press.

Krain, Matthew. 1997. "State-Sponsored Mass Murder: The Onset and Severity of Genocides and Politicides." *Journal of Conflict Resolution* 41 (June): 1–24.

Kruk, Herman. 2002. *The Last Days of the Jerusalem of Lithuania: Chronicles from the Vilna Ghetto and the Camps, 1939–1944,* ed. Benjamin Harshav. New Haven, CT: Yale University Press.

Kulka, Otto D. 2000. "The German Population and the Jews: State of Research and New Perspectives," in Bankier 2000, 271–81.

Kuper, Leo. 1981. *Genocide: Its Political Use in the Twentieth Century.* New Haven, CT: Yale University Press.

Kupper, Alfons. ed. 1969. *Staatliche Akten über die Reichskonkordatsverhandlungen, 1933.* Mainz: Matthias-Grünewald-Verlag.

Lacey, Marc. 2004. "Strife in Congo Town Sows Fear of Return to All-Out War." *New York Times,* December 19, N3.

Lang, Berel. 1999. *The Future of the Holocaust: Between History and Memory.* Ithaca, NY: Cornell University Press.

Lebow, Richard Ned. 2001. "Thucydides the Constructivist." *American Political Science Review* 95 (September): 547–60.

Lemarchand, René. 1994. "Managing Transition Anarchies: Rwanda, Burundi, and South Africa in Comparative Perspective." *Journal of Modern African Studies,* 32 (4): 581–604.

    1995. "Rwanda: The Rationality of Genocide." *Issue: A Journal of Opinion* 23 (2): 8–11.

    1996. *Burundi: Ethnic Conflict and Genocide.* New York: Cambridge University Press.

Lemkin, Raphael. 1944. *Axis Rule in Occupied Europe*. Washington, DC: Carnegie Endowment.

Leonhardt, David. 2004. "Subconsciously, Athletes May Play Like Statisticians." *New York Times*, January 20, F1.

Leslie, R. F., Antony Polonsky, Jan M. Ciechanowski, and Z. A. Pelczynski. 1980. *The History of Poland Since 1863*. Cambridge, UK: Cambridge University Press.

Levendel, Isaac. 1999. *Not the Germans Alone: A Son's Search for the Truth of Vichy*. Evanston, IL: Northwestern University Press.

Levene, Mark and Penny Roberts, eds. 1999. *The Massacre in History*. New York: Berghahn Books.

Leventhal, Gerald S., Jurgis Karuza, Jr., and William R. Fry. 1980. "Beyond Fairness: A Theory of Allocation Preferences," in G. Mikula, ed., *Justice and Social Interaction*. New York: Springer-Verlag, 167–217.

Levine, Hillel. 1991. *Economic Origins of Antisemitism: Poland and Its Jews in the Early Modern Period*. New Haven, CT: Yale University Press.

Levy, Jack S. 2000. "Loss Aversion, Framing Effects, and International Conflict," in M. Midlarsky 2000a, 193–221.

Lewitter, L. R. 1965. "The Partitions of Poland," in A. Goodwin, ed., *The New Cambridge Modern History*, vol. VIII. Cambridge, UK: Cambridge University Press, 333–59.

Lewy, Guenter. 1964. *The Catholic Church and Nazi Germany*. New York: McGraw-Hill.

Libaridian, Gerard. J. 1987. "The Ultimate Repression: The Genocide of the Armenians, 1915–1917," in Wallimann and Dobkowski 1987, 203–35.

Lifton, Robert Jay. 1986. *The Nazi Doctors: Medical Killing and the Psychology of Genocide*. New York: Basic Books.

2000. *Destroying the World to Save It*. New York: Holt.

Lifton, Robert Jay and Eric Markusen. 1990. *The Genocidal Mentality: Nazi Holocaust and Nuclear Threat*. New York: Basic Books.

Lindemann, Albert S. 1997. *Esau's Tears: Modern Anti-Semitism and the Rise of the Jews*. New York: Cambridge University Press.

Loewenberg, Peter. 1971. "The Unsuccessful Adolescence of Heinrich Himmler." *American Historical Review* 76 (June): 612–41.

London, Louise. 2000. *Whitehall and the Jews, 1933–1948: British Immigration Policy, Jewish Refugees and the Holocaust*. Cambridge, UK: Cambridge University Press.

Longman, Timothy. 1995. "Genocide and Socio-Political Change: Massacres in Two Rwandan Villages." *Issue: A Journal of Opinion* 23 (2): 18–21.

Lozowick, Yaacov. 2002. *Hitler's Bureaucrats: The Nazi Security Police and the Banality of Evil*, trans. Haim Watzman. London: Continuum.

Lukowski, Jerzy. 1999. *The Partitions of Poland 1772, 1793, 1795*. London: Longman.

Lukowski, Jerzy and Hubert Zawadzki. 2001. *A Concise History of Poland*. Cambridge, UK: Cambridge University Press.

Luttwak, Edward N. 1987. *Strategy: The Logic of War and Peace*. Cambridge: Belknap Press.

Machiavelli, Niccolò. 1950. *The Prince and The Discourses*. New York: Random House.

MacRaild, Donald M. 1999. *Irish Migrants in Modern Britain, 1750–1922*. New York: St. Martin's Press.

Madsen, Wayne. 1999. *Genocide and Covert Operations in Africa: 1993–1999*. Lewiston, NY: Edwin Mellen Press.

Mahler, Raphael. 1971. *A History of Modern Jewry 1780–1815*. New York: Schocken Books.

Malia, Martin. 1999. *Russia Under Western Eyes: From the Bronze Horseman to the Lenin Mausoleum*. Cambridge: Harvard University Press.

Mamdani, Mahmood. 2001. *When Victims Become Killers: Colonialism, Nativism, and the Genocide in Rwanda*. Princeton, NJ: Princeton University Press.

Mango, Andrew. 2000. *Atatürk*. New York: Overlook Press.

Mann, Michael. 1997. "The Contradictions of Continuous Revolution," in Ian Kershaw and Moshe Lewin, eds., *Stalinism and Nazism: Dictatorships in Comparison*. Cambridge, UK: Cambridge University Press, 135–57.

Manoschek, Walter. 2000. "The Extermination of the Jews in Serbia," in Herbert 2000b, 163–85.

Mansfield, Harvey C. 1996. *Machiavelli's Virtue*. Chicago: University of Chicago Press.

Marashlian, Levon. 1999. "Finishing the Genocide: Cleansing Turkey of Armenian Survivors, 1920–1923," in Richard G. Hovannisian ed., *Remembrance and Denial: The Case of the Armenian Genocide*. Detroit: Wayne State University Press, 113–45.

Markusen, Eric. 1987. "Genocide and Total War: A Preliminary Comparison," in Wallimann and Dobkowski 1987, 97–123.

Marquis, Christopher and Marc Lacey. 2004. "Powell and Annan See Hints of Disaster in Sudan." *New York Times*, July 1, A1, A6.

Marriott, John A. 1947. *The Eastern Question: An Historical Study in European Diplomacy*, 4th ed. Oxford: Clarendon Press.

Marrus, Michael R. 1985. *The Unwanted: European Refugees in the Twentieth Century*. New York: Oxford University Press.

1987. *The Holocaust in History*. Hanover, NH: Published for Brandeis University Press by University Press of New England.

Marrus, Michael R. and Robert O. Paxton. 1982. "The Nazis and the Jews in Occupied Western Europe, 1940–1944." *Journal of Modern History* 54 (December): 687–714.

1995. *Vichy France and The Jews*. Stanford, CA: Stanford University Press.

Martin, Douglass. 2001. "Gerhart Riegner, 90, Dies: Disclosed Holocaust Plans." *New York Times*, December 5, A27.

Martin, Ian. 1998. "Hard Choices After Genocide: Human Rights and Political Failures in Rwanda," in Jonathan Moore, ed., *Hard Choices: Moral Dilemmas in Humanitarian Intervention*. Lanham, MD: Rowman and Littlefield, 157–76.

Martin, Marie A. 1994. *Cambodia: A Shattered Society*, trans. Mark W. McLeod. Los Angeles: University of California Press.

Matthäus, Jürgen. 2004. "Operation Barbarossa and the Onset of the Holocaust, June–December 1941," in Christopher R. Browning, *The Origins of the Final Solution: The Evolution of Nazi Jewish Policy, September 1939–March 1942*. Jerusalem: Yad Vashem, and Lincoln: University of Nebraska Press, 244–308.

Mayer, Arno. 1988. *Why Did the Heavens Not Darken?: The "Final Solution" in History*. New York: Pantheon.

McCarthy, Justin. 1997. *The Ottoman Turks: An Introductory History to 1923*. New York: Longman.

McDermott, Rose. 1992. "Prospect Theory in International Relations: The Iranian Hostage Rescue Mission." *Political Psychology* 13 (June): 237–63.

1998. *Risk-Taking in International Politics: Prospect Theory in American Foreign Policy*. Ann Arbor: University of Michigan Press.

McMurray, Jonathan S. 2001. *Distant Ties: Germany, the Ottoman Empire, and the Construction of the Baghdad Railway*. Westport, CT: Praeger.

Mearsheimer, John J. 2001. *Great Power Politics*. New York: Norton.

Meiggs, Russell. 1972. *The Athenian Empire*. Oxford: Oxford University Press.

Meinecke, Friederich. 1957. *Machiavellism*, trans. Douglas Scott. New Haven, CT: Yale University Press.

Melson, Robert. 1992. *Revolution and Genocide: On the Origins of the Armenian Genocide and the Holocaust*. Chicago: University of Chicago Press.

Melvern, Linda. 2000. *A People Betrayed: The Role of the West in Rwanda's Genocide*. London: Zed Books.

2004. *Conspiracy to Murder: The Rwandan Genocide*. London: Verso.

Merkl, Peter H. 1975. *Political Violence Under the Swastika: 581 Early Nazis*. Princeton, NJ: Princeton University Press.

Michman, Dan. 2003. *Holocaust Historiography: A Jewish Perspective Conceptualizations, Terminology, Approaches and Fundamental Issues*. London: Vallentine Mitchell.

Michman, Joseph. 1989. "The Controversy Surrounding the Jewish Council of Amsterdam: From Its Inception to the Present Day," in Michael R. Marrus, ed., *The Nazi Holocaust: Historical Articles on the Destruction of European Jews, No. 6, The Victims of the Holocaust*, vol. II. Westport, CT: Meckler, 821–43.

Midlarsky, Elizabeth R. 1968. "Aiding Responses: An Analysis and Review." *Merrill-Palmer Quarterly* 14 (3): 229–60.

Midlarsky, Elizabeth R., Stephanie Fagin Jones, and Robin Nemeroff. (forthcoming). "Heroic Rescue During the Holocaust: Empirical and Methodological Perspectives," in R. Bootzin and P. McKnight, eds., *Measurement, Methodology, and Evaluation*. Washington, DC: American Psychological Association.

Midlarsky, Elizabeth R. and Eva Kahana. 1994. *Altruism in Later Life*. Thousand Oaks, CA: Sage Publications.

Midlarsky, Elizabeth R. and Manus I. Midlarsky. 2004. "Echoes of Genocide: Trauma and Ethnic Identity Among European Immigrants." *Humboldt Journal of Social Relations* 28 (2): 38–53.

Midlarsky, Manus I. 1982. "Scarcity and Inequality: Prologue to the Onset of Mass Revolution." *Journal of Conflict Resolution* 26 (March): 3–38.

   1984. "Preventing Systemic War: Crisis Decision-Making Amidst a Structure of Conflict Relationships." *Journal of Conflict Resolution* 28 (December): 563–84.

   1988a. *The Onset of World War*. Boston: Unwin Hyman.

   1988b. "Rulers and the Ruled: Patterned Inequality and the Onset of Mass Political Violence." *American Political Science Review* 82 (June): 491–509.

   1999. *The Evolution of Inequality: War, State Survival, and Democracy in Comparative Perspective*. Stanford, CA: Stanford University Press.

   ed. 2000a. *Handbook of War Studies II*. Ann Arbor: University of Michigan Press.

   2000b. "Identity and International Conflict," in M. Midlarsky 2000a, 25–58.

   2002. "Realism and the Democratic Peace: The Primacy of State Security in New Democracies," in Michael Brecher and Frank Harvey, eds., *Millennial Reflections on International Studies*. Ann Arbor: University of Michigan Press, 107–42.

   2003. "The Impact of External Threat on States and Domestic Societies." *International Studies Review* 5 (December): 13–18.

   2004. "Nihilism in Political Chaos: Himmler, bin Laden, and Altruistic Punishment." *Studies in Conflict and Terrorism* 27 (May–June): 187–206.

   2005. "The Demographics of Genocide: Refugees and Territorial Loss in the Mass Murder of European Jewry." *Journal of Peace Research (special issue on the demography of conflict and violence)* 42 (4): 375–91.

Midlarsky, Manus I., John A. Vasquez, and Peter V. Gladkov, eds. 1994. *From Rivalry to Cooperation: Russian and American Perspectives on the Post-Cold War Era*. New York: HarperCollins.

Miller, Donald E. and Lorna T. Miller. 1993. *Survivors: An Oral History of the Armenian Genocide*. Berkeley: University of California Press.

Mills, Nicolaus and Kira Brunner, eds. 2002. *The New Killing Fields: Massacre and the Politics of Intervention*. New York: Basic Books.

Milton, David and Nancy D. Milton. 1976. *The Wind Will Not Subside: Years in Revolutionary China – 1964–1969*. New York: Pantheon.

Mitchel, John. 1868. *The History of Ireland: From the Treaty of Limerick to the Present Time*. New York: D. and J. Sadlier.

Moore, Bob. 1997. *Victims and Survivors: The Nazi Persecution of the Jews in the Netherlands 1940–1945*. London: Arnold.

Morgenthau, Henry. 1918. *Ambassador Morgenthau's Story*. New York: Doubleday.

Morley, John F. 1980. *Vatican Diplomacy and the Jews During the Holocaust, 1939–1943*. New York: KTAV.

Morris, Stephen, J. 1999. *Why Vietnam Invaded Cambodia: Political Culture and the Causes of War*. Stanford, CA: Stanford University Press.

Morse, Arthur D. 1968. *While Six Million Died: A Chronicle of American Apathy*. New York: Random House.

Most, Benjamin H. and Harvey Starr. 1989. *Inquiry, Logic, and International Politics*. Columbia: University of South Carolina Press.

Murray, Williamson and Allan R. Millett. 2000. *A War to Be Won: Fighting the Second World War*. Cambridge: Belknap Press of Harvard University Press.

Nagy-Talavera, N., 2001. *The Green Shirts and the Others: A History of Fascism in Hungary and Romania*. Iaşi: Center for Romanian Studies.

Neiman, Susan. 2002. *Evil in Modern Thought: An Alternative History of Philosophy*. Princeton, NJ: Princeton University Press.

Neshamit, Sarah. 1977. "Rescue in Lithuania During the Nazi Occupation," in Gutman and Zuroff 1977, 289–331.

Neumann, Franz. 1942. *Behemoth: The Structure and Practice of National Socialism*. New York: Oxford University Press.

Newbury, Catharine. 1995. "Background to Genocide: Rwanda." *Issue: A Journal of Opinion* 23 (2): 12–17.

Newbury, Catharine and David Newbury. 1999. "A Catholic Mass in Kigali: Contested Views of the Genocide and Ethnicity in Rwanda." *Canadian Journal of African Studies* 33 (2 and 3): 292–315.

Ó Gráda, Cormac. 1999. *Black '47 and Beyond: The Great Irish Famine in History, Economy, and Memory*. Princeton, NJ: Princeton University Press.

Obenaus, Herbert. 2000. "The Germans: 'An Antisemitic People.' The Press Campaign After 9 November 1938," in Bankier 2000, 147–80.

O'Neill, Barry. 1999. *Honors, Symbols, and War*. Ann Arbor: University of Michigan Press.

 2001. "Risk Aversion in International Relations Theory." *International Studies Quarterly* 45 (December): 617–40.

Oren, Nissan. 1968. "The Bulgarian Exception: A Reassessment of the Salvation of the Jewish Community," in Livia Rothkirchen, ed., *Yad Vashem Studies on the European Jewish Catastrophe and Resistance, VII.* Jerusalem: Yad Vashem, 83–106.

Ortayli, Ilber. 1999. "Greeks in the Ottoman Administration During the Tanzimat Period," in Dimitri Gondicas and Charles Issawi, eds., *Ottoman Greeks in the Age of Nationalism: Politics, Economy, and Society in the Nineteenth Century.* Princeton, NJ: Darwin Press, 161–67.

Ostrom, Elinor, James Walker, and Roy Gardner. 1992. "Covenants with and Without a Sword: Self-Governance Is Possible." *American Political Science Review* 86 (June): 404–17.

Ould-Abdallah, Ahmedou. 2000. *Burundi on the Brink, 1993–1995: A UN Special Envoy Reflects on Preventive Diplomacy.* Washington, DC: United States Institute of Peace Press.

Padfield, Peter. 1991. *Himmler: Reichsführer-SS.* New York: Henry Holt and Company.

Palmer, Alan. 1992. *The Decline and Fall of the Ottoman Empire.* London: John Murray.

Pascal, Julia. 2000. *The Holocaust Trilogy: Theresa; A Dead Woman on Holiday; The Dybbuk.* London: Oberon Books.

Payne, Stanley G. 1995. *A History of Fascism, 1914–1945.* Madison: University of Wisconsin Press.

Phayer, Michael. 2000. *The Catholic Church and the Holocaust, 1930–1965.* Bloomington: Indiana University Press.

Pipes, Richard. 1993. *Russia Under the Bolshevik Regime.* New York: Knopf.

Póirtéir, Cathal, ed. 1995. *The Great Irish Famine.* Dublin: Mercier Press.

Pók, Attila. 1997. "Germans, Hungarians, and the Destruction of Hungarian Jewry," in Cesarani 1997b, 147–58.

Polonsky, Antony. 1972. *Politics in Independent Poland 1921–1939: The Crisis of Constitutional Government.* Oxford: Clarendon Press.

    ed. 1993. *From Shtetl to Socialism: Studies from Polin.* London: Littman Library of Jewish Civilization.

Polonsky, Antony and Monika Adamczyk-Garbowska. 2001. "Introduction," in Antony Polonsky and Monika Adamczyk-Garbowska, eds., *Contemporary Jewish Writing in Poland: An Anthology.* Lincoln: University of Nebraska Press, ix–l.

Polvinen, Tuomo. 1986. *Between East and West: Finland in International Politics, 1944–1947,* ed. and trans. D. G. Kirby and Peter Herring. Minneapolis: University of Minnesota Press.

Polybius. 1960. *The Histories,* trans. W. R. Paton. Cambridge: Harvard University Press.

Posen, Barry R. 1984. *The Sources of Military Doctrine: France, Britain, and Germany Between the World Wars.* Ithaca, NY: Cornell University Press.

1993. "The Security Dilemma and Ethnic Conflict." *Survival* 35: 27–47.

Pottier, John. 2002. *Re-imagining Rwanda: Conflict, Survival and Disinformation in the Late Twentieth Century.* Cambridge, UK: Cambridge University Press.

Power, Samantha. 2001. "Bystanders to Genocide: Why the United States Let the Rwandan Tragedy Happen." *Atlantic Monthly* 288 (September): 84–108.

   2002a. *A Problem from Hell: America and the Age of Genocide.* New York: Basic Books.

   2002b. "Raising the Cost of Genocide," in Mills and Brunner 2002, 245–64.

Presser, J. 1969. *The Destruction of the Dutch Jews*, trans. Arnold Pomerans. New York: Dutton.

Prunier, Gérard. 1995. *The Rwanda Crisis: History of a Genocide.* New York: Columbia University Press.

Quinn, Kenneth M. 1989a. "Explaining the Terror," in Jackson 1989a, 215–40.

   1989b. "The Pattern and Scope of Violence," in Jackson 1989a, 179–208.

Ragin, Charles C. 1987. *The Comparative Method: Moving Beyond Qualitative and Quantitative Strategies.* Berkeley: University of Carlifornia Press.

Rautkallio, Hannu. 1987. *Finland and the Holocaust: The Rescue of Finland's Jews*, trans. Paul Sjöblom. New York: Holocaust Library.

Raymond, Philippe Ganier. 1985. *L'affiche rouge.* Paris: Marabout, c. Fayard, 1975.

Reid, James J. 1992. "Total War, the Annihilation Ethic, and the Armenian Genocide, 1870–1918," in Richard G. Hovannisian, ed., *The Armenian Genocide: History, Politics, Ethics.* New York: St. Martin's Press, 21–52.

Rhodes, Richard. 2002. *Masters of Death: The SS-Einsatzgruppen and the Invention of the Holocaust.* New York: Knopf.

Riding, Alan., 2001. "French Film Bears Witness to Wartime Complicity." *New York Times*, January 9, E1, E3.

Ridley, Jasper. 1970. *Lord Palmerston.* New York: E. P. Dutton.

Riegner, Gerhart. 1998. *Ne jamais désespérer: soixante années au service du peuple juif et des droits de l'homme.* Paris: Cerf.

Rigg, Bryan M. 2002. *Hitler's Jewish Soldiers: The Untold Story of Nazi Racial Laws and Men of Jewish Descent in the German Military.* Lawrence: University Press of Kansas.

Ringelblum, Emmanuel. 1974. *Notes from the Warsaw Ghetto: The Journal of Emmanuel Ringelblum*, ed. and trans. Jacob Sloan. New York: Schocken Books.

Robbins, Lionel. 1937. "Foreword," in Costantino Bresciani-Turroni, *The Economics of Inflation: A Study of Currency Depreciation in Post-War Germany, 1914–1923*, trans. Millicent E. Savers. London: George Allen and Unwin, 5–6.

Robinson, Jacob. 1972. "Introduction: Some Basic Issues that Faced the Jewish Councils," in Trunk 1972, xxi–xxxv.

Robinson, Thomas, W. 1971. "Introduction," in Thomas W. Robinson, ed., *The Cultural Revolution in China*. Berkeley: University of California Press, 1–20.

Röhl, John C. G. 1994. *The Kaiser and His Court: Wilhelm II and the Government of Germany*, trans. Terence F. Cole. Cambridge, UK: Cambridge University Press.

Rosenbaum, Alan S., ed. 1998. *Is the Holocaust Unique?: Perspectives on Comparative Genocide*. Boulder, CO: Westview.

Rostovtzeff, M. 1960. *Rome*, trans. J. D. Duff. New York: Oxford University Press.

Rummel, Rudolph. 1997. *Power Kills: Democracy as a Method of Nonviolence*. New Brunswick, NJ: Transaction Publishers.

    1998. *Statistics of Democide: Genocide and Mass Murder since 1900*. Münster: Lit Verlag.

Sabrin, B. F., ed. 1991. *Alliance for Murder: The Nazi–Ukrainian Nationalist Partnership in Genocide*. New York: Sarpedon.

Sachar, Howard M. 2002. *Dreamland: Europeans and Jews in the Aftermath of the Great War*. New York: Vintage.

Sajer, Guy. 1971. *The Forgotten Soldier*, trans. Lily Emmet. New York: Harper and Row.

Sanfey, Alan G., James K. Rilling, Jessica A. Aronson, Leigh E. Nystrom, and Jonathan D. Cohen. 2003. "The Neural Basis of Economic Decision-Making in the Ultimatum Game." *Science* 300 (June 13): 1755–58.

Schabas, William A. 2000. *Genocide in International Law: The Crimes of Crimes*. Cambridge, UK: Cambridge University Press.

Schivelbusch, Wolfgang. 2003. *The Culture of Defeat: On National Trauma, Mourning, and Recovery*, trans. Jefferson Chase. New York: Metropolitan Books.

Schmitt, Carl. [1932] 1996. *The Concept of the Political*, trans. J. Harvey Lomax. Chicago: University of Chicago Press.

Scholder, Klaus. 1987. *The Churches and the Third Reich*, vol. I, trans. John Bowden. London: SCM Press.

Schwab, George. 1996. "Introduction," in Schmitt [1932] 1996, 3–16.

Schweller, Randall L. 1996. "Neorealism's Status Quo Bias: What Security Dilemma?." *Security Studies* 5 (Spring): 90–121.

Sciolino, Elaine and Jason Horowitz. 2005. "Saving Jewish Children, But at What Cost?: Vatican Memo Confirms Refusal to Return Baptized Refugees." *New York Times*, January 9.

Secher, Reynald. 2003. *A French Genocide: The Vendée*, trans. George Holoch. Notre Dame, IN: University of Notre Dame Press.

Segev, Tom. 1987. *Soldiers of Evil: The Commandants of the Nazi Concentration Camps*. New York: McGraw-Hill.

Sen, Amartya. 2002. *Rationality and Freedom*. Cambridge: Belknap Press of Harvard University Press.

Senese, Paul D. and John Vasquez. 2004. "Alliances, Territorial Disputes, and the Probability of War: Testing for Interactions," in Paul F. Diehl, ed., *The Scourge of War: New Extensions on an Old Problem.* Ann Arbor: University of Michigan Press, 189–221.

Shaw, Martin. 2003. *War and Genocide: Organized Killing in Modern Society.* Cambridge: Polity.

Shaw, Stanford J., and Ezel Kural Shaw. 1977. *History of the Ottoman Empire and Modern Turkey,* vol. II, *Reform, Revolution, and Republic: The Rise of Modern Turkey, 1808–1975.* New York: Cambridge University Press.

Sicker, Martin. 2001. *The Islamic World in Decline: From the Treaty of Karlowitz to the Disintegration of the Ottoman Empire.* Westport, CT: Praeger.

Sijes, B. A. 1977. "Several Observations Concerning the Position of the Jews in Occupied Holland During World War II," in Gutman and Zuroff 1977, 527–53.

Skocpol, Theda. 1979. *States and Social Revolutions: A Comparative Analysis of France, Russia, and China.* New York: Cambridge University Press.

Sloan, G. R. 1997. *The Geopolitics of Anglo-Irish Relations in the Twentieth Century.* London: Leicester University Press.

Smith, Bradley F. 1971. *Heinrich Himmler: A Nazi in the Making, 1900–1926.* Stanford, CA: Hoover Institution Press.

Smith, Michael Llewellyn. 1998. *Ionian Vision: Greece in Asia Minor, 1919–1922.* Ann Arbor: University of Michigan Press.

Smith, Roger W. 1987. "Human Destructiveness and Politics: The Twentieth Century as an Age of Genocide," in Wallimann and Dobkowski 1987, 21–27.

Snyder, Jack. 1985. "Perceptions of the Security Dilemma in 1914," in Robert Jervis, Richard Ned Lebow, and Janice Gross Stein, eds., *Psychology and Deterrence.* Baltimore: Johns Hopkins University Press, 153–79.

  1991. *Myths of Empire: Domestic Politics and International Ambition.* Ithaca, NY: Cornell University Press.

Sober, Elliott and David Sloan Wilson. 1998. *Unto Others: The Evolution and Psychology of Unselfish Behavior.* Cambridge: Harvard University Press.

Solomons, Israel. 1913. "Lord George Gordon's Conversion to Judaism," paper read before the Jewish Historical Society of England, June 2, 222–65.

Staub, Ervin. 1989. *The Roots of Evil: The Origins of Genocide and Other Group Violence.* New York: Cambridge University Press.

Steele, E. D. 1991. *Palmerston and Liberalism, 1855–1865.* Cambridge, UK: Cambridge University Press.

Steinberg, Jonathan. 1990. *All or Nothing: The Axis and the Holocaust, 1941–1943.* London: Routledge.

Stern, Fritz. 1974. *The Politics of Cultural Despair: A Study in the Rise of the Germanic Ideology.* Berkeley: University of California Press.

Stone, Daniel. 1976. *Polish Politics and National Reform, 1775–1788*. Boulder, CO: East European Monographs, distributed by Columbia University Press.

Strachan, Hew. 2001a. *The First World War*, vol. I, *To Arms*. Oxford: Oxford University Press.

2001b. "Some Quiet on the Western Front." *Times Literary Supplement* 5151 (December 21): 32.

Straus, Scott. 2001. "Contested Meanings and Conflicting Imperatives: A Conceptual Analysis of Genocide." *Journal of Genocide Research* 3 (September): 349–75.

Strauss, Leo. 1999. "German Nihilism." *Interpretation* 26 (Spring): 353–78.

Strong, Donald S. 1941. *Organized Anti-Semitism in America: The Rise of Group Prejudice During the Decade 1930–1940*. Washington, DC: American Council on Public Affairs.

Strong, Tracy B. 1996. "Foreword: Dimensions of the New Debate around Carl Schmitt," in Schmitt [1932] 1996, ix–xxvii.

Tabeau, Ewa and Jakub Bijak. 2003. "Casualties of the 1990s War in Bosnia-Herzegovina: A Critique of Previous Estimates and the Latest Results," paper presented at the IUSSP Seminar on the Demography of Conflict and Violence, Jevnaker, Norway, November.

Tanner, Marcus. 2001. *Ireland's Holy Wars: The Struggle for a Nation's Soul, 1500–2000*. New Haven, CT: Yale University Press.

Taylor, Christopher. 1999. *Sacrifice as Terror: The Rwandan Genocide of 1994*. Oxford: Berg.

Thion, Serge. 1993. "Genocide as a Political Commodity," in Ben Kiernan, ed., *Genocide and Democracy in Cambodia: The Khmer Rouge, the United Nations, and the International Community*. New Haven, CT: Yale University Southeast Asia Studies, 163–90.

Thucydides. 1954. *History of the Peloponnesian War*, trans. Rex Warner. Baltimore: Penguin Books.

Tilly, Charles. 1964. *The Vendée*. Cambridge: Harvard University Press.

Todorov, Tzvetan. 2001. *The Fragility of Goodness: Why Bulgaria's Jews Survived the Holocaust*, trans. Arthur Denner. Princeton, NJ: Princeton University Press.

Tritle, Lawrence A. 2000. *From Melos to My Lai: War and Survival*. London: Routledge.

Trumpener, Ulrich. 1968. *Germany and the Ottoman Empire: 1914–1918*. Princeton, NJ: Princeton University Press.

1984. "Germany and the End of the Ottoman Empire," in Kent 1984, 111–40.

Trunk, Isaiah. 1972. *Judenrat: The Jewish Councils in Eastern Europe Under Nazi Occupation*. New York: Macmillan.

Tushnet, Leonard. 1972. *The Pavement of Hell*. New York: St. Martin's Press.

Tversky, Amos, and Daniel Kahneman. 1981. "The Framing of Decisions and the Psychology of Choice." *Science* 211 (January 30): 453–58.

Uvin, Peter. 1998. *Aiding Violence: The Development Enterprise in Rwanda*. West Hartford, CT: Kumarian Press.

Valentino, Benjamin. 2000. "Final Solutions: The Causes of Mass Killing and Genocide." *Security Studies* 9 (Spring): 1–59.

Van Evera, Stephen. 1999. *Causes of War: Power and the Roots of Conflict*. Ithaca, NY: Cornell University Press.

Vasquez, John. 2000. "Reexamining the Steps to War: New Evidence and Theoretical Insights," in M. Midlarsky 2000a, 371–406.

Verwimp, Philip. 2003. "Testing the Double-Genocide Thesis for Central and Southern Rwanda." *Journal of Conflict Resolution* 47 (4): 423–42.

Vistica, Gregory L. 2001. "What Happened in Thanh Phong." *New York Times Magazine* (April 29): 50–133.

Vital, David. 1999. *A People Apart: The Jews in Europe, 1789–1939*. Oxford: Oxford University Press.

Von Riekhoff, Harald. 1971. *German–Polish Relations, 1918–1933*. Baltimore: Johns Hopkins University Press.

Wallimann, Isidor and Michael N. Dobkowski, eds. 1987. *Genocide and the Modern Age: Etiology and Case Studies of Mass Death*. New York: Greenwood Press.

Waltz, Kenneth N. 1979. *Theory of International Politics*. New York: Random House.

   2000. "Structural Realism After the Cold War." *International Security* 25 (Summer): 5–41.

Walzer, Michael. 2002. "Arguing for Humanitarian Intervention," in Mills and Brunner 2002, 19–35.

Warlimont, Walter. 1964. *Inside Hitler's Headquarters: 1939–1945*, trans. R. H. Barry. London: Weidenfeld and Nicolson.

Wasserstein, Bernard. 1999. *Britain and the Jews of Europe, 1939–1945*, 2nd ed. London: Leicester University Press.

Weber, Eugen. 1964. *Varieties of Fascism: Doctrines of Revolution in the Twentieth Century*. New York: Van Nostrand.

   1965. "Romania," in Hans Rogger and Eugen Weber, eds., *The European Right: A Historical Profile*. Berkeley: University of California Press, 501–74.

Webster, Paul. 1991. *Pétain's Crime: The Full Story of French Collaboration in the Holocaust*. Chicago: Ivan R. Dee.

Weinberg, Gerhard L., ed. 2003. *Hitler's Second Book: The Unpublished Sequel to Mein Kampf*, trans. Krista Smith. New York: Enigma.

Weinreich, Max. 1999. *Hitler's Professors*. New Haven, CT: Yale University Press.

Weisman, Steven R. 2004. "Crisis in Sudan Resists Simple Solutions." *New York Times*, August 8, N6.

Weitz, Eric D. 2003. *A Century of Genocide: Utopias of Race and Nation*. Princeton, NJ: Princeton University Press.

Wertheimer, Jack. 1987. *Unwelcome Strangers: East European Jews in Imperial Germany*. New York: Oxford University Press.

Wistrich, Robert S. 2001. *Hitler and the Holocaust*. New York: Modern Library.

Woodham-Smith, Cecil. 1962. *The Great Hunger: Ireland 1845–1849*. New York: Harper and Row.

Woodward, Susan L. 1995. *Balkan Tragedy: Chaos and Dissolution After the Cold War*. Washington, DC: Brookings Institution Press.

Wyman, David. S. 1984. *The Abandonment of the Jews: America and the Holocaust, 1941–1945*. New York: Pantheon.

    1985. *Paper Walls: America and the Refugee Crisis 1938–1941*. New York: Pantheon.

Yahil, Leni. 1977. "The Uniqueness of the Rescue of Danish Jewry," in Gutman and Zuroff 1977, 617–25.

Yamamoto, Masahiro. 2000. *Nanking*. Westport, CT: Praeger.

Yeats, W. B. 1961. *Essays and Introductions*. New York: Macmillan.

Ye'or, Bat. 1985. *The Dhimmi: Jews and Christians Under Islam*, trans. David Maisel. London: Associated University Presses.

Zuccotti, Susan. 1993. *The Holocaust, the French and the Jews*. New York: Basic Books.

    2000. *Under His Very Windows: The Vatican and the Holocaust in Italy*. New Haven, CT: Yale University Press.

Zucker, Bat-Ami. 2001. *In Search of Refuge: Jews and US Consuls in Nazi Germany 1933–1941*. Portland, OR: Vallentine Mitchell.

INDEX

magnitude of, 233
onset of, 233
and USA, 390–92 *see also* genocide
Tversky, Amos, 89, 103–04n

Uganda, 145, 163, 166, 167, 229, 380
Ukraine, 7, 23, 44, 45–53, 56, 61,
 250, 252, 350
 anti-Bolshevism in, 61
 anti-Semitism in, 61
 occupied by Germany, 67
 opposition to Polish rule, 125
 pogroms against Jews in, 252
 provocations in, 124
 site of first twentieth-century mass
  murder of Jews, 264
 western, 48
 work camps in, 207
Ukrainian nationalists, 45, 47, 61, 136
 deaths from famine, 48
 Nazi connection with, 48–49
 provocations, 124
Ulster, 357, 361
 dispossession of Catholic
  landowners from, 357
UNAMIR, *see* United Nations
 Assistance Mission for Rwanda
uncertainty, 87, 103, 375
 and fog of war, 385
 and memory, 369
 and rationality, 375
 and reliance on memory, 375
 at time of observation, 67
unemployment (US), 237, 243
 German, 138
Union of Jewish Communities of
 Romania, 277
United Kingdom, *see* Britain
United Nations, 18, 145, 166, 167,
 232, 234, 363, 364, 387
 awareness of possibility of mass
  killing, 232
 failures of, 211
 genocide convention, 391
 investigation of Jenin "massacre,"
  363
 in Rwanda, 390
 Security Council, 232, 390, 391

withdrawal of troops from Rwanda,
 364
United Nations Assistance Mission for
 Rwanda (UNAMIR), 145, 166,
 167, 231–32
United Nations Convention on the
 Prevention and Punishment of
 the Crime of Genocide, 25, 27
United States, 29, 76, 118, 139, 141,
 145, 151, 152, 161, 195, 212,
 231, 237–46, 240, 362, 363,
 383, 387
 as affine protector, 384–85
 aid to Allies, 143
 anti-Semitism in, 240, 241–45, 393
 aversion to military involvement,
  391
 awareness of possibility of mass
  killing, 232
 bombing campaign against
  Cambodia, 321
 Catholic Church hierarchy, 363–64
 colonies, 114
 Congress, 244
 consular service, 238–39, 240
 and cynical realpolitik, 384
 disabling UN rescue in Rwanda, 391
 entry into World War II, 91
 experiencing another Somalia, 391
 failure to intervene in *St. Louis*
  incident, 245
 German speakers in, 239
 and Holocaust, 237–46
 horrified after 9/11, 380
 immigration laws, 240
 immigration quotas for Austria and
  Germany, 240
 immobilization of, 392
 incubator of Irish nationalism, 360
 intervention in Haiti, 391–92
 intervention in World War II, 143
 Jews compared with Irish Catholics,
  362–63
 military forces of, 390, 391
 nativism in, 240
 neutrality, 144
 opposition to UNAMIR presence in
  Rwanda, 232, 390, 390